D0161609

A GUIDED TOUR OF COMPUTER VISION

A GUIDED TOUR OF COMPUTER VISION

Vishvjit S. Nalwa
AT&T Bell Laboratories

ADDISON-WESLEY PUBLISHING COMPANY
Reading, Massachusetts • Menlo Park, California • New York
Don Mills, Ontario • Wokingham, England • Amsterdam • Bonn
Sydney • Singapore • Tokyo • Madrid • San Juan • Milan • Paris

Sponsoring Editor: Peter S. Gordon
Associate Editor: Helen M. Goldstein
Production Supervisor: Helen M. Wythe
Developmental and Copy Editor: Lyn Dupré
Design Consultant: David M. Weimer
Jacket Designer: Peter M. Blaiwas

Library of Congress Cataloging-in-Publication Data

Nalwa, Vishvjit S.
A guided tour of computer vision / Vishvjit S. Nalwa.
p. cm.
Includes bibliographical references and index.
ISBN 1-201-54853-4
1. Computer vision. I. Title.
TA1632.N275 1993
006.4′2—dc20

This book was typeset by the author on a *Linotronic 300* Linotype phototypesetter using the Palatino family of typefaces for the text. The Palatino family of typefaces—designed by Hermann Zapf, starting around 1950—is named after Giovanni Battista Palatino, a renowned calligrapher of the Renaissance. The letters of this typeface family derive their elegance from being modeled after letters formed by the natural motion of an edged pen.

Printed by R. R. Donnelley & Sons on New Era Matte paper.

Second printing, with revised Subject Index, 1994.

2 3 4 5 6 7 8 9 10-DO-9594

Euclid alone has looked on Beauty bare.

— Edna St. Vincent Millay
The Harp-Weaver and Other Poems
Sonnet XXII (1923)

A GUIDED TOUR OF COMPUTER VISION

Preface

Vision is such an awesome experience that we allude to it time and again in our language. *Seeing* is believing. Leonardo da Vinci was a man of *vision*. Love is *blind*. We *see* eye-to-eye, and we *foresee*. We exchange *views*, and we maintain *viewpoints*. It is no surprise that the metaphors abound: Vision is without doubt the predominant mode of human perception. It is fast and accurate; it is reliable and nonintrusive; it simultaneously provides both detail and an overview. After all, it is a picture that is worth a thousand words—not a touch, a sound, a taste, or a smell.

I am fascinated by vision, and I wish to share my fascination with you. While I was an undergraduate at the Indian Institute of Technology, Kanpur, a professor of mine had a poster: *Anything is possible with love and understanding*. I believe that the automation of visual perception is possible. Not only will we eventually match human performance, but we will exceed it—however remote such a goal might seem now.

This book is a tutorial on the automation of visual perception. More precisely, it is an account of the principles that underlie attempts to automate visual perception. It grew out of a course that I taught at Princeton University in the spring of 1989. My class there for the most part comprised senior undergraduates and first-year graduate students from the sciences and engineering.

What I emphasize in this book are the fundamental concepts that underlie the deduction of the structure and properties of a possibly dynamic three-dimensional world from its two-dimensional images. In addition, I aim to provide details and pointers, especially to recent developments. The topics I review include image formation, edge detection and image segmentation, line-drawing interpretation, shape from shading, shape from texture, shape from stereo, shape from motion, and shape representation.

I adopt the narrow view of vision here: that vision entails recovering the structure and the properties of the visual world. In particular, I exclude what has come to be termed high-level vision. High-level vision is generally taken to include the recognition of, reasoning about, and ascribing purposiveness to components of the perceived scene. Each of these tasks—as, for instance, model-based object recognition—is typically sought to be performed on the basis of knowledge that is context dependent. What I pursue here is domain-independent, noncognitive, nonpurposive vision: vision for its own sake.

It is my hope that this short book will arouse your curiosity and your interest, and that it will serve as a stepping stone toward an improvement in our collective understanding. My intended audience includes both the novice and the expert: To the novice, I seek to provide a lucid introduction, and to the expert, I aim to provide a fresh perspective.

I have sought to organize this book at three levels of detail. For the curious browser, there are the figures, which together with their captions are self-explanatory when studied in sequence. For the reader with a greater interest, there is in addition the text. Finally, for the serious student, there are the footnotes and the appendices that delve into aspects of the mathematics. From all of you I seek criticisms, corrections, and feedback with respect to fact, content, and style.

Vic Nalwa

Acknowledgments

Tom Binford, my doctoral dissertation advisor at Stanford, introduced me to computer vision as only he could in 1983. I thank him for sharing his perspective of the field with me, and for his support.

I am indebted to several individuals for patiently suffering through various drafts of this book and providing valuable feedback with respect to both content and style. In addition to several anonymous reviewers, I thank the following: Shree Nayar, Hong-Seh Lim, Polly Tremoulet, Sanj Kulkarni, Dave Kriegman, Dorothea Blostein, David Fleet, Larry Matthies, David Lowe, Harry Barrow, Katsu Ikeuchi, and Rick Vistnes.

On matters of aesthetic merit, I turned to Dave Weimer for advice, and on all matters of typography, I consulted Ed Pednault. Dave Weimer not only was a source of valuable advice, but also provided considerable assistance in the production of several figures. I would not have been able to create certain other figures without the help of John Adams, Konstantinos Diamantaras, Jerri Merced, John Dowling, Dave Horn, Behzad Shahraray, Harlyn Baker, Bob Lyons, and Thrasyvoulos Pappas. Rich Drechsler patiently guided me through the integration of the figures and the text into Postscript files that could be printed on a Linotype phototypesetter, and Ward Halligan went out of his way to accommodate my printing needs on one such device.

I take this opportunity to thank Raghavan Varadarajan, who provided a molecular biologist's view of the self-sufficiency of the figures and their captions, and was a source of comfort in times of despair. I thank Kicha Ganapathy, my department head at Bell Laboratories, for his patience and support. I am grateful to Cynthia Regis, Anita Quigley, and Karen Rihacek, all of the Bell Laboratories Library at Holmdel, for their immediate personal attention to my library needs.

I am glad I chose Addison-Wesley to publish this book. The staff there was always responsive, cooperative, and understanding. In particular, I am grateful to the following: Helen Goldstein, the de facto coordinator; Lyn Dupré, the developmental editor in whom I placed my faith; Helen Wythe, the production supervisor; and Peter Gordon, the sponsoring editor.

Finally, I thank my parents for having me, loving me, and imparting to me their value of an education.

Contents

A GUIDED TOUR OF COMPUTER VISION

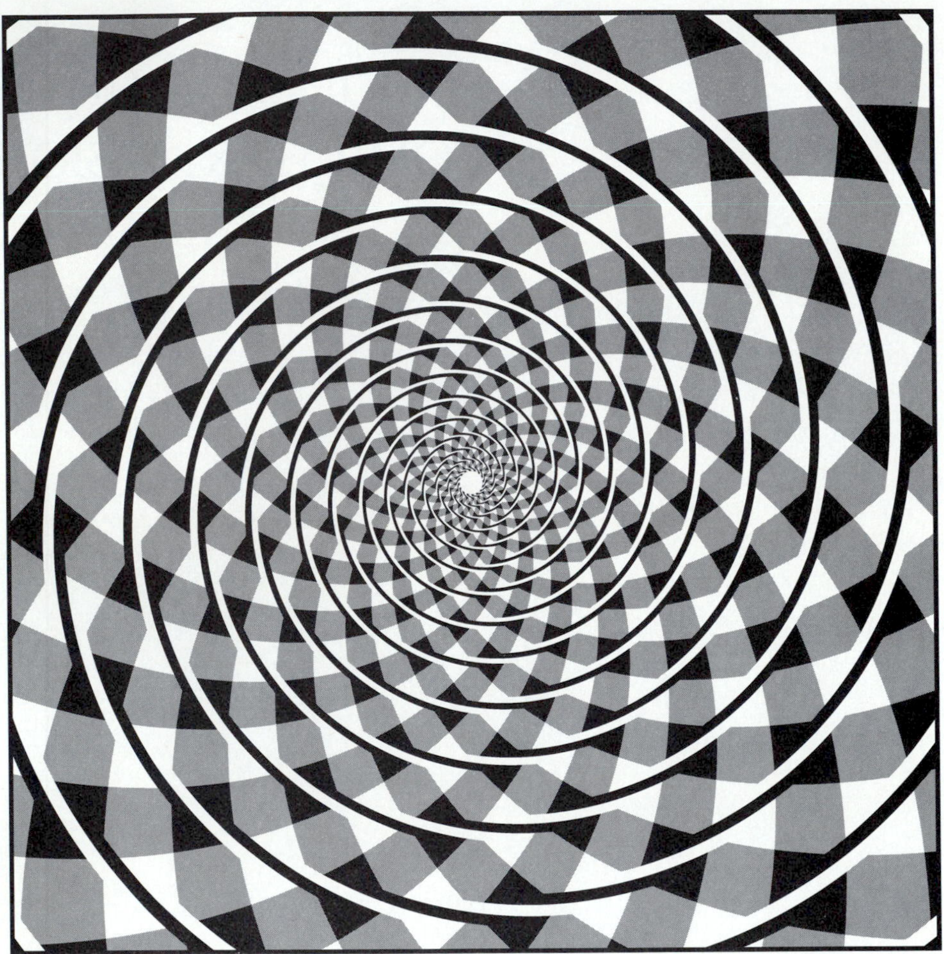

Figure 1.1 Fraser's spiral. Human vision is not quite as infallible as we tend to believe. A case in point is the illusory spiral evoked here by a collection of concentric circles, each circle comprising segments angled toward the center. To convince yourself that there is indeed no spiral, try tracing a spiral with your finger. (After [Fraser 1908].)

Chapter 1

Introduction

If our long-sought quest to create autonomous anthropomorphic automata is to succeed, we must first impart human perceptual capabilities to machines. It has now been well over two decades since several individuals and groups first made concerted efforts to automate visual perception, and yet a sense of frustration seems to prevail. Clearly, this sentiment is prompted to no small extent by the existence of sophisticated human perceptual abilities. We must bear in mind, however, not only that these abilities are the outcome of millions of years of evolution, but also that human perception is fallible; the fallibility of human vision is revealed, for instance, by the well-known Fraser's illusory spiral in Figure 1.1. Nevertheless, perhaps the impatience is justified. Perhaps, computer-vision research has indeed been painstakingly unproductive; or, perhaps, the working framework adopted by the research community is hopelessly flawed. It is too early to tell. This book is an account of the current state of our understanding.

1.1 What Is Computer Vision?

Computer vision, sometimes called **image understanding**, describes the automatic deduction of the structure and properties of a possibly dynamic three-dimensional world from either a single or multiple two-dimensional images of the world. The images may be monochromatic (i.e., "black and white") or colored, they may be captured by a single or multiple cameras, and each camera may be either stationary or mobile.

The structure and properties of the three-dimensional world that we seek to deduce in computer vision include not only geometric properties, but also material properties and the lighting of the world. Examples of geometric properties are the shapes, sizes, and locations of objects, and examples of material properties are the lightness or darkness of surfaces, their colors, their textures, and their material compositions. If the world is changing while it is being imaged, we might also wish to infer the nature of this change, and, perhaps, predict the future.

Why is computer vision difficult to realize? Because, as we shall explore at some length in this book, image formation is a many-to-one mapping: A variety of surfaces with different material and geometrical properties, possibly under different lighting conditions, could lead to identical images. As a result, the inverse imaging problem, given a single image—that is, the problem of inferring from a single image the scene that led to the image—has no unique solution. Equivalently, a single image of a scene does not constrain the imaged scene sufficiently to allow us to recover the scene unambiguously. There are two ways out of this predicament: (1) gather more data (images), and (2) make assumptions about the world. It is, of course, important that every assumption we invoke be tenable, and that we understand the exact role of the assumption well. Hence, we must make all our assumptions explicit, as we shall endeavor to do throughout this book.

Even when the inverse imaging problem is sufficiently constrained to allow a unique solution in principle, there remain the twin practical problems of computability and robustness. Is the solution computable using reasonable resources? Resources include both computing machinery and time. And, is the solution robust? That is, is the solution insensitive to errors in data (i.e., to signal noise), and to errors in computation (e.g., owing to limited precision arithmetic)? Failure on any of these fronts can render an otherwise promising approach useless in practice.

You might wonder whether computer vision is not a form of image processing or pattern recognition. Although there is some overlap, the differences are distinct. **Image processing** is a generic term for the processing of images to produce new images that are more desirable in some fashion; [Pratt 1991] and [Rosenfeld and Kak 1982] are two standard references for image processing. Image processing encompasses the following: **image enhancement**, which modifies images to improve their appearance to human viewers; **image restoration**, which corrects images for degradations (such as motion blur); and **image compression**, which represents images compactly while maintaining acceptable image quality. **Pattern recognition**, or **pattern classification**, on the other hand, classifies patterns into one of a finite (usually small) number of prespecified categories; [Duda and Hart 1973] is the classic reference for pattern recognition. For the most part, the emphasis in pattern recognition is on two-dimensional patterns—for instance, on the letters of the alphabet. Computer vision, in contrast, is concerned with generating descriptions of three-dimensional scenes—scenes that are not constrained to be members of predetermined sets—from two-dimensional images of the scenes.

The purpose of computer vision is to infer the state of the physical world from the inherently noisy and ambiguous images of the world. If the current state of the art is any indication, such a goal is difficult to accomplish in a reliable, robust, and efficient manner. By the same token, such a goal is challenging. One problem in vision is diversity: the inherent diversity in any nontrivial domain with respect to the objects and their relative configurations, and the ensuing diversity in the images, each of which may be acquired from anywhere in any given scene. This diversity necessitates opportunism: Of the many possible sources of information in an image, only a few are typically present, and we must do what we can with what we have.

In addition to the information provided by the images themselves, at times, it might also be possible to bring to bear knowledge about objects, their behavior, and the context. We shall not explore the use of domain-specific knowledge here. Further, we shall restrict ourselves to **passive sensing**—that is, to the sensing of radiation that is already present in the scene, rather than to the sensing of radiation that is actively controlled and introduced by the observer. The latter is termed **active sensing**. Although active sensing—for example, using laser stripes—can greatly simplify the computation of scene structure, it interferes with the state of the world, and is, therefore, not always tolerable. Neither is active sensing always feasible.

The approach to computer vision we shall adopt in this book is a modular one; an alternative approach, for instance, might seek to perform one grand optimization. We, in contrast, shall endeavor to identify and isolate the various sources of information in an image; these sources include, for instance, brightness discontinuities, shading, and motion. One may use each of these sources of information either individually, or in conjunction with the others, to make deductions about the scene. The benefits of a modular approach are more than pedagogic: A modular approach makes it easier to control and monitor the performance of a system, to debug the system, and to understand and improve the system.

Computer vision has several applications less ambitious than the creation of anthropomorphic robots. In fact, one may argue that mimicking human behavior is the wrong agenda for robotics to begin with [Whitney 1986]. Applications of computer vision include the following: automation (e.g., on the assembly line), inspection (e.g., of integrated-circuit chips to detect defects in them), remote sensing (e.g., of possibly hostile terrain to generate its relief maps), human–computer communication (e.g., through gesturing), and aids for the visually impaired (e.g., mechanical guide dogs). See [Brady 1982] for a detailed list of applications.

1.2 A Word About Your Sponsor

You might wonder why computer-vision researchers do not simply build systems that emulate the human visual system, especially considering the wealth of literature in neurophysiology, psychology, and psychophysics. Gregory [Gregory 1978] provides a fascinating introduction to the latter topics; see [Levine and Shefner 1991] and [Kaufman 1974] for more detailed treatments, and [Levine 1985] for an engineering perspective. One good reason why computer-vision researchers do not emulate human vision is that what is known about the human visual system beyond the human eye is largely disjointed, speculative, and meager. Further, although human vision is certainly adequate for most frequently encountered tasks—or is it that our lifestyles are adapted to tasks that can be accommodated by our perceptual faculties—adequacy must not be taken to imply infallibility. The fallibility of human vision is amply demonstrated by the existence of visual illusions, ambiguities, and inconsistencies, one of which was illustrated in Figure 1.1, and several others of which we shall examine in Section 1.2.1. Before we proceed any further, however, let us pause for a moment to consider whether perception has any meaning in the absence of what is commonly understood to be intelligence; such a consideration is especially pertinent given that computer vision has its origins in a field called *artificial intelligence.*

Is visual perception an integral component of what we commonly term intelligence? Perhaps not. Although many researchers subscribe to the view

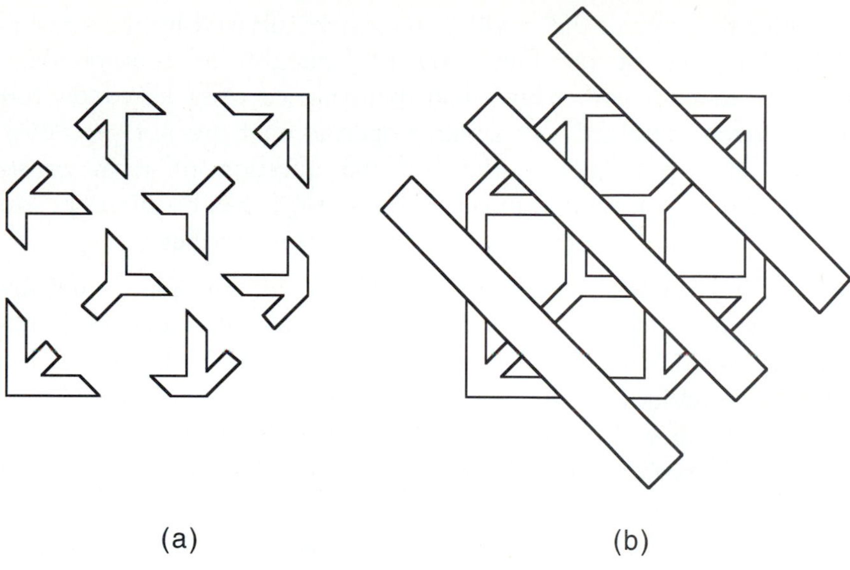

Figure 1.2 Seeing versus thinking. We might argue that seeing and thinking are distinguishable human activities—that seeing is more immediate. Although we can "think" of the fragments in (a) as constituting a cube, it is difficult to "see" a cube. In contrast, we readily "see" a cube in (b), which we can derive from (a) by introducing three "opaque" stripes. Note that the cube in (b) is, in fact, ambiguous: It is the well-known Necker cube, whose vertical face closest to and facing the viewer may reside either in the lower-left corner or in the upper-right corner. (After [Kanizsa 1979], by permission of the Greenwood Publishing Group, Inc., Westport, CT. Copyright © 1979 by Gaetano Kanizsa.)

that perception is inextricably linked to cognition—that what we perceive is often a consequence of logical reasoning—Kanizsa [Kanizsa 1979] argues forcefully that seeing and thinking are clearly distinguishable human activities. He maintains that although thinking and reasoning may lead us to *conceive* of a spatiotemporal phenomenon based on some visual data, *seeing* is more immediate in that it does not require conscious mental effort. Kanizsa buttresses his argument with the two drawings shown in Figure 1.2. Although we can conceive the disjointed fragments in Figure 1.2(a) to constitute a cube, we do not perceive a cube, at least not right away. The introduction of three "opaque" stripes, as in Figure 1.2(b), however, changes our perception: It makes the cube perceptually apparent. Although no one can deny the critical role of perception in the acquisition of information by humans, one could argue that seeing is just a "mechanical act" in that (barring illusions) it does not originate anything.[1] All that the act of seeing does is infer the state of the world to the extent allowed by the sensed data. And, in doing so, it provides food for thought, to conceptualize and classify—to assign membership in an equivalence class based on form or function, thereby implicitly ascribing properties that are not perceived, but rather are only postulated. Although the question of what constitutes intelligence is of considerable intellectual import, it has no direct bearing on our discussion here; hence, we shall not delve into it further.

Even if we were indeed seeking to duplicate human vision—and say that we had a better understanding of its mechanisms—it is not at all obvious that blind emulation would be the recommended route. For one, evolution took its course under a set of physical and computational constraints that are substantially different from the technological barriers that confront us today. A disclaimer is perhaps in order here. Not for a moment am I suggesting that research in biological vision is of little use to the advancement of computer vision. On the contrary, such research is exciting, enlightening, and stimulating. After all, it is biological systems that provide us with the proof of the possibility of high-performance general-purpose vision. However, given that relatively definitive accounts are currently available only for the workings of the human eye (see Section 1.2.2), we are well advised to be cautious in seeking to ground computer vision in what we think we know about human vision.

1.2.1 Visual Illusions, Ambiguities, and Inconsistencies

As already indicated, the fallibility of the human visual system is amply demonstrated by the existence of visual illusions, ambiguities, and inconsistencies, several of which we shall now examine. See [Gregory 1978] and [Frisby 1980] for additional examples.

We already encountered one visual illusion, the well-known Fraser's spiral, in Figure 1.1. You can confirm easily that the spiral in Figure 1.1 is illusory by trying to trace the spiral. Figure 1.3 illustrates several other classical optical illusions.

---

1. This line of reasoning has an important historical precedent. It was used by Lady Lovelace in her mid-nineteenth century account to describe the limitation of Babbage's Analytical Engine, the forerunner of the modern-day computer; see, for instance, p. 284, [Babbage et al. 1961]. It also often lies at the heart of arguments denying the possibility of a thinking machine—see, for instance, [Turing 1950]—but that is another matter. See the book by Penrose [Penrose 1989] in this connection.

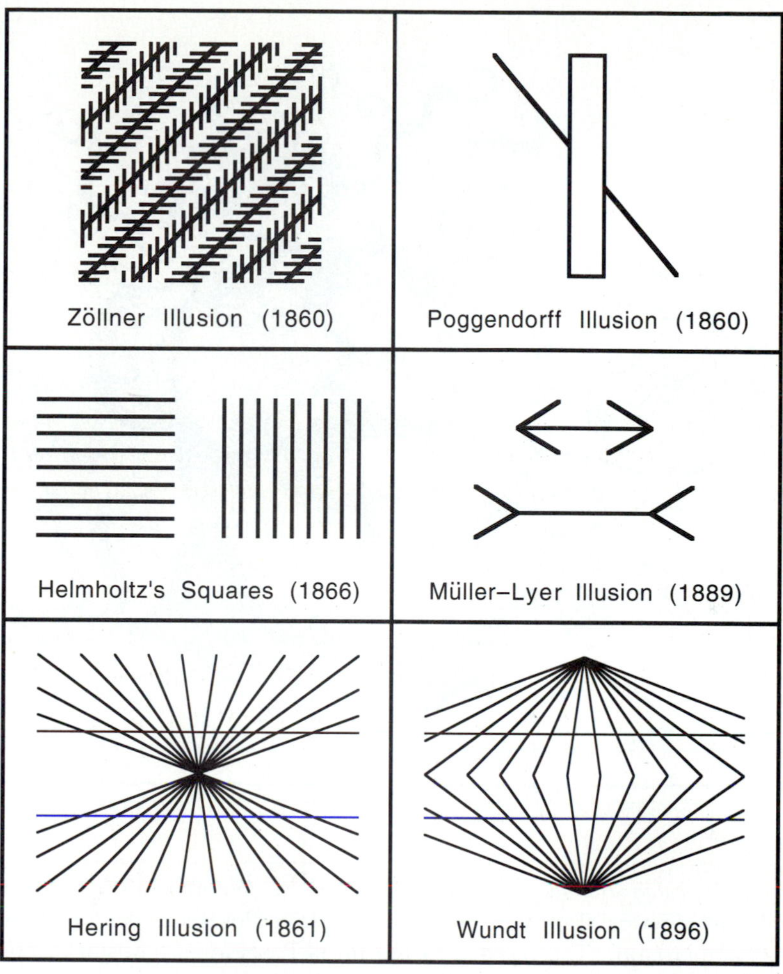

Figure 1.3 Six classical optical illusions. In each of the drawings, geometric truths appear untrue. The illusory effect is so strong that you might wish to have a ruler handy to verify the various assertions. In the Zöllner illusion, the diagonals are parallel, but appear otherwise. In the Poggendorff illusion, the two diagonal straight-line segments seem offset even though they are collinear. Helmholtz's two squares appear rectangular. In the Müller–Lyer illusion, the horizontal line with the reversed arrowheads appears longer than the line with the normal arrowheads, even though both lines have the same length. Finally, in both the Hering and Wundt illusions, the two horizontal and parallel straight lines appear bowed. (See [Boring 1942] for the origins of these optical illusions.)

Figure 1.4 *Poseidon and the Mermaid*, by David M. Weimer, 1990. This India-ink drawing is ambiguous: It may be perceived either as Poseidon, the Greek god of the sea, or as a mermaid. The mermaid's tail fin is Poseidon's moustache. (Courtesy, David M. Weimer.)

At times, a figure may evoke more than a single interpretation—that is, the figure may be ambiguous. The multiple interpretations of a figure may either coexist, or one interpretation may dominate the other(s). Weimer's *Poseidon and the Mermaid*, illustrated in Figure 1.4, is an excellent example of an ambiguous figure: It may be perceived either as Poseidon or as a mermaid. Several other visually ambiguous figures are shown in Figure 1.5.

Finally, it is possible that, although what we perceive from a figure is neither ambiguous nor completely illusory, it is globally unrealizable in that we cannot physically construct the perceived three-dimensional object in its entirety in three-dimensional space. This possibility is illustrated beautifully

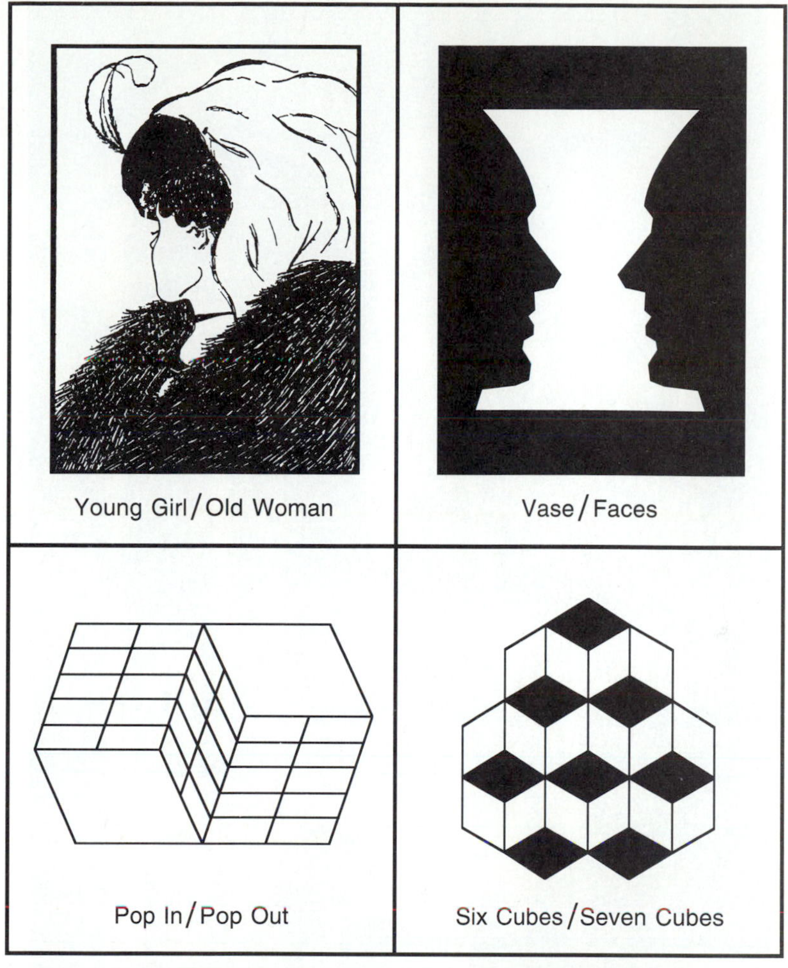

Figure 1.5 Four well-known visual ambiguities. In each of the drawings, two interpretations compete for attention. In the young-girl/old-woman illustration, the young girl's chin is the old woman's nose. The interpretation of the vase/faces illustration depends on whether the black region is seen as the background or as the foreground. Finally, the pop-in/pop-out and six-cubes/seven-cubes ambiguities depend on the spontaneous reversal of the perceived concavities and convexities. (See [Boring 1930] for the origin of the young-girl/old-woman ambiguity, which is based on a cartoon by Hill in 1915; see [Boring 1942] for the origin of the vase/faces ambiguity, which is based on an ambiguous figure by Rubin in 1915; the pop-in/pop-out and six-cubes/seven-cubes ambiguities are based on the Schröder staircase (illustrated in Figure 4.2), which was proposed in 1858 and whose origin is described in [Boring 1942].)

Figure 1.6 *Belvedere*, by Maurits C. Escher, 1958. This well-known lithograph exhibits several geometrical inconsistencies that are not readily apparent. The middle-level pillars cross from the front to the rear, and vice versa; the ladder's base is inside the building, but its top is outside; the topmost level is at right angles to the middle level; the cube being examined by the person on the bench is geometrically impossible. (Copyright © 1990 by M. C. Escher Heirs / Cordon Art – Baarn – Holland.)

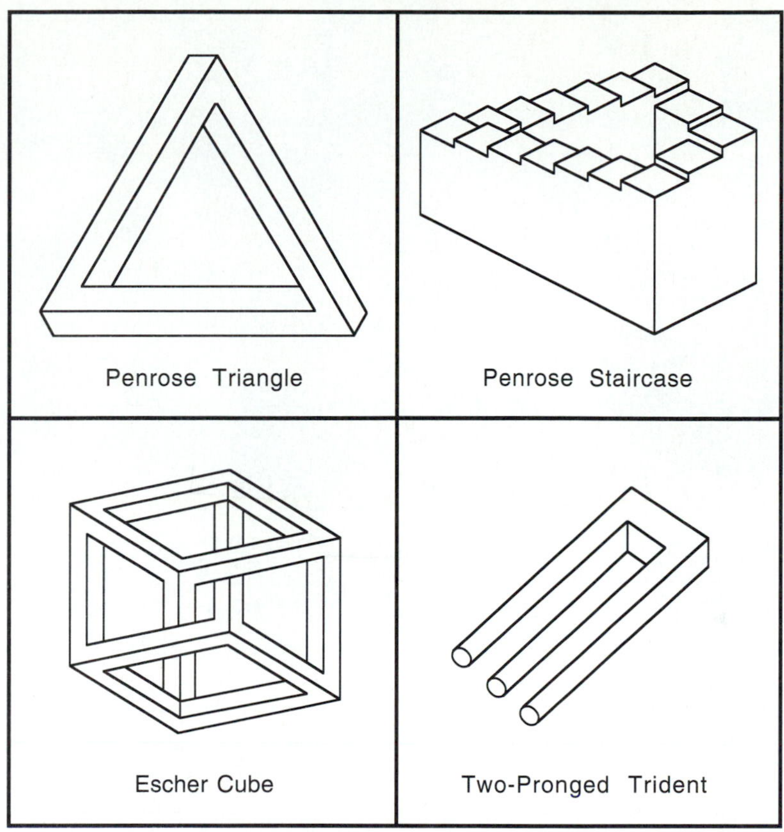

Figure 1.7 Four well-known visual inconsistencies. In each of the drawings, geometrical inconsistency makes the perceived object physically unrealizable. The Penrose triangle (after [Penrose and Penrose 1958]) appears to be a polyhedron, but if it were one, it could not form a closed loop. The Penrose staircase (after [Penrose and Penrose 1958]) descends (ascends) all the way around to the starting step. The Escher cube (after Escher's lithograph, *Belvedere,* 1958) has a top that is inconsistent with its base. Finally, the two-pronged trident (after [Gregory 1965]) appears to terminate in three prongs that have circular cross-sections, whereas the base of the trident appears to have only two prongs with rectangular cross-sections.

by *Belvedere,* the well-known lithograph by Escher reproduced in Figure 1.6. Although the lithograph at first seems to portray a perfectly ordinary scene, a closer examination reveals several geometrical inconsistencies that render the perceived scene physically unrealizable. Figure 1.7 illustrates four other "inconsistent drawings."

Figure 1.8 An image whose interpretation by humans changes when the image is turned upside down. If you turn this photograph of two lava cones with craters upside down, you will perceive it to be the image of two craters with mounds. This reversal of the perceived concavities and convexities is apparently due to an implicit assumption by you, the viewer, that the scene is lit from above. (After [Rittenhouse 1786]. Photograph provided by Associated Press / Wide World Photos, 1972.)

All the examples of visual illusions, ambiguities, and inconsistencies rendered thus far might strike you as contrived. It may seem to you that their success at "manipulating" our visual system depends at least in part on their lack of "realism." After all, if we cannot believe what we see, what are we to believe? This absolute faith in our perceptual faculties is not entirely justified. Consider, for instance, Figure 1.8—a routine photograph of a natural scene showing lava cones with craters at their tips. There seems no cause for confusion here, now that we have a real scene. However, the photograph remains unambiguous only until we turn it upside down: Then, the cones become craters, and the craters become cones.

The various visual illusions, ambiguities, and inconsistencies furnished here are more than just curiosities. They provide us with valuable insights into the nature of human vision, and, in addition, they raise the following all-important question: Is human vision just controlled hallucination? That is, do we infer from our retinal images more than what is supported by the geometry and physics of image formation? Helmholtz, in his justly celebrated *Handbook of Physiological Optics*, first published in the middle of the nineteenth century, expresses the view that, "Every image is the image of a thing merely for him who knows how to read it, and who is enabled by the aid of the image to form an idea of the thing" (p. 24, [Helmholtz 1910], English translation).[2] The implication of this assertion is that it is not as though the human visual system is making precise and exact inferences based on the physics of image formation in the eye, but rather that the human visual system is invoking some rules of thumb that are derived from and biased by the prior experience of the individual, and, perhaps, of the species. As a result, humans may "see" what is not (i.e., hallucinate), and they may not "see" what is (i.e., overlook). Whereas we are quite forgiving when it comes to the performance of humans, we are not quite as charitable when it comes to the performance of machines. Hence, we need ask ourselves this: Do we really wish to make machines see as we do?

1.2.2 The Eye and Beyond

Irrespective of whether or not we seek to emulate human vision—in either one or both of form and function—it is pertinent to ask, what is it exactly that we know about the human visual system? If nothing else, the answer to this question would educate and enlighten us, and would perhaps even suggest strategies for machine vision.

---

2. Hermann von Helmholtz (1821–1894), the author of the *Handbook of Physiological Optics* ([Helmholtz 1909], [Helmholtz 1910], [Helmholtz 1911]), was one of the preeminent scientists of the nineteenth century. He made fundamental contributions to a wide variety of disciplines, including physiology, optics, electrodynamics, mathematics, and meteorology. He is best known, however, for his statement of the law of conservation of energy. Helmholtz was an empiricist—he denied the doctrine of innate ideas and held experience to be the basis of all knowledge—and his empiricism is reflected in his work. Helmholtz's greatest work, the *Handbook of Physiological Optics* (1856–1866), is an epitome of the scientific method. It is the single most important treatise on the physics and physiology of human vision to this day. Helmholtz's inventions in connection with human vision included the ophthalmoscope, which is an instrument for viewing the interior of the eye, and the ophthalmometer, which is an instrument for making measurements of the eye. Helmholtz's other great work on sensory perception, *On the Sensations of Tone as a Physiological Basis for the Theory of Music* (1862), laid the foundations for the science of acoustics.

That the eye is an organ of sight is obvious: All you need to do to verify this assertion is to close your eyes. However, it is not equally obvious what the exact role of the eye might be. Pythagoras and his followers, circa 500 B.C., supported the "emanation hypothesis of vision." According to this hypothesis, visual rays emanate in straight lines from the eye, spreading with immeasurable speed and consummating the act of vision on touching the perceived object. You may think of this mechanism of vision as analogous to how a blind person might discover her surroundings by groping with a long cane. The emanation hypothesis, however strange it may sound now, remained widely accepted in various forms for centuries, until Kepler, in 1604, correctly proposed that the eye is an optical instrument that forms a real inverted image on its back surface; see Figure 2.1. You are referred to Polyak's monumental *The Vertebrate Visual System* [Polyak 1957] both for an extended historical account of investigations into the eye, and for intricate physiological details of the eye.

The human eye is roughly a globe about 2 cm in diameter, free to rotate in its orbit under the control of six extrinsic muscles. Figure 1.9 illustrates the schematic of the horizontal cross-section of the right human eye, viewed from above. Light enters the eye through the tough transparent **cornea**, passes through the watery **aqueous humor** that fills the **anterior chamber**, proceeds to the crystalline **lens**, and then through the gelatinous **vitreous humor**, finally to form an inverted image on the photosensitive **retina**. Directly in front of the lens is an annular opaque muscular membrane, the **iris**, which gives the eye its color. Light can enter the eye only through the circular aperture of the iris, the **pupil**, whose size is controlled by the expansion and contraction of the iris. The lens is held in place by the **suspensory ligament**, through which the **ciliary muscle** adjusts the curvature of the lens. Barring the region of the eye where the cornea is located, the eye is covered by a dense fibrous opaque sheath called the **sclera**, part of which is seen as the white of the eye. Between the sclera and the retina lies the heavily pigmented **choroid**, which absorbs the light that passes through the retina undetected.

The adjustment of the curvature of the lens of an eye by its ciliary muscle is called **accommodation**. Accommodation adapts the eye for clearest vision at a particular distance—in a healthy eye, objects at this distance are imaged on the retina rather than in front of or behind the retina. Objects that are imaged in front of or behind the retina appear blurred to the viewer. **Nearsightedness**, or **myopia**, describes the inability of an eye to bring into focus on its retina objects that are distant from the eye—these objects are

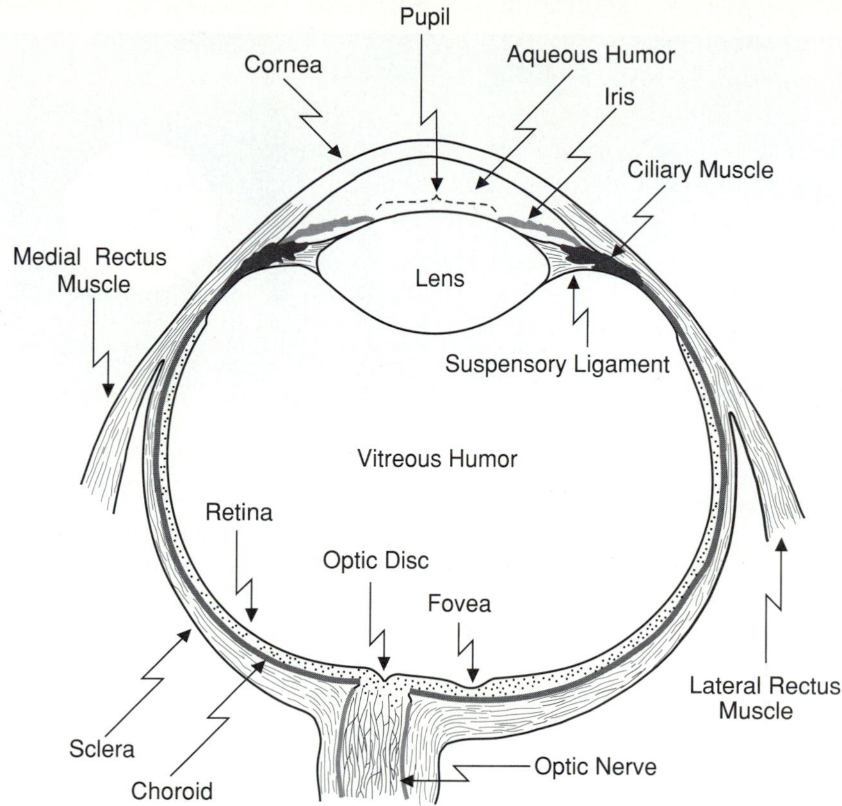

Figure 1.9 Schematic of a horizontal cross-section of a right human eye, viewed from above. Light passes in sequence through the cornea, the aqueous humor, the lens, and the vitreous humor, finally to form an image on the photosensitive *retina*. The retina encodes the image into nerve impulses, and transmits these impulses to the brain via the optic nerve. Clearest vision is realized in a circular depression in the retina called the *fovea*. The optic disc, where the optic nerve leaves the retina, is "blind." The ciliary muscle, which attaches to the lens through the suspensory ligament, controls the curvature of the lens. The iris, which is an opaque annular muscular membrane that gives the eye its color, controls the size of the pupil, which is the aperture in the iris that is the sole entrance for light into the eye. The sclera is a dense, fibrous, opaque sheath covering much of the eye. The choroid is a heavily pigmented layer that lies between the sclera and the retina.

imaged in front of the retina. **Farsightedness**, or **hypermetropia**, describes the inability of an eye to bring into focus on its retina objects that are close to the eye—these objects are imaged behind the retina. Both nearsightedness and farsightedness can usually be corrected by external lenses.

Figure 1.10 Discovery of your blind spot. You can discover your blind spot as follows. First, close your left eye and hold this book in the normal reading position about a foot or so away from your face. Then, look steadily at the white cross with your right eye, and doing so move the book slowly toward and away from your open eye, until, at a particular position of the book, the white disc disappears completely from your view. The white disc will seem to disappear completely from its black background when the retinal image of the disc is formed within your optic disc (see Figure 1.9), which is also known as the *blind spot*. (After [Mariotte 1668] and [Helmholtz 1911].)

The Retina

The **retina** is a complex nervous membrane with a mosaic of photoreceptors that on being stimulated by light produce electrical nervous signals. These signals are transmitted to the brain via the **optic nerve**, evoking the experience of vision. The location on the retina where all the individual nerve fibers constituting the optic nerve come together is called the **optic disc**. This region is free of photoreceptors, and hence, is often called the **blind spot**. (Everyone has a blind spot—you can experience yours by performing the simple experiment outlined in Figure 1.10.) Not far from the blind spot, near the axis of the lens, is a shallow pit with a high concentration of photoreceptors. This pit is the **fovea**. Although only a fraction of a millimeter in diameter, the fovea is of paramount importance as it provides the greatest visual acuity in brightly lit scenes. It is at the fovea that objects are imaged when we direct our gaze toward them.

The retina, which is a fraction of a millimeter thick—that is, about as thick as a few sheets of typing paper—has been the subject of several revealing studies since the advent of the compound microscope. According to its greatest investigator, Ramón y Cajal, "The preference that the best known anatomists and histologists have given to this area is easily understood, since a knowledge of the arrangements of retinal cells is essential for a full understanding of vision and the many problems associated with it" (p. 781, [Ramón y Cajal 1892–1893], English translation). Figure 1.11 shows a photograph of a vertical section of a human retina taken from about 1.25 mm from the center of the fovea; a schematic of the photograph is shown alongside the photograph. The retina in the photograph was stained so that its structure would be highlighted—in a living eye, the retina is largely transparent. The first important point to note is that the optic nerve fibers run close to the vitreous humor, whereas the **rods** and **cones**—the two types of photoreceptors, each named after its shape—are located near the choroid. This arrangement is counterintuitive as it requires that the light pass through almost the entire depth of retinal tissue—complete with blood vessels (not shown in the figure), nerve cells, and nerve fibers—before it can be sensed. At the fovea, however, unlike the rest of the retina, much of the retinal tissue between the photoreceptors and the vitreous humor is displaced to one side, creating a shallow pit that has direct access to light.

The second important point to note with respect to the structure of the retina, illustrated in Figure 1.11, is that the photosensitive rods and cones do not have a continuous physical link to the optic nerve fibers by means of which they transmit signals to the brain. This absence of a physical link was first established by Ramón y Cajal, who showed that the retina comprises three distinct layers of nerve cells, and that these nerve cells communicate with one another through junctions, called **synapses** (see [Polyak 1957]). We shall not delve into the details of the structure and function of the retina—see [Rodieck 1973] for these details. Suffice it to say that, as illustrated in Figure 1.11, the rods and cones transmit signals to the optic nerve fibers, which extend from the **ganglion cells**, by means of the **bipolar cells**. At the input end of the bipolar cells are the **horizontal cells**, and at the output end of the bipolar cells are the **amacrine cells**, both horizontal and amacrine cells providing lateral (synaptic) interconnections between the nerve cells that run vertically in Figure 1.11. These lateral interconnections determine the response of a ganglion cell to a photostimulus within an extended retinal area called the ganglion cell's **receptive field** (see the excellent article by Werblin [Werblin 1973] in this connection). It seems that at least one function of the retinal nerve cells that mediate between the photoreceptors and the optic nerve fibers is to condense the information contained in the light impinging on the retina. This hypothesis is supported by the sheer numbers of the photoreceptors and the optic nerve fibers: Whereas the total number of cones in a human eye is about 6 million, and the total number of

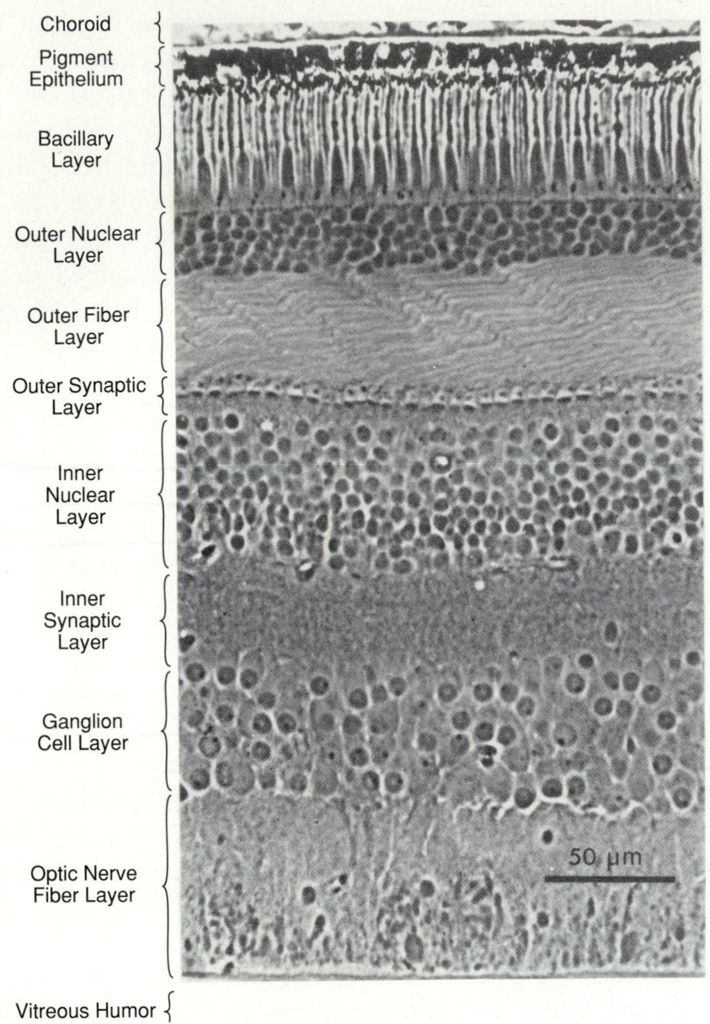

Figure 1.11 The human retina. A photograph of a vertical cross-section of a human retina is shown on this page, and the schematic corresponding to this photograph is shown on the facing page. The photograph, which was obtained through phase-contrast microscopy, is of a retinal section about 0.4 mm thick, this section taken from about 1.25 mm from the center of the fovea. Light strikes the retina through the vitreous humor, which is at the bottom of the photograph, and then proceeds through much of the retinal tissue to be detected by the photoreceptors, which are of two types: *rods* and *cones*. The rods, which are capable of detecting light at much fainter levels than are the cones, facilitate vision in the dark. The cones, on the other hand—which unlike the rods come in three distinct varieties, each variety with a preferred sensitivity to red, green, or blue light—provide us with color vision. At the fovea, which is the region of the retina that provides the clearest vision, the inner layers of the retina that lie between the vitreous humor and the photoreceptors are pushed to one side so that light can impinge more directly on the photoreceptors. It is to accommodate this dislocation of retinal tissue that the

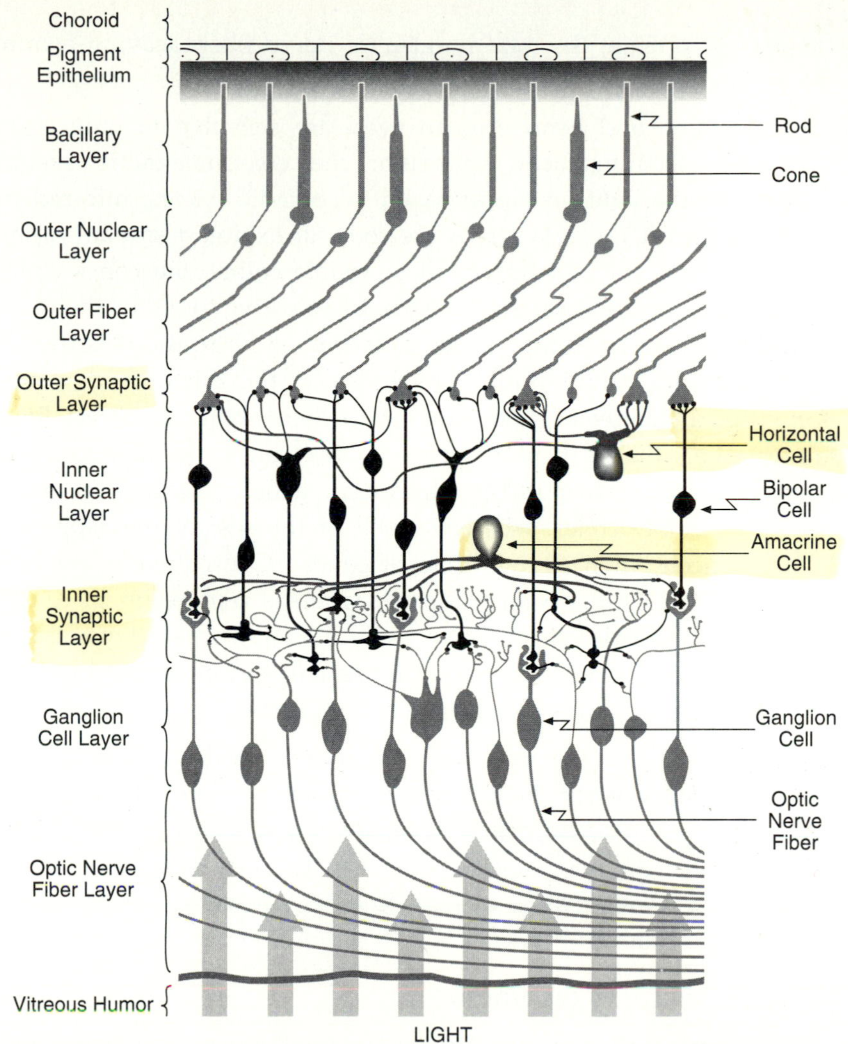

nerve fibers that lead from the nuclei of the rods and cones to the outer synaptic layer have highly slanted trajectories in the neighborhood of the fovea, as in the photograph shown. At the outer synaptic layer, the rod and cone terminals form synapses with the bipolar cells. A *synapse* is a site at which one cell of the nervous system transmits signals to another cell. The bipolar cells lead to the ganglion cells, with which they form synapses at the inner synaptic layer. It is the nerve fibers of the ganglion cells that come together to form the optic nerve, which leads to the brain. As the optic nerve fibers in all number only of the order of 1 million, in contrast to about 125 million rods and cones, the signals that are generated by the rods and cones in response to light impinging on them must of necessity be compacted and encoded before they can be transmitted to the brain. This compaction is accomplished with the aid of horizontal and amacrine cells, which provide lateral synaptic interconnections at the outer and inner synaptic layers, respectively. (Photograph from [Boycott and Dowling 1969] with permission, and schematic after [Polyak 1957].)

rods is about 120 million, the total number of nerve fibers leaving a human eye is only of the order of 1 million (see [Pirenne 1967]).

Rods and cones, and hence human eyes, are sensitive to only a small fraction of the electromagnetic spectrum; the electromagnetic spectrum includes not only the light visible to us but also radio waves, infrared rays, ultraviolet rays, and X rays. Whereas the rods all exhibit a similar variation in sensitivity to light over the spectrum of visible colors, the cones come in three distinct varieties, each variety being most sensitive to either the red, the green, or the blue portion of the visible spectrum. As a result, it is the cones that provide us with color vision. The rods, on the other hand, come in handy for vision in dimly lit scenes owing to their ability to detect light at much fainter levels than can be detected by the cones. In this connection, see, for instance, [Cornsweet 1970]. The fovea, which provides the greatest visual acuity, has only cones, whereas much of the rest of the retina has a much higher concentration of rods than of cones. Consequently, our vision in brightly lit scenes is sharp and colored, whereas our vision in dimly lit scenes is blurred and colorless. (As an aside, it might interest you to learn that it is the absence of rods from the fovea that prompts astronomers to "look off" the fovea when they wish to detect faint stars.)

All in all, the human eye is a truly remarkable device. To this day, no feat of human engineering has come even remotely close in performance. The sensitivity of the human eye approaches the absolute limit set by the quantum nature of light, and the maximum visual acuity of the human eye is high enough for the wave nature of light to have a bearing; see, for instance, [Pirenne 1967] and [Barlow 1981].

The Visual Pathways to the Brain

Although the past two centuries have witnessed substantial gains in our understanding of the structure and function of the human eye, "the more central parts of the visual system have little that is not at the moment mysterious" (p. 7, [Barlow 1981]). It is the conversion of representations of retinal images into knowledge of the world that constitutes the barrier to our understanding of human vision. Although we do have an idea of the major visual pathways from the eyes to the brain, we know little of what happens in the brain.

Figure 1.12 illustrates the major visual pathways from the eyes to the brain. From each eye emerges an **optic nerve**, which carries electrical nervous signals from the eye to the brain. The fibers constituting each optic nerve can be divided into two groups: those that originate on the inner nasal side of the eye, and those that originate on its outer temporal side. Fibers

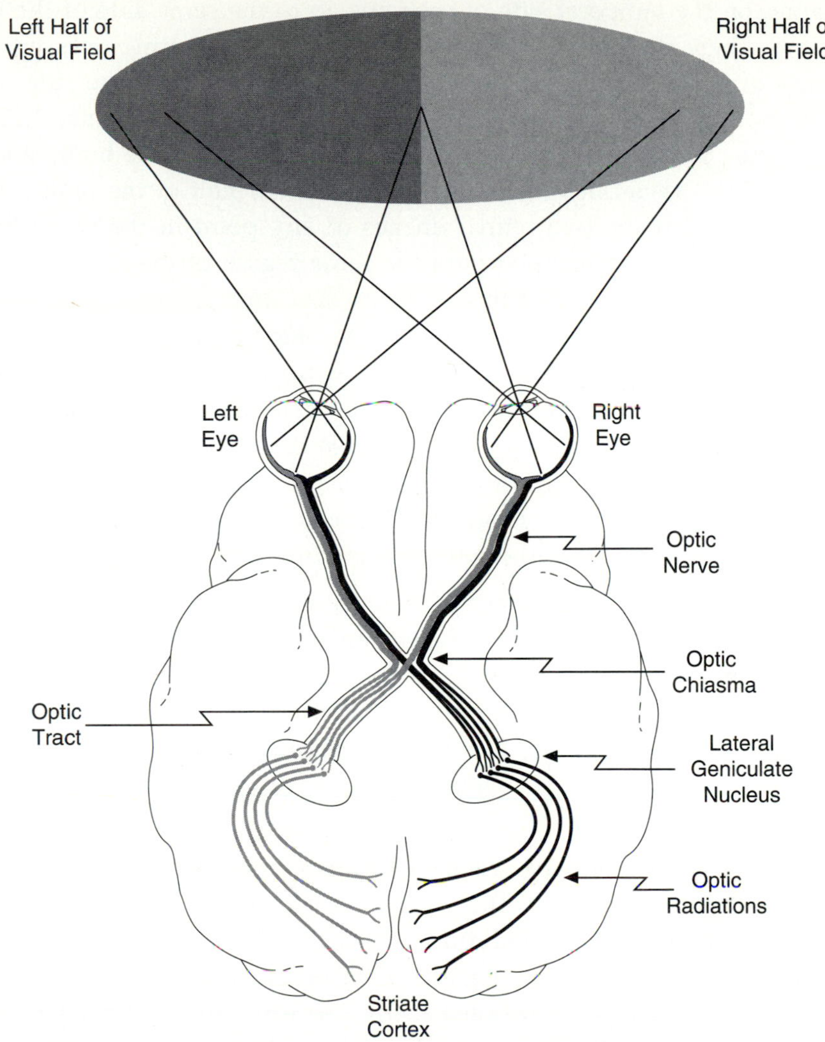

Figure 1.12 The major visual pathways from the eyes to the brain. The pattern of light striking each retina is encoded into nerve impulses, and these impulses are transmitted to the brain via the optic nerve that emerges from the retina. The left half of the visual field, which is imaged on the right half of each retina, is transmitted to the right half of the brain; the right half of the visual field, which is imaged on the left half of each retina, is transmitted to the left half of the brain. The cross-over of optic nerve fibers that is necessary to realize such a mapping takes place at the optic chiasma. From the optic chiasma, the nerve fibers proceed to the lateral geniculate nuclei via the optic tracts; from the lateral geniculate nuclei, nerve impulses are transmitted to the striate cortex of the brain via the optic radiations. It is important for binocular stereoscopic depth perception that each of the possibly two retinal images of a point in the visual field be mapped onto the same region of the brain.

originating on the temporal side of each eye go to the same side of the brain as the eye where they originate. In contrast, fibers originating on each nasal side cross over at the **optic chiasma** and proceed to the opposite side of the brain as the eye where they originate. Thus, as indicated in Figure 1.12, the left half of the visual field is mapped onto the right half of the brain, and the right half of the visual field is mapped onto the left half of the brain. What is important is that the two retinal images of any point in the scene that is visible to both eyes are mapped onto the same region of the brain. It is the disparity between the two retinal images that makes stereoscopic depth perception possible within the field of view shared by the two eyes, also called the **stereoscopic field.**[3] (The term *stereoscopic* literally implies the seeing of objects in three dimensions. However, its use here is more specific: *Stereoscopic* is taken to mean the seeing of objects in three dimensions on the basis of the retinal disparity between the images formed in the left and the right eye. As we shall see at length in this book, it is possible to perceive an object in three dimensions without the use of both eyes.)

To appreciate the significance of stereoscopic vision, you may perform the following simple experiment. Set up an uncapped pen on its end on a flat surface, perhaps with the aid of a few books, and then withdraw your hands some few feet away from the pen. Then, keeping your head stationary, try to cap the pen, first with one eye closed, and then with both eyes open. You should find it much easier to cap the pen with both eyes open.

Returning to the primary visual pathways from the eyes to the brain illustrated in Figure 1.12, from the optic chiasma, the nerve fibers proceed in two groups, the **optic tracts**, each tract comprising fibers that originate on the same side of each of the two retinas. Most of the nerve fibers constituting each of the two optic tracts proceed to the corresponding **lateral geniculate nucleus**, which is mainly a relay station where the nerve fibers make their first postretinal synapse. From the two lateral geniculate nuclei, signals are transmitted via the **optic radiations** to the **striate cortex**, which gets its name from its striped appearance in a fresh human brain. The importance of the

3. It seems that binocular animals that are predators have both eyes in front of their heads, like humans, and as a result, they have a large stereoscopic field of view. Binocular stereoscopic vision is important to predators as it allows them to judge accurately without moving the distance to their prey. In contrast to binocular predators, binocular prey have one eye on either side of their heads, an arrangement that provides prey with a large total field of view at the expense of a large stereoscopic field. A large total field of view allows prey to determine whether a predator is present over a large range of directions, and such a determination is clearly of higher priority to prey than is the accurate estimation of the distance of a predator.

fovea is manifested in the striate cortex by the disproportionately large area dedicated to the fovea there. In comparison to what we know of the human eye, little is known of what happens in the region of the brain dedicated to vision; see [Kuffler, Nicholls, and Martin 1984], [Peters and Jones 1985], and [Hubel 1988] for perspectives on the state of our understanding.

1.3 What Is to Come

This book aims to lead you gently through a guided tour of computer vision, stopping along the way to emphasize concepts and their significance. For the more seasoned among you, there shall be details and pointers, especially to recent developments. Although these details and pointers, which can safely be ignored without loss of continuity, may at first seem obscure to those among you who are unfamiliar with the terrain, they could later serve as guide maps for unaccompanied explorations. There are no prerequisites per se to join this tour. Curiosity and interest are taken for granted.

Figure 1.13 provides a sketch of a plausible schema for a general-purpose computer-vision system. By **general purpose** here is meant "without restriction to a particular task or domain." The boxes in the figure represent data, and the arrows indicate processes and the direction of data flow. The computer-vision paradigm in Figure 1.13 is by far the most common; hence, for purposes of discussion, let us adopt it here too.

In the computer-vision paradigm of Figure 1.13, the three-dimensional scene is first viewed by one or multiple cameras to produce either monochromatic or colored images. We shall restrict ourselves to monochromatic images in this book. The images thus acquired are processed so that the brightness discontinuities within the images are detected—these discontinuities are termed *edges*—and perhaps also so that the images are segmented into relatively homogeneous image regions. Then, the images and their edge and homogeneous-region maps are used to constrain the possible interpretations of the imaged world. Currently, the most widely investigated processes used to constrain the three-dimensional world are based on the following image characteristics: line drawings (i.e., edge maps of images), shading (i.e., variation in image brightness), variation in image texture, the disparity between images in stereo image pairs, and image evolution under motion of the camera relative to the scene. The significance of edges, shading, texture, stereo, and motion in the interpretation of images is highlighted by Figures 3.1, 5.1, 6.1, 7.1, and 8.1, respectively. The three-dimensional constraints derived from images may be either local (e.g., the depths, orientations, and reflectances of surface points), or global (e.g., the

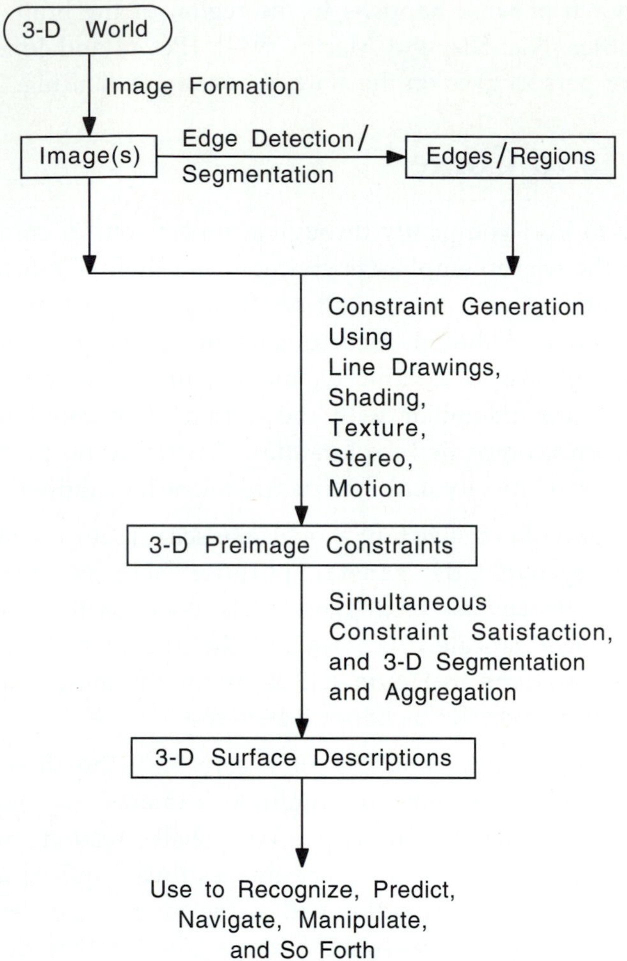

Figure 1.13 A plausible schema for general-purpose computer vision. *Computer vision* describes the automatic deduction of the structure and properties of a (possibly dynamic) three-dimensional world from its two-dimensional image(s). The boxes in the figure denote data, the arrows indicate processes and the direction of data flow, and 3-D is an abbreviation for three-dimensional. The term *preimage* in the figure refers to the imaged scene. In general, the preimage of any point in the range of a mapping is the point or collection of points in the domain of the mapping that map onto the particular point in the range—in the context of imaging, the mapping is image formation, whose domain is the three-dimensional world and whose range is the two-dimensional image.

restriction of a surface to be a surface of revolution). At any rate, once a collection of such constraints has been derived, surface descriptions may be generated by simultaneously enforcing all the preimage constraints (i.e., constraints on the imaged scene) and partitioning the data into sets arising from independent surfaces. These descriptions, preferably simultaneously metric and symbolic, may serve a variety of purposes: recognition, prediction, navigation, manipulation, and the performance of other tasks that require cognition and planning. (The **preimage** of any point in the range of a mapping is the point or collection of points in the domain of the mapping that map onto the particular point in the range—in the context of imaging, the mapping is image formation, whose domain is the three-dimensional world and whose range is the two-dimensional image.)

Although modularity is a convenient design procedure, and the absence of feedback avoids tricky control problems, it is clear that in Figure 1.13, the strict demarcation between the various processes (and data) and the restriction to forward data flow are both potentially limiting to robustness. For instance, edge detection is likely to proceed better in conjunction with the interpretation of edges. All the processes in Figure 1.13 could conceivably be modulated by succeeding data; as in all feedback loops, stability would be the primary ensuing concern. Nevertheless, despite its obvious limitations, as Figure 1.13 does represent the currently most popular paradigm, its components are what we shall discuss.

In Chapter 2, we shall discuss three aspects of image formation: geometry, radiometry, and sensing. This discussion will lay the foundation for the treatment of other topics. In Chapter 3, we shall examine edge detection and image segmentation. First, we shall consider popular schemes to detect edge fragments in images, and then, we shall turn our attention to the organization of such fragments into extended edges, and the description of these edges; subsequently, we shall review image-segmentation techniques. In Chapters 4, 5, 6, 7, and 8, we shall review the fundamentals of, and examine the progress made toward, constraining the imaged world using line drawings, shading, texture, stereo, and motion, respectively. These topics are at the heart of computer-vision research today. Owing to the limited success to this point of such efforts in generating robust three-dimensional preimage constraints, simultaneous constraint satisfaction and three-dimensional segmentation and aggregation have received relatively scant attention in the literature. Hence, we shall not devote a separate chapter to these topics. In Chapter 9, we shall first examine the attributes that make a representation desirable, and then, we shall discuss several shape-representation strategies in this light. Finally, in Chapter 10, we shall consider pointers to some of the topics that have not previously received our attention. These topics include the following: so-called high-level tasks, such as object recognition, that may require three-dimensional surface descriptions; industrial applications; active range finding; and color vision.

1.4 A Bibliographical Note

Computer vision, as we know it today, had its beginnings in the seminal work of Roberts [Roberts 1965], who developed computer programs to deduce the three-dimensional structure and arrangement of a few simple trihedral-vertex polyhedra from their digital images. Roberts's modest success with his *blocks world* prompted high hopes. Back in the 1960s, the emerging and ambitiously named field, *artificial intelligence*, was arousing spectacular short-term expectations. Soon, however, researchers realized that visual perception is a nontrivial intellectual enterprise, and that techniques developed to analyze polyhedral scenes almost never lend themselves to more general settings.

Since the early work of Roberts, substantial time and effort have been devoted to computer vision, and the ensuing results have been documented in several publications. The principal among these publications are the journals *IEEE Transactions on Pattern Analysis and Machine Intelligence* (*IEEE PAMI*), *International Journal of Computer Vision* (*IJCV*), and *Computer Vision, Graphics, and Image Processing* (*CVGIP*), now with the subtitle *Image Understanding* (*CVGIP: IU*). Other journals of interest include *Artificial Intelligence*, *Biological Cybernetics*, *Journal of the Optical Society of America A*, *Pattern Recognition Letters*, *Pattern Recognition*, *IEEE Transactions on Robotics and Automation*, *International Journal of Robotics Research*, and *IEEE Transactions on Systems, Man, and Cybernetics*. Occasionally, survey articles surface in the *Computing Surveys* and the *Proceedings of the IEEE*. The most prominent conferences in the field are the *International Conference on Computer Vision* (*ICCV*) and the *IEEE Computer Society Conference on Computer Vision and Pattern Recognition* (*CVPR*). Other related conferences include the *International Conference on Pattern Recognition*, the *International Symposium on Robotics Research*, the *IEEE International Conference on Robotics and Automation*, and the *International Joint Conference on Artificial Intelligence*. New results obtained at several U.S. universities are first reported in the proceedings of the *Image Understanding Workshop*, which is organized at regular intervals by the Defense Advanced Research Projects Agency (DARPA) of the United States. It is not uncommon to also find references to reports and memoranda—however, as only a minuscule fraction of the audience has ready access to any such document, this author finds the practice ill-advised.

Two popular books on the subject are *Computer Vision* by Ballard and Brown [Ballard and Brown 1982], and *Robot Vision* by Horn [Horn 1986]; the latter provides an in-depth coverage of relatively few topics. Several survey articles and collections of papers have also been published. Among the surveys, the two most prominent are [Barrow and Tenenbaum 1981a] and [Brady 1982]; both are slightly dated; however, the former provides a valuable historical perspective. Among the collections of papers, the most significant one that comprises papers not published elsewhere is [Hanson and Riseman 1978]; this collection includes two fairly influential position papers, one by Marr [Marr 1978], and the other by Barrow and Tenenbaum [Barrow and Tenenbaum 1978]. In addition to the various books and surveys, every year, Rosenfeld publishes a handy exhaustive bibliography in *CVGIP*. Given that most theoretical results are of largely untested utility, and experimental claims of unsubstantiated robustness, computer-vision books and surveys of necessity reflect personal perspectives. This book will be no different.

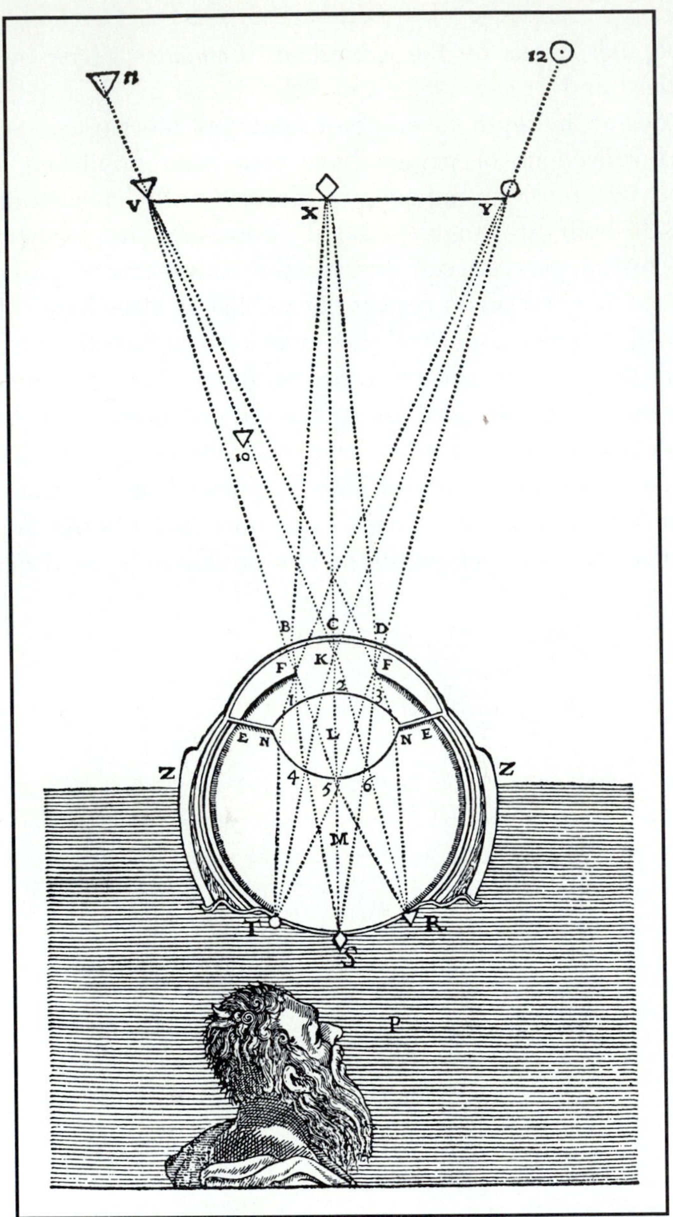

Figure 2.1 Image formation on the retina, according to Descartes. Descartes removed the eye of an ox, scraped its back to make it transparent, and then observed on it from a darkened room "not perhaps without wonder and pleasure" the inverted image of a scene (see [Pirenne 1967]). Such an experiment was performed originally by Scheiner, first with the eyes of sheep and oxen, and then, in 1625, with a human eye; the formation of an inverted retinal image was proposed by Kepler in 1604 (see [Polyak 1957]). (From Descartes's *La Dioptrique*, 1637.)

Chapter 2

Image Formation

In Chapter 1, we discussed some salient aspects of the human visual system—in particular, of the human eye. As illustrated in Figure 2.1, the human eye forms an inverted image of the scene on its retina. The retina, in turn, as we saw in Chapter 1, senses the image, encodes it, and then transmits the encoded image to the brain. The role of a camera in a

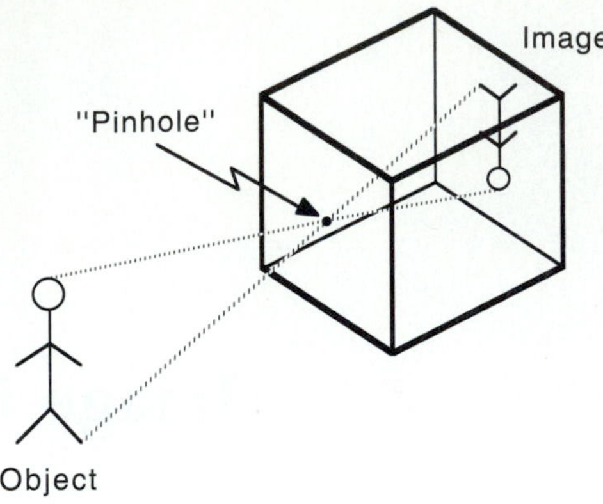

Figure 2.2 Pinhole camera. A pinhole camera is the simplest device to form an image of a three-dimensional scene on a two-dimensional surface: Straight rays of light pass through a "pinhole" and form an inverted image on a surface.

computer-vision system is analogous to the role of the eye in the human visual system. Let us now explore the relationship between the three-dimensional world and its two-dimensional image produced by a camera. This relationship is at the heart of every nonheuristic attempt to recover the properties of a scene from its one or multiple images. Hence, it is important that we understand this relationship well.

Our discussion here will proceed along three lines: geometry, radiometry, and sensing. First, we shall study the geometry of image formation. Then, we shall examine the relationship between the amount of light radiating from a surface and the amount of light impinging on the image of the surface. Finally, we shall turn our attention to the sensing of the image—that is, to the conversion of the image into a representation that is amenable to storage, processing, and analysis by an electronic computer. A word of caution: All the models presented in this chapter are just first-order approximations that will certainly be in need of refinement as computer vision advances.

2.1 Geometry

The simplest imaging device is a **pinhole camera** of the type illustrated in Figure 2.2. Ideally, a pinhole camera has an infinitesimally small aperture—a "pinhole"—through which light enters the camera and forms an image on the camera surface facing the aperture. Geometrically, the image is formed by straight rays of light that travel from the object through the aperture to

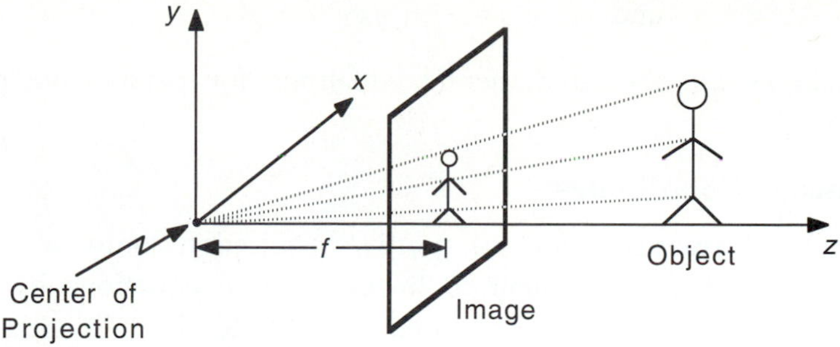

Figure 2.3 Perspective projection. In *perspective projection*, each object point is projected onto a surface along a straight line through a fixed point called the *center of projection*. (Throughout this book, we shall use the terms *object* and *scene* interchangeably.) The projection surface here is a plane. Perspective projection closely models the geometry of image formation in a pinhole camera (see Figure 2.2), except, in perspective projection, we are free to choose the location of the projection surface such that the image is not inverted.

the image plane; here, as elsewhere, we use the terms *object* and *scene* interchangeably. Such a mapping from three dimensions onto two dimensions is called *perspective projection*. Let us first examine perspective projection, and then let us examine two linear approximations to perspective projection. Subsequently, we shall consider the role of a lens in image formation.

2.1.1 Perspective Projection

Perspective projection, also known as **central projection**, is the projection of a three-dimensional entity onto a two-dimensional surface by straight lines that pass through a single point, called the **center of projection**. Perspective projection closely models the geometry of image formation in a pinhole camera.

As illustrated in Figure 2.2, the image in a pinhole camera is inverted. As far as analysis goes, this inversion of the image is mildly inconvenient. Hence, it is customary instead to consider the geometrically equivalent configuration of Figure 2.3 in which the image is on the same side of the center of projection as the scene, and, as a result, the image is not inverted. Now, if we denote the distance of the image plane from the center of projection by f, and we denote the object coordinates and the image coordinates by the subscripts o and i, respectively, then it is clear from similar triangles that

$$x_i = \frac{f}{z_o} x_o \quad \text{and} \quad y_i = \frac{f}{z_o} y_o .$$

These equations are the fundamental equations for perspective projection onto a plane.

Homogeneous Coordinates

The preceding equations for perspective projection onto a plane are nonlinear. It is often convenient to linearize these equations by mapping each point (x, y, z) in three-dimensional space onto the following line that passes through the origin in four-dimensional space: $(X, Y, Z, W) = (wx, wy, wz, w)$, where w is a dummy parameter that sweeps a straight line in four-dimensional space. The new coordinates, (X, Y, Z, W), are called **homogeneous coordinates**. (Historically, the use of homogeneous coordinates in computer vision goes back to Roberts in 1965 [Roberts 1965].) Although the homogeneous coordinates of a point in three-dimensional space are not unique as every point in three-dimensional space is represented by a whole family of points in four-dimensional space, the homogeneous coordinates are unambiguous if we exclude the origin in four-dimensional space. That is, barring the origin, every point in four-dimensional space represents no more than a single point in three-dimensional space. Specifically, (X, Y, Z, W), $W \neq 0$, in four-dimensional space represents the single point $(x, y, z) = (X/W, Y/W, Z/W)$ in three-dimensional space. Despite their redundancy, homogeneous coordinates are extremely useful as they allow us to express several otherwise nonlinear transformations linearly; see, for instance, [Ballard and Brown 1982] and [Wolberg 1990]. In homogeneous coordinates, perspective projection onto a plane may be expressed as follows:

$$\begin{bmatrix} X_i \\ Y_i \\ Z_i \\ W_i \end{bmatrix} = \begin{bmatrix} f & 0 & 0 & 0 \\ 0 & f & 0 & 0 \\ 0 & 0 & f & 0 \\ 0 & 0 & 1 & 0 \end{bmatrix} \begin{bmatrix} X_o \\ Y_o \\ Z_o \\ W_o \end{bmatrix},$$

where, once again, the subscripts o and i denote the object coordinates and the image coordinates, respectively. You can easily verify the equivalence of this linear expression to the preceding nonlinear equations for perspective projection by making the following two substitutions: $(X_i, Y_i, Z_i, W_i) = (\alpha x_i, \alpha y_i, \alpha z_i, \alpha)$ and $(X_o, Y_o, Z_o, W_o) = (\beta x_o, \beta y_o, \beta z_o, \beta)$. Although the exact definition of a linear transform must await Section 2.3.2, it is sufficient to note here that a transform is linear if and only if it can be expressed as a matrix multiplication, as in the preceding expression for perspective projection in homogeneous coordinates.

Figure 2.4 Photograph illustrating a vanishing point. Parallel straight lines converge at a single point under perspective projection. This point is called the *vanishing point* of the straight lines. (Photograph by Herbert Gehr, from the magazine *Life*, July 1947, © Time Warner, Inc.)

Vanishing Point and Vanishing Line

An important concept in the context of perspective projection is that of a vanishing point. The **vanishing point** of a straight line under perspective projection is that point in the image beyond which the projection of the straight line cannot extend. That is, if the straight line were infinitely long in space, the line would appear to "vanish" at its vanishing point in the image. As the vanishing point of a straight line depends only on the orientation of the line, and not on the position of the line, the notion of a vanishing point is frequently explained in the context of parallel lines. Barring the degenerate case where parallel lines are all parallel to the image plane, parallel straight lines in space project perspectively onto straight lines that on extension intersect at a single point in the image plane. The common intersection of the straight lines in the image, which is the vanishing point, corresponds to "points at infinity" in the receding direction of the parallel straight lines in space. The photograph in Figure 2.4 illustrates a vanishing point beautifully.

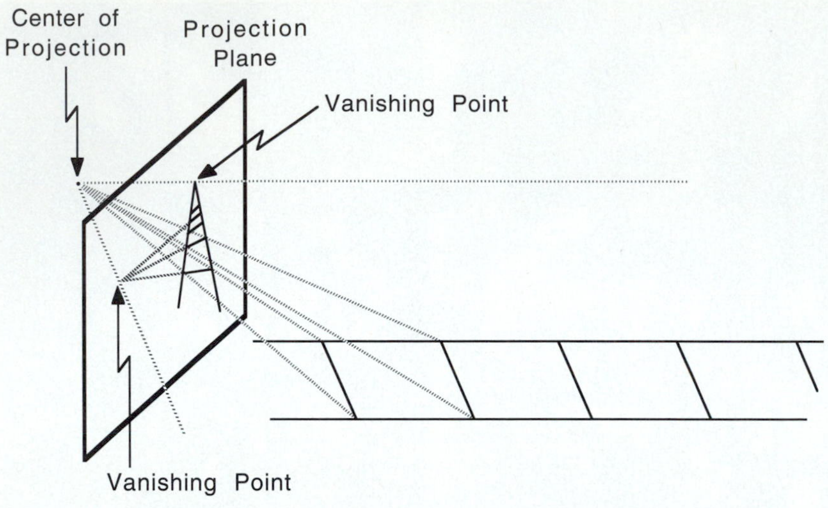

Figure 2.5 The vanishing point. The *vanishing point* of a straight line under perspective projection is that point on the projection surface at which the line would appear to "vanish" if the line were infinitely long in space. The location of the vanishing point of a straight line depends only on the orientation of the straight line in space, and not on the line's position: For any given spatial orientation, the vanishing point is located at that point on the projection surface where a straight line passing through the center of projection with the given orientation would intersect the projection surface.

As illustrated in Figure 2.5, the vanishing point of any given straight line in space is located at that point in the image where a parallel line through the center of projection intersects the image plane. It follows easily that the vanishing point of every straight line that is confined to some plane—actually, for every straight line that is parallel to this plane—lies somewhere along a particular straight line in the image plane. This line, called the **vanishing line** of the plane, is located where a parallel plane through the center of projection intersects the image plane.

Planar Versus Spherical Perspective Projection

Although it is to the geometry of Figure 2.3 that most people refer when they speak of perspective projection, this geometry is not always the most convenient to analyze. In Figure 2.3, the image is formed at the intersection of a cone of projection rays with a plane. Let us call projection along a cone of projection rays onto a plane **planar perspective projection**. The image in planar perspective projection depends on more than just the position of the center of projection: It also depends on the orientation and position of the

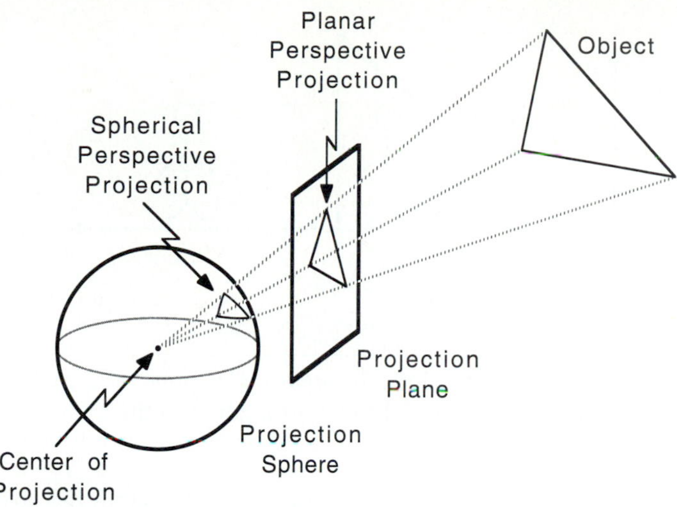

Figure 2.6 Planar and spherical perspective projection. In perspective projection, each object point is projected along a straight line through the center of projection: In *planar perspective projection*, the projection surface is a plane, and in *spherical perspective projection*, the projection surface is a sphere that is centered at the center of projection.

imaging surface, which is a plane. We can remove such a dependence by instead projecting the scene onto a unit sphere that is centered at the center of projection, as illustrated in Figure 2.6; the unit sphere in this context serves as a convenient device to represent the two-dimensional manifold of projection rays.[1] Let us call projection along a cone of projection rays onto a

1. It is noteworthy that the earliest extant geometrical investigation of vision, the treatise *Optics* by Euclid [Euclid c. 300 B.C.], confined itself to the study of the relative orientations of projection rays. Although the premise of the *Optics* that object points are visible when rays emitted by the eye are incident on them is now known to be false, the geometrical analysis therein remains accurate, and is, in fact, remarkable. For instance, the proof of the following proposition of the *Optics* contains the seeds of the notion of a vanishing point: "Parallel lines, when seen from a distance, appear not to be equally distant from each other" (p. 358, [Euclid c. 300 B.C.], English translation). We shall have further occasion to appreciate the present-day relevance of the *Optics* to computer vision.

Euclid, the author of the *Optics*, is best known for his *Elements*, a treatise without equal in the history of mathematics. The *Elements* lay the foundations of axiomatic geometry, and has been used as a text virtually unchanged for over 2000 years. Despite the preeminence of the *Elements*, all that is known with certainty of Euclid's life is that he founded a school at Alexandria circa 300 B.C. and taught mathematics there. An anecdote relates that, on being asked by a student what he would gain by learning geometry, Euclid called his slave and said, "Give him three obols [ancient Greek coins] since he must needs make gain by what he learns" (see [Gillispie 1971]).

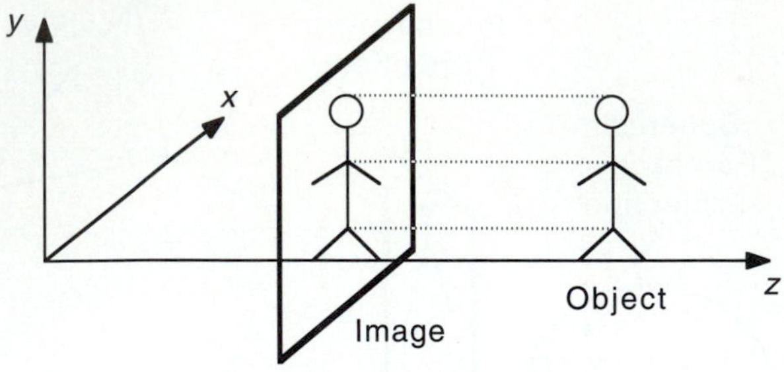

Figure 2.7 Orthographic projection. In *orthographic projection*, each object point is projected onto a plane along a straight line orthogonal to the plane.

sphere, which is not necessarily of unit radius but is centered at the center of projection, **spherical perspective projection**. Under spherical perspective projection, straight lines map onto great-circle arcs—that is, they map onto arcs of circles that are centered at the center of the sphere. Once again, the vanishing point of a straight line is located at that point in the image where a parallel line through the center of projection intersects the imaging surface; hence, we now get two vanishing points for *every* orientation of a straight line. It is not difficult to see that an image formed under planar perspective projection along with its center of projection defines the corresponding image under spherical perspective projection. Of course, we can go from spherical perspective projection to planar perspective projection too.

2.1.2 Orthographic Projection

Orthographic projection, as illustrated in Figure 2.7, is the projection of a three-dimensional entity onto a plane by a set of parallel rays orthogonal to this plane. In the figure, we have $x_i = x_o$ and $y_i = y_o$, where, once again, the subscripts o and i denote the object coordinates and the image coordinates, respectively. Under conditions that we shall examine in this section, orthographic projection closely approximates perspective projection up to a uniform scale factor. When valid, such an approximation is extremely convenient as orthographic projection, unlike perspective projection, is a linear transformation in three-dimensional space.

Consider the perspective-projection geometry of Figure 2.3 once again. As the object is moved away from the center of projection along the z-axis, the image size clearly decreases. More important, the magnification factor (f/z_o) in the perspective-projection equations becomes less sensitive to z_o. That is, $f/(z_o + \Delta z_o)$ tends to be more closely approximated by (f/z_o) as

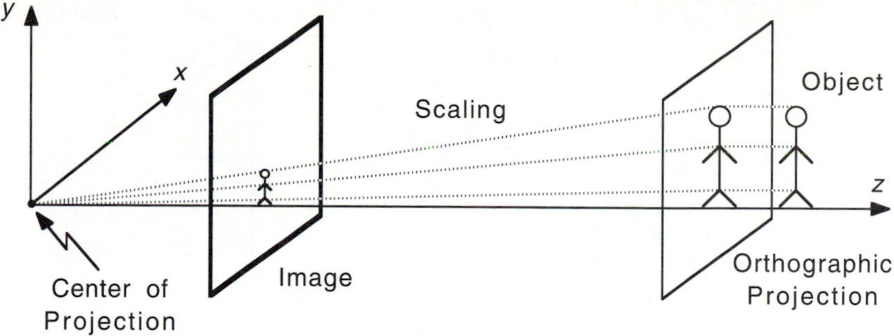

Figure 2.8 Approximation of perspective projection by orthographic projection. Perspective projection onto a plane can be approximated by orthographic projection, followed by scaling, when (1) the object dimensions are small compared to the distance of the object from the center of projection, and (2) compared to this distance, the object is close to the straight line that passes through the center of projection and is orthogonal to the image plane (this line is the z-axis here).

$(z_0/\Delta z_0)$ tends to become large. This increasingly close approximation of $f/(z_0+\Delta z_0)$ by (f/z_0) might lead you to believe that, whenever the average depth of an object is large compared to the object's range of depths, perspective projection can be approximated by orthographic projection up to the scale factor (f/z_0). Such a hypothesis, however, is incorrect.

Two conditions are necessary and sufficient for perspective projection to be approximated closely by orthographic projection up to a uniform scale factor:

1. The object must lie close to the optical axis; in consistency with the terminology for the imaging geometry of a lens in Section 2.1.4, the **optical axis** here is defined as the line through the center of projection that is orthogonal to the image plane.
2. The object's dimensions must be small.

Both *close* and *small* here are with respect to the distance of the object from the center of projection. Figure 2.8 graphically illustrates the approximation of perspective projection as a two-step process: orthographic projection onto a nearby plane parallel to the image plane, and then, perspective projection onto the image plane. The latter is equivalent to uniform scaling. It is not difficult to see that the two projections in tandem approximate direct perspective projection closely only when both the conditions specified here are satisfied. To verify this assertion, you need simply to consider projections of various wire-frame cuboids, each cuboid with one face parallel to the image plane.

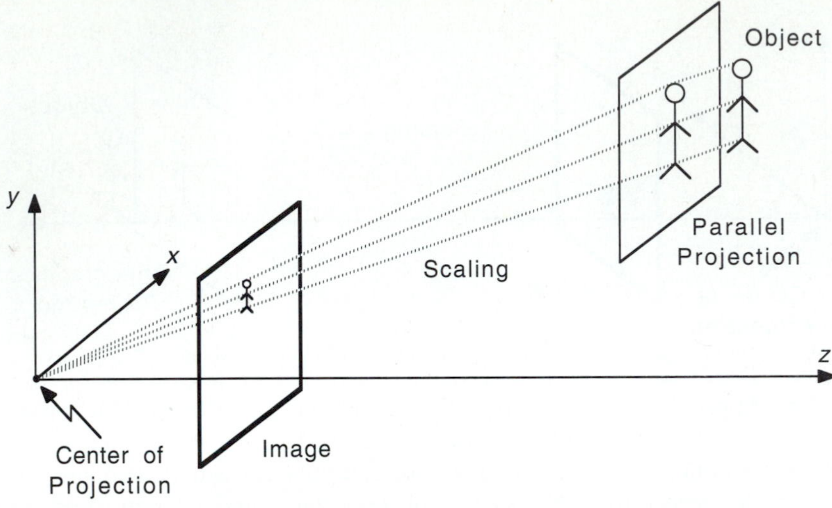

Figure 2.9 Approximation of perspective projection by parallel projection. *Parallel projection* onto a plane is a generalization of orthographic projection in which all the object points are projected along a set of parallel straight lines that may or may not be orthogonal to the projection plane. Perspective projection onto a plane can be approximated by parallel projection, followed by scaling, whenever the object dimensions are small compared to the distance of the object from the center of projection. The direction of parallel projection in such an approximation is along the "average direction" of perspective projection.

2.1.3 Parallel Projection

Parallel projection is a generalization of orthographic projection in which the object is projected onto the image plane by a set of parallel rays that are not necessarily orthogonal to this plane. Parallel projection, like orthographic projection, is a linear transformation in three-dimensional space. Under conditions that we shall examine in this section, parallel projection too provides a convenient approximation to perspective projection up to a uniform scale factor.

As illustrated in Figure 2.9, perspective projection can be approximated by parallel projection up to a uniform scale factor whenever the object's dimensions are small compared to the average distance of the object from the center of projection. The direction of parallel projection is along the "average direction" of perspective projection. When the object, in addition to being *small*, is *close* to the optical axis, the parallel-projection direction can be taken to lie along the optical axis, and we get orthographic projection.

Even when the dimensions of the scene are not small compared to the average distance of the scene from the center of projection, it may be possible

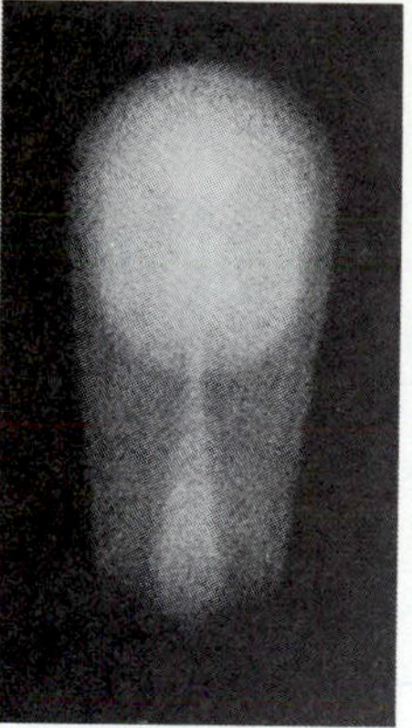 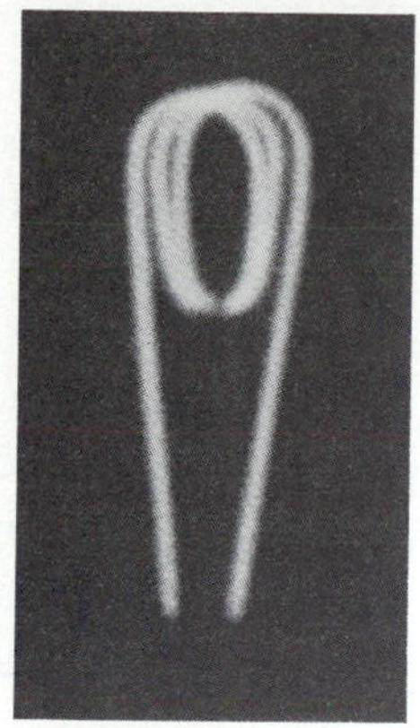 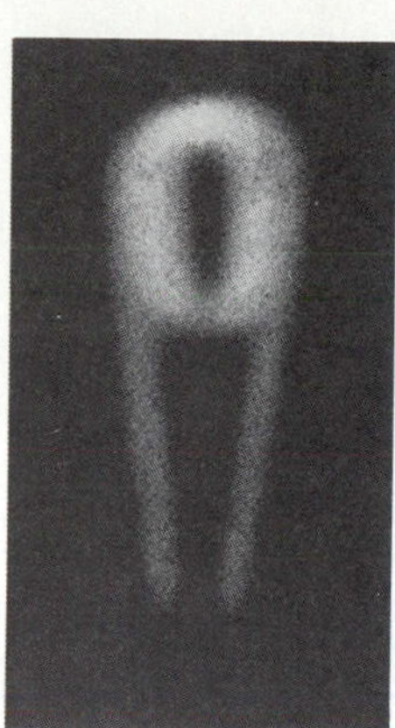

Figure 2.10 Three pinhole-camera photographs (enlarged) of an incandescent filament, each photograph acquired with a circular aperture of a different size. From left to right, the diameter of the aperture is 0.06 inch, 0.015 inch, and 0.0025 inch, respectively; in each case, the distance between the aperture and the image plane is 4 inches. Simple ray tracing would lead us to believe that, as the aperture size is decreased, the image will become sharper. However, when the aperture is reduced below a certain size, rectilinear ray tracing is inadequate for purposes of analysis, and we need to consider *diffraction*, a term used to describe the bending of light rays around the edges of opaque objects. Diffraction, whose extent is inversely related to the ratio of the width of the aperture to the wavelength of the incident light, increasingly blurs the image as the aperture is reduced beyond a certain point. (From [Ruechardt 1958] with permission.)

to partition the scene into smaller subscenes, each of whose dimensions are small compared to its average distance from the center of projection. Under such circumstances, we could approximate perspective projection of the whole scene by a set of parallel projections, each parallel projection applying to a different subscene and having its own projection direction and scale factor. Such an approximation seems to have been proposed first by Ohta, Maenobu, and Sakai [Ohta, Maenobu, and Sakai 1981]; this approximation has subsequently been termed **paraperspective projection** by Aloimonos and Swain [Aloimonos and Swain 1988].

2.1.4 Imaging with a Lens

Thus far, in this chapter, we have considered a pinhole camera, its imaging geometry, and approximations to this geometry. Let us now turn to imaging with a lens. As the size of the aperture of a pinhole camera is reduced, simple ray tracing would lead us to believe that the image will become progressively sharper. However, as demonstrated by the photographs in Figure 2.10, the image will become sharper only up to a point. Below a certain aperture size, rectilinear ray tracing is inadequate for purposes of analysis, and we need to consider **diffraction**, a term used to describe the bending of light rays around the edges of opaque objects. In general, the smaller the width of the aperture relative to the wavelength of the incident light, the more pronounced is the diffraction; see [Ruechardt 1958] for an elementary and readable account of diffraction and related optical phenomena. As the aperture size is reduced, in addition to an increase in the image blurring due to diffraction, there is a decrease in the image intensity (i.e., in the image brightness), the image intensity being directly proportional to the area of the aperture. These considerations lead us to use lenses, the aim of using a lens being to duplicate the pinhole geometry without resorting to undesirably small apertures.

Under ideal circumstances, a lens gathers all the light radiating from an object point toward the lens's finite aperture, and brings this light into focus at a single distinct image point. However, lenses have limitations of their own. The principal limitation of lenses is that, strictly speaking, a lens can bring into focus only those object points that lie within one particular plane parallel to the image plane. We are assuming here, as elsewhere, that the lens is *thin* and that its **optical axis**—that is, its axis of rotation—is perpendicular to the imaging surface, which is a plane. As illustrated in Figure 2.11, a thin lens ideally obeys the **thin-lens equation**, which is also known as the **lens law**:

$$\frac{1}{u} + \frac{1}{v} = \frac{1}{f},$$

where u is the distance of an object point from the plane of the lens, v is the distance of the focused image of the object point from this plane, and f is the focal length of the lens. It is clear from this equation that, as the object distance u becomes increasingly large with respect to the focal length f, the image distance v approaches f. In fact, the **focal length** of a lens can be defined as the distance from the plane of the lens at which any object point that is located at infinity is brought into focus. Axial object points located at infinity are brought into focus at the **focal point**, which is located on the optical axis at a distance f from the lens; the plane perpendicular to the optical axis at the focal point is called the **focal plane**. Even when objects are not quite at infinity, it is often reasonable to assume that they are brought into focus approximately on the focal plane. Unless stated otherwise, we shall assume throughout this book that the objects are brought into focus on the focal plane, and that the image plane is coincident with the focal plane. As we discussed earlier, the purpose of using a lens is to duplicate the pinhole geometry while maintaining a reasonable aperture size. The aperture

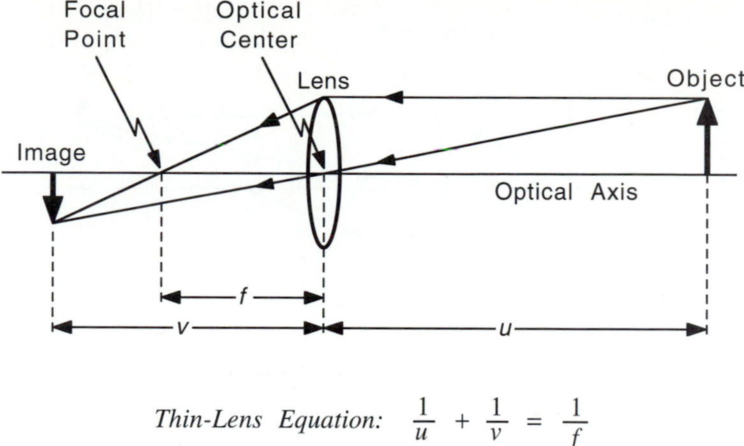

Thin-Lens Equation: $\frac{1}{u} + \frac{1}{v} = \frac{1}{f}$

Figure 2.11 Thin-lens equation: $1/u + 1/v = 1/f$, where u is the distance of an object point from the plane of the lens, v is the distance of the image of the object point from this plane, and f is the focal length of the lens. The *thin-lens equation,* also known as the *lens law,* governs the relationship between the distances of an object and its image from the lens, both distances measured along the lens's *optical axis,* which is the axis of rotation of the lens. As illustrated, we can geometrically determine the position of the image of an off-axis object point by invoking the following two rules: (1) all rays parallel to the optical axis of the lens are deflected by the lens to pass through the lens's focal point, which is at a distance f from the lens along its optical axis; and (2) all rays through the lens's *optical center,* which is a central point in the lens along its optical axis, pass through the lens undeflected. Thus, the optical center of the lens plays the role of a "pinhole" in a pinhole camera (see Figure 2.2), the purpose of using a lens being to duplicate the pinhole geometry while gathering light over a much larger aperture than is possible with a pinhole camera.

here, as elsewhere, is assumed to be circular, and, for all practical purposes, to be in the plane of the lens. As illustrated in Figure 2.11, the effective center of perspective projection for a thin lens is at the lens's **optical center**, which is a central point in the lens along its optical axis through which light rays may be assumed to pass undeflected.

The **field of view** of an imaging device describes the cone of viewing directions of the device. This cone, which comprises all the directions from which rays of light strike the image plane after passing through the effective center of projection of the lens, is almost always chosen to be symmetrical about the optical axis of the lens. For any given size of an image, the field of view of an imaging device is inversely related to the magnification of the lens, and, hence, to its focal length (see Figure 2.11). **Wide-angle lenses** have

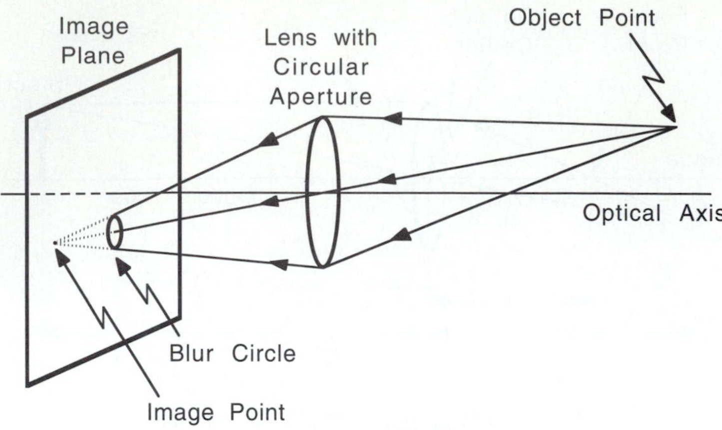

Figure 2.12 Misfocus blur. When a lens brings the image of an object point into focus either in front of or behind the image plane, rather than on the image plane, what appears on the image plane is a blur. If the in-focus image is farther from the lens than the image plane, then this blur has the same shape as the aperture through which light crosses the lens; if the in-focus image is closer to the lens than the image plane, then this blur has the inverted shape of the aperture. As is geometrically evident from the figure, the size of the blur is proportional to the size of the aperture—if we assume that the aperture lies in the plane of the lens, then the factor of proportionality, which may be used as an index of the misfocus, is the ratio of the distance of the in-focus image from the image plane to the distance of the in-focus image from the plane of the lens.

small focal lengths, and, as a result, they have large fields of view. **Telephoto lenses**, on the other hand, have large focal lengths, and, as a result, they have small fields of view. As a practical matter, the perspective imaging geometry of an imaging device is approximated closely by orthographic projection (up to a uniform scale factor) whenever a telephoto lens is used to view a distant scene that has a relatively small range of depth. Clearly, such an approximation is inappropriate when a wide-angle lens is used.

Now, as is clear from the thin-lens equation, for any given position of the image plane, only points within one particular object plane are brought into focus on the image plane by an ideal thin lens. As illustrated in Figure 2.12, points that do not lie within the particular plane brought into focus are imaged as **blur circles**—also known as **circles of confusion**—each blur circle being formed by the intersection of the corresponding cone of light rays with the image plane. As is clear from the figure, the diameter of a blur circle is proportional to the diameter of the aperture. Hence, as the aperture size is decreased, the range of depths over which the world is approximately in focus, better known as the **depth of field**, increases, and errors in focusing become less important. This increase in depth of field, of course, is accompanied by a reduction in the image intensity, to compensate for which it might be necessary to use longer exposure times for image sensing. Clearly, we have a fundamental tradeoff here: loss of resolution (i.e., discriminability) in space, versus that in time—equivalently, image blur due to misfocus, versus image blur due to motion during image capture. This tradeoff, of course, is precisely what aperture-adjustment mechanisms in cameras allow us to control.

Aberrations and Diffraction

Although lenses allow us to overcome some of the limitations of a pinhole camera, they are not without problems. Every lens typically exhibits several imperfections or aberrations. An **aberration** of a lens is any failure of the lens to bring together at the following specific point all the light radiating toward the lens from a single object point: the point that lies along the straight line through the object point and the optical center of the lens, at a distance governed by the lens law (see Figure 2.11).

There are several types of aberrations that a lens might exhibit; for an extensive discussion of aberrations, see the *Manual of Photogrammetry* [Slama 1980] and [Hecht and Zajac 1974]. To begin with, not only does an ideal lens bring into focus just one plane, but also this plane depends on the wavelength of the incident light; this dependence is a consequence of the dependence of the refractive index of the lens on the wavelength of the incident light. As a result, we have **chromatic aberrations** that are caused by radiation at different wavelengths from a single point being brought into focus at different points, which has the effect of blurring the image. Even with monochromatic radiation—that is, with radiation at a single wavelength—the image may be blurred owing to the inability of the lens to bring into focus at a single point all the light rays radiating toward the lens from a single object point. **Spherical aberration** describes the failure of a lens to bring into focus at a single point monochromatic light rays originating at a single point on the optical axis of the lens; **coma** and **astigmatism** describe the failure of the lens to do the same for monochromatic rays from an off-axis point. The three-dimensional blurring of individual image points is not the only possible aberration. Even when a lens is capable of bringing into focus at a single point all the radiation of every wavelength impinging on the lens from a single object point, we are not guaranteed a perfect image. That is, we are not guaranteed an image that is perfect in the sense of its being a planar perspective projection of the scene when this scene is planar

Figure 2.13 Image distortion. Even when a lens brings the image of each object point into focus at a single point on the image plane, we are not guaranteed a perfect image: The geometry of the image may not conform to a planar perspective projection of the scene. Such an aberration, termed *image distortion*, causes straight lines in the scene to appear bowed in the image, as in the ceiling of the room in the photograph shown.

and orthogonal to the optical axis of the lens. The image of such a scene may be brought into focus not on a plane, but instead on a curved surface—such an aberration is termed **curvature of field**. Further, even when a planar scene that is orthogonal to the optical axis of the lens is brought into focus on a single plane that is orthogonal to the optical axis of the lens, the image may be distorted—such an aberration is simply called **distortion**. Image distortion, which is illustrated for a general scene in Figure 2.13, is of particular concern when a wide-angle lens is used. Manufacturers of optical equipment seek to minimize the net effect of the various aberrations on the overall image quality by designing complex lens systems that are composed of several carefully selected and aligned individual lens elements. A reduction in the aperture size is also helpful in reducing the effect of aberrations on the image, but such a reduction could lead to an unacceptable reduction in the intensity of the image.

Even if a lens were perfectly free of aberrations, the physical nature of light would preclude a perfect image. We would still need to take into account the effects of **diffraction**, which, as we saw earlier, describes the deviation of light from a rectilinear path at the edges of opaque objects. A lens whose image quality is limited by diffraction—rather than by aberrations—is said to be **diffraction limited**. As a result of diffraction, the image of a point object formed by an aberration-free lens obeying the lens law is not a point on the image plane even when this plane is at the distance v dictated by the lens law. In particular, if the aperture of the lens is circular, then the image of a point object is a circular disc surrounded by progressively fainter rings; such a diffraction pattern is called the **Airy pattern**, after the astronomer who first derived its equation in the early nineteenth century. The radius of the central disc of the Airy pattern is $1.22\,\lambda v/d$, where λ is the wavelength of the incident light, v is the distance of the image plane from the lens, and d is the diameter of the circular aperture of the lens; see, for instance, [Hecht and Zajac 1974] and [Goodman 1968]. Thus, in a diffraction-limited imaging system, we can improve the image quality in two ways: (1) by increasing the size of the aperture, and (2) when feasible, by reducing the wavelength of the light forming the image. The former strategy, which also increases the brightness of the image, is adopted in the design of telescopes, and the latter strategy is adopted in the design of microscopes.

Camera Calibration

Despite all the approximations and problems with lenses, it must be emphasized that perspective projection is an extremely useful and convenient model for the geometry of image formation by a lens. We must, however, always bear in mind that that's just what perspective projection is: It is a model.

To derive three-dimensional geometric information from an image, it is necessary to determine the parameters that relate the position of a scene point to the position of its image. This determination is known as **camera calibration**, or, more accurately, as **geometric camera calibration**. Let us assume that the perspective-projection model is valid. Let us further assume a global coordinate frame for the scene, and an independent two-dimensional frame for the image. We need to relate the spatial positions and orientations of these two frames, and to determine the position of the center of projection. In addition, to account for the transformation undergone by an image between its capture on the image plane and its display, we need to determine two independent scale factors, one for each image coordinate axis.

As perspective projection and image scaling along any direction in the image are both linear transformations in homogeneous coordinates, each of these operations, and, therefore, the complete mapping from a scene position to its image position, can be expressed as a multiplicative matrix in homogeneous coordinates. Given the image positions and scene coordinates of six points, it is straightforward to derive a closed-form solution to this matrix (see [Ballard and Brown 1982]); more points offer greater robustness. Ganapathy [Ganapathy 1984] has shown that this matrix, in turn, provides closed-form solutions to the six **extrinsic camera parameters** and to the four **intrinsic camera parameters**. Of the six extrinsic camera parameters, three are for the position of the center of projection, and three are for the orientation of the image-plane coordinate frame. Of the four intrinsic camera parameters, two are for the position of the origin of the image coordinate frame, and two are for the scale factors of the axes of this frame. Although the distance of the image plane from the center of projection cannot be modeled independently of the scale factors of the axes of the image, as indicated in our discussion of lenses, this distance is often well approximated by the focal length of the lens. On the other hand, if the scale factors of the image axes are known a priori, this distance too may be calibrated.

Typically, camera calibration is pursued using a known calibration object whose images exhibit a large number of distinct points that can be identified easily and located accurately in the image. Clearly, it is desirable that the calibration object be easy to generate and to measure accurately, and that the shape of the object be conducive to simplifying the calibration computations. One object that meets these criteria comprises either one or multiple planar rectilinear grids [Tsai 1986].

Tsai [Tsai 1986] argues that, in practice, it is necessary to model and calibrate image distortion in addition to the ideal-case parameters we have discussed. He reviews previous calibration techniques, and then describes a now widely used calibration procedure designed for accuracy, robustness, and efficiency. Also of interest here is the work by Fischler and Bolles [Fischler and Bolles 1981], who investigate the determination of the extrinsic camera parameters under knowledge of the intrinsic camera parameters; this problem is called the **exterior camera-orientation problem**. In particular, Fischler and Bolles show that, given the image positions and scene locations of three points, the extrinsic camera parameters have at most four solutions, each solution expressible in closed form.

2.2 Radiometry

Section 2.1 elucidated the geometric relationship between the world and its image. Let us now consider the **radiometric relationship** between the world and its image. That is, let us consider the relationship between the amount of light radiating from a surface point, called the **scene radiance**, and the amount of light incident at the image of the surface point, called the **image irradiance**. Although both radiance and irradiance are informally termed **brightness**, their units of measurement are quite different, as we shall see next. The treatment here follows [Horn 1986].

The **irradiance** of a surface is the amount of light incident on the surface; irradiance is measured as power per unit irradiated area (in metric units, watts per square meter). The **radiance** of a surface in any direction is the amount of light emitted by the surface in that direction; radiance is measured as power per unit foreshortened radiating area in the direction of radiation, per unit solid angle (in metric units, watts per square meter, per steradian). As illustrated in Figure 2.14, the **foreshortened area** of a surface in any direction is the area of the surface under orthographic projection in that direction; for a planar surface patch, the foreshortened area is simply the product of the actual area of the patch with the cosine of the angle between the surface normal and the direction of projection. As also illustrated in Figure 2.14, the **solid angle**, in steradians, of a cone of directions originating at a point is the area spanned by the cone on a unit sphere centered at the point; thus, the solid angle subtended by a small surface patch at a distant point is the foreshortened area of the patch in the direction of the point divided by the square of the distance of the patch from the point. In Figure 2.14, the irradiance of the surface located at the point P is the ratio of the following two terms: (1) the total power of the light incident on the surface at P within some small surface area δA; to (2) the area δA. The radiance of this surface at the point P in the direction $\mathbf{t}$ is the ratio of the following two terms: (1) the total power of the light emitted by a small surface area δA at P within a small cone of directions about $\mathbf{t}$; to (2) the product of the foreshortened area of the radiating surface patch δA at P in the direction $\mathbf{t}$ with the solid angle of the cone of directions about $\mathbf{t}$.

Consider an ideal thin lens once again. Assume that the object distance u is much greater than the focal length f of the lens, and that the image plane is at a distance f from the lens; then, as discussed in Section 2.1.4, the image will be brought into focus approximately on the image plane. Further assume that the object distance u is much greater than the diameter d of the circular aperture of the lens. Then, the direction of radiation from an object

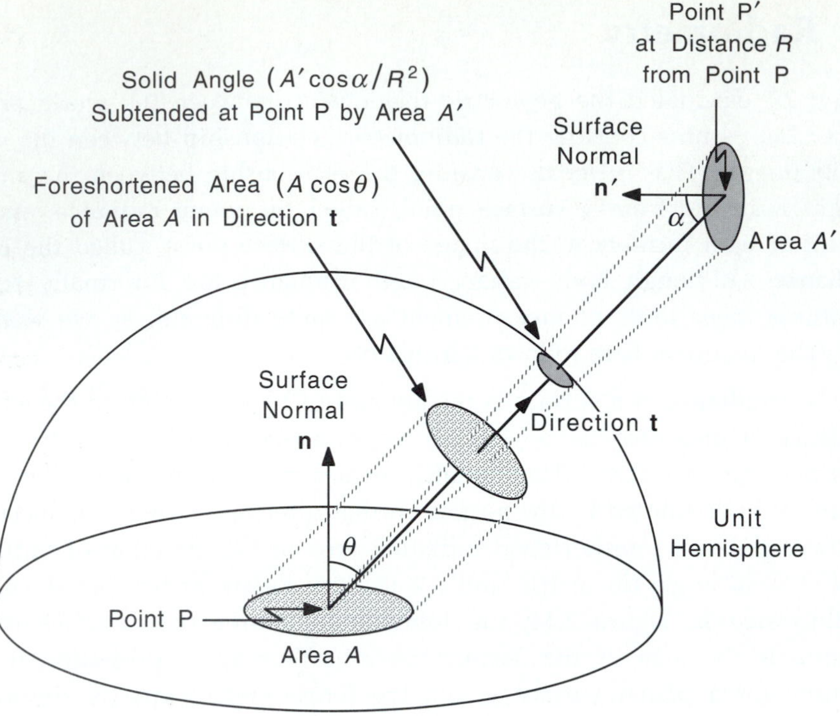

Figure 2.14 Foreshortened area and solid angle. The *foreshortened area* of a surface patch in any direction is the area of the patch under orthographic projection in that direction. In the figure, the planar surface patch located at the point P with area A has the foreshortened area $A \cos\theta$ in the direction $\mathbf{t}$, where $\mathbf{t}$ forms an angle θ with the surface normal $\mathbf{n}$. A *solid angle* is the three-dimensional analog of an ordinary angle: Just as an ordinary angle at a point is measured in radians by the arc-length that the angle spans on a unit circle centered at the point, the solid angle at a point is measured in steradians by the area that the angle spans on a unit sphere centered at the point. (A unit circle and a unit sphere are a circle and a sphere, respectively, each with a radius of unit length.) Thus, the solid angle subtended by a surface patch at a point is the area of the patch under spherical perspective projection onto a unit sphere centered at the point. In the figure, if the dimensions of the surface patch located at the point P′ are small compared to the distance of this patch from the point P, then the solid angle subtended at P by this patch will be approximately the following: $A' \cos\alpha / R^2$, where A' is the area of the surface patch, α is the angle between the surface normal $\mathbf{n}'$ of the patch and the direction from the patch toward P, and R is the distance of the patch from P. To verify this approximate expression for the solid angle, note that the area of the perspective projection of the patch onto a unit sphere is approximately the same as the area of the perspective projection of the patch onto a plane tangent to the sphere, and the latter perspective projection is closely approximated by orthographic projection followed by scaling (as illustrated in Figure 2.8).

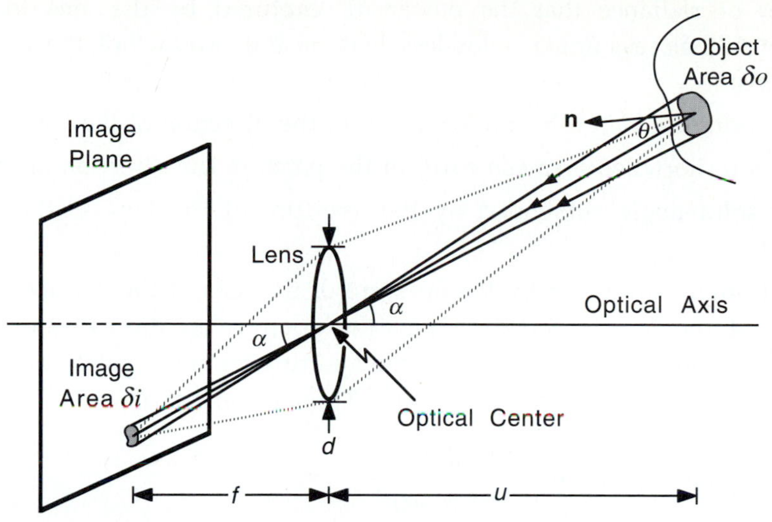

Figure 2.15 Radiometry of image formation by a thin lens. Light rays radiating from the object surface patch δo toward the aperture of the lens are captured by the lens, and are projected onto the image area δi. The object distance u and the focal length f of the lens are not to scale in the figure: The thin-lens equation dictates that u be much greater than f for the image to be brought into focus at a distance f from the lens. It is assumed here that u is much greater than both f and the diameter d of the circular aperture through which light crosses the lens. The light incident on a surface is called the *irradiance* of the surface, and is measured in units of power per unit incident surface area. The light emitted by a surface in a particular direction is called the *radiance* of the surface in that direction, and is measured in units of power per unit foreshortened radiating area (in the direction of radiation) per unit solid angle (subtended at the point of radiation). Both radiance and irradiance are informally termed *brightness*. In the figure, if we equate the light captured by the lens from the object area δo to the light projected by the lens onto the image area δi, we arrive at the following important relation between the radiance *Rad* of a surface and the irradiance *Irrad* of its image: $Irrad = Rad\ (\pi/4)\ (d/f)^2 \cos^4\alpha$, where d is the diameter of the circular aperture through which light crosses the lens, f is the focal length of the lens, and α is the angle between the optical axis of the lens and the direction from the lens toward the object area.

point to any point on the lens will be approximately constant. Let us denote the angle between this direction and the optical axis of the lens by α, as illustrated in Figure 2.15.

Consider Figure 2.15. Let *Rad* be the radiance in the direction of the lens of an infinitesimal object surface patch with area δo and surface normal $\mathbf{n}$; let δi be the area of the image of the patch; let $\mathbf{n}$ form an angle θ with the direction from the object patch toward the lens. Then, it follows from the definition of radiance that the power δP captured by the lens from the surface patch δo, assuming a lossless lens, is the product of the following three terms:

1. The radiance *Rad* of the surface patch in the direction of the lens
2. The foreshortened area ($\delta o \cos\theta$) of the patch in the direction of the lens
3. The solid angle subtended by the aperture of the lens at the surface patch

The solid angle subtended by the aperture of the lens at the surface patch is the ratio of the foreshortened area of the aperture in the direction of the patch to the square of the distance of the aperture from the patch; that is, it is the ratio of $\pi(d/2)^2\cos\alpha$ to $(u/\cos\alpha)^2$. Thus, we arrive at

$$\delta P \;=\; Rad\ (\delta o \cos\theta)\ \frac{\pi\,(d/2)^2\cos\alpha}{(u/\cos\alpha)^2}\,.$$

Now, as ($\delta o \cos\theta$) is the foreshortened area of δo in the direction of the lens, and ($u/\cos\alpha$) is the distance of δo from the lens, $(\delta o \cos\theta)/(u/\cos\alpha)^2$ is simply the solid angle subtended by the surface patch δo at the optical center of the lens. But this solid angle, as illustrated in Figure 2.15, is the same as the solid angle subtended by the image patch δi at the optical center of the lens; that is, it is the same as $(\delta i \cos\alpha)/(f/\cos\alpha)^2$. Making the substitution, we get

$$\delta P \;=\; Rad\ \pi\,(d/2)^2\cos\alpha\ \frac{(\delta i \cos\alpha)}{(f/\cos\alpha)^2}\,.$$

Rearranging, and denoting the image irradiance by *Irrad*, we finally arrive at

$$Irrad \;=\; \frac{\delta P}{\delta i} \;=\; Rad\ \frac{\pi}{4}\left(\frac{d}{f}\right)^2\cos^4\alpha\,.$$

This relation is of fundamental importance. Let us call it the **fundamental radiometric relation** between the radiance *Rad* of the scene and the irradiance *Irrad* of the scene's image. Recall here that f is the focal length of the lens, d is the diameter of the circular aperture of the lens, and α is the angle between the optical axis of the lens and the direction from the lens toward the distant object point that is being imaged. The ratio (f/d)—that is, the ratio of the focal length f of the lens to the diameter d of the circular aperture of the lens—is called the **f-number** of the lens.

The fundamental radiometric relation tells us that the image irradiance is proportional to the scene radiance. The factor of proportionality is the product of ($\pi/4$), a constant, $(d/f)^2$, the square of the inverse of the f-number, and $\cos^4\alpha$, where α is the angle between the optical axis of the lens and the direction from the lens toward the object point being imaged. The dependence of the image irradiance on $(\pi d^2/4)$, which is the area of the aperture of the lens, is to be expected as the amount of light captured by the lens from a distant object point is proportional to the area of the aperture of the lens. The dependence of the image irradiance on $(1/f)^2$ is also explained easily: The size of the in-focus image is proportional to the distance of this image from the lens, and, for objects that are far away, this distance is the focal length f of the lens; it follows that the image area is proportional to f^2, and, hence, the image irradiance is proportional to $(1/f)^2$. Both the area of the aperture and the focal length of the lens are constant over any image. In contrast, the $\cos^4\alpha$ term—whose physical significance in the fundamental radiometric relation is not as immediately apparent—varies over the image. Even the $\cos^4\alpha$ term, however, may be assumed constant when the field of view is sufficiently small. More generally, we can factor this term out by calibrating points on the camera's image plane for their orientation with respect to the optical center of the lens; such a calibration is subsumed by the camera calibration that we discussed earlier in Section 2.1.4.

2.3 Sensing

Thus far, we have considered the relationship between the scene and its image formed on the image plane. This image, however, is not amenable to processing by an electronic computer: This image must first be sensed. Conceptually, sensing an image entails converting the "optical image" into an "electrical image." A variety of devices can be used for this purpose; see, for instance, [Ballard and Brown 1982].

In our discussion of radiometry in Section 2.2, we disregarded the wavelength of the incident light because the relationship between the scene radiance and the image irradiance is independent of this wavelength. Now, however, we must take into account not only the spectral composition of the image irradiance—that is, the composition of the image irradiance as a function of its wavelength λ—but also the possible dependence of the image irradiance on time t. Let us denote the image irradiance by $Irrad(x, y, t, \lambda)$, where (x, y) are the position coordinates of points on the image plane. Then, the "electrical image" $E(x, y)$ at any particular time instant $t = t_o$ is given by the following expression:

$$E(x, y) \;=\; \iint Irrad(x, y, t, \lambda)\; s(\lambda)\; \tau(t - t_o)\; d\lambda\, dt\,,$$

where $s(\lambda)$ is the spectral sensitivity of the imaging device, and $\tau(t)$ is the imaging device's temporal window (i.e., its temporal weighting function) positioned at time $t = 0$. Color cameras typically incorporate three different spectral sensitivity functions, each sensitivity function leading to either the "red," the "green," or the "blue" color component of the colored image. In this book, we shall restrict ourselves to monochromatic (i.e., "black and white") images that are acquired using a single spectral sensitivity function.

Conceptually, what we have now is an "electrical image" that is captured at time $t = t_0$ and that is defined for continuously varying image coordinates (x, y). Let us first consider how this image is represented in a digital computer as an array of digits, and then, let us look at some of the salient properties of the digital image vis-à-vis the image irradiance. You must bear in mind that the demarcation between, and the ordering of, the various steps we are executing here to make the transition from image irradiance to a digital image are motivated by reasons of conceptual simplicity, rather than by the existence of direct one-to-one physical correlates in a practical imaging device.

2.3.1 Sampling and Quantization

If we are to process, store, or manipulate an image with a digital computer, what we need is a **digital image**—that is, an array of integers in which each integer represents the image irradiance at a discrete time at a discrete point on the image plane. The generation of such an image at any particular time entails first **sampling** the continuously defined image at a discrete set of locations on the image plane, and then **quantizing** each sample. That is, it entails first determining the value of the continuously defined image at each of several discrete image locations—each discretely located value of the image being called a **sample** of the image—and then assigning to each sample, a discrete integer label that is representative of the range within which the sample lies. Familiar examples of quantization include the conversion of reals to integers by truncation or rounding. Sampling discretizes the domain of a function, and quantization discretizes its range. Figure 2.16 illustrates the sampling and quantization of a cone. (For an extended discussion on sampling and quantization, see [Rosenfeld and Kak 1982].)

Although we are primarily interested in two-dimensional images here—these images, perhaps, time varying—sampling and quantization may be pursued in any number of dimensions. In general, any signal may have either a continuous domain or a discrete domain; further, the signal may have either a continuous range or a discrete range. A signal that has both a continuous domain and a continuous range is called **analog**, and a signal that has both a discrete domain and a discrete range is called **digital**. When a signal is simply described as **discrete**—without any further qualification—it

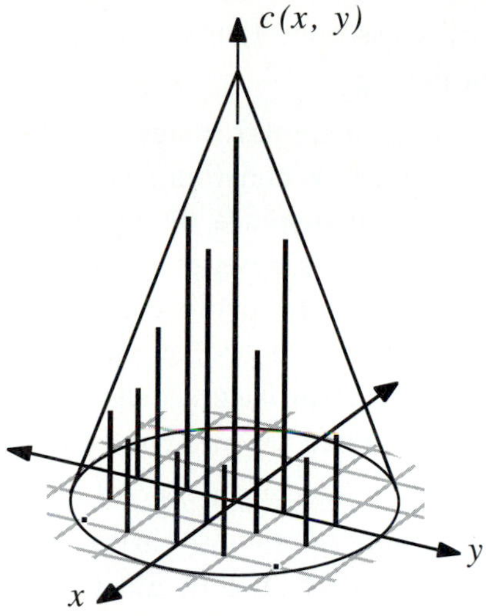

Figure 2.16 Sampling and quantization. *Sampling* discretizes the domain of a function, ideally assigning to each discrete point of the domain the value of the function at the point. *Quantization* discretizes the range of a function, mapping the value of the function at every point onto one of several discrete values. With respect to ideal sampling, note that the value of a function at any point is the same as the weighted integral of the function with respect to a unit impulse located at the point. A *unit impulse* at a point is, by definition, a function that is nonzero at only that point, and that has a unit integral. In the figure, sampling discretizes the x–y plane over which the cone $c(x, y)$ is defined by permitting only integer values for x and y; quantization discretizes the magnitude of $c(x, y)$ at every point by truncating the nonintegral part of the magnitude. For clarity, only those quantized samples of the cone are shown that are in the front half-plane. Now, an image is a two-dimensional function whose domain is the image plane, and whose range is the range of values that the image irradiance at a point might assume. An image that has been sampled and quantized is called a *digital image,* and each quantized sample constituting a digital image is called a *pixel* (an abbreviation for *picture element*); at any image point, any measure of the image irradiance—whether sampled or unsampled, quantized or unquantized—is called the *image intensity* at the point. Throughout this book, we shall assume each digital image to comprise samples that are located on a square grid, and we shall assume each pixel to take on an integral value that is related monotonically to the brightness of the image sample the pixel represents. Then, a digital image is an array of integers (pixels) in which each integer represents the (quantized) brightness of the image at a (sampled) point on a square grid on the image plane. We digitize images to make them amenable to processing by a digital computer, which is the most common category of computer today.

is generally assumed that this description applies to the domain of the signal. When a signal is simply described as **continuous**—without any further qualification—it is generally assumed that this description applies to both the domain and the range of the signal.

Each quantized sample in a digital image is called a **pixel**, which is an abbreviation for *picture element*. When there is no cause for confusion, we shall also use *pixel* as a unit of distance on the image plane to denote the smallest intersample spacing. The integer value of a pixel at any image location is called the **image intensity** or the **gray level** at that image location. Whereas the term *gray level* refers to one of the discrete quantization levels that a pixel might assume, the term *image intensity* is more general in that it refers to any measure—quantized or unquantized, sensed or not—of the image irradiance at a point.

Although a digital image is just an array of numbers, it is rarely displayed as such. Humans find it difficult to visualize the underlying optical image from such a representation. Hence, it is standard practice to display a digital image as an array of adjoining uniformly gray areas, each area representing an individual pixel with respect to both the pixel's location and the pixel's brightness.

It is natural to wonder what is lost in the process of sampling and quantization, the former being a discretization of space (i.e., of the image plane), and the latter of amplitude (i.e., of the image intensity). Let us consider sampling first. Fortunately for us there is the well-known **Whittaker–Shannon sampling theorem**. This theorem is described at length in [Rosenfeld and Kak 1982], [Goodman 1968], and [Bracewell 1978]; see also Appendix A2.1 on the Fourier transform at the end of the chapter. The central notion of the sampling theorem is straightforward: Any continuous function that is limited in how rapidly it can vary—that is, a continuous function that is so-to-speak bandlimited—can *completely* characterized by its samples so long as these samples are spaced less than a particular interval apart. The maximum permissible spacing between the samples of a signal is inversely proportional to the signal's **bandlimit**, which, loosely speaking, is a measure of the degree of "variability" of the signal. The (minimum) sampling rate that corresponds to the maximum permissible intersample spacing is called the **Nyquist rate**. If a signal is sampled (significantly) above or below its Nyquist rate, the signal is said to be **oversampled** or **undersampled**, respectively. The sampling theorem applies to every dimension over which the signal varies, and its applicability does not depend on the total number of such dimensions; for instance, in time-varying imagery, the sampling theorem applies to each of the two dimensions of the image plane, and to time.

The sampling theorem may come to you as a surprise if you are not already familiar with it. Whereas it is clear that any function can be interpolated with increasing accuracy as the spacing between the samples of the function is decreased, it is not equally clear that (1) it may be possible to reconstruct the function *exactly*, and (2) it may not help to increase the number of samples beyond a certain limit. Perhaps, a simple example would help here. Consider the familiar family of polynomials: $f(x) = \sum_{i=0}^{n} c_i \, x^i, \; n \geq 0$. Now, for $n = 0$, the function $f(x)$ is a constant, and it is clear that one sample characterizes the function completely; for $n = 1$, $f(x)$ is a straight line, and two samples suffice to characterize the function completely; and so on. As the degree of "variability" (indexed by n here) increases, we need more samples. Moreover, having more than n independent samples serves no purpose under ideal circumstances. Whereas, what we have here is a family of functions expressed as the weighted sum of elementary polynomials, it is clear that a similar argument could be made for functions that are expressed as the weighted sum of some other elementary functions. In signal processing, it is customary to express functions as the weighted sum of sines and cosines of varying frequencies, which leads us to the Fourier transform, but we shall not delve into that here. For more on the Fourier transform, and on the interpretation of the sampling theorem under it, see Appendix A2.1 at the end of the chapter.

Although the locations at which a continuously defined image is sampled may be arranged in a variety of configurations, for reasons of practical convenience, these locations are almost always chosen to lie on a rectangular grid on the image plane. For illustrative purposes, let us assume a square grid of sampling locations throughout this book, each sampling location having integral coordinates m and n along the x- and y-axes of the image, respectively. Then, the image intensity I of the digital image at the image location (m, n) can be expressed as follows:

$$I(m,\, n) \;\; = \;\; Quantize\left[\iint E(x,\, y) \;\; \omega(x-m,\, y-n) \;\; dx\, dy \right],$$

where $E(x, y)$ is the previously defined "electrical image," *Quantize* is a function that discretizes its argument, and $\omega(x, y)$ is the window function associated with the sampling of the continuously defined "electrical image." Before we discuss quantization, let us look into the role of $\omega(x, y)$ more closely.

Ideal sampling requires that the sampling window $\omega(x, y)$ be the Dirac delta function $\delta(x, y)$, but such a sampling window is neither feasible nor desirable. The **Dirac delta function** $\delta(x, y)$, by definition, has a unit integral over the x–y plane and is zero everywhere except at the origin. Hence, if

$\omega(x, y)$ were $\delta(x, y)$, then $\iint E(x, y)\, \omega(x-m, y-n)\, dx\, dy$ would reduce to $E(m, n)$, which is the sample of $E(x, y)$ at $(x, y) = (m, n)$. Now, the sampling theorem tells us that a signal is characterized adequately by its samples only when the signal is sampled finely enough as dictated by the signal's bandlimit. But, as we shall soon see, the irradiance over the image plane could well exhibit intensity variations that are sharp enough to cause the "electrical image" $E(x, y)$ to be undersampled by $\delta(x, y)$. In practice, of course, the sampling-window function cannot simultaneously have a zero extent and a unit integral; that is, $\omega(x, y)$ cannot be $\delta(x, y)$, which is simply a convenient mathematical device. In practice, the sampling-window function $\omega(x, y)$ is determined by the finite area of each of the identical individual sensor elements that are used to measure the image irradiance over the image plane. More precisely, $\omega(x, y)$ represents the sensitivity of each individual sensor element to image irradiance at different locations over the sensor's area, just as the spectral-window function $s(\lambda)$ represents the sensitivity of each individual sensor element to image irradiance at different wavelengths. Analogously to the spatial sampling window $\omega(x, y)$, and to the spectral window $s(\lambda)$, the temporal window $\tau(t)$ of the imaging device determines the weighting of the image irradiance over time. If, instead of a single image, we were to consider a sequence of images of a time-varying scene, the role of $\tau(t)$ in temporal sampling would be analogous to the role of $\omega(x, y)$ in spatial sampling.

Undersampling a continuously defined image over the image plane leads to a phenomenon known as **aliasing**. The most common manifestation of aliasing in an image is the jagged appearance of oblique image-intensity edges—that is, of oblique image contours across which the image intensity changes abruptly. Figure 2.17(b) shows an aliased 64×64 synthetic image of a circular disc of radius 24 pixels; each sample in Figure 2.17 is represented by a uniformly gray 1-pixel square. Figure 2.17(b) was derived by sampling the image shown in Figure 2.17(a) at each of a 64×64 square array of image locations by the delta function $\delta(x, y)$. That is, Figure 2.17(b) was derived by putting $\omega(x, y) = \delta(x, y)$ and letting m and n each take on 64 equispaced values in the expression $\iint E(x, y)\, \omega(x-m, y-n)\, dx\, dy$, where $E(x, y)$ describes the image in Figure 2.17(a). Figure 2.17(c) shows the outcome of replacing the delta sampling function, used to derive Figure 2.17(b), by the two-dimensional Gaussian function

$$G(x, y) \;=\; (1/(2\pi\sigma_{\text{blur}}^2))\; \exp(-[x^2 + y^2]\,/\,(2\sigma_{\text{blur}}^2)),$$

where σ_{blur} is a parameter that is chosen to be 0.9 pixel here. (See Figure 3.7 for a plot of a two-dimensional Gaussian.) Whereas the delta function (owing to its impulsive nature and unit integral) provides a pointwise sample

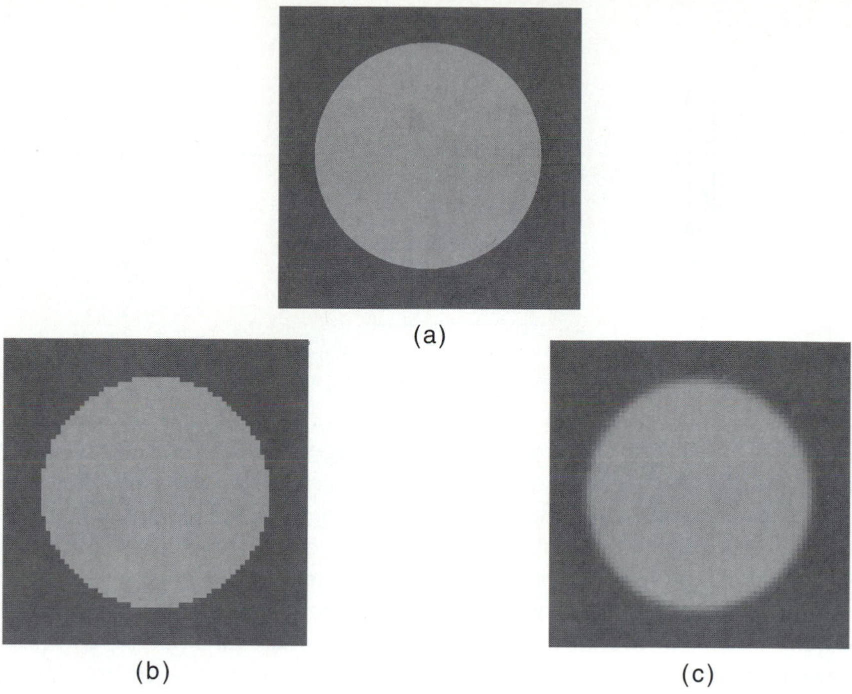

Figure 2.17 Image aliasing. In a sampled image, the most common visually apparent manifestation of the phenomenon known as *aliasing* is the jagged appearance of image-region boundaries that were smooth prior to the sampling of the image. We are assuming here that the sampled image is displayed as a collection of abutting polygonal areas, each of which represents a single image sample with respect to both the position of the sample and its brightness; in the figure, each image sample is displayed as a uniformly bright square. **(a)** An unsampled synthetic image of a circular disc. **(b)** Image aliasing on sampling the image in (a) by a 64×64 grid of unit impulses—that is, on sampling the image in (a) by assigning to each point of a 64×64 square grid superimposed on the image the weighted integral of the image with respect to a unit impulse located at the point. **(c)** Image aliasing on sampling the image in (a) by a 64×64 grid of unit two-dimensional Gaussians—that is, on sampling the image in (a) by assigning to each point of a 64×64 square grid superimposed on the image the weighted integral of the image with respect to a unit two-dimensional Gaussian centered at the point. A Gaussian is a function that is shaped roughly like a bell, and a unit Gaussian is a Gaussian with a unit integral. As illustrated, image aliasing is less pronounced when the image is sampled by a nonimpulsive function, rather than by an impulse—that is, when the sample at an image point is not the weighted integral of the image there with respect to an impulse, but with respect to some other function. In general, image aliasing is caused by the spacing between the samples of the original image being too large to allow the sampling function used to capture adequately the spatial variations in the intensity (i.e., brightness) of the original image—see Figure 2.18 in this context.

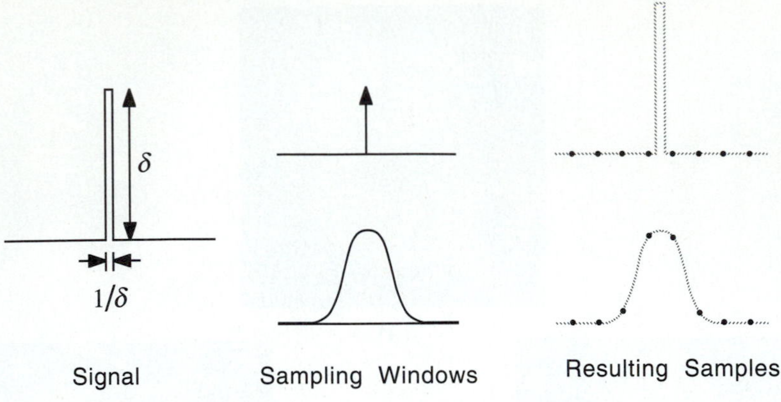

Figure 2.18 The effect of the shape of the sampling window on the recoverability of a continuously defined signal from that signal's discrete samples. The choice of the *sampling window*—that is, of the function used to weight a continuously defined signal in the computation of that signal's samples—directly affects the recoverability of the original signal from that signal's discrete samples. This effect of the choice of the sampling window is demonstrated here by sampling a one-dimensional rectangular pulse that is uniformly zero except for a short interval $1/\delta$, within which the pulse is uniformly δ. The rectangular pulse is shown on the left; two choices of the sampling window are shown in the middle; for each sampling window, one possible set of samples of the pulse is shown on the right, each sample in a set being represented by a solid black dot. As the figure illustrates, the impulsive sampling function (represented by $\uparrow$), with its zero extent and unit integral, may "miss" the rectangular pulse completely, whereas the bell-shaped function will, in effect, provide impulsive samples of a smoothed version of the pulse.

of the signal at each location, the Gaussian function (owing to its bell shape and unit integral) provides the local weighted average of the signal at each location; see Figure 2.18 for a one-dimensional illustration of these outcomes of the application of the two sampling functions. A sampling window that computes a local weighted average of the original signal smooths the signal implicitly, thereby reducing the signal's bandlimit. Clearly, the circular shape of the disc in Figure 2.17(a) is more perceptible in Figure 2.17(c) than it is in Figure 2.17(b).

As illustrated in Figure 2.18, undersampling may result in more than just signal distortion: It may cause sharp intensity variations to be lost completely. A bandlimiting sampling window can smooth such variations, making them more amenable to recovery from their samples. Of course, then the recovery would provide only a smoothed signal, but a smoothed signal is better than nothing. Optimally, we would like a window function that avoids aliasing by bandlimiting the image just enough, as dictated by the

Figure 2.19 Gray-scale contouring. Gray-scale contouring is illustrated here in a synthetic digital image of a matte sphere—this sphere illuminated from the top-right-front corner. *Gray-scale contouring* is a phenomenon in which a quantized image exhibits image contours across which the image intensity changes abruptly owing to the quantization of the intensity of the original image, rather than due to an abrupt change in the unquantized intensity. The term *gray scale* here denotes the set of discrete values onto which the image intensity is mapped on quantization, each individual discrete quantization level being called a *gray level*. Gray-scale contouring is caused by an insufficient number of quantization levels being available within some range of intensity variation; this inadequacy of quantization levels, as illustrated, leads to distinct bands of uniform brightness where the image should be shaded smoothly. In the digital image here, as elsewhere in this book, each pixel is represented by a square of fixed size whose brightness is monotonically related to the value of the pixel.

sampling theorem. The price we pay for oversmoothing is the unnecessary loss of detail.

Whereas sampling need not result in a loss of information, quantization affords no such luxury. As is evident from the examples of converting reals to integers by truncation or rounding, quantization is a many-to-one mapping; as a result, quantization is, in general, irreversible. Sampling, in general, is a many-to-one mapping too; it is only by restricting the domain of continuous signals that are being sampled to be sufficiently bandlimited that we are able to ensure that no two distinct continuous signals map onto the same discrete signal. We saw artifacts of image undersampling in Figure 2.17. The synthetic image of a smoothly shaded matte sphere in Figure 2.19 illustrates artifacts of image-intensity quantization. In the image in Figure

2.19, an inadequate number of gray levels has led to bands of uniform intensity—each of these bands accompanied by abrupt intensity changes—where the image should be shaded smoothly. This phenomenon of abrupt intensity changes across image contours due to intensity quantization is called **gray-scale contouring**; see, for instance, [Pratt 1991].

Quantization may be viewed as a source of signal **noise**, which is a term describing undesirable signal corruption. Quantization noise is additive; that is, if the original signal were $s(.)$ and the quantized signal were $f(.)$, then we could write $f(.) = s(.) + q(.)$, where $q(.)$ represents the quantization noise. The statistics of $q(.)$ depend on both the statistics of $s(.)$ and the quantization strategy. For instance, returning to our examples of converting reals to integers by rounding or truncation, whereas rounding places an upper bound of 0.5 on the magnitude of $q(.)$, truncation places an upper bound of 1.0 on this magnitude.

Quantization noise is not the only noise in our digital-image representation of image irradiance. There are several other noises, many of these noises inherent to the nature of sensing—for example, photoelectronic and thermal noises (see [Andrews and Hunt 1977]). If we assume that the overall image noise $\eta(m, n)$ is additive, then we can express a digital image $I(m, n)$ that is acquired at time $t = t_o$ as follows:

$$I(m, n) = \int\int \Big\{ \Big[\int\int Irrad(x, y, t, \lambda)\ s(\lambda)\ \tau(t - t_o)\ d\lambda\, dt \Big] \;\omega(x-m, y-n) \Big\}\, dx\, dy \;+\; \eta(m, n).$$

Here, $\omega(x, y)$ should be interpreted as a "system blurring function" that incorporates not just the spatial sampling characteristics of the identical individual sensor elements, but also any misfocus blur and other image imperfections arising from the use of a lens.

For purposes of analysis and investigation, the noise $\eta(m, n)$ is almost always assumed to be **independently identically distributed (i.i.d.)**. That is, it is almost always assumed that each sample $\eta(i, j)$ of the noise is independent of every other sample $\eta(k, l)$, where $(i, j) \neq (k, l)$, and that every sample has an identical probability density function. (See Appendix A2.2 at the end of the chapter for a concise introduction to the probability density function of a random variable and other related concepts.) The probability density function that the image noise η is most commonly assumed to have is the zero-mean one-dimensional Gaussian: $f(z) = (1/\sqrt{2\pi\sigma^2})\ \exp(-[z - m]^2/(2\sigma^2))$, where m is the mean (zero here) of the random variable z, and σ is its standard deviation. The Gaussian function, which has the familiar bell shape illustrated in Figure 2.20, is so widely used

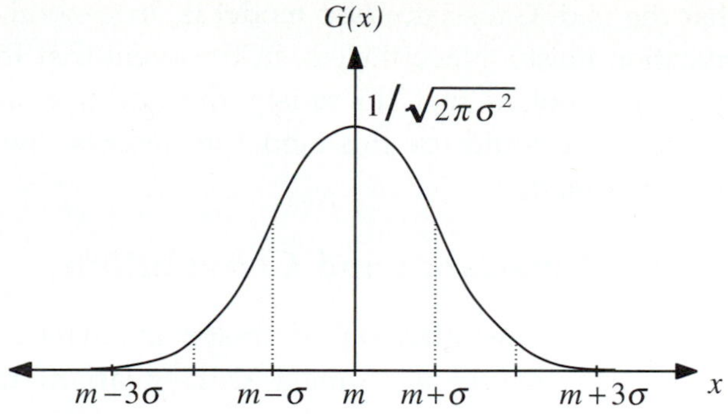

Figure 2.20 The one-dimensional Gaussian. The *one-dimensional Gaussian* has the following form: $G(x) = (1/\sqrt{2\pi\sigma^2}\,) \exp(-[x-m]^2/(2\sigma^2))$, where m is the *mean* of the Gaussian, and σ is its *standard deviation*. The Gaussian is a bell-shaped function that is centered about its mean and that has a width proportional to its standard deviation. As expressed here, the Gaussian has a unit integral. A multidimensional Gaussian is a generalization of a one-dimensional Gaussian: Along every dimension of a multidimensional Gaussian, the multidimensional Gaussian varies as a one-dimensional Gaussian. The Gaussian—in both one and multiple dimensions—is a widely used function, often finding application in its one-dimensional manifestation as a convenient mathematical model for the probability of a random number taking on an arbitrary value as a function of that value. The Gaussian probability model not only finds experimental confirmation in many natural phenomena, but it also has a mathematical justification when the random number in question is the result of a large number of individual random events.

that the area under it is frequently tabulated for various intervals. This area, which determines the probability of the random variable z taking on a value within a particular range, is 0.683 for the interval $m \pm \sigma$, 0.954 for the interval $m \pm 2\sigma$, 0.997 for the interval $m \pm 3\sigma$, and, of course, 1 for the interval $\pm\infty$.

Although the assumption that the noise is i.i.d. zero-mean Gaussian is convenient, this assumption is not always valid. Consider, for instance, image quantization noise—that is, the error in the intensity of the image as a result of intensity quantization. First, as in the image in Figure 2.19, image quantization noise is generally not independent at adjoining pixels. Second, the probability density function of quantization noise is almost never a Gaussian (e.g., see [Oppenheim and Schafer 1975]). Last, the statistics of image quantization noise are often different for different pixels; for instance, in the event of **image saturation** or **clipping**, which describes the quantization of image intensities above a certain level onto a single gray level, the quantization noise clearly depends on the intensity of the pixel.

Thus, we see that the i.i.d. Gaussian noise model is, in general, inappropriate for image quantization noise. Nevertheless, in the event that the image noise is dominated by other noises that do satisfy the additive i.i.d. zero-mean Gaussian noise model, we could use this model to describe the overall image noise to a close approximation.

2.3.2 Linear Shift-Invariance and Convolution

If we ignore noise, the transformation of image irradiance into a digital image described in this chapter is a **linear shift-invariant transformation**. The notion of a linear shift-invariant transformation is an important one, and is worth dwelling on a little.

A transform $T\{.\}$ is said to be a **linear transform** if it satisfies the following property:

$$T\{\mathrm{a}\,g(x,\,y) + \mathrm{b}\,h(x,\,y)\} \;=\; \mathrm{a}\,T\{g(x,\,y)\} + \mathrm{b}\,T\{h(x,\,y)\}$$

for all input functions g and h, and all constants a and b. In other words, a transform is linear if it satisfies the following two conditions:

1. In response to an input that is the sum of any two functions, the output of the transform is the sum of the individual outputs of the transform in response to each of the two functions separately.
2. In response to an input that is the product of any function with any constant, the output of the transform is the product of the constant with the output of the transform in response to just the function.

Note that linear equations, in general, *do not* constitute linear transforms; for instance, you can easily verify that the function f satisfying $f(x) = \mathrm{m}x + \mathrm{c}$ *does not* satisfy the definition of a linear transform. Whereas, in general, a linear set of equations expressed in matrix notation comprises a matrix multiplication followed by an addition, a transform is linear if and only if it can be expressed as just a matrix multiplication; see, for instance, [Aleksandrov, Kolmogorov, and Lavrent'ev 1969].

A transform $T\{.\}$ is said to be a **shift-invariant transform** if it satisfies the following property: Given $T\{i(x,\,y)\} = o(x,\,y)$,

$$T\{i(x - x_o,\, y - y_o)\} \;=\; o(x - x_o,\, y - y_o)$$

for all input functions i and all shifts $(x_o,\, y_o)$. In other words, a transform is shift-invariant if the only effect that an arbitrary shift in the input to the transform has on the output of the transform is to shift the output by an amount identical to the shift in the input. This definition is for a continuous-input continuous-output system—that is, for a system whose input and output functions are defined over continuously varying x and y.

For a discrete-input or discrete-output system—that is, for a system whose input or output is defined over only discrete x and y—the shifts (x_o, y_o) are naturally restricted to be discrete. However, if the discrete functions in question actually represent continuous functions that are sampled adequately as dictated by the sampling theorem—an assumption we shall frequently invoke implicitly—then we may apply the definition of shift-invariance to the underlying continuous functions, rather than to their samples.

It is worth pointing out here that the composite of a sequence of transformations that are all either linear, shift-invariant, or linear shift-invariant is also linear, shift-invariant, or linear shift-invariant, respectively. Further, the order of the individual transformations in the sequence is immaterial as far as the final output is concerned. See [Goodman 1968] and [Bracewell 1978] for an introduction to linear shift-invariant systems—that is, to systems whose input–output transformation is linear shift-invariant.

As we just discussed, in a system whose input–output relation is shift-invariant, a displacement in the input by a certain amount induces an equal displacement in the output. In particular, if the input is some elementary function, its displacement induces an equal displacement in the system's elementary-input response. Now, if a system is not only shift-invariant, but also linear, then the response of the system to any sum of weighted and displaced elementary functions will be the sum of the correspondingly weighted and displaced responses of the system to each of the elementary functions individually. In particular, if we denote a set of elementary two-dimensional functions by $\{e_i(x, y)\}$ and the corresponding set of responses of a linear shift-invariant system by $\{h_i(x, y)\}$, then the response of the system to $\sum_i w_i e_i(x - x_i, y - y_i)$ will be $\sum_i w_i h_i(x - x_i, y - y_i)$, where $\{w_i\}$ is the set of weights. It follows that, if we can (conceptually) decompose an input to a linear shift-invariant system into a weighted sum of displaced elementary functions, then we can compute the output of the system in response to this input in a straightforward fashion if we know the elementary-input responses of the system. Thus, we see that the input–output relation of a linear shift-invariant system is specified completely by the set of responses of the system to any set of elementary functions in terms of which all input functions can be described. For a continuous-input system, one such set of elementary functions comprises sines and cosines of varying frequencies; see Appendix A2.1 on the Fourier transform in this connection.

It turns out that the specification of a linear shift-invariant system's **impulse response**—that is, its response to a unit impulse—completely characterizes the input–output relation of the system. (A continuous unit impulse $\delta(x, y)$ is the **Dirac delta function**, which has a unit integral and is zero everywhere except at the origin; a discrete unit impulse $\delta(m, n)$ is the **Kronecker delta function**, which is one at the origin and zero elsewhere.) Now, any continuous signal $i(x, y)$ can be expressed as the following integral of displaced and weighted impulses:

$$i(x, y) = \int_{-\infty}^{+\infty} \int_{-\infty}^{+\infty} i(u, v)\; \delta(x-u, y-v)\; du\, dv\,.$$

This property is known as the **sifting property** of the unit impulse as the unit impulse $\delta(x-u, y-v)$ *sifts* out the value of $i(u, v)$ at the location $(u, v) = (x, y)$. But as an integral, by definition, is just an infinite sum in the limit, the output $o(x, y)$ of any continuous-input continuous-output linear shift-invariant system with impulse response $h(x, y)$ and input $i(x, y)$ can be expressed as follows:

$$\begin{aligned} o(x, y) &= \int_{-\infty}^{+\infty} \int_{-\infty}^{+\infty} i(u, v)\; h(x-u, y-v)\; du\, dv \\ &= \int_{-\infty}^{+\infty} \int_{-\infty}^{+\infty} i(x-u, y-v)\; h(u, v)\; du\, dv\,. \end{aligned}$$

This operation of computing the weighted integral of one function with respect to another function that has first been reflected about the origin, and then variably displaced, is termed **convolution**—more specifically, **continuous convolution**. The two functions are said to be *convolved*, and the preceding relationship is expressed compactly as $o = i * h$, or, equivalently, $o = h * i$. Figure 2.21 provides a straightforward illustration of a continuous convolution in one dimension.

The strict definition of convolution requires that, for two functions to be convolved, one of the two functions be reflected about the origin—for example, $h(x, y) \rightarrow h(-x, -y)$—before the weighted integral be computed under the variable displacement of this function. However, when there is no cause for confusion, we shall also use the term *convolution* to describe the computation of the straightforward weighted integral under the variable displacement of a function that has not been first reflected. There is no inconsistency here, as long as it is understood that the latter convolution is *not* with respect to the weighting function as such, but rather is with respect to the reflection of the weighting function about the origin. To take a specific example, $h(-x, -y) * i(x, y) = \int_{-\infty}^{+\infty} \int_{-\infty}^{+\infty} h(u-x, v-y)\; i(u, v)\; du\, dv$, which is simply the weighted integral of $i(x, y)$ with respect to $h(x, y)$ under the variable displacement of the latter. Of course, reflection of the weighting function about the origin is redundant when this function is symmetric about the origin—in the example here, when $h(x, y) = h(-x, -y)$.

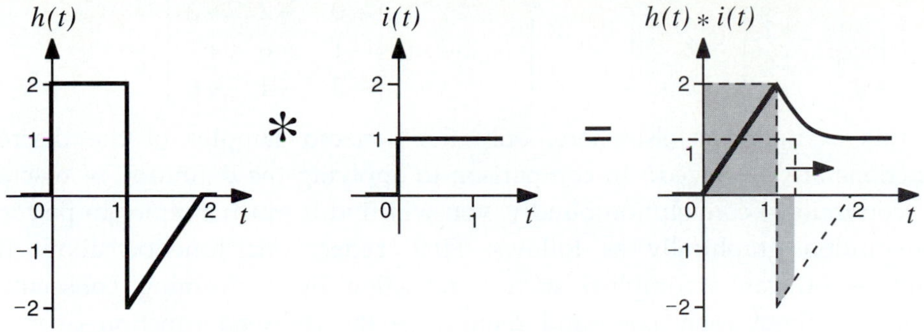

Figure 2.21 Convolution. *Convolution*, denoted by $*$ in the figure, is the operation of computing the weighted integral (sum in the case of discrete functions) of one function with respect to another function that has first been reflected about the origin, and then variably displaced. In one continuous dimension, $h(t) * i(t) = \int h(t-\lambda)\, i(\lambda)\, d\lambda = \int h(\lambda)\, i(t-\lambda)\, d\lambda$. If either of two functions that are convolved together is symmetric about the origin—as, for instance, a Gaussian is—then computing the convolution of the two functions reduces to computing the weighted integral (sum in the case of discrete functions) of one function with respect to the other function under variable displacement between the two functions. In particular, under such circumstances, there is no need to reflect one function about the origin to compute the convolution of the two functions.

The definition of discrete convolution is completely analogous to that of continuous convolution; both continuous convolution and discrete convolution are denoted by $*$, and the qualifiers *continuous* and *discrete* are invariably dropped. **Discrete convolution** is the weighted sum of one discrete function (e.g., a digital image) with respect to another discrete function (e.g., a mask of weights) that has first been reflected about the origin and then variably displaced. For instance, in two dimensions, if $I(m, n)$ and $H(m, n)$ are two discrete functions, then

$$I(m, n) * H(m, n) = \sum_{i=-\infty}^{+\infty} \sum_{j=-\infty}^{+\infty} I(i, j)\, H(m-i, n-j)$$

$$= \sum_{i=-\infty}^{+\infty} \sum_{j=-\infty}^{+\infty} I(m-i, n-j)\, H(i, j).$$

Just as the output of a continuous-input continuous-output linear shift-invariant system with input $i(x, y)$ and impulse response $h(x, y)$ is $i(x, y) * h(x, y)$, the output of a discrete-input discrete-output linear shift-invariant system with input $I(m, n)$ and impulse response $H(m, n)$ is $I(m, n) * H(m, n)$. A simple numerical example of a two-dimensional discrete convolution is instructive here:

$$\begin{bmatrix} -1 & +1 \\ -2 & +2 \end{bmatrix} * \begin{bmatrix} 0 & 2 \\ 1 & 3 \end{bmatrix} = \begin{bmatrix} 0 & -2 & +2 \\ -1 & -6 & +7 \\ -2 & -4 & +6 \end{bmatrix}.$$

In this example, as elsewhere, only the nonzero samples of the discrete functions are displayed. In comparison to applying the definition of discrete (or continuous) convolution blindly, you will find it much simpler to perform convolution graphically as follows: First, reflect one function about the origin—you can accomplish such a reflection by performing consecutive reflection about each axis—and then, slide the reflected function over the other function, noting the weighted sum (or integral) at each position.

Convolution, both continuous and discrete, exhibits several important properties. Four of these properties are the following:

1. Commutativity: $f * g = g * f$.
2. Associativity: $f * (g * h) = (f * g) * h$.
3. Distributivity over addition: $f * (g + h) = f * g + f * h$.
4. If f or g is differentiable, then $(f * g)' = f' * g$ or $(f * g)' = f * g'$, respectively, where $'$ denotes differentiation.

See [Bracewell 1978] for a detailed and intuitive introduction to convolution.

As indicated earlier, the impulse response of a linear shift-invariant system determines the input–output relation of the system completely. In the context of imaging systems, the impulse response is better known as the **point spread function**. This function, typically bell-shaped—on interpolation, in the case of a digital image—describes the intensity variation of the image of an isolated point object located on a uniformly black background.

An important characteristic of an effectively continuous-input continuous-output linear shift-invariant system is that, given a sinusoidal input, the system output is also sinusoidal with the same frequency—in the case of a multidimensional system, with the same frequency and orientation. However, the amplitude and position of the input sine wave may undergo a change on passing through a linear shift-invariant system. For instance, if the input to a two-dimensional linear shift-invariant system is $A_i \sin(2\pi ux + 2\pi vy + k_i)$, then the output of the system will be of the type $A_o \sin(2\pi ux + 2\pi vy + k_o)$, where A_o and k_o are constants that depend not only on A_i and k_i, but also on u and v. Note that the function $A \sin(2\pi ux + 2\pi vy + k)$ is a sine wave that is oscillating in the x–y plane with frequency $\sqrt{u^2 + v^2}$ in the direction $\tan^{-1}(v/u)$ with respect to the x-axis; this wave is constant in the direction orthogonal to its direction of oscillation, the amplitude of the wave is A, and the position of the wave is determined by k. The sinusoidal-input sinusoidal-output property of a linear shift-invariant system is easily verified from the input–output convolution relation we examined earlier. The change in the amplitude and the position of an input sine wave—this change depending on the frequency and orientation of the wave—is, of course, determined completely by the system's impulse response. On the other hand, the impulse response of a linear shift-invariant system is determined completely by knowledge of the system's responses to all possible sinusoidal inputs. The latter complete determination makes perfect sense: We can always determine the response of any linear shift-invariant system to an arbitrary input, including an impulse, by first decomposing the input signal into a sum (integral) of shifted and scaled sine waves, each wave with a particular frequency and orientation, and then summing (integrating) the individual shifted and scaled responses of the system. The possibility of the decomposition of a signal into a sum (integral) of shifted and scaled sine waves is intimately linked to the notion of the Fourier transform, a concept we shall examine briefly in Appendix A2.1.

In conclusion, it is clear that linear shift-invariance is an extremely convenient attribute for a system to possess. It is equally clear that the best we can hope for, in practice, is that this property, like the additive i.i.d. zero-mean Gaussian noise assumption, will be satisfied approximately by the relationship between the image irradiance and the digital image. Nevertheless, the first-order model for the digital image described in this chapter remains quite useful, and often is adequate.

A2.1 The Fourier Transform

You may wonder whether an arbitrary function can be decomposed into a sum/integral of shifted and scaled sinusoids of various frequencies and orientations. Such a decomposition is intimately linked to the notion of the Fourier transform, a ubiquitous tool in signal processing that we shall examine briefly here in two dimensions. First, note that any arbitrarily shifted and scaled sine wave with a particular frequency and orientation can be expressed as the weighted sum of a sine wave and a cosine wave, both with the same frequency and orientation as the original wave, but each with zero displacement; for instance,

$$A\sin(2\pi ux + 2\pi vy + k) \;=\; [A\sin(k)]\,\cos(2\pi ux + 2\pi vy) \;+\; [A\cos(k)]\,\sin(2\pi ux + 2\pi vy).$$

Here, the function $A\sin(2\pi ux + 2\pi vy + k)$ is a sine wave that is oscillating in the x–y plane with frequency $\sqrt{u^2 + v^2}$ in the direction $\tan^{-1}(v/u)$ with respect to the x-axis; this wave is constant in the direction orthogonal to its direction of oscillation, the amplitude of the wave is A, and the position of the wave is determined by k. Now, the Fourier transform, in effect, decomposes a function into an integral of scaled (but undisplaced) sinusoids and cosinusoids of various frequencies and orientations, each sinusoid and cosinusoid with the same frequency and orientation being represented together as the weighted sum of two complex conjugate exponentials, for instance, as follows:

$$B\cos(2\pi ux + 2\pi vy) \;+\; C\sin(2\pi ux + 2\pi vy) \;=$$
$$[(B - iC)/2]\ \exp(+i[2\pi ux + 2\pi vy]) \;+\; [(B + iC)/2]\ \exp(-i[2\pi ux + 2\pi vy]),$$

where i is the imaginary square root of -1, and $\exp(iz) = \cos(z) + i\sin(z)$.

The **Fourier transform** Ψ of a two-dimensional function $f(x, y)$ is defined as follows:

$$F(u, v) \;=\; \Psi\{f(x, y)\} \;\triangleq\; \int_{-\infty}^{+\infty}\int_{-\infty}^{+\infty} f(x, y)\ \exp(-i[2\pi ux + 2\pi vy])\ dx\,dy\,.$$

Both $f(x, y)$ and $F(u, v)$ may, in general, be complex-valued. The Fourier transform, when it exists, is a unique mapping from the so-called function domain, which is the x–y plane here, to the so-called Fourier domain, which is the u–v plane here. In other words, there is a one-to-one correspondence between every function and that function's Fourier transform.

The **inverse Fourier transform** Ψ^{-1} expresses the original function $f(x, y)$ as an integral of complex exponentials that are weighted as follows by the Fourier transform $F(u, v)$ of $f(x, y)$:

$$f(x, y) \;=\; \Psi^{-1}\{F(u, v)\} \;=\; \int_{-\infty}^{+\infty}\int_{-\infty}^{+\infty} F(u, v)\ \exp(+i[2\pi ux + 2\pi vy])\ du\,dv\,.$$

It follows from this expression that the values of the Fourier transform at every pair of points (u, v) and $(-u, -v)$ encode the sinusoidal and cosinusoidal components of the original function that have the frequency $\sqrt{u^2 + v^2}$ and the orientation $\tan^{-1}(v/u)$ with respect to the x-axis. Specifically,

$$F(u, v)\ \exp(+i[2\pi ux + 2\pi vy]) \;+\; F(-u, -v)\ \exp(-i[2\pi ux + 2\pi vy])$$

expands to the following weighted sum of a cosinusoid and a sinusoid:

$$[F(u, v) + F(-u, -v)]\ \cos(2\pi ux + 2\pi vy)$$
$$+\; i\,[F(u, v) - F(-u, -v)]\ \sin(2\pi ux + 2\pi vy)\,.$$

If $f(x, y)$ is a function that is real-valued everywhere, then, for all u and v, $[F(u, v) + F(-u, -v)]$ will be real and $[F(u, v) - F(-u, -v)]$ will be imaginary—equivalently, the real part of $F(u, v)$ will be symmetric about the origin, and the imaginary part of $F(u, v)$ will be antisymmetric about the origin.

Without getting into the intricacies of the Fourier transform—for instance, into the conditions for the existence of the Fourier transform's defining integrals—let us examine several of its salient properties, expressed here as theorems.

Duality Theorem:

If $\Psi\{f(x, y)\} = F(u, v)$,
then $\Psi\{F(x, y)\} = f(-u, -v)$.

Linearity Theorem:

If $\Psi\{g(x, y)\} = G(u, v)$ and $\Psi\{h(x, y)\} = H(u, v)$,
then $\Psi\{ag(x, y) + bh(x, y)\} = aG(u, v) + bH(u, v)$.

Similarity Theorem:

If $\Psi\{f(x, y)\} = F(u, v)$,
then $\Psi\{f(ax, by)\} = (1/|ab|)\, F(u/a, v/b)$.

Shift Theorem:

If $\Psi\{f(x, y)\} = F(u, v)$,
then $\Psi\{f(x - x_o, y - y_o)\} = F(u, v) \exp(-i[2\pi u x_o + 2\pi v y_o])$.

Parseval's Theorem:

If $\Psi\{f(x, y)\} = F(u, v)$,
then $\int_{-\infty}^{+\infty}\int_{-\infty}^{+\infty} |f(x, y)|^2\, dx\, dy = \int_{-\infty}^{+\infty}\int_{-\infty}^{+\infty} |F(u, v)|^2\, du\, dv$.

Convolution Theorem:

If $\Psi\{g(x, y)\} = G(u, v)$ and $\Psi\{h(x, y)\} = H(u, v)$,
then $\Psi\{g(x, y) * h(x, y)\} = G(u, v)\, H(u, v)$.

Owing to the importance of convolution in linear shift-invariant systems as explained in Section 2.3.2, the convolution theorem is of particular interest. What it tells us is that convolution in the function domain is equivalent to multiplication in the Fourier domain. From this result, and the duality theorem, it follows that multiplication in the function domain is equivalent to convolution in the Fourier domain.

Owing to the one-to-one correspondence between a function and its Fourier transform, when convenient, we may choose to carry out, or perhaps just visualize, an operation in the Fourier domain rather than in the function domain. A prime example of such an operation is convolution, which, as we have just seen, is equivalent to the much simpler operation of multiplication in the other domain. The **Whittaker–Shannon sampling theorem**, alluded to in Section 2.3.1, is also visualized conveniently in the Fourier domain. Now, a function is said to be **bandlimited** if the function's Fourier transform is zero beyond some frequency in every direction in the Fourier domain; the smallest frequency beyond which the Fourier transform of a function is zero in a particular direction in the Fourier domain is called the **bandlimit** of the function in that direction. What sampling a function uniformly by the Dirac delta function does to the function's Fourier transform is replicate the transform in various directions. In two dimensions, if the function is sampled along the x- and y-axes at uniform intervals X and Y, respectively, then the Fourier transform of the function will be replicated along the u- and v-axes at uniform intervals $1/X$ and $1/Y$, respectively (cf. the similarity theorem). Now, a function can be recovered *exactly* from its samples only so long as the nonzero portion of the function's Fourier transform does not overlap in the Fourier domain with the nonzero portions of the replicas of the function's Fourier transform. The minimum sampling rate that guarantees this absence of overlap is called the **Nyquist rate**. When a function is sampled at less than its Nyquist rate, the nonzero portion of the function's Fourier transform will overlap with the nonzero portions of the replicas of the function's Fourier transform, and we will get **aliasing**.

The standard engineering reference for the notion of a Fourier transform is [Bracewell 1978]. The second chapter of [Goodman 1968] provides a concise summary of the concepts that we have discussed here—and of other related concepts—specifically in the context of two-dimensional functions.

A2.2 Probability Density and Distribution

The **distribution function** F_α of a random variable α is defined for any real number z by

$$F_\alpha(z) \triangleq \text{probability}\{\alpha \leq z\};$$

that is, it is the probability of α taking on a value less than or equal to z. The **probability density function** f_α of a random variable α is, by definition,

$$f_\alpha(z) \triangleq \frac{d\,F_\alpha(z)}{dz};$$

that is, it is the probability per unit interval of α taking on a value between z and $z + \Delta z$ in the limit $\Delta z \rightarrow 0$. Hence, $F_\alpha(z) = \int_{-\infty}^{z} f_\alpha(p)\, dp$. Clearly, the probability that α has a value between $-\infty$ and $+\infty$ must be 1, and, hence, we must have $\int_{-\infty}^{+\infty} f_\alpha(z)\, dz = F_\alpha(\infty) = 1$.

Note that the distribution function of a random variable provides the *cumulative probability* of the random variable assuming a value less than or equal to some real number, whereas the probability density function of a random variable provides the *relative probability* of the random variable assuming a value equal to some real number. Strictly speaking, for any random variable, the probability density function, as defined, exists only if the distribution function of the random variable is differentiable—a condition not met if the random variable can take on only discrete values. The term **probability distribution**—as opposed to the term *distribution function*—is often used to describe the relative probabilities of a random variable taking on various values: This term refers to the probability density function when the random variable is continuous, and to the set of individual probabilities of the random variable when the random variable is discrete.

Two important measures of a random variable are its mean and variance. The **mean** m_α or **expected value** $E[\alpha]$ of a random variable α is, by definition,

$$m_\alpha \;=\; E[\alpha] \;\triangleq\; \int_{-\infty}^{+\infty} z\, f_\alpha(z)\, dz\,.$$

It follows that the expected value of any function of α, say $h(\alpha)$, which itself is a random variable, is given by $E[h(\alpha)] = \int_{-\infty}^{+\infty} h(z)\, f_\alpha(z)\, dz$. An important property of expected values is that the expectation of a sum of random variables is the sum of their expectations; that is, $E[\,\Sigma_{i=1}^{n} \alpha_i\,] = \Sigma_{i=1}^{n} E[\alpha_i]$. The **variance** $\mathrm{var}(\alpha)$ of a random variable α—or, equivalently, the square of the **standard deviation** σ_α of the random variable α—is, by definition, the expected value of the square of the deviation of the random variable from its mean; that is,

$$\mathrm{var}(\alpha) \;=\; \sigma_\alpha^2 \;\triangleq\; E[(\alpha - m_\alpha)^2] \;=\; \int_{-\infty}^{+\infty} (z - m_\alpha)^2\, f_\alpha(z)\, dz\,.$$

Equivalently, $\sigma_\alpha^2 = E[(\alpha - m_\alpha)^2] = E[(\alpha - E[\alpha])^2] = E[\alpha^2] - E^2[\alpha]$.

The **joint distribution function** $F_{\alpha\beta}$ and **joint probability density function** $f_{\alpha\beta}$ of two random variables α and β are defined as follows:

$$F_{\alpha\beta}(u, v) \;\triangleq\; \text{probability}\{\alpha \le u \text{ and } \beta \le v\}\,,$$

$$f_{\alpha\beta}(u, v) \;\triangleq\; \frac{\partial^2 F_{\alpha\beta}(u, v)}{\partial u\, \partial v}\,.$$

Hence, $F_{\alpha\beta}(u, v) = \int_{-\infty}^{u} \int_{-\infty}^{v} f_{\alpha\beta}(p, q)\, dp\, dq$. The **conditional distribution function** $F_{\alpha|\beta}$ and **conditional probability density function** $f_{\alpha|\beta}$ of a random variable α, given another random variable $\beta = v$, are defined as follows:

$$F_{\alpha|\beta}(u \mid \beta = v) \;\triangleq\; \text{probability}\{\alpha \le u \text{ given } \beta = v\}\,,$$

$$f_{\alpha|\beta}(u \mid \beta = v) \;\triangleq\; \frac{d\, F_{\alpha|\beta}(u \mid \beta = v)}{du}\,.$$

Hence, $F_{\alpha|\beta}(u \mid \beta = v) = \int_{-\infty}^{u} f_{\alpha|\beta}(p \mid \beta = v)\, dp$.

Two random variables α and β are said to be **independent** if the probability of one taking on some value or set of values is independent of the other taking on some value or set of values. For such variables, we have the following relations: $F_{\alpha\beta}(u, v) = F_\alpha(u)\, F_\beta(v)$, $f_{\alpha\beta}(u, v) = f_\alpha(u)\, f_\beta(v)$, $F_{\alpha|\beta}(u \mid \beta = v) = F_\alpha(u)$, and $f_{\alpha|\beta}(u \mid \beta = v) = f_\alpha(u)$.

The standard engineering reference for these and related concepts in probability theory is [Papoulis 1984]. The first chapter of [Ross 1983] provides a concise summary.

Figure 3.1 *The Archer*, working model, by Henry Moore, 1964. On the left is an image of a working model of a sculpture, and on the right is an artist's rendering of some of the salient brightness edges in the image. An *edge* in an image is an image contour across which the intensity of the image changes abruptly; an image-intensity edge may or may not correspond to a physical edge of an object. It is sometimes said that the objective of science is to describe nature economically. Analogously, one purpose of edge detection in an image is to strip away some of the redundancy of sensing—to encode and describe the information contained in the image in a form more economical than that in which the information impinges on the sensors [Attneave 1954]. (Photograph, courtesy The Henry Moore Foundation, Much Hadham, England.)

Chapter 3

Edge Detection and Image Segmentation

When we speak of an *edge* in everyday conversation, we generally refer to a contour in space along which a surface either terminates or undergoes a sudden change in orientation. The concept of an edge in an image is related to this everyday notion: An **edge** in an image is an image contour across which the brightness of the image changes abruptly—perhaps in magnitude or in the rate of change of magnitude. Figure 3.1 illustrates an artist's rendering of some of the salient brightness edges in a photograph. In this chapter, we shall first discuss the automatic detection of edges in an image, and then we shall discuss the segmentation of an image into regions that have smoothly varying intensities in their interiors.

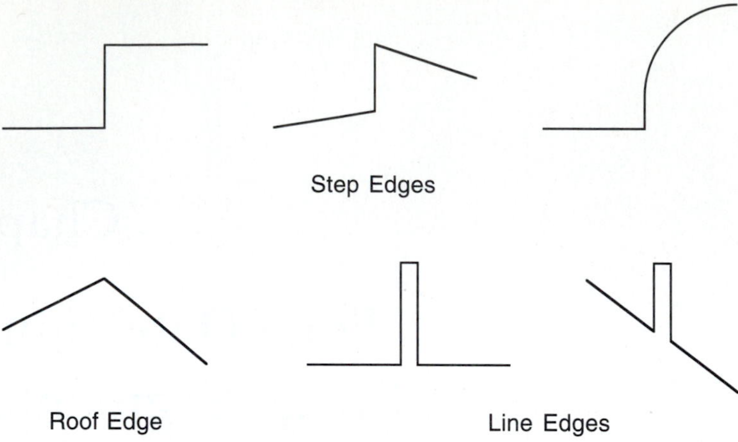

Figure 3.2 Profiles of various types of image-intensity edges as they would appear in an image in the absence of blurring, sampling, or quantization by the imaging system. A *step edge* exhibits a discontinuity in the magnitude of the image intensity, a *roof edge* exhibits a discontinuity in the first derivative of the image intensity, and a *line edge* comprises two step edges that are close together. Step edges are the most common among these three types of edges; hence, we shall restrict ourselves almost exclusively to step edges in this book.

Recall from Chapter 2 that what is available to us in a digital image is a set of quantized samples of the optical image formed on the image plane. Clearly, these samples have their sole significance in the optical image they represent. As this optical image is characterized by the image-irradiance function defined over the image plane, we can freely talk about the characteristics of the continuously defined intensity surface underlying a digital image.

A **step edge** in a digital image refers to an image contour across which the magnitude of the underlying (continuously defined) intensity function changes abruptly. A **roof edge** refers to a contour (other than a step edge) across which the orientation of the underlying intensity surface changes abruptly. For purposes of analysis and investigation, these abrupt changes are modeled as (mathematical) discontinuities. Figure 3.2 shows the profiles of some step and roof edges. It also contains examples of **line edges**, which are frequently just pairs of adjacent parallel step edges (however, see also the end of Section 5.1.2).

Our focus here shall be primarily on step edges. Step edges are by far the most commonly occurring and widely studied edges. For purposes of analysis and design of edge detectors, it is almost always assumed that the step edges are ideal in that, barring noise and blurring by the imaging

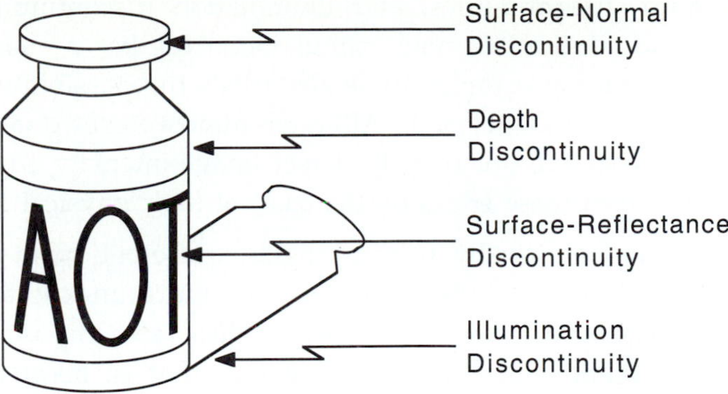

Figure 3.3 Physical events in a scene that may lead to intensity edges in an image of the scene. Among the various physical events in a scene that may lead to intensity edges in an image of the scene, the principal events are discontinuities in the surface normal, in surface reflectance, in illumination, and in depth. Notice that a discontinuity in depth may simultaneously be a discontinuity in the surface normal.

system, the intensities on their two sides are constant. The difference between the intensities on the two sides of a step edge is called the step edge's **contrast**.

Although edge detection often leads to the segmentation of an image into regions with smoothly varying intensities in their interiors, it need not do so. Although edges form the boundaries of smoothly varying image-intensity regions, and nonedges form these regions' interiors, clearly edges need not be always closed (see Figures 4.14 and 4.15). Under a variety of circumstances, it is image segmentation that is specifically desired. Then, techniques geared directly toward image segmentation (rather than toward edge detection) are often preferred; such techniques circumvent the problems of dangling and fragmented edges, at times by absorbing these edges into image segments, and at others by completing these edges across smoothly shaded image regions. Although our focus here shall be on edge detection, we shall also review several prominent image-segmentation techniques.

Before we discuss edge detection, let us pause to consider why we seek to detect edges in the first place. As we saw in Chapter 2, the image irradiance is proportional to the scene radiance, and hence discontinuities in the image intensity correspond to discontinuities in the scene radiance. Discontinuities in the scene radiance, in turn, may result from one of several causes, each cause interesting and informative in its own right. Figure 3.3 illustrates the principal scene events that lead to intensity edges in an image. These events include surface-normal discontinuities, depth discontinuities, surface-reflectance discontinuities, and illumination discontinuities. Notice that a depth discontinuity may simultaneously be a surface-normal discontinuity. For glossy surfaces, there also exists the possibility of edges of specular reflections (see Figure 3.1). Although almost never done in practice, it is in principle desirable not only to detect image-intensity edges, but also to distinguish between these edges on the basis of their physical causes.

Edges are also noteworthy from a slightly different point of view: an information-theoretic one. Under this view, the more unexpected an event, the more information that event conveys. Edges are important precisely because they represent image nonredundancies—that is, because the image intensity (gradient) on either side of a step (roof) edge cannot be predicted by an examination of the other side. This viewpoint was first elaborated by Attneave in his classic paper, "Some Informational Aspects of Visual Perception" [Attneave 1954]; the roots of information theory lie in the seminal paper by Shannon, "A Mathematical Theory of Communication" [Shannon 1948]. The aim of vision is the abstraction of the structure of the world from the world's images, and edge detection is a crucial data-reduction step in almost all proposals to meet this aim.

Edges, as mentioned earlier, are image contours across which the underlying intensity surface is discontinuous. The detection of such contours is almost always performed as a two-step process: first, the detection of short linear edge segments called **edgels** (abbreviation for *edge elements*), and then, the aggregation of edgels into extended edges, and, perhaps, the parametric description of these edges. We shall examine edgel detection first, and then we shall examine edgel aggregation and edge description. Finally, we shall consider a few direct techniques of image segmentation.

3.1 Edgel Detection

All edgel detectors seek to verify the existence of short linear edge segments that are postulated to lie across image windows (i.e., subimages) that have the same shape and size as the operator kernel. (The *kernel* of an operator, literally the core, is the part of the operator that makes use of the intensity of the image; the kernel of a convolution operator is the operator's nonzero part.) The image windows over which an edgel detector is applied need not be disjoint. In fact, in almost all implementations, they are positioned at 1-pixel intervals along each sampling direction. Such a spacing of image windows provides redundancy at the expense of extra computation, assuming that we can identify multiple responses of the operator to a single edge, and that we can distinguish such responses from multiple responses to multiple edges.

Most edgel detectors fall into one of two classes: difference operators or parametric-model matchers. Difference operators seek to estimate derivatives of the underlying intensity surface by computing weighted differences between pixel intensities, the underlying idea being that large image gradients reflect abrupt intensity changes. Parametric-model matchers, on the other hand, seek to determine whether the pixel intensities within an image window conform to some parameterized edgel model. Various operators belonging to each of these two classes are discussed in this chapter. First, however, let us consider how we can evaluate the performance of an operator.

3.1.1 Operator Evaluation

Several elements are common to the evaluation of all feature detectors. Ideally, a detector should respond positively to the presence of the feature that it is seeking to detect, and negatively to that feature's absence. However, owing to the presence of noise, such behavior of a detector is not always feasible. Hence, one index of an operator's performance is the statistical likelihood of the operator's **true positives**, or, equivalently, of its **false negatives**—that is, of its positive, or negative, responses in the presence of instances of the feature, respectively. These statistics are a function of the signal's *signal-to-noise ratio*, a term defined in reference to the particular feature that is sought to be detected.

Given models of the feature and the noise, it is relatively straightforward to establish the true-positive and false-negative statistics of an operator using **Monte Carlo simulations**. (*Monte Carlo*—after the famous gambling resort—is a general term used to describe any technique that uses random numbers to find an approximate solution to a problem that might otherwise be difficult to solve.) It is much more difficult to quantify the statistical likelihood of an operator's **false positives**—that is, of the operator's positive responses in the absence of the feature. The reason for the difficulty is that the space of nonfeatures has no single characteristic model. Often, what is done to obtain false-positive statistics is to determine the operator's response to a constant signal that is corrupted by noise.

Thus, we see that the design and evaluation of an operator must take into account two types of errors: (1) the rejection of a correct hypothesis, termed a *false negative* or a **type-I error**; and (2) the acceptance of an incorrect hypothesis, termed a *false positive* or a **type-II error**. In addition to the false-negative and false-positive statistics, when pertinent, we would also like to know the accuracy with which the operator estimates the parameters of a feature when the feature is detected correctly; this accuracy is, in general, a function of the signal-to-noise ratio. Unfortunately, few edge detectors have been characterized in the fashion described here, making it difficult to offer objective comparisons of the various proposals.

3.1.2 Difference Operators

It is clear that, at a step edge, the underlying intensity surface of an image has a large gradient pointing across the edge. Researchers often exploit this phenomenon to detect edges, typically by thresholding the magnitude of the intensity gradient everywhere on the image—that is, by declaring edges at all image points where the intensity gradient is above a certain cutoff, called the *threshold*. Thresholding may be followed by thinning the output, perhaps by retaining only those gradients that are locally maximum in the direction of the gradient; this selective retention is sometimes called *nonmaximum suppression*. **Thresholding** is a general term that we shall encounter in several contexts: It denotes the use of one or more discrete numerical cutoffs, called **thresholds**, to classify a numerical entity.

The **gradient** of a function $f(x, y)$ is, by definition, the vector $\vec{\nabla} f(x, y) \triangleq [\partial f/\partial x \quad \partial f/\partial y]$. Now, the image-intensity gradient—both its magnitude and its direction—can be estimated in a variety of ways. If we assume that the sampled intensity surface is continuously differentiable—smoothing by the sampling window makes this assumption tenable—then the simplest approach is to devise difference operators that estimate the directional derivatives of the image intensity in any two orthogonal directions at a single point. If we denote these orthogonal directional derivatives of the image intensity by Δ_1 and Δ_2, then the magnitude of the image-intensity gradient is given by $\sqrt{\Delta_1^2 + \Delta_2^2}$, and the direction of the image-intensity gradient with respect to the direction of the Δ_1 estimate is given by $\tan^{-1}(\Delta_2/\Delta_1)$.

Before we move on to techniques for estimating Δ_1 and Δ_2, a few quick observations on the gradient are worthwhile. The gradient $\mathbf{G}(x, y)$ of a surface $z = f(x, y)$ at any point (x_o, y_o) defines the tangent plane to the surface at that point. This plane can be expressed as follows: $\mathbf{G}(x_o, y_o) \cdot [(x - x_o) \quad (y - y_o)] = z$, where $\mathbf{G}(x, y) = [\partial f/\partial x \quad \partial f/\partial y]$. It follows easily that the first directional derivative of the surface in any direction in the x–y plane, say in the direction of the unit vector $\mathbf{n}$, is simply the dot product $\mathbf{G} \cdot \mathbf{n}$.

The simplest gradient operator, the **Roberts' cross operator** [Roberts 1965], uses the two masks shown in Figure 3.4(a) to compute, at the center of a 2×2 window, Δ_1 and Δ_2 along the diagonals of the window. Constant

Δ_1		Δ_2	
0	1	1	0
-1	0	0	-1

(a)

Δ_1			Δ_2		
-1	0	1	1	1	1
-1	0	1	0	0	0
-1	0	1	-1	-1	-1

(b)

Δ_1			Δ_2		
-1	0	1	1	2	1
-2	0	2	0	0	0
-1	0	1	-1	-2	-1

(c)

Δ_1				Δ_2			
-3	-1	1	3	3	3	3	3
-3	-1	1	3	1	1	1	1
-3	-1	1	3	-1	-1	-1	-1
-3	-1	1	3	-3	-3	-3	-3

(d)

Figure 3.4 Gradient operators. **(a)** *Roberts' cross operator.* **(b)** 3×3 *Prewitt operator.* **(c)** *Sobel operator.* **(d)** 4×4 Prewitt operator. We can estimate a directional derivative of the image intensity at a point in a digital image by applying an appropriate mask, of the types illustrated here, to the image at that point—that is, by computing the weighted sum of the pixels in the neighborhood of the image point with respect to the weights provided by a suitable mask. If, for instance, we denote the four entries of a 2×2 mask, such as a Roberts' cross mask, by a, b, c, and d, and we denote four identically arranged image pixels by I_a, I_b, I_c, and I_d, respectively, then, by appropriately choosing a, b, c, and d, we can estimate variously oriented directional derivatives of the image intensity at the center of the four image pixels by computing the weighted sum $(aI_a + bI_b + cI_c + dI_d)$. In each pair of masks illustrated here, the two masks provide equally scaled estimates of the directional derivatives in two orthogonal directions at the image point where the masks are centered; the Roberts' cross masks provide scaled estimates of the directional derivatives along the diagonals of the masks, and the other pairs of masks provide scaled estimates of the directional derivatives along the horizontals and the verticals of the masks. If we denote any two equally scaled and orthogonally directed directional derivatives of the image intensity at an image point by Δ_1 and Δ_2, then the magnitude of the gradient of the image intensity at the image point is proportional to $\sqrt{\Delta_1^2 + \Delta_2^2}$, and the orientation of the gradient with respect to the direction of the Δ_1 estimate is given by $\tan^{-1}(\Delta_2/\Delta_1)$. Along step edges in the image intensity, the gradient of the image intensity has a large magnitude and the direction of the gradient is orthogonal to the step-edge contour.

multiplicative factors have been omitted from the figure as these factors do not affect the relative magnitudes of the gradients computed at different image points—these factors, however, are important in determining the relative sensitivities of the various operators to noise. Two masks equivalent to the Roberts' cross masks, but providing estimates for Δ_1 and Δ_2 along the image coordinate axes at the center of a 2×2 window, rather than along the diagonals of the window, are the following:

$$\begin{bmatrix} -1 & +1 \\ -1 & +1 \end{bmatrix} \quad \text{and} \quad \begin{bmatrix} +1 & +1 \\ -1 & -1 \end{bmatrix}$$

(constant multiplicative factors have been omitted once again). We can easily derive these masks from the Roberts' cross masks by invoking the directional-derivative relation described earlier. Further, we can show that these masks, and, equivalently, those constituting the Roberts' cross operator, in effect provide the gradient of the least-squares-error planar surface fitted over a 2×2 window [Brooks 1978].[1]

We can derive a different gradient estimator, the **Prewitt operator** [Prewitt 1970], by fitting a least-squares-error quadratic surface over a 3×3 image window, and then differentiating the fitted surface. A **quadratic** is a second-order polynomial in up to two independent variables; a quadratic surface is a function of the type $f(x, y) = \Sigma \Sigma_{i+j \leq 2} a_{ij} x^i y^j$, where a_{ij} are the coefficients, and a quadratic curve is a curve of the type $\Sigma \Sigma_{i+j \leq 2} a_{ij} x^i y^j = 0$, where a_{ij} are the coefficients. Two masks that result from differentiating the least-squares-error quadratic surface fitted over a 3×3 image window are illustrated in Figure 3.4(b); these masks provide (scaled) estimates of the directional derivatives along the image coordinate axes at the center of the window. We can show that fitting a least-squares-error planar surface over a 3×3 image window, rather than a least-squares-error quadratic surface, would lead to the same set of masks [Brooks 1978].

Difference masks, such as those illustrated in Figure 3.4, seek to accentuate variations in the intensity of an image by computing the differences between weighted combinations of the pixel intensities within the

1. If the pixel intensities in a digital image are denoted by $I(m, n)$, where m and n are the image coordinates, then we obtain the **least-squares-error fit** of a function $f(m, n)$ to the data $I(m, n)$ by minimizing $\xi^2 = \Sigma_m \Sigma_n (I(m, n) - f(m, n))^2$. Here, $I(m, n)$ are the actual image intensities, and the minimization is carried out with respect to the parameters of $f(m, n)$ that we seek to determine. For instance, if $f(m, n) = \Sigma_i \Sigma_j c_{ij} m^i n^j$, then the minimization is with respect to c_{ij}, the coefficients of the bivariate polynomial. We accomplish the minimization of ξ^2 that we seek by equating to zero each of ξ^2's partial derivatives with respect to the parameters of $f(m, n)$. In the case of the bivariate polynomial, this operation corresponds to setting all $\partial \xi^2 / \partial c_{ij}$ equal to 0.

span of the mask. As we shall see, difference masks succeed not only in accentuating actual intensity variations that underlie a digital image, but also in accentuating image noise. The opposite effect—that of suppressing intensity variations, including those due to image noise—is accomplished by employing **averaging masks** or **smoothing masks**, which, in contrast to difference masks, have all positive weights. Now, within a constant-intensity region, a difference mask ought to provide a zero response as there is no intensity variation within such a region; within a constant-intensity region, an averaging mask ought to provide a response that is equal to the constant image intensity of the region, as the average of a constant is the constant itself. It follows that the sum of the weights of a difference mask must be equal to 0, and the sum of the weights of an averaging mask must be equal to 1.

Two masks closely related to the Prewitt operator are the masks of the **Sobel operator** that are illustrated in Figure 3.4(c). (For the record, Pingle [Pingle 1969] seems to have been the first person to describe the Sobel operator, attributing it to Sobel.) On application to an image, each Sobel mask in effect provides the (scaled) average of either the image's horizontal or vertical directional derivatives that we obtain by using the 2×2 masks that we discussed in the context of the Roberts' cross operator. We can establish this property of the Sobel masks by noting the following two convolutions that derive the two Sobel masks by convolving each of the 2×2 horizontal and vertical directional-derivative masks with a 2×2 averaging mask (that has all 1s, barring the scale factor $1/4$):

$$\begin{bmatrix} 1 & 1 \\ 1 & 1 \end{bmatrix} * \begin{bmatrix} -1 & +1 \\ -1 & +1 \end{bmatrix} = \begin{bmatrix} -1 & 0 & +1 \\ -2 & 0 & +2 \\ -1 & 0 & +1 \end{bmatrix}, \quad \text{and}$$

$$\begin{bmatrix} 1 & 1 \\ 1 & 1 \end{bmatrix} * \begin{bmatrix} +1 & +1 \\ -1 & -1 \end{bmatrix} = \begin{bmatrix} +1 & +2 & +1 \\ 0 & 0 & 0 \\ -1 & -2 & -1 \end{bmatrix}.$$

Recall that discrete convolution is the weighted sum of one discrete function with respect to another function that has been first reflected about the origin, and then variably displaced—here, as elsewhere, only the nonzero samples of the discrete functions are displayed. It follows from the preceding equalities that the application of the Sobel masks to an image is equivalent to the execution of either of the two following sequences of operations. First, compute the horizontal and vertical directional derivatives of the image using the 2×2 difference masks, and then, average each result with a 2×2 mask that has all 1s. Equivalently, first, average the image with a 2×2 mask that has all 1s, and then, compute the horizontal and vertical directional derivatives of the averaged image using the 2×2 difference masks.[2]

As noted by Prewitt [Prewitt 1970], an obvious shortcoming of her 3×3 masks is that they do not use the image intensity at the center of the window. To overcome this shortcoming, she proposed the masks illustrated in Figure 3.4(d). These masks provide the (scaled) directional derivatives in the horizontal and vertical directions at the center of a 4×4 window, once again by implicitly fitting a least-squares-error quadratic surface.

In the tradition of Prewitt, Haralick [Haralick 1984] proposed fitting a particular class of cubic surfaces (in the least-squares sense) over square image windows. Then, edges are declared at those pixels with gradients above some threshold that have within their immediate neighborhood a negatively sloped zero-crossing of the second directional derivative taken in the direction of the gradient. Such zero-crossings correspond to local first–directional-derivative maxima in the direction of the gradient. This approach is clearly a reasonable strategy to localize step edges, a task that simple gradient-thresholding schemes fail to accomplish. Haralick offers experimental evidence in support of his claim that his operator improves over several previously proposed operators with respect to false positives and false negatives; the operators Haralick considers include the 3×3 Prewitt gradient operator, and the Marr–Hildreth operator, which we shall consider later in this section.

In the same paper referred to earlier, Prewitt [Prewitt 1970] describes an alternative to the preceding techniques to estimate the image gradient. This

---

2. It is instructive to go through the exercise of establishing explicitly that each Sobel mask indeed provides the (scaled) average of either the image's horizontal or vertical directional derivatives, each of these derivatives estimated using 2×2 masks—or, equivalently, that each Sobel mask provides either the (scaled) horizontal or the (scaled) vertical directional derivatives of the averaged image, each of these derivatives estimated using 2×2 masks. Let us denote the discrete image by $I(m, n)$; the 2×2 averaging mask with all 1s by $A(m, n)$; the 2×2 horizontal and vertical directional-derivative masks by $R_H(m, n)$ and $R_V(m, n)$, respectively; and the corresponding Sobel masks by $S_H(m, n)$ and $S_V(m, n)$, respectively. Then, for reasons explained in Section 2.3.2, we can express the weighted sums that we compute by applying the Sobel masks to the image by the following two convolutions: $S_H(-m, -n) * I(m, n)$ and $S_V(-m, -n) * I(m, n)$. Expanding each Sobel mask into the convolution of the 2×2 averaging mask with the appropriate horizontal or vertical 2×2 directional-derivative mask, and invoking the associativity and commutativity properties of convolution, we reach the following equalities:

$$\begin{aligned} S_H(-m, -n) * I(m, n) &= [A(-m, -n) * R_H(-m, -n)] * I(m, n) \\ &= A(-m, -n) * [R_H(-m, -n) * I(m, n)] \\ &= R_H(-m, -n) * [A(-m, -n) * I(m, n)], \end{aligned}$$

and the analogous relations for the vertical mask. This establishes the sought result.

-1	1	1
-1	-2	1
-1	1	1

0°

1	1	1
-1	-2	1
-1	-1	1

45°

1	1	1
1	-2	1
-1	-1	-1

90°

1	1	1
1	-2	-1
1	-1	-1

135°

(a)

-100	-100	0	100	100
-100	-100	0	100	100
-100	-100	0	100	100
-100	-100	0	100	100
-100	-100	0	100	100

0°

-100	32	100	100	100
-100	-78	92	100	100
-100	-100	0	100	100
-100	-100	-92	78	100
-100	-100	-100	-32	100

30°

100	100	100	100	100
-32	78	100	100	100
-100	-92	0	92	100
-100	-100	-100	-78	32
-100	-100	-100	-100	-100

60°

100	100	100	100	100
100	100	100	100	100
0	0	0	0	0
-100	-100	-100	-100	-100
-100	-100	-100	-100	-100

90°

100	100	100	100	100
100	100	100	78	-32
100	92	0	-92	-100
32	-78	-100	-100	-100
-100	-100	-100	-100	-100

120°

100	100	100	32	-100
100	100	92	-78	-100
100	100	0	-100	-100
100	78	-92	-100	-100
100	-32	-100	-100	-100

150°

(b)

Figure 3.5 Edge templates. **(a)** Prewitt masks in four directions. **(b)** *Nevatia–Babu masks* in six directions. Each template is tuned to a step edge in a particular direction such that, when the template is applied to a digital image at a point where there is a step edge with the orientation of the template, the template provides a response with a large magnitude. We can use the magnitude of the largest response from the responses of variously oriented templates that are applied at an image point—each template from a set of templates of the type of which two subsets are shown here—to determine whether a step edge is present at the image point. The orientation of a step edge detected in such a fashion is given by the orientation of the template that provides the largest response.

alternative proceeds as follows. First, apply a set of oriented difference operators to the image window, each operator providing a (scaled) estimate of the first derivative in a different direction. Then, take the maximum response of the various difference operators to provide a (scaled) estimate of the gradient magnitude, and take the corresponding operator direction to provide an estimate of the gradient direction. Four of the eight masks proposed by Prewitt are shown in Figure 3.5(a). Similarly inspired edge templates that compute *edge strengths* in various directions were proposed subsequently by Kirsch [Kirsch 1971], and later by Nevatia and Babu [Nevatia and Babu 1980]. The masks constituting the **Nevatia–Babu operator** are shown in Figure 3.5(b).

A simple example is instructive here. Figure 3.6(a) is a 64×64 synthetic digital image of a circular constant-intensity region—of radius 24 pixels—located on a darker constant-intensity background. This image was generated in two steps. First, the continuously defined intensity pattern was convolved with the following two-dimensional Gaussian: $G(x, y) = (1/(2\pi\sigma_{\text{blur}}^2)) \exp(-[x^2 + y^2] / (2\sigma_{\text{blur}}^2))$, $\sigma_{\text{blur}} = 0.6$ pixel. Then, the pattern that resulted was sampled by an integer-valued square grid, and each sample was quantized to take on an integral value in the range 0 to 255. In the figure, each sample is represented by a uniformly gray 1-pixel square. (See Section 2.3.1 for the reasoning behind this procedure of synthetic-image generation.) Let us denote the intensity difference between the circular disc and its background by *step-size*. Parts (b), (c), and (d) of Figure 3.6 were synthesized in the same fashion as was part (a), except that each sample was corrupted (prior to quantization) with independently identically distributed (i.i.d.) zero-mean additive Gaussian noise whose standard deviation was σ_{noise} (see Section 2.3.1). The **signal-to-noise ratio (SNR)**, defined here as SNR $\triangleq$ *step-size*$/\sigma_{\text{noise}}$, in each of parts (b), (c), and (d) is 16, 8, and 4, respectively. Figure 3.6(e) and Figure 3.6(f) are the (scaled) image-intensity gradient magnitudes estimated in Figure 3.6(b) and Figure 3.6(d), respectively, by application of the Roberts' cross operator. Figure 3.6(g) and Figure 3.6(h) are the (scaled) image-intensity gradient magnitudes estimated in Figure 3.6(b) and Figure 3.6(d), respectively, by application of the 3×3 Prewitt operator. Figure 3.6(i) and Figure 3.6(j) are the (scaled) image-intensity gradient magnitudes estimated in Figure 3.6(b) and Figure 3.6(d), respectively, by application of the Nevatia–Babu masks. In none of the displayed image-intensity gradient estimates is any thresholding performed; that is, in no case is the response of an operator suppressed when this response lies below a certain value, called the *threshold*. Although each of the three operators is less effective on the noisier image than it is on the less noisy image, the performance of the three operators on the noisier image is markedly different: The Roberts' cross operator is the least effective, whereas the Nevatia–Babu operator is the most effective. Note, however, that in the low-noise case, the Roberts' cross operator gives the thinnest edge response, whereas the Nevatia–Babu operator gives the thickest edge response. (See the discussion in Section 3.1.4 for an explanation of these differences in performance.)

The surface-fitting methods adopted by Prewitt and Haralick to estimate the image gradient implicitly smooth the underlying intensity surface by projecting it onto the space of functions spanned by the chosen basis. An alternate method of smoothing the image is to convolve it with some local averaging filter that has all positive weights summing up to unity. The filter used most often is a discretized version of the two-dimensional Gaussian: $G(x, y) = (1/(2\pi\sigma^2)) \exp(-[x^2 + y^2]/(2\sigma^2))$, where σ determines the width of the filter, and the factor $(1/(2\pi\sigma^2))$ ensures that the integral of $G(x, y)$ is unity. Two currently popular edge detectors based on Gaussian smoothing are described next.

The first, the **Marr–Hildreth operator** [Marr and Hildreth 1980], convolves the image with a discretized version of the Laplacian of a Gaussian, and then takes the resulting zero-crossings—which can be shown to form closed contours—to constitute edges. As $\nabla^2(G * I) = (\nabla^2 G) * I$—where $\nabla^2 = \partial^2/\partial x^2 + \partial^2/\partial y^2$ is the Laplacian operator, G is a Gaussian, I is the image, and $*$ denotes convolution—convolving the image with the Laplacian of a Gaussian is equivalent to first smoothing the image with the Gaussian, and then computing its Laplacian. It is easy to verify that the Laplacian of a Gaussian (like the Gaussian itself) is an isotropic operator; that is, it is rotationally symmetric. Figure 3.7 illustrates the three-dimensional appearances of a Gaussian and its Laplacian. As the $\nabla^2 G$ operator is isotropic, it is clear that the two orthogonal axes along which the second partial derivatives are computed can be oriented in any fashion. In particular, along an ideal straight step edge, we can orient one axis along the edge and the other axis across the edge. Then, as the second partial derivatives in both these directions are zero at the edge, and the second partial derivative across the edge becomes nonzero as we move away from the edge, it is apparent that the $\nabla^2 G$ operator produces zero-crossings along the edge. Although the response of the operator is also zero within constant-intensity regions, we do not get zero-crossings within such regions. See Figure 3.16 for an illustration of the performance of the Marr–Hildreth operator. Marr and Hildreth recommend that convolution with the $\nabla^2 G$ operator be carried out at several different scales—that is, for several different values of the σ of the Gaussian G—and that, then, the various zero-crossings be combined to produce the final edge image. The primary justification of the Marr–Hildreth operator is biological: Some low-level retinal computations seem to resemble convolutions with Laplacians of Gaussians. Although convolution of an image with Laplacians of Gaussians has been shown to facilitate image compression [Burt and Adelson 1983], neither Marr and Hildreth, nor any other author, has made a strong case for the use of such convolutions in detecting intensity edges underlying digital images. (In the biological sciences, Srinivasan, Laughlin, and Dubs [Srinivasan, Laughlin, and Dubs 1982] have expressed a similar view,

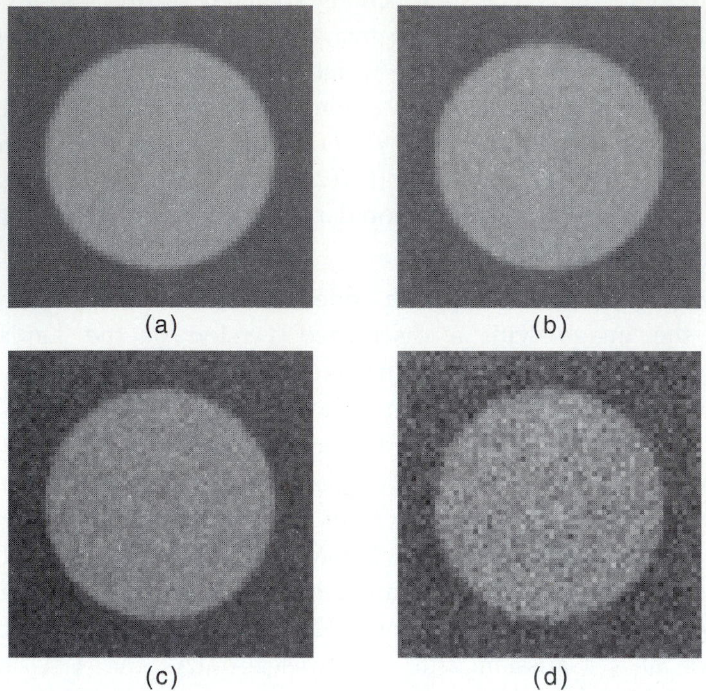

Figure 3.6 Difference operators applied to a synthetic digital image. We can use image operators such as those described in Figure 3.4 and Figure 3.5 to detect step edges in the image intensity of a digital image. As these operators all compute the differences between various weighted combinations of the pixel intensities within the span of the operator, they are generically termed *difference operators*. Illustrated here are the results of applying three different difference operators to synthetic digital images that are corrupted by *additive, independently identically distributed (i.i.d.), zero-mean Gaussian noise* as follows: Each sample of the synthetic digital image has had added to it, independently and prior to quantization, a random number from among a Gaussian distribution of random numbers whose mean is zero and whose standard deviation is σ_{noise}. **(a)** A 64×64 digital image of a circular constant-intensity region that spans 48 pixels horizontally and vertically along its diameter and is located on a darker constant-intensity background, the difference in intensity between the foreground and the background being denoted by *step-size*. **(b)** Same as (a), except now the image is corrupted by additive i.i.d. zero-mean Gaussian noise whose standard deviation σ_{noise} is such that the *signal-to-noise ratio*, defined as $\text{SNR} \triangleq$ *step-size*$/\sigma_{\text{noise}}$, is SNR = 16. **(c)** Same as (b), except SNR = 8. **(d)** Same as (b), except SNR = 4. **(e)** Roberts' cross applied to (b). **(f)** Roberts' cross applied to (d). **(g)** 3×3 Prewitt operator applied to (b). **(h)** 3×3 Prewitt operator applied to (d). **(i)** Nevatia–Babu operator applied to (b). **(j)** Nevatia–Babu operator applied to (d). In the case of the Roberts' cross and Prewitt operators, at each image point the (scaled) estimate of the magnitude of the gradient of the image intensity at the point is displayed; in the case of the Nevatia–Babu operator, at each image point the (scaled) maximum from among the responses of the various individual masks applied at the image point is displayed. In the images

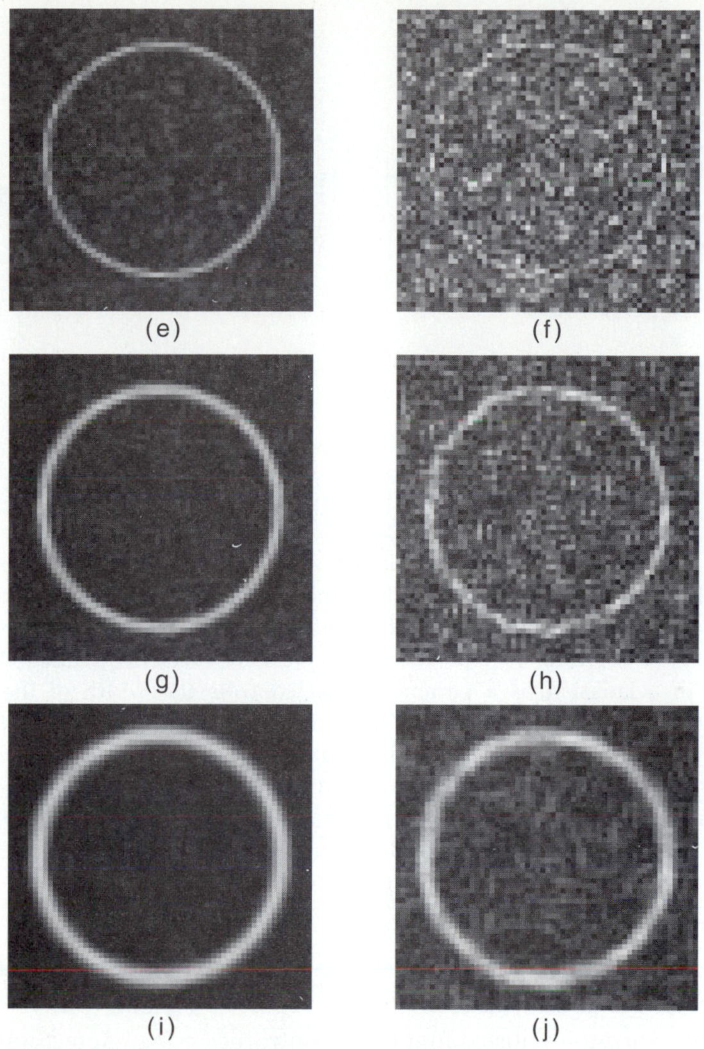

(e) (f)

(g) (h)

(i) (j)

displayed here, a large response of a difference operator may be taken to indicate a step edge in the image intensity, the distinction between a large response and a small response being based on whether the response is greater than or less than a certain (usually ad hoc) threshold. The operation of using one or more thresholds to classify a numerical entity—in the context here, to classify the response of a difference operator as arising from a step edge in the image intensity—is called *thresholding*. Thresholding is not performed in any of the images displayed here. The displayed outcomes of the application to the images of three different difference operators illustrate that, in general, as the size of an operator is increased, the operator becomes less sensitive to image noise. This decrease in sensitivity to image noise, however, is bought at a price: As the operator size is increased, there is a deterioration in the ability of the operator to discriminate between and detect adjacent image-intensity edges that simultaneously fall within the span of the operator.

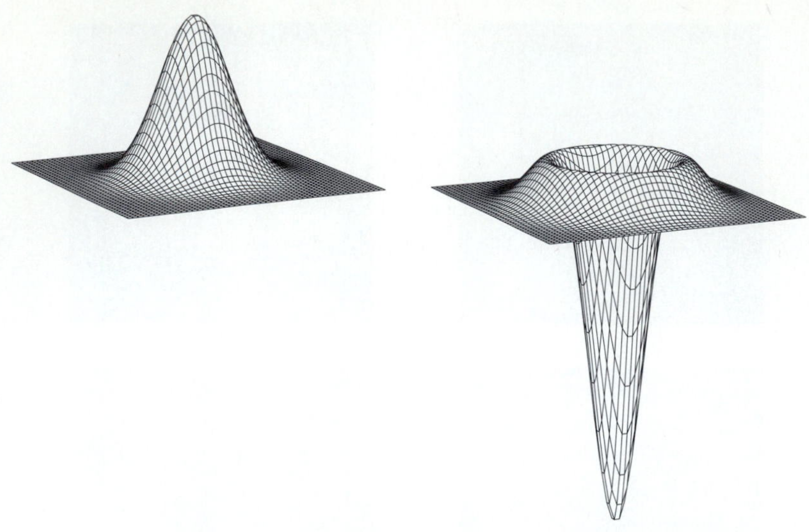

Figure 3.7 The two-dimensional Gaussian and its Laplacian. A plot of a two-dimensional Gaussian is shown on the left, and that of its Laplacian is shown on the right. A *two-dimensional Gaussian* that is located at the origin has the following form: $G(x, y) = (1/(2\pi\sigma^2)) \exp(-[x^2 + y^2] / (2\sigma^2))$, where σ, called the *standard deviation* of the Gaussian, is a parameter that controls the width of the Gaussian. The *Laplacian of a Gaussian* is, by definition, the following: $\nabla^2 G(x, y) \triangleq \partial^2 G(x, y)/\partial x^2 + \partial^2 G(x, y)/\partial y^2$. As illustrated, a Gaussian is shaped like a bell, whereas its Laplacian is shaped like an inverted Mexican hat. Both functions, plotted here in the range $\pm 4\sigma$, are rotationally symmetric, and asymptotically 0. The Gaussian, as expressed here, has a unit integral over the x–y plane; the Laplacian of a Gaussian has a zero integral over the x–y plane.

discussing the plausibility of the various roles attributed to retinal computations; see also [Barlow 1981].) Several authors have repeatedly pointed out various shortcomings of isotropic edge detectors; see, for instance, [Haralick 1984], [Canny 1986], and [Nalwa and Binford 1986]. Nevertheless, the Marr–Hildreth operator remains popular.

The other popular operator that uses Gaussian smoothing is the **Canny operator** [Canny 1986]. It detects edges at the zero-crossings of the second directional derivative of the smoothed image in the direction of the gradient where the gradient magnitude is above some threshold. That is, conditional on the magnitude of the gradient of the smoothed image being greater than some threshold, it seeks out zero-crossings of $\partial^2 (G * I)/\partial \mathbf{n}^2$, which is the same as $\partial([\partial G/\partial \mathbf{n}] * I)/\partial \mathbf{n}$, where I is the image, G is a Gaussian, $*$ denotes convolution, and $\mathbf{n}$ is the direction of the gradient of the smoothed image. These zero-crossings correspond to first-directional-derivative

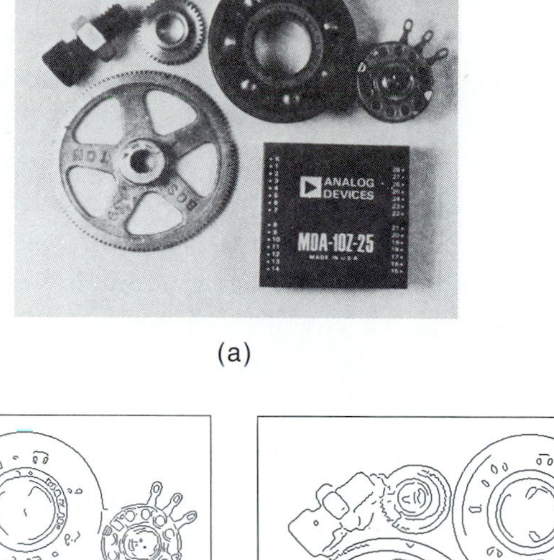

(a)

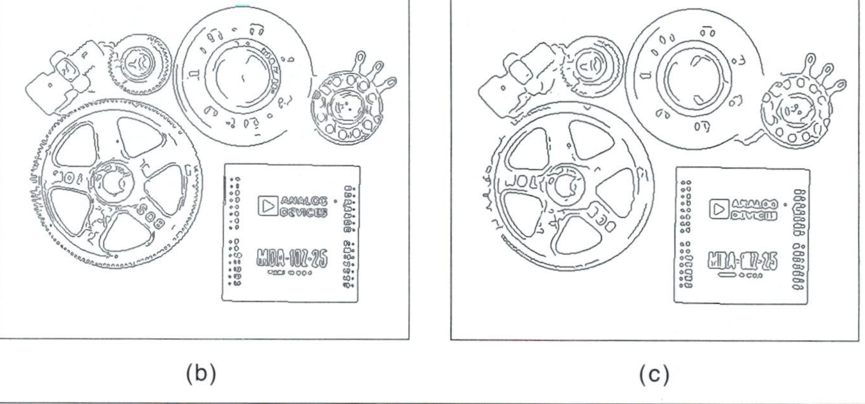

(b) (c)

Figure 3.8 The Canny edge operator applied to a parts image. **(a)** Original image (576×454). **(b)** Output for $\sigma = 1.0$. **(c)** Output for $\sigma = 2.0$. The *Canny operator* first smooths the image by convolving it with a two-dimensional Gaussian—say, of standard deviation σ—and then, it declares step edges at those image locations where the magnitude of the gradient of the image intensity is locally maximum with respect to the gradient magnitudes along the direction of the gradient. (From [Canny 1986] with permission, © 1986 IEEE.)

maxima and minima in the direction of the gradient—clearly, the maxima in magnitude are a reasonable choice for locating edges. See Figure 3.8 for an illustration of the performance of the Canny operator. Canny's proposal is similar to that of Haralick—and its roots, in fact, go back to Prewitt [Prewitt 1970]—except here, Gaussian smoothing is used instead of surface fitting. Two thresholds are used for the gradient magnitude: one threshold that is low, to extend and complete edge segments that are detected using another threshold that is high. As previously suggested by Marr and Hildreth, Canny too suggests that the outputs of multiple filters at different scales be integrated. Canny derives his filter by optimizing a certain performance index that favors true positives, true negatives, and the accurate localization of detected edges. However, his analysis is restricted to linear-shift-invariant filters that detect unblurred one-dimensional continuous steps; further, although his performance index is reasonable, several other equally justifiable performance criteria are possible and these criteria would lead to different filters. The point here is that it is not sufficient to have a so-called optimal filter: We must also ask, optimal with respect to what? and optimal under what assumptions? Gaussian smoothing is an isotropic operation, and, as we shall soon see, smoothing along an edge contour is desirable, but that across it is not. Canny goes on to suggest nonisotropic alternatives to Gaussian smoothing. Canny's operator—in its basic single-scale second-directional-derivative–of–Gaussian form—is fairly straightforward to implement and, as Figure 3.8 illustrates, performs reasonably well. Hence, it is widely used.

It is worth pointing out here that Torre and Poggio [Torre and Poggio 1986] have suggested a unified theoretical framework for the investigation of difference operators. Their framework is based on the theory of regularization of ill-posed problems.[3] They use their framework first to establish several geometrical and topological properties of edges detected by differential operators, and then briefly to discuss the relationship among five operators that are well known: Binford [Binford 1981], Shanmugam–Dickey–Green [Shanmugam, Dickey, and Green 1979], Marr–Hildreth [Marr and Hildreth 1980], Haralick [Haralick 1984], and Canny [Canny 1986].

Processing at Multiple Resolutions or Scales

The idea of using operators of multiple sizes, or, as is often said, processing at **multiple scales**, is an important one. We referred to this idea earlier in the context of the Marr–Hildreth and Canny operators; let us now give this

3. **Regularization** is a technique that seeks to provide a unique and robust approximate solution to a problem that otherwise might not have such a solution by modifying the problem in a controlled fashion. In particular, it is used to "solve" a class of problems termed **ill-posed**. A problem is said to be *ill-posed* if it fails to satisfy one of the following conditions: a solution exists, is unique, and is stable (see [Tikhonov and Arsenin 1977]). Typically, regularization works by converting an inverse problem (e.g., given $y = f(x)$, find x from y) into one of minimizing the sum of two terms: an error term measuring the conformance of the solution to the data (e.g., $\int [y - f(x)]^2 dx$), and a regularization term imposing a penalty for the lack of smoothness in the solution (e.g., $\lambda \int [d^2 f(x)/dx^2]^2 dx$). The relative weights of the two terms are controlled by the regularization parameter (λ in the example here). Regularization has been proposed by Poggio, Torre, and Koch [Poggio, Torre, and Koch 1985] as a general framework for solving a wide variety of so-called low-level vision problems; see also [Bertero, Poggio, and Torre 1988] and [Marroquin, Mitter, and Poggio 1987] in this connection.

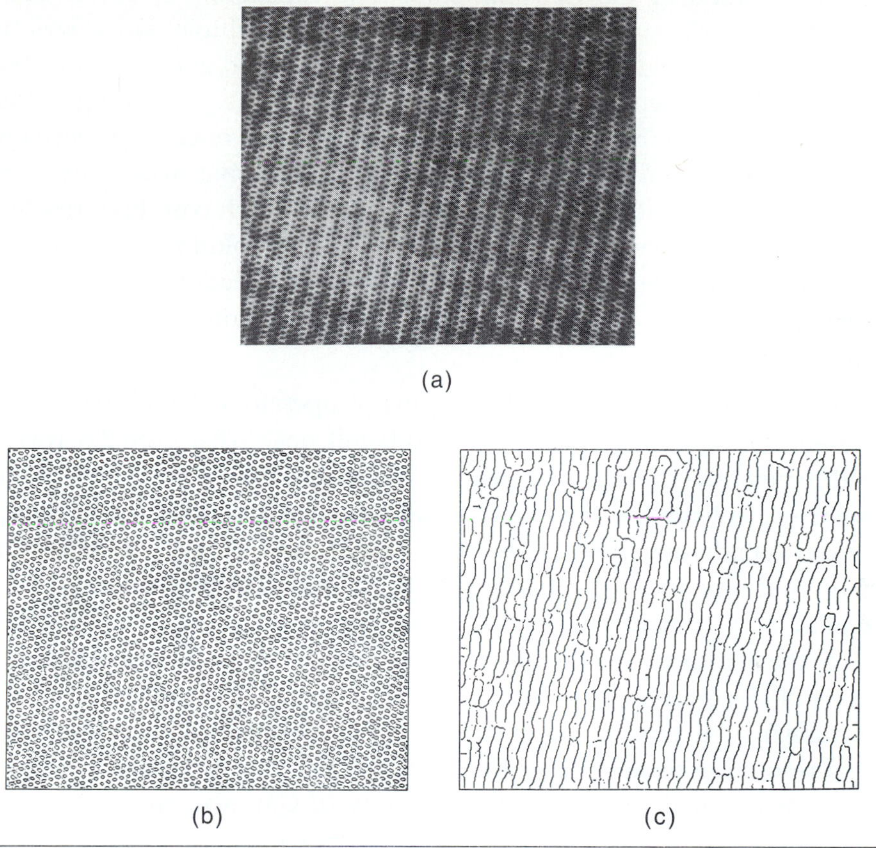

Figure 3.9 Edges at two different scales detected by the Canny operator in an image of a wipe cloth. The term *scale* here denotes a level of resolution, or, equivalently, a level of detail; *scale* also has the more usual connotation of the enlargement or reduction of an entity while the entity's proportions are maintained; we shall depend on the context to distinguish between these two uses of *scale*. **(a)** Original image (576×454). **(b)** Edges at $\sigma = 1.0$. **(c)** Edges at $\sigma = 5.0$. As the standard deviation σ of the smoothing Gaussian of the Canny operator is increased, the coarser details of the image gain in emphasis at the expense of the finer details; see also Figure 3.10 in this connection. (From [Canny 1986] with permission, © 1986 IEEE.)

idea the attention it deserves. Many objects, especially ones that are textured, may be described usefully at a variety of scales. At the finest scale (i.e., at the highest resolution), the texture becomes important; at the coarsest scale (i.e., at the lowest resolution), the gross shape is primary. This varying relative prominence of texture and gross structure is illustrated in Figure 3.9 with the image of a wipe cloth to which the Canny operator has been applied, first with $\sigma = 1$ pixel, and then with $\sigma = 5$ pixels (σ here is the standard deviation of the Gaussian smoothing function). In the context of edge detection, the idea of using operators of multiple sizes was first proposed by Rosenfeld and Thurston in 1971 [Rosenfeld and Thurston 1971]. It has since been invoked in several other contexts (e.g., shading, texture, stereo, motion, shape representation), finding use most often as a mechanism to reduce computation: low-cost low-resolution processing over a coarse grid (applied to the smoothed data) serving to guide high-cost high-resolution processing over a finer grid. Although the lower-resolution grids are often chosen to be regular subsets of the highest-resolution grid, irregular tessellations are also possible; see, for instance, [Montanvert, Meer, and Rosenfeld 1991].

The problem of combining the outputs of operators at multiple scales in a coherent and systematic manner is a difficult one. This problem was first tackled for the one-dimensional case by Witkin in 1983 [Witkin 1983]; a more formal treatment for the two-dimensional case was provided by Koenderink in 1984 [Koenderink 1984a] (see also [Yuille and Poggio 1986]). These authors, as do most other authors, investigate and establish several desirable properties of Gaussian smoothing as a mechanism of varying resolution. Varying the width of the Gaussian with which a signal is smoothed varies the level of discernible detail in the smoothed signal: The larger the width of the Gaussian, the greater the smoothing of the original signal, the less the level of resolution or detail, and the fewer the samples necessary to represent the smoothed signal. One attractive property of Gaussian smoothing is that consecutive convolution with a series of Gaussians, each Gaussian with a particular standard deviation σ_i, is equivalent to a single convolution with the Gaussian of standard deviation $\sqrt{\Sigma_i \sigma_i^2}$. More significantly, Koenderink has established that Gaussian convolution provides the unique way to vary resolution if we insist that the operation of resolution variation be homogeneous, be isotropic, and, most important, not introduce spurious detail as the resolution is decreased. Figure 3.10 illustrates the evolution of an image under Gaussian convolution as σ is varied between 1 and 16 pixels, doubling at each step. Now, the most common technique for combining results at multiple scales is to track the results through **scale space**—that is, through a continuum of variation in resolution. This strategy is illustrated in Figure 3.11 for a one-dimensional signal whose zero-crossings of the second derivative have been tracked after the signal has first been embedded in scale space using a one-dimensional Gaussian.

Koenderink [Koenderink 1984a] has pointed out that convolving an image with a Gaussian is equivalent to finding the solution to the diffusion—or, heat-conduction—equation, with the image providing the initial condition, and a decrease in resolution corresponding to the passage of

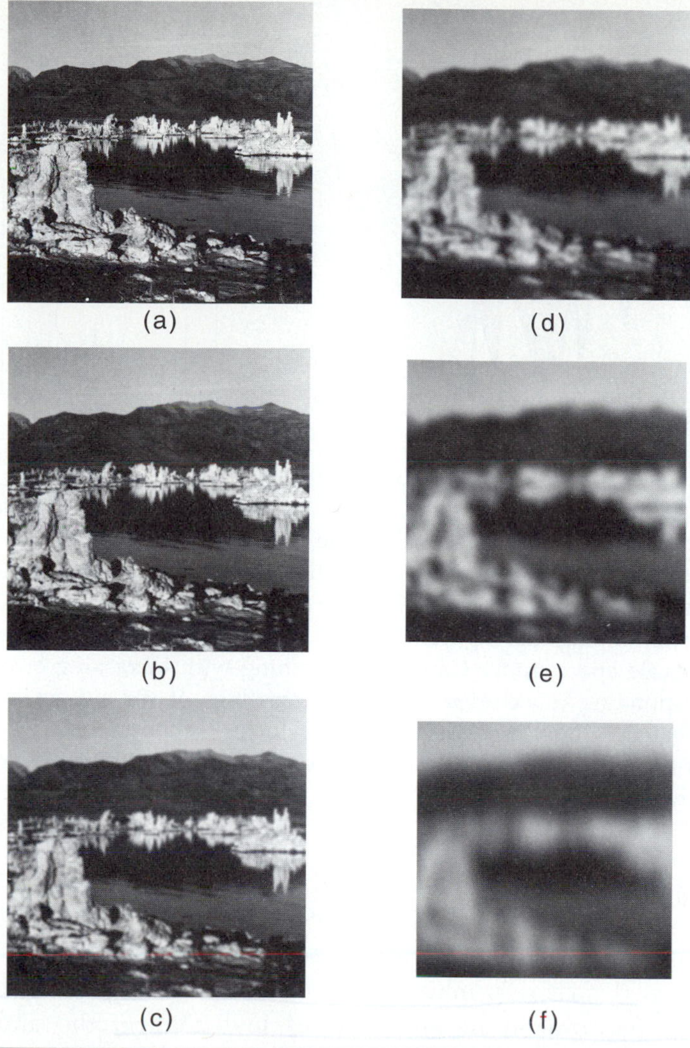

Figure 3.10 The evolution of an image under increasing Gaussian smoothing. Convolving an image with a Gaussian, or with some other function that has all positive weights that sum (integrate) up to unity, smooths the intensity variations in the image: The broader the smoothing function, the greater the smoothing of the intensity variations. The image here is convolved with a discrete Gaussian that is derived as follows from a continuously varying Gaussian of standard deviation σ: First, the continuously varying Gaussian is sampled identically to the digital image, and then, the samples are all normalized (scaled) so that their sum is unity. **(a)** Original image (600×600). **(b)** $\sigma = 1$. **(c)** $\sigma = 2$. **(d)** $\sigma = 4$. **(e)** $\sigma = 8$. **(f)** $\sigma = 16$. As the σ of the smoothing Gaussian is increased, the characteristics of the image at increasingly lower spatial resolutions (i.e., at increasingly coarser scales) become apparent. Note that, in addition, as σ is increased, the convolution of the image with the Gaussian is defined over a smaller area. (Photograph by David N. Horn, *Mono Lake, California*, 1987.)

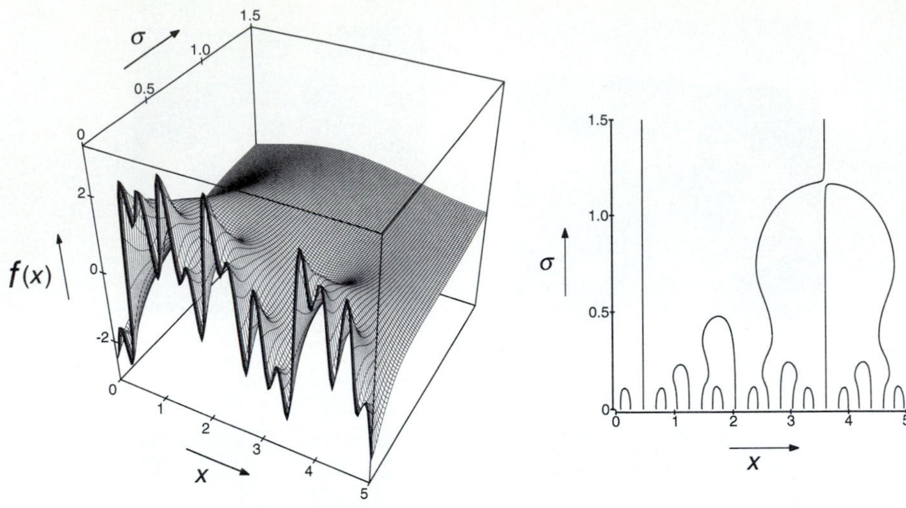

Figure 3.11 Scale space. We can relate the characteristics of a signal at various scales (i.e., at various resolutions) by embedding the signal in *scale space*, which has the added dimension of variable resolution. The notion of scale space is illustrated here with a one-dimensional signal. On the left is a one-dimensional signal $f(x)$ as it evolves in scale space under Gaussian smoothing with increasing σ; on the right are the corresponding trajectories of the zero-crossings of the second derivative of $f(x)$. Note that it is only because the original unsmoothed signal is defined well beyond the range $0 \leq x \leq 5$ that the signal continues to be defined over this range under smoothing.

time. Interestingly, Perona and Malik [Perona and Malik 1990] have suggested anisotropic diffusion (i.e., diffusion that is direction dependent) as a mechanism to detect edges at varying scales. The anisotropy is conceived to be such that diffusion is inhibited in directions of large intensity change, whereas it is encouraged in directions of low change, the aim being to encourage the formation of uniform-intensity regions that have boundaries across which the intensity gradient is high. It is argued that, not only does anisotropic diffusion, like isotropic diffusion, not introduce spurious detail at low resolution, but anisotropic diffusion has the added advantage of preserving the location of homogeneous-region boundaries. However, as noted by Perona and Malik, anisotropic diffusion is unsuitable for noisy images as it inhibits the smoothing not only of edges, but also of noise.

3.1.3 Parametric-Model Matchers

An alternative to performing edgel detection by thresholding the image gradient is developing an edgel model and computing its degree of match to the image data. Such an approach is, in general, computationally more

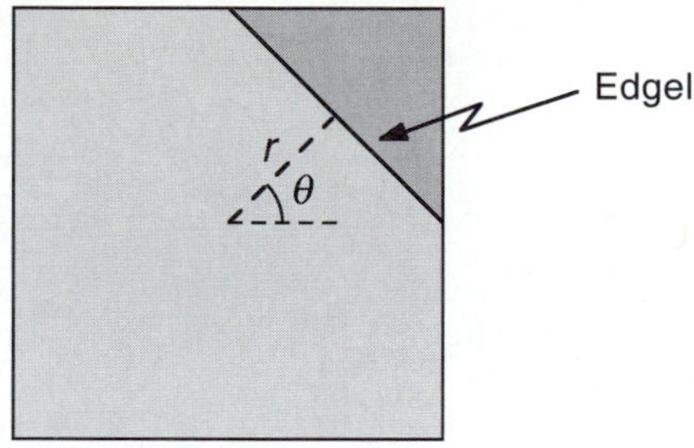

Figure 3.12 An ideal step edgel. An *edgel* (an abbreviation for *edge element*) in an image is a short, linear segment of an image-intensity edge. An ideal step edgel, which is an edgel with constant image intensity on either side, has four degrees of freedom: orientation, position, and the constant intensities on the two sides of the step. The term *degrees of freedom* denotes the independently variable parameters of an entity.

expensive than is using difference operators. However, parametric-model matching may provide superior performance with respect to edgel detection, and, further, may provide a richer description of edgels.

The most widely cited parametric-model matcher is the **Hueckel operator**; [Hueckel 1971] contains the original proposal, and [Hueckel 1973] contains an extension to deal with line edges. This operator uses an ideal step-edgel model with the four degrees of freedom illustrated in Figure 3.12: orientation, position, and constant image intensity on either side of the step. The **degrees of freedom** of an entity are the entity's independently variable parameters; for example, a sheet of paper lying flat on a table has three degrees of freedom—two for its location, and one for its orientation. Although we could do the matching here by seeking the least-squares-error fit of the parametric model to the image window, as the model is nonlinear in its parameters, such an approach would be iterative over the four parameters, and, hence, would be computationally expensive. To reduce the computational requirements, Hueckel suggests that both the image data and the model be represented (over circular windows) by their first eight coefficients in a particular two-dimensional orthonormal series expansion. Then, we could minimize a weighted sum of square errors between the two sets of coefficients, rather than between the image pixels and model samples. Hueckel claims that such a minimization requires iteration over just one parameter: the orientation of the edgel. An edgel is declared present if the weighted least-squares error between the two sets of coefficients is "small," and the step size—that is, the magnitude of the intensity difference between

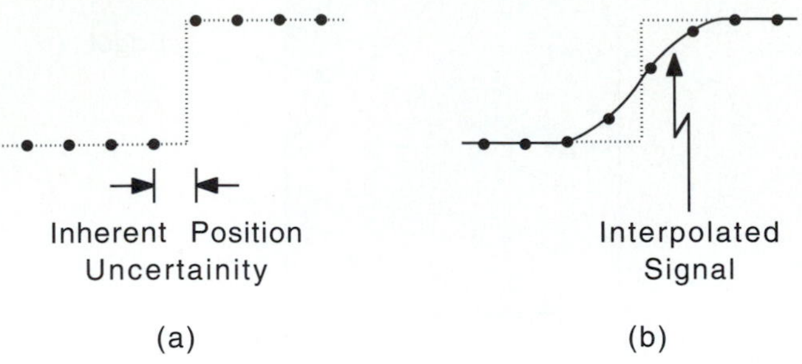

Figure 3.13 The relative recoverabilities of a blurred step edge and an unblurred step edge from their respective samples. A blurred (i.e., smoothed) step edge is more amenable to recovery from its ideal (i.e., pointwise) samples than is an unblurred step edge. **(a)** Samples of a blur-free one-dimensional step edge. **(b)** Interpolated samples of a blurred one-dimensional step edge. As is apparent from the figure, if a step edge is (in effect) blurred *prior* to being sampled—see Figure 2.18 in this connection—then we can deduce the position of the original edge from that edge's samples to subsample accuracy.

the two sides of the step—is "large." Hueckel's work prompted several similar attempts to fit step-edgel models to image data using orthogonal series expansions (see [Rosenfeld and Kak 1982]).

Another parametric-model matcher is the **Nalwa–Binford operator** [Nalwa and Binford 1986]. It uses the same four step-edgel parameters as the Hueckel operator, except that it takes into account the system blurring function described in Section 2.3.1; this function is assumed to be a Gaussian with constant σ. As illustrated in Figure 3.13, a blur-free digital imaging system would result in inherent uncertainty in the location of a step edge; smoothing prior to sampling makes subpixel localization of the step edge possible as a blurred step edge, unlike an unblurred step edge, is amenable to recovery from its samples. The Nalwa–Binford operator circumvents search in four-parameter space by exploiting the observation that the intensity surface underlying a step edgel in a digital image ideally varies only in the direction across the edgel, and not in the direction along the edgel. Such a surface—a surface such as the one illustrated in Figure 3.14 that is constant along some direction—is termed a **one-dimensional surface**. The strategy adopted by Nalwa and Binford to detect edgels is as follows. First, fit a least-squares-error one-dimensional cubic (i.e., third-order polynomial) surface over a 5×5 window to estimate the orientation of the underlying intensity surface; this surface fitting is iterative over orientation. Then, fit over the image window, in the least-squares sense, each of a one-dimensional

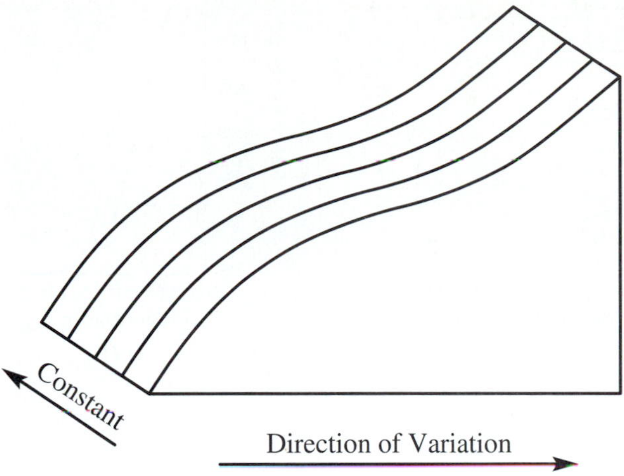

Figure 3.14 A one-dimensional surface. A *one-dimensional surface*, by definition, is a surface that is constant along some direction. The variation in the image intensity that underlies a linear edge segment in a digital image can be modeled as a one-dimensional surface. When valid, the invocation of a one-dimensional–surface model for the image intensity provides edge detection with an increased robustness to image noise. (From [Nalwa and Binford 1986] with permission, © 1986 IEEE.)

model-edgel surface and a one-dimensional quadratic (i.e., second-order polynomial) surface, both these one-dimensional surfaces with the previously estimated orientation. Fitting the model-edgel surface is iterative over edgel position, and fitting the quadratic surface is noniterative. The one-dimensional quadratic surface, which has the same number of parameters as does the model-edgel surface—namely, four—is used to model nonedgels. Hence, if the least-squares error of the quadratic fit is greater than that of the model-edgel fit, declare a step edgel; otherwise, do not. Nalwa and Binford recommend subsequent thresholding on the estimated step size at two and one-half times the standard deviation of the image noise σ_{noise}. This recommendation is based on Monte Carlo simulations leading to the true- and false-positive statistics illustrated in Figure 3.15(a) and Figure 3.15(b), respectively. Figure 3.15(c) and Figure 3.15(d) show the root-mean-square errors in the estimates of the orientations and positions of randomly generated synthetic step edgels, respectively, as a function of the *signal-to-noise ratio (SNR)* defined as *step-size*$/\sigma_{\text{noise}}$. The authors claim that their operator is substantially superior to the Marr–Hildreth operator; a comparison of the two operators' performance on a particular image is reproduced in Figure 3.16 (see [Nalwa and Binford 1986] for implementation details).

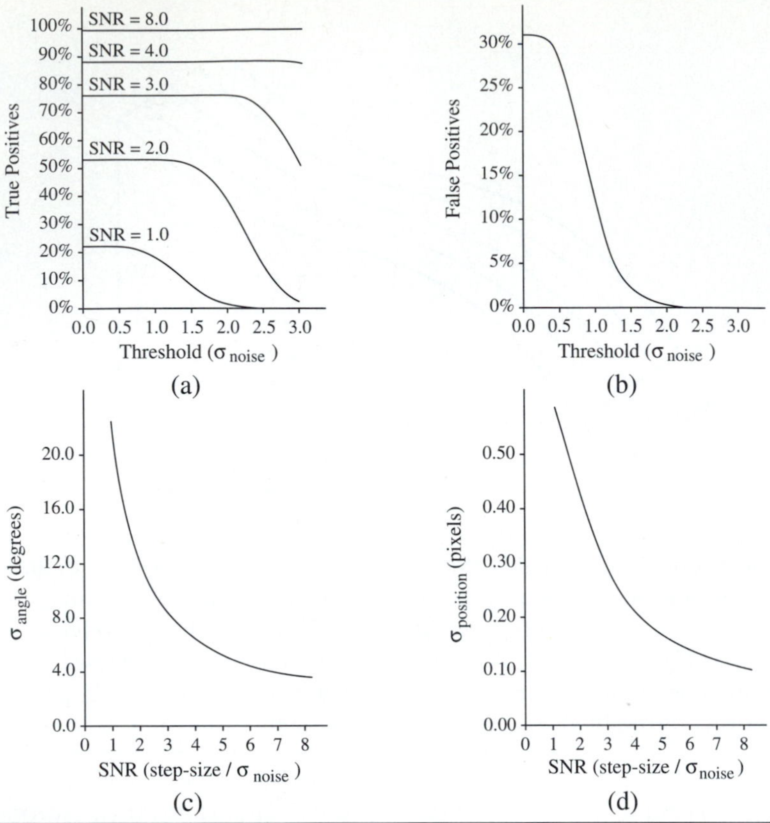

Figure 3.15 Characterization of an edge detector. Any detector, including an edge detector, may be characterized by the likelihoods of its true positives and its false positives. *True positives* and *false positives* are the affirmative (i.e., positive) responses of the detector in the presence and absence, respectively, of the entity that is sought to be detected. In addition to specifying the likelihoods of a detector's true and false positives, we might also specify the accuracy with which the detector estimates the parameters of its true positives. One particular edge detector, the Nalwa–Binford operator, is statistically characterized here in this fashion on the basis of its performance on a large number of 5×5 synthetic image windows, each window corrupted by additive i.i.d. zero-mean Gaussian noise whose standard deviation is σ_{noise}. The term *image window*, here, and elsewhere, denotes a small image that is typically part of a larger image. **(a)** True positives: Percentages of synthesized step edges at various SNRs, where SNR $\triangleq$ *step-size*$/\sigma_{\text{noise}}$, that are detected as having a *step-size* above a certain threshold, which is expressed in units of σ_{noise} in the figure. **(b)** False positives: Percentage of synthesized noisy image windows, each window with a constant underlying intensity, that are falsely declared to contain step edges, each step edge with an estimated *step-size* above a certain threshold. **(c)** Root-mean-square error in the estimates of the orientations of the true positives that are detected in (a) with a zero threshold, as a function of the SNR. **(d)** Root-mean-square error in the estimates of the positions of the true positives that are detected in (a) with a zero threshold, as a function of the SNR. (From [Nalwa and Binford 1986] with permission, © 1986 IEEE.)

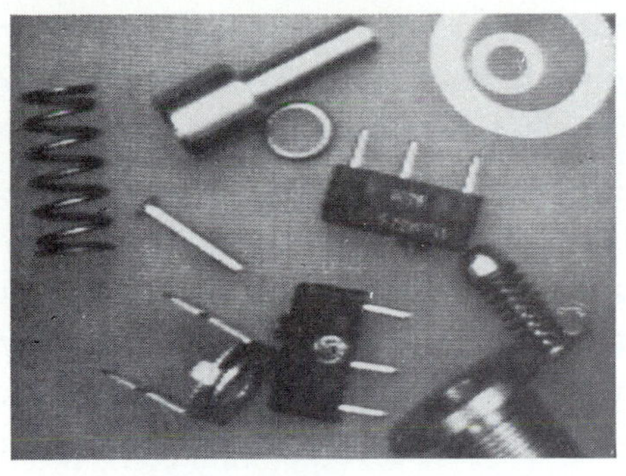

(a)

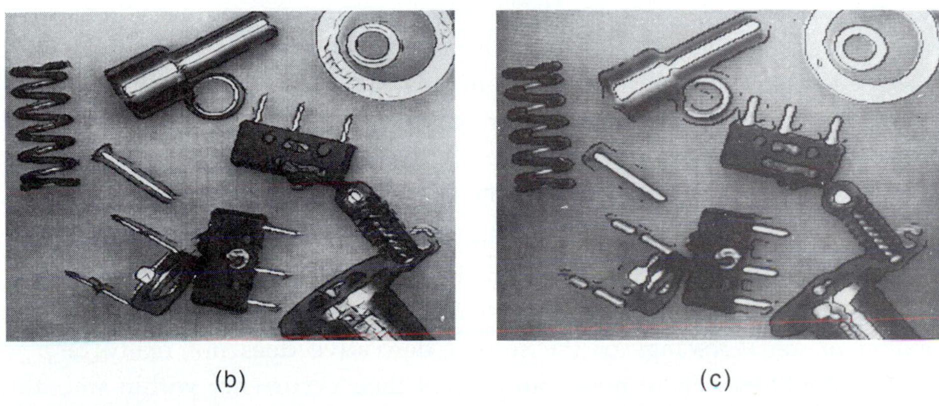

(b) (c)

Figure 3.16 The Nalwa–Binford and Marr–Hildreth edge operators applied to a bin-of-parts image. **(a)** Original image (256×256). **(b)** Edges detected by the Nalwa–Binford operator superimposed on the original image. **(c)** Edges detected by the Marr–Hildreth operator superimposed on the original image. The *Nalwa–Binford operator* detects step edges in an image by fitting parameterized one-dimensional surfaces over each of an array of overlapping image windows, declaring a step edge in a particular orientation to be present in an image window under the following condition: The least-squares error of fitting a parameterized one-dimensional step-shaped surface in the particular orientation to the image window is less than the least-squares error of fitting a one-dimensional quadratic-polynomial surface in the same orientation to the image window. The *Marr–Hildreth operator* convolves the image with the Laplacian of a Gaussian (see Figure 3.7), and then, it declares step edges to be present at the zero-crossings of the convolved image. (From [Nalwa and Binford 1986] with permission, © 1986 IEEE.)

3.1.4 Issues and Tradeoffs in Edgel Detection

The preceding description of several well-known edgel detectors was brief. For a more thorough review, see [Blicher 1984]; see also [Pratt 1991]. Now, let us focus our attention on some of the basic issues and tradeoffs in edge detection. In this context, this author strongly recommends the paper by Prewitt [Prewitt 1970], which is remarkable for its depth and clarity.

As reflected in our discussion of edgel operators, most of the work thus far has been based on discrete approximations to differential operators. Although step edges do exhibit large first derivatives and zero-crossings of the second derivative, these conditions are only necessary for the existence of step edges; they are not sufficient. It is well known that derivatives and their discrete approximations emphasize noise.[4] In fact, the higher the order of the derivative or difference, the more pronounced the effect. In the context of edge detection, the significance of this property of derivatives (and their discrete approximations) is that image noise, rather than actual intensity variation, may prompt large image gradients and zero-crossings of the second directional derivative. An operator such as the Marr–Hildreth operator [Marr and Hildreth 1980], which computes not just the second derivative across the edge but also that along the edge, is necessarily more noise sensitive than an operator such as Canny's [Canny 1986], which computes the second derivative only across the edge. Computation of the second derivative along the edge emphasizes intensity fluctuations due to noise in that direction, while serving no purpose in edge detection.

Difference operators have other drawbacks in addition to their sensitivity to noise. Operators that threshold on the first derivative respond not just to edges, but also to sufficiently steep smooth shading. Finding local gradient maxima or zero-crossings of the second derivative does not really help us because small amounts of noise can prompt their occurrence within smoothly shaded image regions. For instance, both the Nevatia–Babu [Nevatia and Babu 1980] and Canny [Canny 1986] operators return false edges within smoothly shaded regions. Even in the absence of noise, it is not difficult to

4. To see the effect that differencing has on signal noise, let us consider a discrete one-dimensional signal x_i corrupted by additive i.i.d. zero-mean noise η_i with variance σ_η^2. Say, $y_i = x_i + \eta_i$. Then, the first difference between two adjacent samples of y_i can be expressed as $(y_{i+1} - y_i) = (x_{i+1} - x_i) + (\eta_{i+1} - \eta_i)$. The signal noise here, $(\eta_{i+1} - \eta_i)$, has mean $E[\eta_{i+1} - \eta_i] = 0$, and variance $E[(\eta_{i+1} - \eta_i)^2] = E[\eta_{i+1}^2 - 2\eta_{i+1}\eta_i + \eta_i^2] = 2\sigma_\eta^2$. (Note that, as the noise is zero-mean i.i.d., $E[\eta_{i+1}\eta_i] = E[\eta_{i+1}]\,E[\eta_i] = 0$.) Thus, we see that the variance of the noise in the first difference is double that in the original signal. Similar computations can be carried out for two-dimensional discrete signals, and for higher-order differences.

see that we can have zero-crossings of the second derivative in the absence of a step edge. These zero-crossings are essentially points of inflection (i.e., curvature sign changes) and need not correspond to edges, as in the case of a corrugated intensity surface.

Whereas difference operators tend to err on the side of false positives, model matchers tend to err on the side of false negatives, the reason being that the latter do not take into account all possible intensity variations that might accompany a step edge in practice. Both the Hueckel and Nalwa–Binford operators model only variations in position, orientation, and constant intensities: They do not model intensity variations on either side of the step, such as those illustrated, for instance, in Figure 3.2. Hence, although they are less likely to respond to smooth shading, they are also less likely to respond to actual edges that do not (at least approximately) conform to the invoked edgel model. The Nalwa–Binford operator explicitly seeks to discriminate against smooth shading by modeling nonedgels by a one-dimensional quadratic surface, the criterion for edgel detection being that the image data conform more closely to the edgel model than to the nonedgel model. Unlike difference operators, model matchers provide us with estimates of edgel parameters. However, these estimates often are provided at the expense of greater computation, and these estimates are likely to be biased in the presence of unmodeled intensity variations.

Many of the issues in edge detection span both difference operators and model matchers. For instance, consider surface fitting, which has been used both as a means of estimating derivatives, as by Prewitt [Prewitt 1970] and by Haralick [Haralick 1984], and as a classification technique, as by Hueckel [Hueckel 1971] and by Nalwa and Binford [Nalwa and Binford 1986]. The key issue in surface fitting is the choice of a basis—of a set of functions to be fit over the image data. Clearly, we must choose a basis that can represent the underlying intensity variations adequately. However, adequacy of representation is not enough. We must also seek a basis that will provide this adequacy with a minimal number of parameters. For instance, consider a set of noisy samples of a planar surface (e.g., of $f(x, y) = ax + by + c$). Now, it is clear that fitting a constant (e.g., $f(x, y) = c$) to the data is inadequate. It is also clear that fitting a plane to noisy data, in general, will not yield zero error. What is not equally clear is that, although a higher-order polynomial (e.g., a quadratic in x and y) might yield a smaller error, this fit is less desirable than is a planar fit as it models not just the underlying intensity variations, but also fluctuations due to noise. To be more specific, if we have 9 points in all to begin with, clearly, a bivariate cubic polynomial with its 10 coefficients will fit the data with zero error;

however, this fit might not at all resemble the plane we are seeking. The moral is that although adequacy of a basis is necessary, it is not sufficient. Given that the samples of an image within a window may, in general, arise from a variety of intensity fluctuations, no single basis can, in general, suffice (in the sense described) in all cases. If we restrict ourselves to a single choice, we shall obtain incorrect results when the basis is inadequate and noise-sensitive results when the basis is not minimal. Hence, if we are seeking to model the intensity variation underlying an image window accurately, we must fit a variety of bases, examine the resulting errors, and then decide which basis is appropriate for the particular data; this procedure, which can be formalized, is standard practice in statistical analysis.

The importance of interpreting a digital image as a set of quantized samples of a continuously varying function cannot be overemphasized. As demonstrated clearly by the root-mean-square positional-error statistics in Figure 3.15(d) from [Nalwa and Binford 1986], once a digital image is provided such an interpretation, subpixel edge localization is the natural outcome. In a sequel, Nalwa [Nalwa 1987] demonstrates how we can improve the resolution of an edgel detector substantially by simply interpolating the image prior to processing. Figure 3.17 illustrates this resolution improvement for the Nalwa–Binford operator. (It is of interest to note here that Barlow [Barlow 1979] has suggested that the first thing the human visual cortex does to the retinal images transmitted from the eyes to the brain is to perform explicit discrete spatial interpolation on these images.)

The noise characteristics of an operator depend on the size of the operator. The larger the operator, the more it implicitly averages out random noise[5] (perhaps before computing first- or higher-order derivatives). This phenomenon was illustrated vividly for gradient operators in Figure 3.6, where we saw that the 5×5 Nevatia–Babu operator performs more effectively on the high-noise image than does the 3×3 Prewitt operator,

---

5. To see the effect that averaging has on signal noise, let us consider a discrete one-dimensional signal x_i corrupted by additive i.i.d. zero-mean noise η_i with variance σ_η^2. Say, $y_i = x_i + \eta_i$. Then, the weighted average of y_i can be expressed as follows: $\Sigma_i\, w_i y_i = \Sigma_i\, w_i x_i + \Sigma_i\, w_i \eta_i$, where w_i are the weights (all positive), $\Sigma_i\, w_i = 1$, and all summations are implicitly between $i = 1$ and $i = n$. The signal noise here, $\Sigma_i\, w_i \eta_i$, has mean $E[\,\Sigma_i\, w_i \eta_i\,] = \Sigma_i\, w_i\; E[\,\eta_i\,] = 0$, and variance $E[\,(\Sigma_i\, w_i\, \eta_i)^2\,] = \Sigma_i\, w_i^2\; E[\,\eta_i^2\,] = \sigma_\eta^2\; \Sigma_i\, w_i^2$. (Note that, as the noise is zero-mean i.i.d., $E[\,\eta_i\, \eta_j\,] = E[\eta_i]\, E[\eta_j] = 0$ for $i \neq j$.) Thus, we see that the variance of the noise in the average is $\Sigma_i\, w_i^2$ times that in the original signal. As all the w_i are positive, $\Sigma_i\, w_i^2 < (\,\Sigma_i\, w_i)^2$, and as, further, $\Sigma_i\, w_i = 1$, it is clear that $\Sigma_i\, w_i^2 < 1$. In particular, if all the weights are equal and the average is taken over n samples, then $\Sigma_i\, w_i^2 = 1/n$. Similar computations can be carried out for a two-dimensional signal.

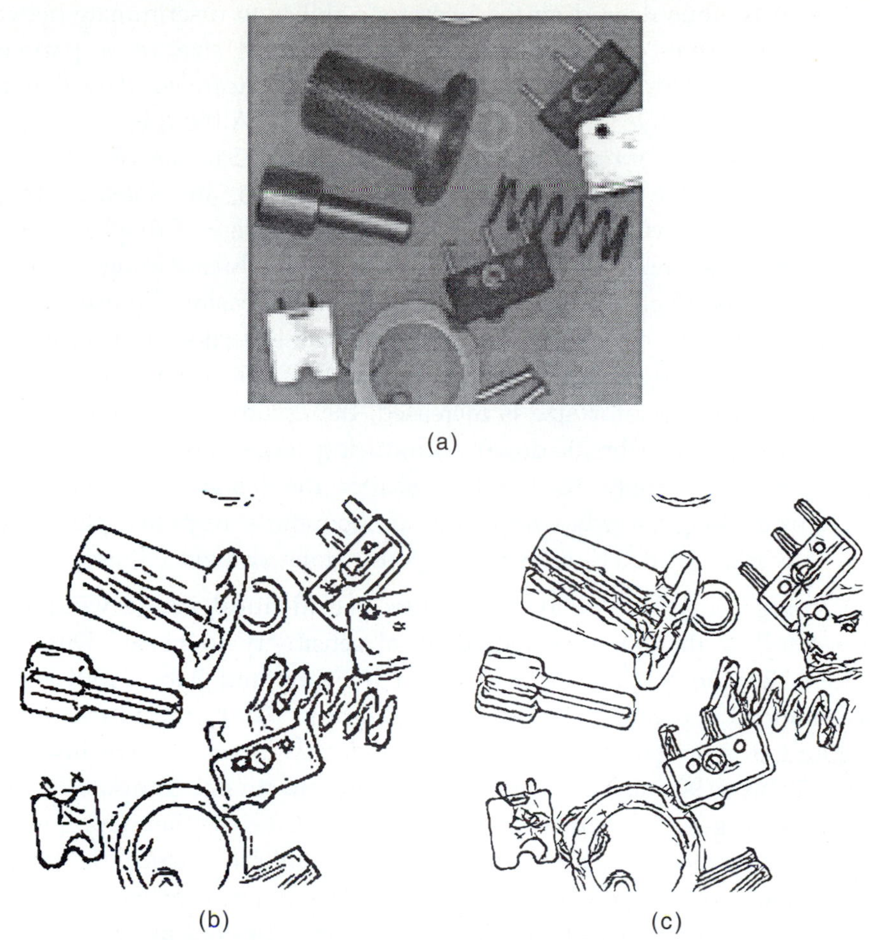

(a)

(b) (c)

Figure 3.17 Improvement of the resolution of an edge detector by image interpolation. We can improve the resolution of an edge detector—that is, we can improve its ability to detect and discriminate between edges that adjoin one another in a digital image—by interpolating the image prior to pursuing edge detection. **(a)** Original bin-of-parts image (128×128). **(b)** Nalwa–Binford operator applied to the original image. **(c)** Nalwa–Binford operator applied to the image after first interpolating the image onto a grid with twice the linear resolution of the original grid. (From [Nalwa 1987] with permission, © 1987 IEEE.)

which in turn performs more effectively than does the 2×2 Roberts' cross. (In this connection, recall that the 3×3 Sobel masks can, in fact, be explicitly construed as 2×2 difference masks followed by or preceded by a 2×2 averaging mask.) However, increasing an operator's size also increases the likelihood of the operator overlapping several edges or corners simultaneously, thus degrading the operator's ability to discriminate between and detect adjacent edges. Hence, as the window size of a particular operator is increased, we trade off resolution for improved detection and localization of locally straight resolvable edges. Although, among the operators whose performance is illustrated in Figure 3.6, the Nevatia–Babu operator would give the thickest response even to an isolated straight edge—as it would overlap the edge for the largest range of displacements—this thickest response reflects only that simple thresholding is not a mechanism of localization, only one of detection. Increasing the operator size adversely affects not only resolution, but also the detection and localization of high-curvature edges because of the invalidity of the straight-edgel model. In general, as the operator size is increased, the assumptions invoked in the operator's design may break down, introducing large and unknown biases. Similar comments apply to window shape; for instance, a decrease in window size along an edge improves an operator's response along high-curvature edges, but deteriorates the response along straight edges.

Of course, just because two operators use identical image windows, it does not follow that they exhibit identical sensitivity to noise. Directional operators, like the Nevatia–Babu operator [Nevatia and Babu 1980] and the Nalwa–Binford operator [Nalwa and Binford 1986], introduce implicit averaging that is largely along the edge, rather than across it. For instance, a Nevatia–Babu mask aligned with a step edge effectively computes (scaled) weighted averages of the intensities on the two sides of the step, and then provides the difference. (Contrary to what you might suspect, the Hueckel operator does not provide directional smoothing because of its use of basis functions that exhibit two-dimensional variation.) In contrast to directional smoothing, isotropic smoothing—as, for instance, by a Gaussian in the case of the Marr–Hildreth operator [Marr and Hildreth 1980] and the simplest version of the Canny operator [Canny 1986]—provides simplicity and uniformity at the expense of smoothing across edges. Whereas smoothing along an edge is desirable as such smoothing (ideally) averages noisy samples representing a single intensity, smoothing across an edge is not desirable as the latter smoothing averages intensities that are inherently different. The latter smoothing also adversely affects the ability of an operator to discriminate between and detect edges that are close together, and, in general, the operator's ability to localize step edges exhibiting intensity fluctuations on either side; see, for instance, [Nalwa and Binford 1986]. The more the smoothing across an edge, as would happen as the σ of a blurring Gaussian is increased, the more the deterioration of these abilities.

Finally, let us take a slightly closer look at the effect of image sampling and quantization on edge detection. Consider intensity quantization first. As we saw in Figure 2.19, intensity quantization can cause smoothly varying intensity surfaces to have a "staircase" appearance in a phenomenon known as *gray-scale contouring*. As a result, local examination of an image may indicate step edges where none exist. To get a clearer idea of how such step edges may come about, consider that we can generate the step $\{0\ 0\ 0\ 1\ 1\ 1\}$ by simply rounding the samples of the linear intensity profile $(0.15x)$. Similarly, sampling and quantization of the linear profile $(0.6x - 0.8)$ can yield a step of two gray levels spanning a 5-pixel window: $\{0\ 0\ 1\ 2\ 2\}$. Of course, much larger steps are possible with nonlinear profiles. The immediate implication of the false-contouring phenomenon is that local edge detectors cannot cope with fundamental ambiguities resulting from intensity quantization. Now consider image sampling. As confirmed by Figure 2.17, where a circular disc is sampled by a square grid, all regular sampling grids are inherently anisotropic (e.g., see [Rosenfeld and Kak 1982]). As a consequence, edge detection, localization, and resolution in a digital image are all necessarily orientation dependent.

3.2 Edgel Aggregation and Edge Description

What an edgel detector typically produces are short linear disjointed edge segments, each segment with an orientation and a position. These segments by themselves are generally of little use until they are aggregated into extended edges. Whereas substantial effort has been directed toward edgel detection, relatively little attention has been paid to the aggregation of edgels into extended edges and the parametric description of these edges. These topics are touched on now.

If an edgel detector tracks the edge whenever it discovers a new edgel (e.g., [Hueckel 1973]), then postprocessing to aggregate the edgels may be unnecessary. However, most inherently parallel edgel detectors need to be followed by edgel aggregation. Work on this problem broadly falls into two categories: global and local. Global strategies have been formulated as graph searches for minimum cost paths, each edgel forming a node in a graph and the cost of connecting two edgels depending on their proximity, relative orientation, and contrasts, among other factors. Montanari [Montanari 1971] proposed the use of dynamic programming (see Footnote 1 in Section 7.2.2) for this purpose, whereas Martelli [Martelli 1976] and Ramer [Ramer 1975] advocated the use of heuristic search (see [Nilsson 1980]). Local methods for edgel aggregation extend edges by seeking the most "compatible" candidate edgel in the neighborhood of an edge termination (e.g., [Nevatia and Babu 1980], [Nalwa and Pauchon 1987]). Although global methods can incorporate domain knowledge into their cost functions, and are more robust to noisy edgel data—that may result, perhaps, from either one or both of an ill-designed edgel detector and a high noise level in the image—these advantages are bought at the expense of a relatively high computational cost.

Once the edgels have been aggregated into extended edges, we are faced with the task of describing these edges. Barrow and Popplestone [Barrow and Popplestone 1971] suggested a plot of the edge's tangent versus the edge's arc-length for this purpose. Such a representation has several attractive features—among them, circles map onto straight lines, and straight lines map onto horizontal straight lines, these mappings facilitating the detection of circular edges and straight edges, respectively. The chief hindrance to using the tangent versus arc-length plot is the problem of estimating this plot robustly. Following the approach of Turner [Turner 1974], Nalwa and Pauchon [Nalwa and Pauchon 1987] used this plot to fit straight lines and conic sections (i.e., ellipses, hyperbolas, and parabolas) to extended edges. Conics have been used for curve fitting by several other researchers; see, for instance, [Turner 1974], [Bookstein 1979], and [Pavlidis 1983]. Whenever we choose to fit a curve to a set of data on the basis of a particular error criterion that depends on the distance of the data from the curve, an important accompanying concern is the estimation of this distance. This problem is often nontrivial, and crude approximations show up in the fitted curves having systematic deviations from the optimum fit. Several attempts have been made to formulate estimates for the distance of a point from a conic (e.g., see [Turner 1974], [Bookstein 1979], [Sampson 1982], [Pavlidis 1983], [Nalwa and Pauchon 1987]); although an exact solution is possible, it is impractical (see [Nalwa and Pauchon 1987]).

Before we proceed, it is worth mentioning that extended edges, like other curves, can be described at varying levels of detail; that is, they can be described at varying resolutions. Such a description is commonly referred to as a *description at multiple scales*; we discussed multiple scales earlier, in Section 3.1.2, in the context of edge detection. Mokhtarian and Mackworth [Mokhtarian and Mackworth 1986] and Lowe [Lowe 1989] have specifically investigated the concerns that arise in multiple-scale descriptions of curves.

To give you an idea of how an edgel-aggregation and edge-description system may proceed, an example from [Nalwa and Pauchon 1987] is now outlined. Figure 3.18(a) is a 64×64 image of an industrial part. Figure 3.18(b) shows the image's edgels (detected by the Nalwa–Binford operator) mapped onto a 128×128 grid. Thinning leads to the minimally connected graph of Figure 3.18(c). This graph is segmented into edges by simple contour following, with decisions at junctions being based on the compatibility of the orientations of the edgels across the junction. Figure 3.18(d) shows the edgel centers of one of the linked edges, and Figure 3.18(e) provides a polygonal approximation to this edge. Figure 3.18(f) is the tangent versus arc-length plot, the so-called ψ–s plot, of the edge; the tangent along the edge is available from the parameters of the edgels constituting the edge, and the arc-length along the edge is estimated from the edge's polygonal approximation. The ψ–s plot of the edge is used to discover straight lines (constant ψ), inflections (extrema in ψ–s plot), and tangent discontinuities (very large slope in ψ–s plot) in the edge. Also, the initial choice of knots (i.e., endpoints of fitted curve segments) is based on a polygonal approximation to the ψ–s plot. Figure 3.18(g) is the image-plane plot corresponding to Figure 3.18(f). Finally, Figure 3.18(h) shows the fitted straight lines and conics, and also the final set of knots. Both position and tangent continuity are preserved at the knots in the curve fitting here. Away from the detected corners, the root-mean-square distance of the edgel centers from the fitted curves is less than 0.2 pixel, and the maximum distance is less than 0.5 pixel.

The Hough Transform

In the context of fitting curves to edgel data, an interesting and useful tool that has a broad spectrum of applications other than curve fitting is the Hough transform. Whereas the transform has its roots in a proposal by Hough in 1962 (see [Duda and Hart 1972]), the original proposal has since undergone various extensions and analyses (e.g., [Ballard 1981], [Brown 1983]). The key idea is as follows. Suppose that we are given a set of points—or a set of some other local curve features, such as points with assigned tangents—and that we know the parametric form of the curve to which these points belong. Then, we may determine the parameters of the curve underlying the points in two steps. First, map each point, via the **Hough transform**, onto the set of all possible parameter values for which the curve passes through the given point. Then, find the intersection of all the sets of parameter values that are thus mapped. This intersection provides the sought values of the parameters of the underlying curve. An example should elucidate the procedure.

Consider a set of points, each point with an assigned tangent, belonging to a circle whose parameters we seek to determine. Now, a circle has three degrees of freedom: two for the position of its center, and one for its radius. However, any circle passing through a fixed point with an assigned tangent

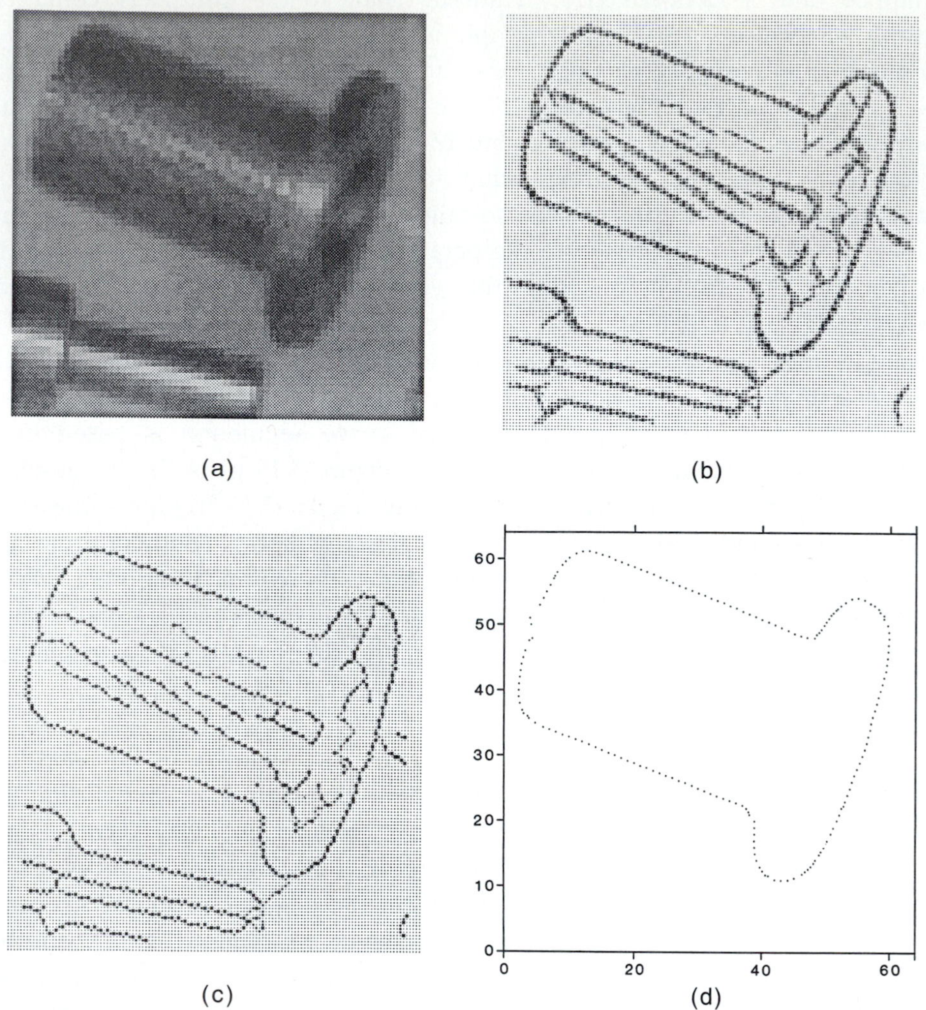

Figure 3.18 Edgel aggregation and edge description. Illustrated is an approach to aggregate locally detected edgels (i.e., short, linear edge segments) into extended edges, and then to describe these edges. The strategy adopted here for the description of edges makes use of the *tangent versus arc-length plot*, the so-called ψ–s plot, which represents a curve by the orientation ψ of the curve's tangent as a function of the length s of the curve between the point of tangency and a fixed point from which the curve extends; a ψ–s plot of a curve determines the curve unambiguously up to a translation. **(a)** Original image (64×64). **(b)** Edgels (detected by the Nalwa–Binford operator) mapped onto a 128×128 grid; the largest dots represent edgel centers, the mid-sized dots represent edgel extensions, and the smallest dots represent the underlying grid. **(c)** Minimally connected graph of edgel centers that is obtained by the thinning of the edgel extensions in (b). **(d)** One of several sets of edgel centers from (c), each set comprising edgel centers that have been aggregated into an edge by simple graph following in (c), with the

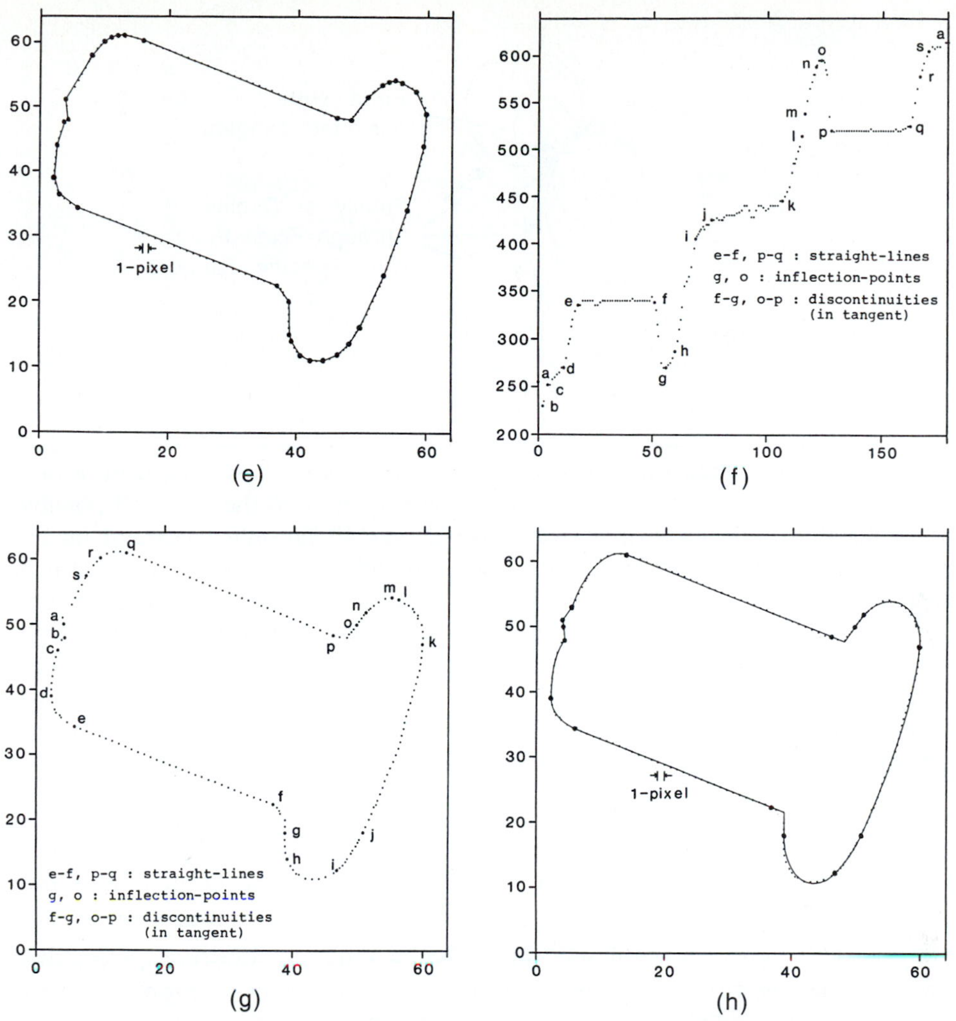

decision of which branches at a junction pair into a single edge being based on the differences between the orientations of the various edgels that lie immediately across the junction. **(e)** A polygon fitted to the points in (d), with the vertices of the polygon highlighted. **(f)** Tangent (ψ) versus arc-length (s) plot for the underlying edge in (d), with estimates for ψ (in degrees, measured counterclockwise from the horizontal) from the original edgel data, with estimates for s (in units of the digital-image interpixel spacing) from the polygonal fit in (e), and with letters corresponding to the letters in (g). **(g)** Same as (d), except now with letters indicating the initial choice of *knots*—a term describing points between which curve segments are fitted to a collection of points—this choice corresponding to the vertices of a polygon fitted (but not shown) to the ψ–s data in (f). **(h)** Final placement of knots accompanied by straight lines and conics fitted between these knots to the edgel data in (d), the fitted curves describing the edge underlying the edgel data compactly. (From [Nalwa and Pauchon 1987] with permission.)

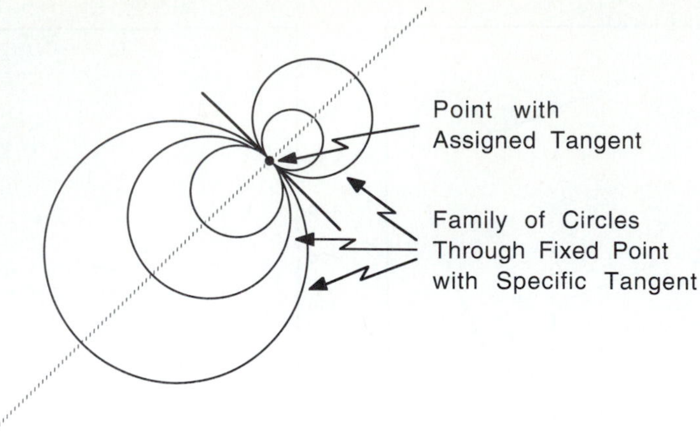

Figure 3.19 The Hough transform. The *Hough transform* maps each feature of a curve, whose parametric form is assumed to be known, onto the set of all possible values that the parameters of the curve could take if the only constraint on the curve were that the particular feature belong to the curve. Now, a circle that is constrained to pass through some fixed point with a particular tangent has one degree of freedom: This single independently variable parameter, as illustrated, could be the location of the circle's center along the straight line that passes through the given point and is orthogonal to the tangent at the point. It follows that, if we are seeking to fit a circle to a point with an assigned tangent, then the Hough transform of this point with its assigned tangent has one degree of freedom.

has only one degree of freedom: As illustrated in Figure 3.19, the center of the circle must lie on the line that is orthogonal to the tangent and that passes through the point, and fixing the circle's center determines the circle's radius. Hence, given a point with an assigned tangent, the three parameters of the underlying circle are constrained to a one–degree-of-freedom set in the parameter space. This set, the Hough transform, is a curve for "well-behaved" problems such as the one here. If we denote the point by (x_o, y_o), and the angle made by its assigned tangent with the negative-x direction by θ_o, then the Hough transform is given by

$$\begin{aligned} x_o &= x_c + r \sin \theta_o , \\ y_o &= y_c + r \cos \theta_o , \end{aligned}$$

where (x_c, y_c) are the coordinates of the center of the circle, and r is the circle's radius. Similarly, every other point plus tangent will generate a corresponding constraint curve. The parameters of the underlying circle must lie on all these curves; hence, they must lie at the intersection.

If the constraint sets have no common intersection, then there is no curve of the specified parametric form that satisfies the given data, and if the intersection is not a single point, then the solution is ambiguous. In the presence of noise (or of multiple underlying parametric curves), the parameter space may be quantized into an array of "buckets," each feature point casting a vote in every bucket that overlaps its constraint set, and the bucket with the maximum number of votes (or, in the case of multiple underlying curves, the buckets with local maxima in votes) determining the parameters. Note that this strategy provides the curve that "fits" the maximum number of feature points, rather than one that minimizes some error measure over *all* feature points. Further, as intersections of constraint sets of adjacent feature points are treated no different from those of distant feature points, relative locations of feature points are not a consideration during curve fitting here. (See [Ballard and Brown 1982] for an excellent introduction to the Hough transform and its variants.)

3.3 Image Segmentation

The **segmentation** of an image is the division of the image into fragments, or segments, each of which is homogeneous in some sense, but the union of no two adjacent segments is homogeneous in the same sense; the sense in which we are seeking each image segment to be homogeneous here is that the segment not exhibit any abrupt intensity changes in its interior. As indicated earlier, although edge detection often leads to the segmentation of an image into regions with smoothly varying intensities in their interiors, it need not do so. As it is image segmentation that is often desired, several techniques have been developed specifically for this purpose. These methods can be fairly robust, and are sufficient for certain applications. Three prominent approaches are discussed here: pixel classification, splitting and merging, and relaxation. For a more extensive treatment see [Ballard and Brown 1982], [Rosenfeld and Kak 1982], and [Pavlidis 1977]; see also [Zucker 1976a] and [Haralick and Shapiro 1985].

3.3.1 Pixel Classification

The simplest approach to segment an image is to classify each pixel based on its gray level—that is, to partition the gray scale into intervals, and assign every pixel with a gray level within a particular interval to a single class. This operation, commonly referred to as **segmentation by thresholding**, is essentially a quantization-coarsening transformation [Prewitt 1970]. The central concern here is how to choose the thresholds; see [Weszka 1978] for a survey of threshold-selection techniques. One possibility is to take advantage of the multimodal nature of typical gray-level histograms: Large coherent image regions typically generate modes (maxima), whereas edges, which

(a)

(b)

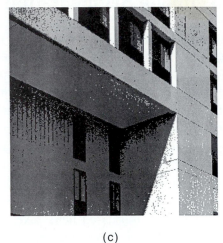

(c)

Figure 3.20 Segmentation of an image based on the valleys in the image's gray-level histogram. The *segmentation* of an image is the division of the image into fragments, or segments, each of which is homogeneous in some sense, but the union of no two adjacent segments is homogeneous in the same sense; the sense in which we are seeking each image segment to be homogeneous here is that the segment not exhibit any abrupt intensity changes in its interior. The *gray-level histogram* of an image is a plot of the number of image pixels that assume each gray level—that is, it is a plot of the number of image pixels that assume each discrete value that the quantized image intensity can take. **(a)** Original image (256×256). **(b)** Gray-level histogram of the image accompanied by a candidate set of thresholds that demarcate gray-level intervals within each of which pixels may be categorized as belonging to a single class. **(c)** Segmentation of the image into four classes of regions based on the thresholds in (b).

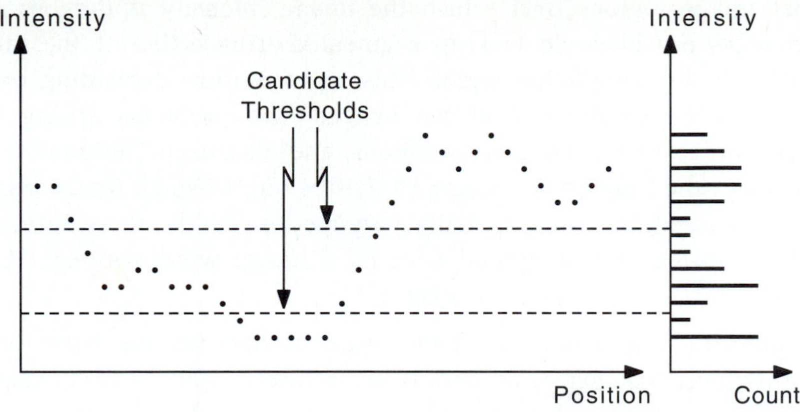

Figure 3.21 Limitations of image segmentation that is based on an image's gray-level histogram. Two fundamental limitations of image segmentation that is based on an image's gray-level histogram are illustrated here with the aid of a digital (i.e., sampled and quantized) one-dimensional intensity profile that is accompanied by its gray-level histogram and a candidate set of thresholds. As is clear from the figure, depending on the overall gray-level statistics of the image pixels, locally distinct edges may go undetected, whereas smoothly varying regions may end up segmented.

comprise a range of intermediate gray levels over a smaller area, typically generate antimodes (minima) [Prewitt 1970].

Figure 3.20 shows an image, its gray-level histogram with candidate thresholds, and the corresponding image segmentation. Several problems with this approach are apparent. First, pixels assigned to a single class need not form coherent regions as the spatial locations of pixels are completely ignored during segmentation here. Second, threshold selection is not always straightforward: There may be a large number of local minima, and, further, some minima may be plateaued. One possibility is to choose thresholds whose image isobrightness contours, on the average, exhibit large intensity gradients along their lengths [Prewitt 1970]; such a strategy incorporates some local-neighborhood information into the segmentation process.

A third shortcoming of the histogram-based approach as described here is that it is unable to segment the image along edges whose adjoining gray levels fall within a single gray-scale interval; this shortcoming is a direct consequence of ignoring the image locations of pixels. Figure 3.21 illustrates both this shortcoming and several other limitations of thresholding-based segmentation with a one-dimensional intensity profile that is accompanied by its gray-level histogram and a candidate set of thresholds. It is clear from the figure that image regions over which the image intensity undergoes large overall changes are likely to end up segmented irrespective of the rate of change of intensity within the region, this segmentation depending on the gray-level statistics of the rest of the image. The problems arising from gradual but large overall intensity variations, and also from "hidden" modes (i.e., maxima in the gray-level histogram) that belong to small image regions, are often addressed by using spatially varying thresholds, these thresholds derived from histograms computed over local image windows (e.g., [Chow and Kaneko 1972], [Beveridge et al. 1989]).

The preceding approach to image segmentation on the basis of the image's gray-level histogram, as described, is rarely used in itself. Several variations are possible. One possibility is to use color images and the statistics of their color components (e.g., [Ohlander, Price, and Reddy 1978], [Beveridge et al. 1989]). Although this strategy does not overcome the fundamental limitations of pixel-based segmentation in principle, it drastically reduces their manifestation in practice. Another possibility is to use histograms of image features that are computed over the pixels. For instance, we could use the histograms of the magnitudes of the image-intensity gradient; thresholding the image-intensity gradient, of course, is precisely what several edge detectors pursue to classify pixels into edge pixels and nonedge pixels. Multiple image features can be used in a variety of ways. They can be combined into a single one-dimensional histogram; for example, we could weight the gray-level statistics of pixels by some function of the image gradient at each pixel [Weszka and Rosenfeld 1979]. Alternately, we could use multiple features to cluster pixels in a multidimensional feature space (e.g., [Coleman and Andrews 1979], [Schachter, Davis, and Rosenfeld 1979]). Almost all pixel-classification approaches to image segmentation incorporate some degree of heuristic postprocessing to make their outputs "presentable." Small isolated regions are often suppressed, adjoining regions merged, and so forth (e.g., [Ohlander, Price, and Reddy 1978], [Beveridge et al. 1989]).

The fundamental drawback of histogram-based approaches to image segmentation is their inherent disregard for spatial coherence. Pappas and Jayant [Pappas and Jayant 1988] seek to overcome this shortcoming by iteratively refining an initial pixel-based segmentation. They invoke a Markov-random-field image model (see Section 3.3.3) to impose spatial coherence on the segmentation, and process over multiple-sized image windows to accommodate gradual variations in intensity within individual image segments. Figure 3.22 provides a sample result.

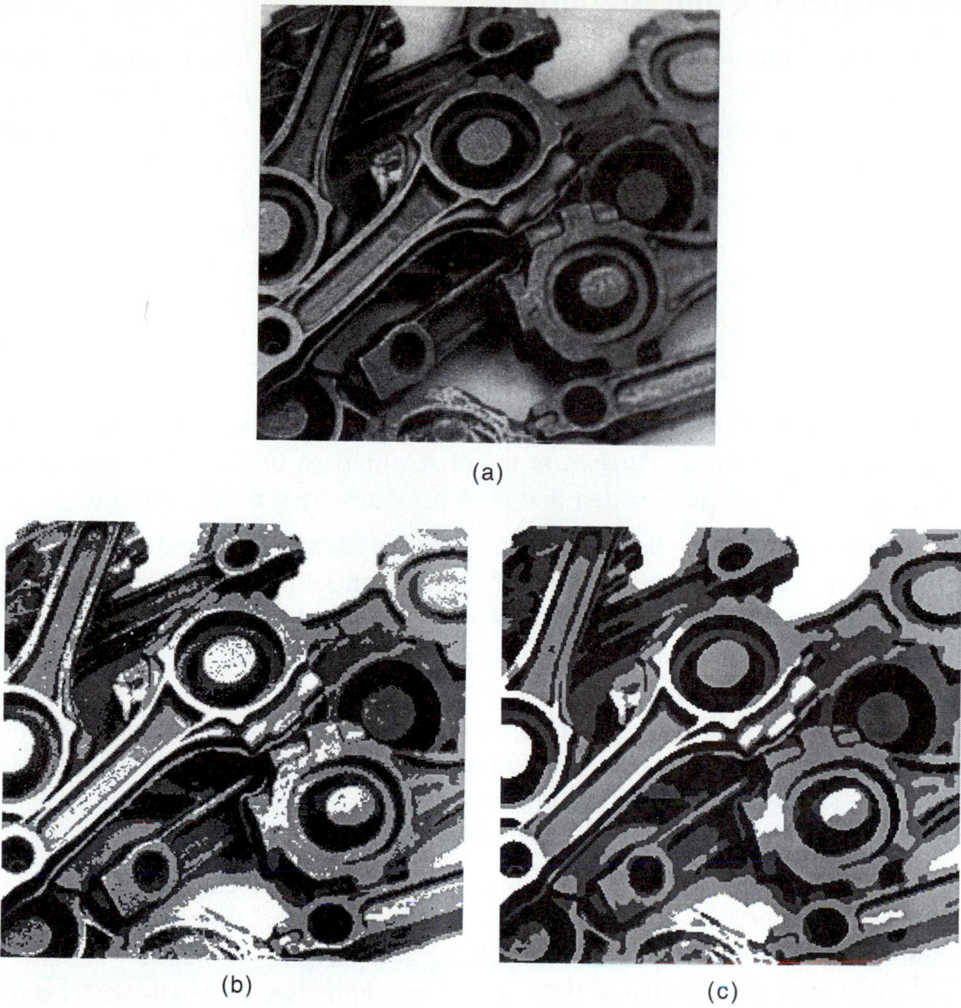

Figure 3.22 Segmentation of an image based on the image's gray-level histogram, and the subsequent imposition of spatial coherence on the segmentation. **(a)** Original image (256×256). **(b)** Segmentation of the image based on the image's gray-level histogram. **(c)** Result of iterative refinement of the segmentation in (b), this refinement depending on a Markov-random-field image model to impose spatial coherence on the segmentation, and on processing over multiple-sized image windows to accommodate smooth intensity variations within individual image segments. An image satisfies the *Markov-random-field (MRF) model* if the conditional probability of a pixel assuming some gray level, given the gray levels over the rest of the image, depends on only the gray levels of the pixel's neighbors. (From [Pappas and Jayant 1988] with permission, © 1988 IEEE.)

3.3.2 Splitting and Merging

Image segmentation can be defined as the partitioning of an image I into subsets S_i, $i = 1, \ldots, m$, such that, given a logical predicate H that checks whether one or more image regions are homogeneous, the following four conditions are met [Horowitz and Pavlidis 1976]:

1. $I = \bigcup_{i=1}^{m} S_i$.
2. $S_i \cap S_j = \emptyset$ for all $i \neq j$.
3. $H(S_i) = \mathit{true}$ for all i.
4. $H(S_i \cup S_j) = \mathit{false}$ for all adjacent S_i and S_j, $i \neq j$.

Note that neither the partition, nor the number of image segments m, is required to be unique. Further, m is not required to be minimum owing to the large computational burden that such a requirement would impose.

Merging schemes begin with a partition satisfying condition 3—for instance, a collection of individual pixels—and then proceed to fulfill condition 4 by gradually merging adjacent image regions. **Splitting** schemes, on the other hand, begin with a partition satisfying condition 4—for instance, the whole image—and then proceed to satisfy condition 3 by gradually splitting image regions. A generalization of these two approaches is a **split-and-merge** strategy that uses both splitting and merging to take a partition possibly satisfying neither condition 3 nor condition 4 to produce a segmentation that satisfies both conditions [Horowitz and Pavlidis 1976].

Several variations are possible within the preceding framework. Differences between the various proposals arise in the choice of the homogeneity predicate, and in the splitting and merging strategies. We shall not delve into the details of these variations here (see [Pavlidis 1977] and [Rosenfeld and Kak 1982]).

Pixel classification based on partitioning the gray scale can be regarded as invoking a rather crude homogeneity predicate that checks whether all pixel gray levels lie within a single interval. A more sophisticated approach is to use a predicate that checks whether the error in approximating the pixel data by some function is less than some threshold, an idea first suggested by Pavlidis [Pavlidis 1972]. The approximating function might be a constant [Horowitz and Pavlidis 1976], a (possibly sloped) plane [Haralick 1980], or some other function. Besl and Jain [Besl and Jain 1988] pursue this idea to its logical conclusion and suggest variable-order surface fitting not only to segment the image, but also to describe the intensity variation within each image segment. The approximating surface they choose for each data set is the lowest-order bivariate polynomial, of up to the fourth order, that has a

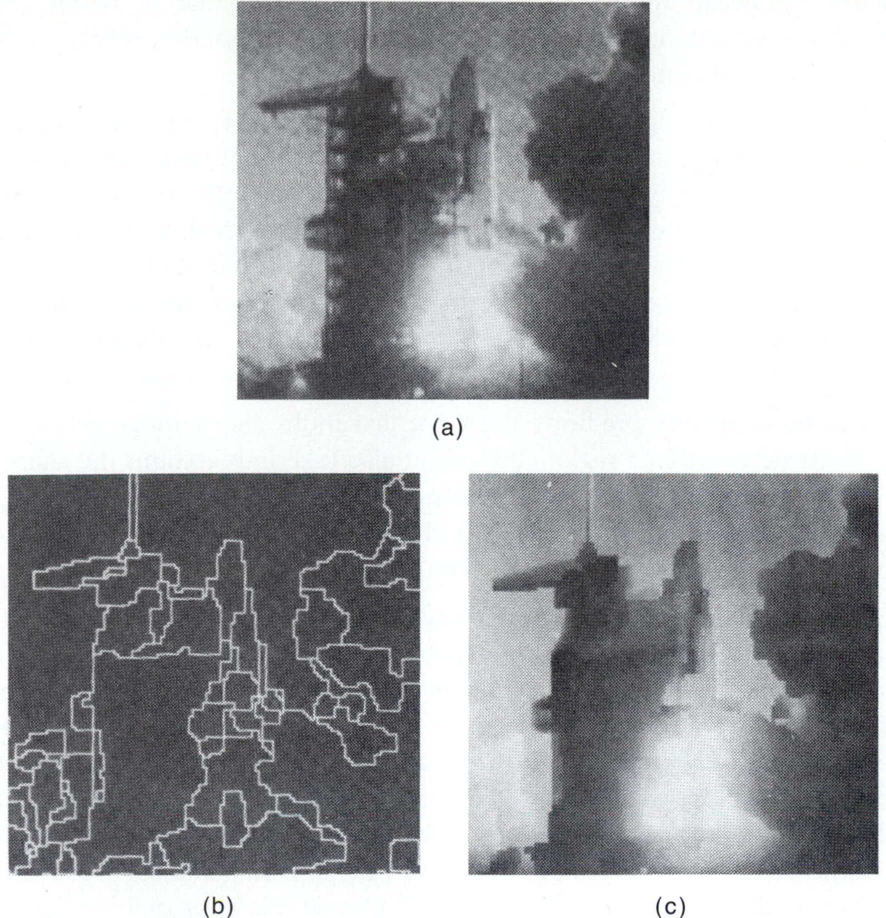

(a)

(b)

(c)

Figure 3.23 Segmentation of an image by region growing. The image here is segmented by a region-growing technique that makes the determination of whether a set of pixels belong to a single coherent image region based on the least-squares errors of fitting multiple-order bivariate polynomial surfaces (of up to the fourth order) to the pixels. **(a)** Original image of a space-shuttle launch (256×256). **(b)** Segmentation of the image. **(c)** Reconstruction of the image based on the least-squares-error polynomial surfaces that are fitted to the image segments in (b). (From [Besl and Jain 1988] with permission, © 1988 IEEE.)

least-squares error less than some threshold (cf. comments on surface fitting in Section 3.1.4). In addition, they require that the signs of the fitting errors, at the level of individual pixels, exhibit an unsystematic spatial distribution; this requirement is premised on the assumption that systematic fitting errors are more likely to be due to the inadequacy of a fit than to be due to random signal noise. Figure 3.23 illustrates the performance of this approach on an image of a space-shuttle launch. In reference to the figure, note that close similarity between an image and its reconstruction that is based on a particular segmentation (set of edges) does not necessarily reflect on the quality of the segmentation (edge detection).

The surface-fitting approach to image segmentation assumes implicitly that we are seeking to partition the intensity surface that underlies the image into smoothly varying regions. Image segmentation into smoothly varying intensity regions is not what we always seek. We may seek to classify image regions based on their texture. For instance, Gupta and Wintz [Gupta and Wintz 1975] use a merging strategy that compares either one or both of the first- and second-order statistics of pixel gray levels in adjacent regions. Section 6.1 delves in some detail into various texture-discrimination criteria.

The homogeneity predicate need not just index the homogeneity of the image intensity within a region, but might also take into account the shape of the region boundary. Brice and Fennema [Brice and Fennema 1970] suggest that merging of adjacent regions should be encouraged in such a way as to shorten or smoothen the image-segment boundaries.

Finally, Feldman and Yakimovsky [Feldman and Yakimovsky 1974] pursue the following domain-dependent strategy. First, an initial (nonsemantic) image partition is interpreted in terms of a domain model, and then the pair of adjacent regions most likely to belong to a single world object is merged. Subsequently, a fresh interpretation is performed, and again a pair of adjacent regions merged. This iteration continues until the probability that the regions and their boundaries are correctly interpreted, given the context (domain model) and the image, is maximized. Tenenbaum and Barrow [Tenenbaum and Barrow 1977] pursue this approach further.

3.3.3 Relaxation

Let us now turn our attention to a particular class of techniques that has several applications in addition to image segmentation: the class of locally cooperative and parallel processes, called *relaxation*. We already encountered one such process in our discussion of scale space (Section 3.1.2)—namely, diffusion, in which each pixel's intensity is modified on the basis of the deviation of this intensity from the intensities of neighboring pixels. See [Davis and Rosenfeld 1981] for a survey of relaxation techniques; see [Rosenfeld, Hummel, and Zucker 1976] for the origins of relaxation; see [Hummel and Zucker 1983] for a foundational treatment. The book by Rosenfeld and Kak [Rosenfeld and Kak 1982] also addresses various concerns in relaxation; further, it provides several applications of relaxation to image segmentation.

A typical paradigm for (probabilistic) **relaxation** comprises the following three steps:

1. A list of candidate labels (e.g., interpretations)—each label in a list with its own confidence level—is independently assigned to each to-be-labeled entity (e.g., to an image pixel).
2. The confidence level of each label in a list is reinforced or inhibited based on the compatibility of the label to the current states of the neighboring lists of labels, the compatibility between various neighboring labels being measured on the basis of some a priori model.
3. Step 2 is repeated several times, this repetition facilitating the propagation of local constraints over larger neighborhoods.

The principal concern with relaxation processes is their slow, and even possible lack of, convergence. Terzopoulos [Terzopoulos 1986] provides a multiresolution strategy (see Section 3.1.2) to speed up the convergence of relaxation processes in the specific context of images.

The relaxation process as described is deterministic, with each iteration monotonically increasing the conformance of the label assignments to the model. There lies the danger in such an approach that the process might converge to a local optimum, rather than to the global optimum. To overcome this possible pitfall, Geman and Geman [Geman and Geman 1984] proposed a stochastic approach that has led to a whole new class of computer vision algorithms. (See [Blake and Zisserman 1987] for a deterministic but less general approach to the same problem.) Let us assume that each to-be-labeled entity (e.g., pixel) is assigned a single label from an ordered and possibly continuous set of labels (e.g., image gray levels), and that we have available an objective function that measures the degree of conformance of the label assignments to some model. This function is sought to be maximized. Then, paraphrasing Geman and Geman, **stochastic relaxation** informally proceeds as follows.

A local change is made to the label assignments based on the current values of the labels at and in the neighborhood of where the change is made. This change is random, and is generated by sampling a local conditional probability distribution for the true labels given the current label assignments. The sampled probability distribution depends on the objective function and on a global control parameter T, called the "temperature." At low temperatures, the local conditional distributions concentrate on states that increase the objective function, whereas at high temperatures, these distributions are essentially uniform. The limiting cases, $T = 0$ and $T = \infty$, correspond respectively to greedy algorithms (such as gradient ascent) and undirected (i.e., "purely random") changes. High temperatures induce a loose coupling between neighboring labels, and low temperatures induce a tight coupling. Local maxima are avoided by beginning at high temperatures, where many of the stochastic changes will actually decrease the objective function, and then gradually lowering the temperature. If the temperature is lowered too rapidly, or insufficient time is spent at temperatures near the freezing point, there lies the danger that the process might converge to a local maximum. As relaxation proceeds, and the temperature is lowered, the process behaves increasingly like iterative improvement.

The gradual reduction of temperature here simulates annealing, which is a physical process by which we can drive certain substances to their low-energy highly regular states by first raising the temperature of the substance, and then gradually lowering the temperature in a carefully controlled fashion. Consequently, *stochastic relaxation* is often described as **simulated annealing.**[6] You can think of simulated annealing as successive stochastic optimization of an objective function at increasingly finer resolutions. It must be emphasized here that simulated annealing, and, hence, stochastic relaxation, is a computational strategy appropriate for only computationally prohibitive problems that can be (meaningfully) formulated as the optimization of some objective function.

Relaxation methods are particularly well suited to image segmentation when the gray levels of the individual pixels can be modeled by a **Markov random field (MRF)**. The principal characteristic of such a field is that the conditional probability of any site (pixel) having a particular value (gray level), given the values at all other sites, is the same as its conditional probability of having that value given the values at only neighboring sites. See [Cross and Jain 1983] and [Besag 1974] for more complete and formal characterizations. MRF models provide a convenient mechanism to impose

---

6. Two bibliographical comments are in order here. First, at each individual temperature, simulated annealing proceeds as the well-known **Metropolis algorithm** [Metropolis et al. 1953] used in statistical physics to compute the equilibrium state of a large collection of interacting individual particles at a particular temperature. Second, the idea of using simulated annealing as an optimization procedure was first proposed independently by Kirkpatrick, Gelatt, and Vecchi [Kirkpatrick, Gelatt, and Vecchi 1983] and by Černý [Černý 1985], both of whom used it for combinatorial optimization. Černý's description of a Monte Carlo algorithm to find approximate solutions to the traveling-salesman problem is particularly lucid. (The *traveling-salesman problem* is to determine the shortest path by which a "traveling salesman" can tour N cities. This problem is the classical example of a large class of combinatorial problems for each of which every known exact solution essentially requires the consideration of all the possibilities.)

local constraints. Thus far, much of the image segmentation work using such models has been directed toward degraded piecewise-constant-intensity synthetic images. (However, see also [Pappas and Jayant 1988], and the references given in the discussion on texture discrimination in Section 6.1.1.) For such images, segmentation is equivalent to restoration. Although several objective functions are possible, the most common approach is to adopt a Bayesian framework and to compute the maximum a posteriori (MAP) estimate of the original image given the degraded image—that is, to maximize the conditional probability of the estimate being the true undegraded image given the degraded image.[7] Geman and Geman [Geman and Geman 1984] pursue one such approach using stochastic relaxation to restore piecewise-constant-intensity images that have been degraded by noise and possibly also blurring. Figure 3.24 provides a sample result. Marroquin, Mitter, and Poggio [Marroquin, Mitter, and Poggio 1987] optimize a different objective function using stochastic relaxation at a fixed temperature to restore

---

7. Given a set of observations d of data δ, which depends in a known statistical fashion on a set of parameters ρ, there are several methods we could adopt to estimate the parameters ρ from the data $\delta = \mathrm{d}$. Among the various methods, the two most prominent are the maximum likelihood approach and the Bayesian approach. The fundamental difference between these two approaches is that, whereas the maximum likelihood approach views the sought parameters as unknown constants, the Bayesian approach views them as random variables with known a priori probability distributions.

The **maximum likelihood (ML) estimate** of a set of parameters ρ, given a set of observations $\delta = \mathrm{d}$, is the value p of the set of parameters that maximizes the probability$\{\delta = \mathrm{d}$ given $\rho = p\}$. The probability$\{\delta = \mathrm{d}$ given $\rho = p\}$ is called the **likelihood** of ρ with respect to the observations $\delta = \mathrm{d}$.

The **Bayesian approach**, in contrast, uses the observations $\delta = \mathrm{d}$ to transform the known a priori probability distribution of the parameters ρ into an a posteriori probability distribution of ρ given $\delta = \mathrm{d}$. It accomplishes this transformation by invoking the well-known **Bayes' rule**:

$$\text{probability}\{\rho = p \text{ given } \delta = \mathrm{d}\} = \frac{\text{probability}\{\delta = \mathrm{d} \text{ given } \rho = p\} \ \text{probability}\{\rho = p\}}{\text{probability}\{\delta = \mathrm{d}\}},$$

where we can evaluate the denominator on the right-hand side, probability$\{\delta = \mathrm{d}\}$, by simply summing, over all possible p, the numerator on that side—this numerator being equal to the probability$\{\delta = \mathrm{d}$ and $\rho = p\}$. The **maximum a posteriori (MAP) estimate** of ρ is that p for which the a posteriori probability of ρ, given $\delta = \mathrm{d}$, is maximum. The Bayesian approach hinges on the assumption that the a priori probability distribution of the sought parameters is available—an assumption that is not always tenable.

Note that the denominator of the a posteriori probability as expressed by Bayes' rule is independent of the parameters ρ, and hence this denominator is just a scale factor. Now, in the event that all possible values of ρ are equally likely, the a priori probability of ρ in the numerator will also become a scale factor, and the MAP estimate and the ML estimate will become one and the same thing. A good reference for these concepts is [Duda and Hart 1973].

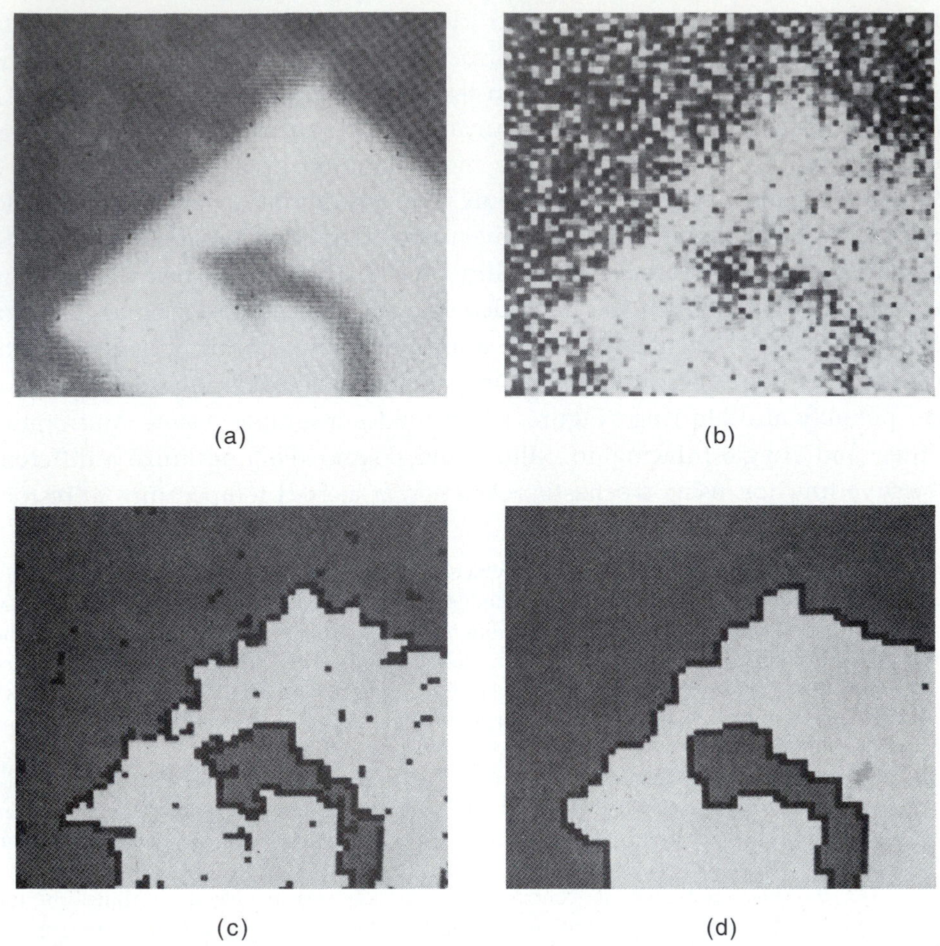

Figure 3.24 Segmentation of an image by stochastic relaxation. Stochastic relaxation is used in the figure to restore—or equivalently, here, to segment—an image whose intensity was originally piecewise constant. **(a)** Original blurred image of a road sign (64×64). **(b)** Image in (a) with noise added. **(c)** Restoration of image in (b) after 100 iterations. **(d)** Restoration of image in (b) after 1000 iterations. *Stochastic relaxation* seeks to optimize an objective function by employing a computational strategy that simulates annealing. *Annealing* is a physical process by which we can drive certain substances to their low-energy highly regular states by first raising the temperature of the substance, and then gradually lowering the temperature in a carefully controlled fashion. In the image restoration here, the objective function that is being optimized favors large constant-intensity image regions with short boundaries (shown in black), these boundaries having a preferred structure that we shall not discuss. (From [Geman and Geman 1984] with permission, © 1984 IEEE.)

piecewise-constant-intensity noisy images. Of course, relaxation is not the only technique to restore or segment images that are modeled by MRFs (e.g., see [Hansen and Elliott 1982], [Besag 1986]). On the other hand, relaxation may be used for image segmentation even when the MRF model is not invoked (e.g., [Geman et al. 1990]).

3.4 Discussion

Although edge detection has come a long way since Roberts' cross, major improvements still seem feasible. Almost all the effort thus far has been directed toward the detection of short linear edge elements. Relatively little attention has been devoted to the detection and localization of edge junctions, corners, and terminations. These features of edges are important precisely for the same reason that edges are important in images: At such points along their lengths, edges exhibit nonredundancy [Attneave 1954]. In addition to the detection of junctions and corners, global grouping of edgels into extended edges and the description of these edges have also received scant attention. Perhaps, the inherent computational complexity of global processes has been a discouraging factor. Relaxation-type iterative processes might offer help here (e.g., [Rosenfeld and Kak 1982], [Zucker et al. 1988]).

As indicated in the introduction to this chapter, most of the attention in edge detection has been on step edges rather than on roof edges. This emphasis on step edges seems justified for two reasons—one, pragmatic, and the other, conceptual. As roof edges are, by definition, discontinuities in the orientation of the intensity surface, their detection implicitly requires the detection of step changes in the first derivatives of the surface, and, as we saw earlier, derivatives emphasize signal noise. It follows that the detection and localization of roof edges will, in general, be less robust than that of step edges, and, further, it would require larger neighborhoods, which imply lower resolution. The second reason why the emphasis on step edges may be justified is more fundamental. Whereas step edges are directly correlated with the structure and configuration of the scene as illustrated in Figure 3.3, roof edges may be artifacts of secondary illumination—that is, of the illumination of a surface patch by light reflected off other surface patches [Forsyth and Zisserman 1991]. (Secondary illumination, which may be substantial, is also important from the standpoint of the detection and localization of step edges as it often leads to intensity variations on either side of such edges, as illustrated in Figure 5.14 [Forsyth and Zisserman 1991]. Perhaps the next generation of step-edgel detectors will take into account such variations, at least to a first order.)

Note that we considered only single-pass local edgel detectors in this chapter. In particular, we did not discuss iterative algorithms and global approaches. As of now, global approaches do not perform well in comparison to noniterative local methods. On the other hand, constraint-propagating iterative processes might offer viable alternatives to the edgel–detection-and-aggregation paradigm. Although attempts along these lines have been reported in the literature (e.g., [Blake and Zisserman 1987]), the results have been relatively weak with respect to sensitivity and resolution. In connection with global approaches, Leclerc [Leclerc 1989] has proposed an interesting formulation that poses edge detection as a problem of generating a "minimal" image description.

As far as image segmentation is concerned, what almost every system provides is a partition of the image pixels, rather than one of the image plane (and the underlying intensity surface). One approach to partition the image plane, given a partition of the image pixels, is to detect edges (to subpixel accuracy) in the neighborhood of pixel-partition boundaries. This strategy, however, may lead to fragmented and dangling edges, thus defeating the whole purpose of segmentation. A more viable alternative might be to use deformable piecewise smooth curves that have an affinity for edges [Kass, Witkin, and Terzopoulos 1988], the initial configuration of the curves being determined by the pixel-partition boundaries.

Finally, it is plausible that edge detection and image segmentation are inherently limited in the absence of feedback from modules that make use of the edges and the image segmentation—this feedback, perhaps, based on the context and on a priori expectations (e.g., see [Feldman and Yakimovsky 1974]). This possibility, of course, is no excuse for deriving from the image less information than the image can provide.

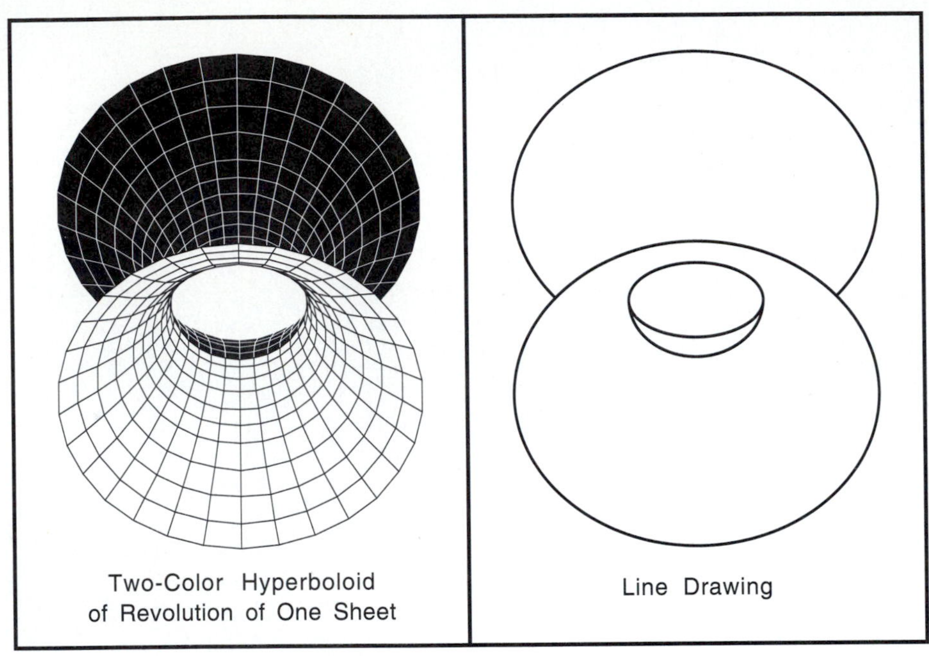

Figure 4.1 A surface and its line drawing, which evokes an interpretation at variance with the surface. A *line drawing* is a representation of the brightness edges in an image; see, for instance, Figure 3.1 for an illustration of brightness edges in an image. Brightness edges in an image arise principally from the following scene events: surface-normal discontinuities, depth discontinuities, surface-reflectance discontinuities, and illumination discontinuities (see Figure 3.3). Although we are often successful at interpreting a line drawing correctly—that is, we are often successful at inferring correctly from a line drawing the scene it represents—we may on occasion be misled by a line drawing. A case in point is the line drawing on the right, which, in fact, is the line drawing of the surface on the left. The surface on the left is a hyperboloid of revolution of one sheet whose one half is black and whose other half is white. A *hyperboloid of revolution of one sheet* is a surface that we can generate by revolving a hyperbola about its nonintersecting axis of symmetry—the grid lines in the rendering of this surface here have been retained solely for illustrative purposes. (After [Nalwa 1988a].)

Chapter 4

Line-Drawing Interpretation

A **line drawing** is a representation of the brightness edges in an image. In this chapter, we shall study the deduction of the three-dimensional structure of a scene from its line drawing. We humans are remarkably adept at inferring from a line drawing the scene the line drawing represents; this observation is confirmed, for instance, by the line drawing we previously encountered in Figure 3.1. However, as the line drawing in Figure 4.1 demonstrates, we are not infallible in our interpretation of line drawings.

Notwithstanding line drawings such as the one in Figure 4.1, which demonstrates our fallibility in line-drawing interpretation, we exhibit a consistently reliable ability to infer the three-dimensional structure of a scene from its line drawing (e.g., [Kennedy 1974]). More often than misinterpret a line drawing, we might find a line drawing to be ambiguous. However, even when we do find a line drawing to be ambiguous, as in the case of the two

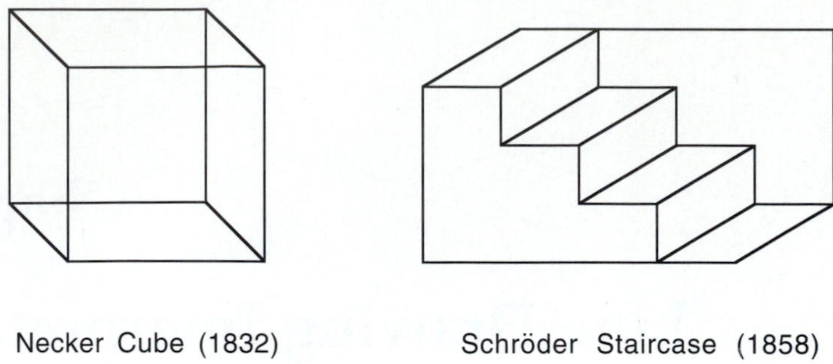

Necker Cube (1832) Schröder Staircase (1858)

Figure 4.2 Two well-known ambiguous line drawings: The Necker cube and the Schröder staircase. In each of the two drawings, depth reversal of the vertical plane that is perceived to be facing the viewer and in front, with the vertical plane that is perceived to be parallel to the first plane but behind, leads to an alternate interpretation of the figure. A convenient technique to perceive the alternate interpretation of either figure is to invert the figure slowly, while continuing to look at the figure. (See [Boring 1942] for a historical account of the two line drawings.)

well-known drawings in Figure 4.2, the number of different interpretations is usually small—often two—and one of the interpretations is usually correct. The drawing on the left in Figure 4.2, the Necker cube, is generally interpreted as a cube, either with its lower vertical face closer to the viewer than its upper vertical face, or vice versa. The drawing on the right, the Schröder staircase, is interpreted as a staircase that is viewed either from above or from below. Our ability to interpret line drawings is remarkable if we take into account that all depth information is lost under projection of a three-dimensional scene onto a two-dimensional image, as illustrated in Figure 4.3 for perspective projection. Let us now study line-drawing interpretation in the context of computer vision.

As already indicated, a line drawing of an image is a representation of the discontinuities in the intensity of the image. As we saw in Chapter 3, image-intensity discontinuities may result from various events in the scene. The principal among these events are surface-normal discontinuities, depth discontinuities, surface-reflectance discontinuities, and illumination discontinuities (shadow edges). Each of these scene events was illustrated in Figure 3.3. Note once again that a depth discontinuity may simultaneously be a surface-normal discontinuity; such a depth discontinuity is to be distinguished from a depth discontinuity across which the surface normal varies continuously, as across the apparent boundary of a sphere.

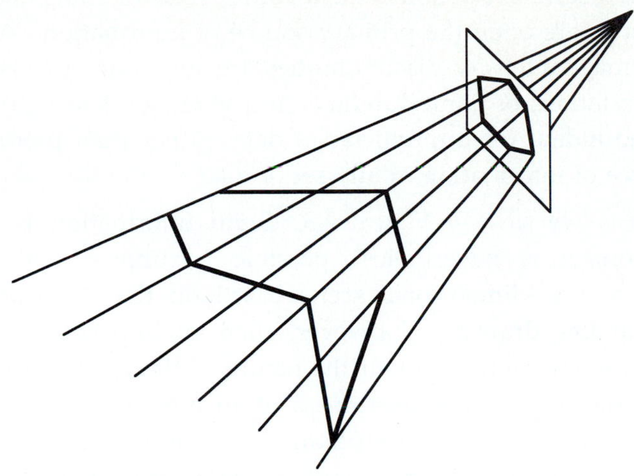

Figure 4.3 The inherent ambiguity of a line drawing. Owing to the complete loss of the depth information in a scene under projection of the scene, the line drawing of any scene event—such as a surface-normal discontinuity, or a depth discontinuity—can only restrict the spatial location of the event to a bundle of rays. As illustrated, under perspective projection, the rays in this bundle all converge at the center of projection; under orthographic projection (not shown), the rays are all parallel to the direction of projection. (After [Barrow and Tenenbaum 1981b].)

Discontinuities in surface normal, illumination, and surface reflectance all lead to **viewpoint-independent edges**—that is, to edges whose three-dimensional spatial locations are independent of the viewpoint. In contrast, continuous–surface-normal depth discontinuities lead to **viewpoint-dependent edges**—that is, to edges whose three-dimensional spatial locations depend on the viewpoint. Consider, for instance, the two straight depth discontinuities that lie on either side of a circular cylinder, and how the spatial locations of these discontinuities vary as you move about the cylinder. The distinction between viewpoint-independent and viewpoint-dependent edges is important: The nature of the conclusions we can draw about the scene from its line drawing in the two cases is substantially different. For brevity, and following common practice, we shall interchangeably use the terms **limbs** and **apparent contours** for continuous–surface-normal depth discontinuities.

Images have a high degree of redundancy. Typically, there are many sources of information in addition to line drawings from which the characteristics of viewed surfaces may be deduced from their images—for instance, shading and texture. However, we could argue—either based on human performance [Barrow and Tenenbaum 1981b] or independent of it—that line drawings are often the primary source of information. As explained in Chapter 3, image-intensity discontinuities are important precisely because they are manifestations of nonredundancy in the image data [Attneave 1954], and it is nonredundant (or unpredictable) data, rather than predictable data, that is the source of information in any set of data.

Although, as we saw in Figure 4.3, depth information is indeed lost under projection, it is nevertheless possible to impose some nontrivial constraints on a three-dimensional scene based on the configuration of its two-dimensional line drawing. However, such an imposition requires that we invoke certain assumptions about the nature of the world and the world's relationship to the image. The usefulness of an inference is, of course, only as good as the validity of the assumptions underlying it. It is almost always assumed that the imaged surfaces are opaque, and that perspective or orthographic projection is an accurate model of the imaging geometry. Under these and other (sometimes implicit) assumptions, line-drawing interpretation typically seeks to aggregate lines into surfaces, and to derive both qualitative and quantitative restrictions on the viewed surfaces. Much of the research to this point has been devoted to the so-called **blocks world**—to a world comprising only polyhedra—and to the extensions of such a world. Progress on the more general problem has been slow and disjointed. Let us discuss both these efforts in turn.

4.1 Polygonal Planar Surfaces

The major analytic focus in line-drawing interpretation has been on the interpretation of the projections of the surface-normal discontinuities and depth discontinuities of opaque polyhedra—or more generally, on the interpretation of the projections of such discontinuities of opaque polygonal planar surfaces. The first systematic analysis was reported by Huffman in his brilliant paper, "Impossible Objects as Nonsense Sentences" [Huffman 1971]. This work, one of the cornerstones of nonheuristic research in computer vision, is discussed at length next. This discussion is followed by a brief description of other work in the tradition of Huffman, and by a short account of a different approach.

4.1.1 Line Labeling

Huffman [Huffman 1971] sought to analyze line drawings representing the surface-normal discontinuities of opaque polyhedra. Although he restricted his attention to polyhedra with trihedral vertices (i.e., vertices formed by exactly three faces), his basic techniques are equally applicable to more general polyhedra. Further, his analysis is valid for both orthographic and perspective projection.

Huffman's [Huffman 1971] first key observation was the need for the **general-viewpoint assumption**: the assumption that the perturbation of the camera viewpoint would not affect the configuration of the line drawing. The term *viewpoint* here is to be interpreted differently under perspective and orthographic projection: When the viewing geometry is modeled by perspective projection, the *viewpoint* is the center of projection, and when the viewing geometry is modeled by orthographic projection, the *viewpoint* is the direction of projection. What the general-viewpoint assumption entails is that certain specific properties of the line drawing persist under perturbation of the viewpoint—only such persistent properties can be gainfully employed to make deductions about the imaged three-dimensional world. (See [Nalwa 1988a] for a more precise mathematical formulation of the general-viewpoint assumption.) Here, the general-viewpoint assumption rules out the possibility of the accidental alignment of image features. "In the case of pictures of polyhedra this eliminates the possibility of pictures in which two vertices of the objects in the scene are, by coincidence, represented at the same point in the picture, or two edges in the scene are seen as a single line in the picture, or a vertex is seen exactly in line with an unrelated edge" (p. 298, [Huffman 1971]). The general-viewpoint assumption is at the heart of line-drawing interpretation, both in human and machine. That humans invoke this assumption is strikingly demonstrated by the subjective contours of Kanizsa [Kanizsa 1979], two examples of which are provided in Figure 4.4. Without the general-viewpoint assumption, meaningful line-drawing interpretation is not feasible. The general-viewpoint assumption has been invoked, although sometimes unknowingly, in all nonheuristic attempts to interpret line drawings since Huffman. The hopelessness of the situation in the absence of this assumption may be gauged from the observation that we must then allow arbitrary planar curves to project onto straight lines in the line drawing. Worse still, a straight line in a line drawing need not be the projection of a space curve at all: It could be the projection of a planar patch along some direction parallel to the plane.

Huffman [Huffman 1971] proposed the following taxonomy of line labels for the visible projections of surface-normal discontinuities in space: $\uparrow$ (occluding), + (nonoccluding convex), and − (concave). These labels, illustrated in Figure 4.5 for a nonpolyhedral object, have the following interpretations: + and − respectively denote convex and concave edges along which both faces forming the edge in space are visible, and $\uparrow$ denotes an

Figure 4.4 The general-viewpoint assumption. The *subjective contours of Kanizsa*—such as the two subjective contours here, each of which suggests a white occluding triangle in space—indicate that we humans implicitly assume that the alignment of image features is not an accident of the viewpoint. In other words, we implicitly invoke the *general-viewpoint assumption* according to which the viewpoint of the camera, or the artist, is in a *general* position in the following sense: The perturbation of the viewpoint would not affect certain specific properties of the figure that are being used to provide the two-dimensional figure with a three-dimensional interpretation. The term *viewpoint* in the general-viewpoint assumption is to be interpreted as the center of projection when the viewing geometry is modeled by perspective projection, and it is to be interpreted as the direction of projection when the viewing geometry is modeled by orthographic projection. In our interpretation of each of the two figures here, we are assuming implicitly that the alignment in the figure of various points along each individual straight side of the perceived white occluding triangle is nonaccidental—that this collinear arrangement of points along each perceived straight edge would persist if the viewpoint under which the figure is acquired were perturbed. If it were not for this assumption of persistence, we would have to allow the possibility of each perceived straight edge being nonstraight in space, and perhaps even discontinuous: Each edge could, in principle, take any of a variety of shapes within the plane that contains both the projection of the edge in the figure, and the viewpoint under which the figure is acquired (see Figure 4.3). The general-viewpoint assumption is at the heart of line-drawing interpretation. It is invoked in all the work on line-drawing interpretation in computer vision, and, unless stated otherwise, we shall implicitly invoke it throughout this book. (After [Kanizsa 1979], by permission of the Greenwood Publishing Group, Inc., Westport, CT. Copyright © 1979 by Gaetano Kanizsa.)

occluding edge, which is necessarily convex. A **convex edge** is an edge along which the (perhaps, partially) visible angle between the two faces forming the edge in space is greater than 180°. A **concave edge** is an edge along which the visible angle between the two faces forming the edge in space is

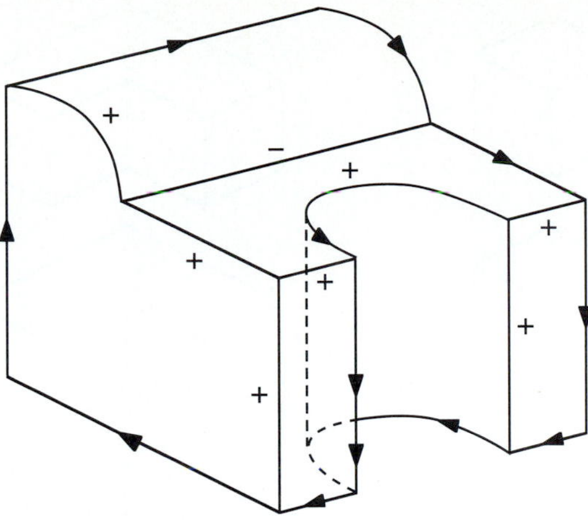

Figure 4.5 Line labels. In any line drawing, an edge that is caused by a depth discontinuity in space can be classified as *occluding*; we are assuming here, as throughout this book, that the viewed surfaces are opaque. A line-drawing edge that is caused by a surface-normal discontinuity in space can be classified as *convex* or *concave*, depending on whether the (perhaps, partially) visible angle between the surfaces adjoining the edge in three-dimensional space is greater than or less than 180°, respectively. An occluding edge is labeled by an arrow (↑) that is oriented along the edge such that the occluding surface is to the right of the arrow, a convex edge that is not an occluding edge is labeled by a plus (+), and a concave edge is labeled by a minus (–). Every line-drawing edge that is caused by a surface-normal discontinuity in three-dimensional space can be labeled at any point by one, and only one, of the labels +, –, and ↑. Whereas in line drawings of polyhedra we are assured that every edge caused by a surface-normal discontinuity in space will have a single unique label along its entire length, we have no such assurance in line drawings of nonpolyhedra. In the line drawing of the nonpolyhedral object shown, notice the change in the line label of one of the curved edges from + to ↑.

less than 180°. An **occluding edge** is a convex edge along which only one of the two faces adjoining the edge in space is visible in the line drawing. The label ↑ along an occluding edge, by convention, is so directed along the edge that, on looking along the arrow, both the faces adjoining the edge in space lie to the right of the arrow, one face behind the other. Having proposed this taxonomy, Huffman makes another key observation, this time regarding the proposed line labels: Every line (in the domain of polyhedra) must have a single label along its entire length, else the pair of surfaces (planes) forming the edge would need to have nonconstant orientation. Figure 4.5 provides an example of a line drawing (of a nonpolyhedral object) with a varying line label. Armed with his line labels and this insight, Huffman systematically derived a complete junction catalog—that is, a catalog of all the possible

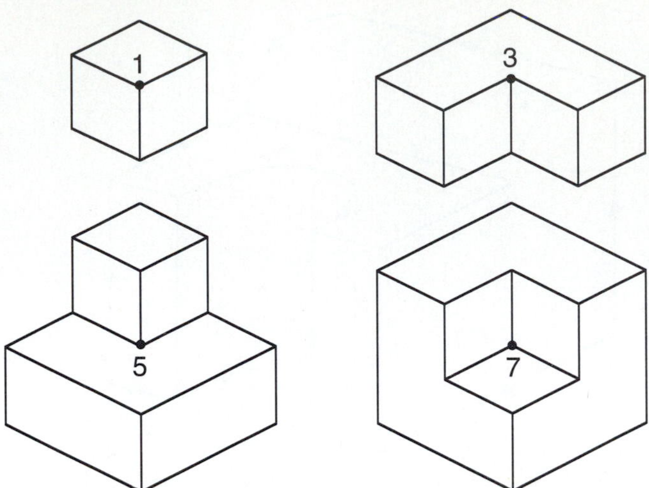

Figure 4.6 The four basic ways in which three planar surfaces can form a vertex of a polyhedron. A vertex of a polyhedron that is formed by exactly three planar surfaces is called a *trihedral vertex*. Although the planar surfaces in the figure are shown to be mutually orthogonal, from our standpoint, it is not this orthogonality that is important, but rather that three independently oriented planes divide space into eight subspaces, and each of these subspaces may either be filled with (opaque) solid matter, or be empty of it. Illustrated here are the four unique configurations in which exactly three planar surfaces meet at a vertex. In each instance, the numbering of the vertex reflects the number of subspaces occupied by (opaque) solid matter. (After [Huffman 1971].)

configurations in which noncotangent labeled lines may meet at a common point in a line drawing. His derivation begins with the observation that there are four basic ways in which three planar surfaces may come together to form a vertex. The four basic configurations of three planar surfaces at a vertex are illustrated in Figure 4.6; although the planes in the figure are shown to be mutually orthogonal, the mutual orthogonality of the planes is not necessary for the argument. Note that three independently oriented planes divide space into eight subspaces; the vertex numbering in Figure 4.6 reflects the number of these subspaces that are occupied by solid matter. Now, each vertex can be viewed from any of the eight subspaces that remain unoccupied. Within each such unoccupied subspace, the appearance of the vertex in the line drawing remains the same with respect to the number, the labels, and the configuration ("V," "W," or "Y") of the lines forming the vertex. Figure 4.7 illustrates all possible distinct appearances of the vertices shown in Figure 4.6. In any line drawing, in addition to V-, W-, and Y-

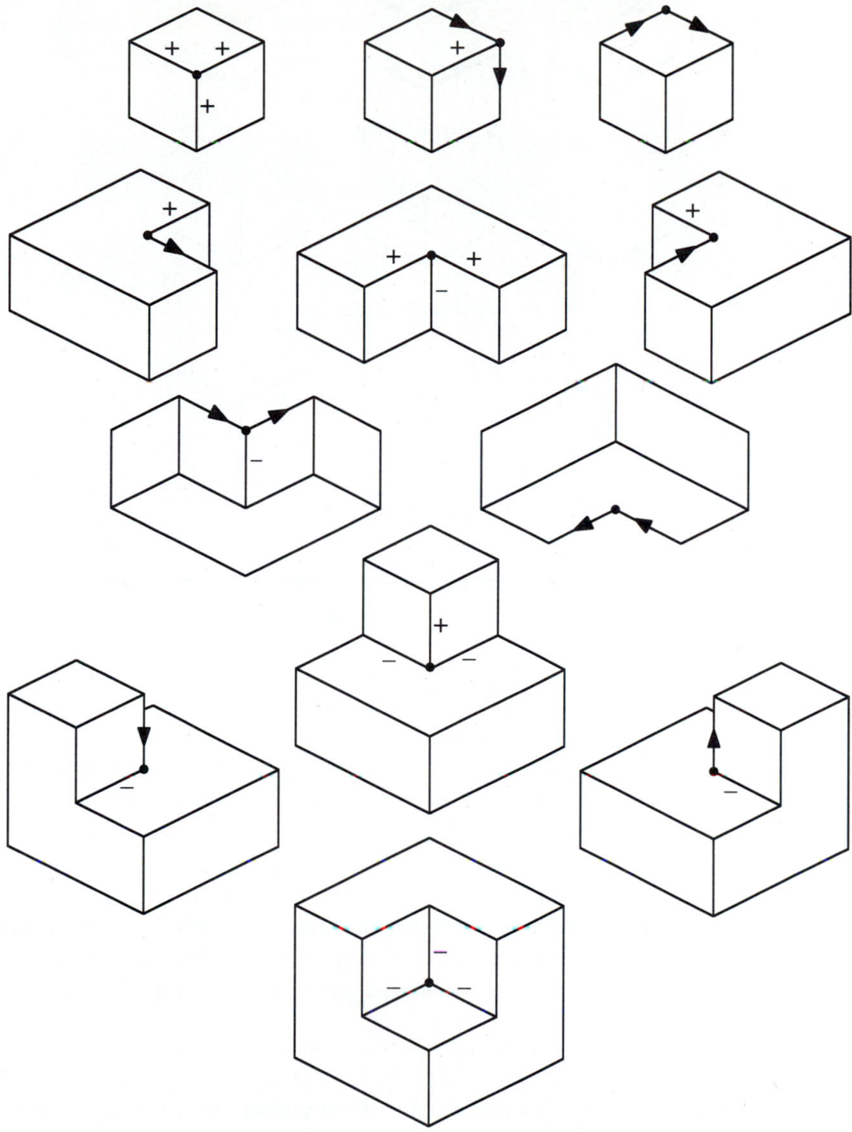

Figure 4.7 All possible distinct appearances of trihedral vertices of polyhedra. Each edge is labeled according to whether it is occluding (↑), nonoccluding convex (+), or concave (–), with the arrow along an occluding edge oriented such that the occluding surface is to the right of the arrow. This catalog of all possible distinct appearances of trihedral vertices of polyhedra is derived from Figure 4.6 by considering the appearance of each numbered vertex from within each of the unoccupied subspaces adjoining the vertex. (After [Huffman 1971].)

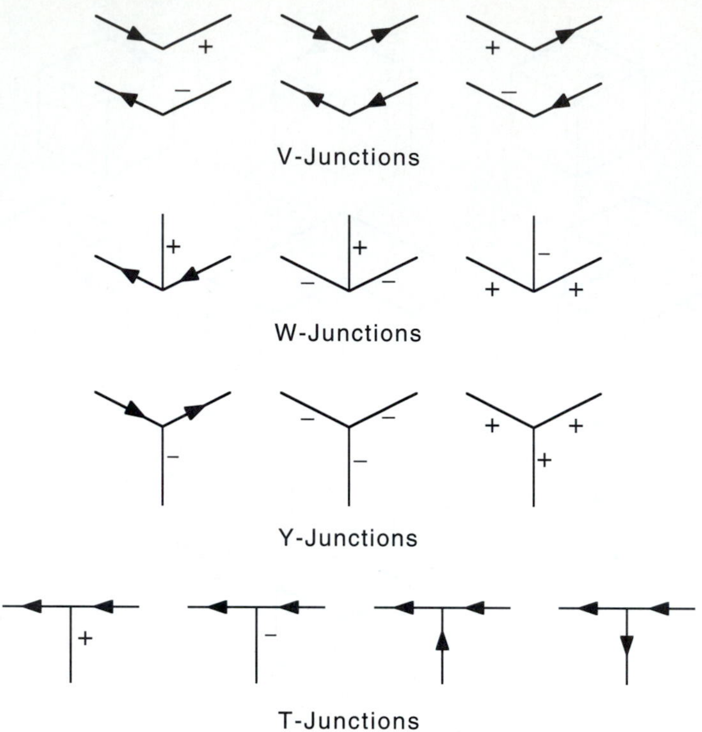

Figure 4.8 The complete junction catalog for line drawings of trihedral-vertex polyhedra: V-junctions, W-junctions, Y-junctions, and T-junctions. Each junction is named after its shape. In line drawings of polyhedra, the term *junction* denotes the meeting of two or more noncotangent lines; when nonpolyhedral objects are included, the term *junction* in addition denotes the meeting of cotangent lines that have different curvatures. The illustrated junction catalog derives its power from its number of entries being a very small fraction of the total number of combinatorially possible ways in which the variously shaped junctions could be labeled. (After [Huffman 1971].)

junctions, another type of junction, the **T-junction**, is also possible—this junction is formed by the partial occlusion of an edge by an occluding edge. The complete catalog of labeled junctions is illustrated in Figure 4.8. Note that simple combinatorics would suggest a much larger junction dictionary; for instance, any particular junction formed by three lines, each line with four labeling possibilities (nonoccluding convex, concave, and occluding in one of two senses), can be labeled in $4^3 = 64$ distinct ways.

The stated aim of Huffman's 1971 paper was to gain insights into the problem of line-drawing interpretation by developing a procedure to determine whether a line drawing is physically unrealizable by trihedral-vertex polyhedra—that is, whether the represented object is impossible (in the domain of trihedral-vertex polyhedra). Huffman made no attempt to derive any quantitative results. Clearly, a necessary condition for a line drawing to be physically realizable is that we be able to label the drawing's junctions on the basis of the preceding dictionary without assigning different labels to the two ends of any straight-line segment. Note, however, that multiple consistent labelings are not ruled out. As the set of all consistent labelings of a line drawing encompasses all the possible valid interpretations of the line drawing—while this set is a small subset of the set of all the combinatorially possible labelings of the line drawing—several strategies have been proposed in the literature to derive the consistent labelings of a line drawing (e.g., [Waltz 1975]). We shall not delve into these strategies here.

Figure 4.9(a) from [Huffman 1971] illustrates a line drawing for which no consistent labeling is possible. Although consistent labeling is necessary, as noted by Huffman, it is not sufficient to guarantee a physically realizable scene. Figure 4.9(b) illustrates a consistently labeled impossible polyhedron, the so-called Penrose triangle. (Although the Penrose triangle is generally attributed to Penrose and Penrose [Penrose and Penrose 1958]—and this explains its name—this impossible polyhedron appears to have been conceived independently much earlier, in 1934, by Oscar Reutersvärd (see [Ernst 1986]).) It is also worth noting here that it might be possible to assign to a line drawing of a realizable scene labels that are consistent with the junction catalog but are physically unrealizable. An example of such a labeling is provided in Figure 4.9(c). Although Huffman did derive additional necessary conditions, over and above consistent labeling, for the physical realizability of a line drawing, he was unable to provide sufficient conditions. As noted by Mackworth [Mackworth 1977], the basic deficiency of the consistent-labeling approach is that it enforces only the qualitative constraint that each edge be either exclusively nonoccluding convex, exclusively concave, or exclusively occluding in one of two senses: In particular, the line-labeling approach does not require that the surfaces be planar. Observe that the Penrose triangle shown in Figure 4.9(b) is physically realizable, with its assigned labels, if we allow nonplanar surfaces.

It is not intended to discuss at length the large body of additional work devoted to the labeling of line drawings of polygonal planar surfaces. Instead, you are provided with a flavor of the literature and appropriate references. Huffman's junction dictionary was independently arrived at by Clowes [Clowes 1971]. This work was followed by a series of articles

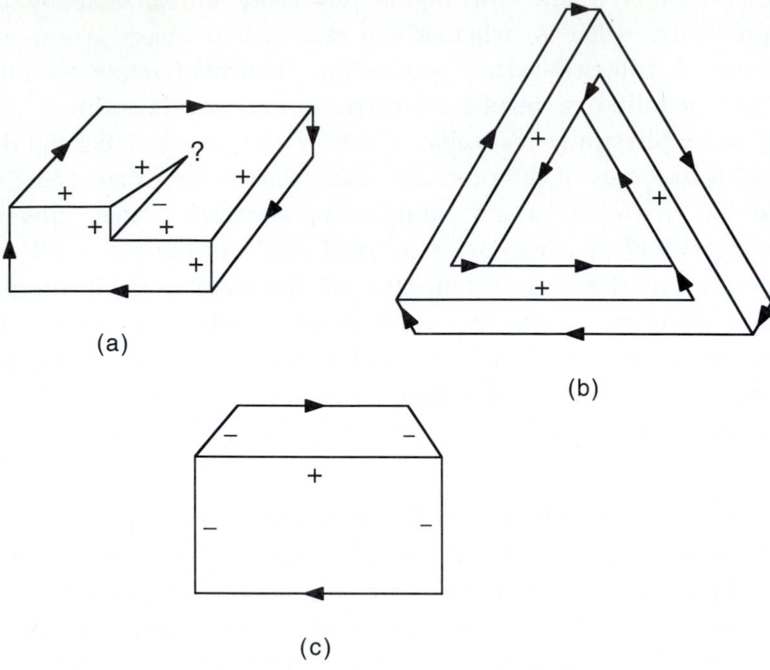

Figure 4.9 Physical realizability of a line drawing by trihedral-vertex polyhedra. For a line drawing comprising straight-line segments to be physically realizable by trihedral-vertex polyhedra, it is necessary, but not sufficient, that it be possible to assign to each straight-line segment in the line drawing a single label (from among +, −, and ↑) such that the line labels across every junction are consistent with the junction catalog for trihedral-vertex polyhedra illustrated in Figure 4.8. **(a)** A line drawing with no consistent labeling (after [Huffman 1971]). **(b)** A consistent labeling of a line drawing of an impossible polyhedron (after [Huffman 1971]). **(c)** A physically realizable line drawing with a consistent labeling that cannot be realized by any polyhedron (after [Mackworth 1977]).

attempting to extend it in various directions. Waltz [Waltz 1975] extended the Huffman–Clowes labeling set to include shadow boundaries and cracks, and, in addition, proposed three illumination categories for regions adjoining each edge: illuminated region, projected-shadow region, and region facing away from light source. A single point-light-source was assumed. Mackworth [Mackworth 1973] adapted an idea of Huffman [Huffman 1971] to propose the so-called gradient space for the analysis of orthographically projected line drawings of polyhedral objects; the restriction to trihedral vertices was removed, and various necessary conditions for the validity of a line drawing were derived. (The gradient space, described at length in Section 5.1.1, is simply a device to represent surface-normal orientations.)

The investigations of Huffman [Huffman 1971], Clowes [Clowes 1971], Waltz [Waltz 1975], and Mackworth [Mackworth 1973], and also those preceding the Huffman–Clowes formulation, are all discussed succinctly by Mackworth in [Mackworth 1977]. Huffman ([Huffman 1977a], [Huffman 1977b]) went on to propose the use of a so-called dual space to remove the trihedral-vertex assumption from his earlier work [Huffman 1971]; orthographic projection was assumed, and once again, a necessary but insufficient condition was derived. Draper [Draper 1981] provides a detailed critique of Mackworth's gradient-space approach and Huffman's dual-space approach, and also a demonstration of their validity under perspective projection; he goes on to propose an alternative technique, called *sidedness reasoning*, that is valid under both orthographic and perspective projection. Kanade [Kanade 1980] extended Huffman's junction dictionary to allow for polygonal planar surfaces that are configured such that no more than three surfaces of different orientations meet at any vertex, and no more than three edges of different orientations are involved at any vertex; orthographic projection was assumed; also, a general viewpoint was assumed implicitly. Kanade's domain, termed the *origami world* after the Japanese art of paper folding, is a superset of the Huffman–Clowes domain as the planar surfaces are not assumed to bound polyhedra. Finally, work on domains comprising both polygonal-planar surfaces and polyhedra seems to have been brought to a halt by Sugihara [Sugihara 1984], who showed that the existence of a solution to a particular set of algebraic equalities and inequalities is both necessary and sufficient for a labeled line drawing to represent a valid scene under orthographic projection. Such an approach to determining the physical realizability of a line drawing, we might argue, as Huffman argued earlier in a broader context, provides "an exceptionally weak claim since it is equivalent to saying that a picture is realizable if and only if it is possible to determine locations of planes in the scene that intersect and obscure each other in ways that yield the lines of the given picture" (pp. 508–509, [Huffman 1977b]).

4.1.2 Nonlabeling Constraints

Labels of lines in a line drawing provide only one class of qualitative constraints on the viewed three-dimensional scene—for example, the convexity or the concavity of a polyhedron along each of its visible edges. Of course, labels are not the only constraints that can be deduced from a line drawing. Although most of the work in line-drawing interpretation has been dedicated to line labeling, there have been a few other approaches. We shall discuss one of these approaches here, and several others in Section 4.2.2 in the context of nonplanar surfaces.

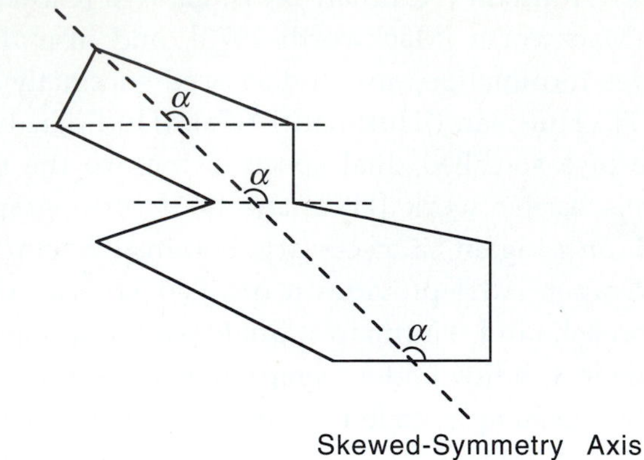

Figure 4.10 Skewed symmetry. A *skewed symmetric figure* is a planar figure that exhibits pointwise symmetry at a fixed angle α about some axis, called the *axis of skewed symmetry* of the figure. In other words, in a skewed symmetric figure, every straight line that is oriented at an angle α with respect to the axis of skewed symmetry intersects the figure equidistantly on either side of the axis. If α is a right angle, the figure is said to exhibit *bilateral* or *mirror symmetry*. A planar figure that is bilaterally symmetric exhibits skewed symmetry under orthographic projection.

Kanade [Kanade 1981] proposed two heuristics to interpret line drawings of his polygonal-planar-surface world described in the Section 4.1.1. Once again, orthographic projection and a general viewpoint were assumed. The first heuristic suggests that parallel lines in a line drawing be interpreted as projections of parallel lines in space. This heuristic is actually a constraint under the general-viewpoint assumption in the sense that the inference it draws from an observation is both necessary and sufficient to produce the observation. As pointed out by Kanade, it fails only for viewing directions confined to a single plane, and such a confinement is disallowed under general viewpoint. The second heuristic by Kanade suggests that a skewed symmetry in a line drawing be interpreted as the projection of a bilateral symmetry in space. A **skewed symmetry**, as illustrated in Figure 4.10, is the pointwise symmetry of a two-dimensional planar figure at some fixed angle about an axis. When this fixed angle is a right angle, we have bilateral (mirror) symmetry. For the skewed-symmetry heuristic to be an actual constraint—that is, for the inference it draws to be not only sufficient to produce the observation, but also necessary—Kanade's world must exclude all skewed symmetric figures. This exclusion is necessary because both skewed symmetric and bilaterally symmetric figures exhibit skewed symmetry under orthographic projection. Such a restriction on the domain is fairly limiting; this restriction excludes, for instance, all nonisosceles triangles.

4.2 Nonplanar Surfaces

As might be expected, the tools, techniques, and results developed for polygonal planar surfaces are not directly applicable to nonplanar surfaces. In his pioneering work on polyhedral objects, Huffman [Huffman 1971] presented some preliminary thoughts on the appearance of junctions in line drawings of some simple smooth nonplanar surfaces. He introduced a new label for limbs (i.e., continuous–surface-normal depth discontinuities), and expanded the junction dictionary to include cusps formed by cotangent lines. Unfortunately, Huffman's observations were quite informal in nature, and although he promised a more detailed paper, he never delivered one.

Let us begin here by familiarizing ourselves with some basic terminology from differential geometry. See the delightful book by Hilbert and Cohn-Vossen, *Geometry and the Imagination* [Hilbert and Cohn-Vossen 1952], for a lucid conceptual introduction to differential geometry, and see the book by Lipschutz [Lipschutz 1969] for a concise analytical treatment. A scalar- or vector-valued function is said to be $\mathbf{C}^n$ if it is n **times continuously differentiable**—that is, if all its first- through nth-order derivatives exist and are continuous. Functions that are just continuous are denoted by C^0, and functions whose derivatives of all orders exist are denoted by C^∞. Note that, as a differentiable function must necessarily be continuous, the existence of all the mth-order derivatives of a function implies the existence of, and the continuity of, all its $(m-1)$th-order derivatives. A scalar- or vector-valued function is said to exhibit an n**th-order discontinuity** if it exhibits a discontinuity in any of its nth-order derivatives.

Surfaces that are C^2—that is, twice continuously differentiable—are of particular interest to us. All points on such surfaces belong to one of four classes: elliptic, hyperbolic, parabolic, or planar. These four types of points are illustrated in Figure 4.11. Loosely speaking, an **elliptic point** is one where the surface is locally cup-shaped—that is, it is curved the same way (either convexly or concavely) in every direction. A **hyperbolic point** is one where the surface is locally saddle-shaped—that is, it is curved one way in some directions and the other way in others. A **parabolic point** is one where the surface has a locally conical nature in that it is not at all curved in one direction, but is curved (one way) in every other. And a **planar point** is one where the surface is locally flat—that is, it is not curved in any direction.

A surface that comprises only parabolic points is called a **developable surface**. Such a surface has the notable property that we can construct it by bending a planar surface without stretching that surface. Every developable surface must be either a cylinder, a cone, or a tangent surface of a space

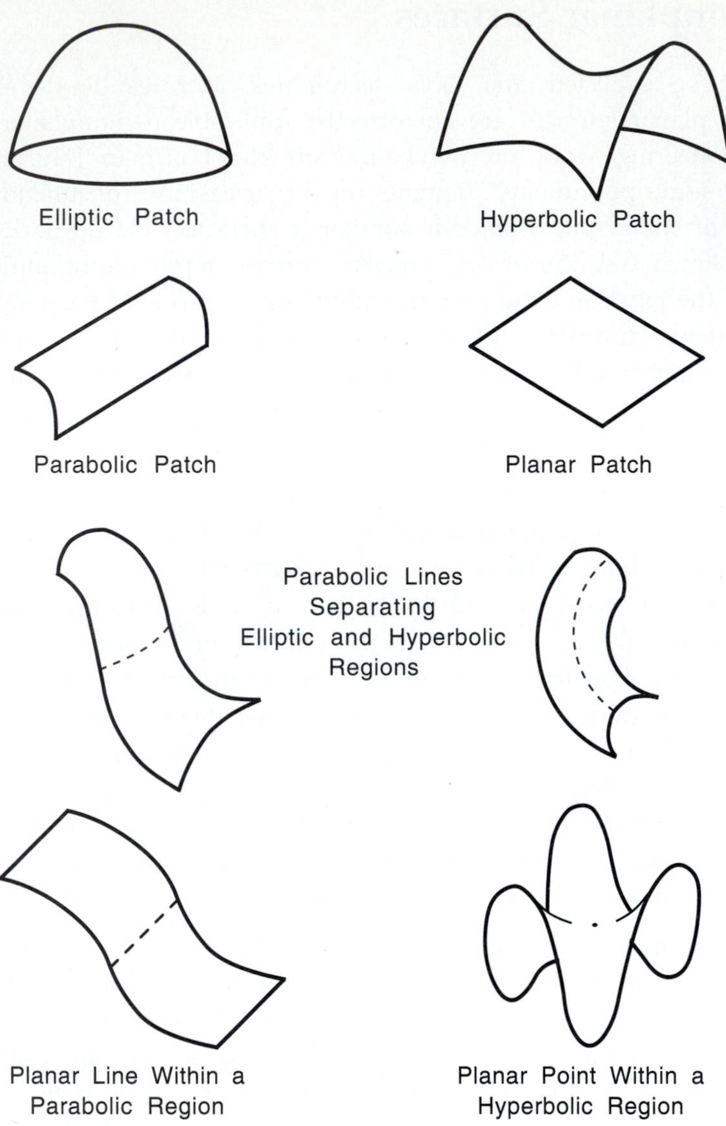

Figure 4.11 Elliptic, hyperbolic, parabolic, and planar points illustrated on a variety of surfaces. At an *elliptic point*, the surface is locally cup-shaped; at a *hyperbolic point*, it is locally saddle-shaped; at a *parabolic point*, it is locally cylindrical; at a *planar point*, it is locally planar. Elliptic, hyperbolic, parabolic, and planar patches are surfaces that respectively comprise elliptic, hyperbolic, parabolic, and planar points; parabolic and planar lines are lines that respectively comprise parabolic and planar points. From top to bottom, left to right, the surfaces illustrated may be characterized as parts of an egg, a saddle, a cylinder, a plane, a bell, a torus, a children's slide, and finally, the most interesting monkey saddle, which gets its name from its ability to accommodate a monkey's tail.

curve. A **cylinder** is a surface that is swept by a straight line as the line moves along a space curve while the line maintains its orientation. For instance, a straight line that moves along a circle, while the line remains orthogonal to the plane of the circle, sweeps out a *circular cylinder*. A **cone** is a surface that is swept by a straight line as the line moves along a space curve while the line continues to pass through a fixed point in space, called the *vertex* of the cone. For instance, a straight line that moves along a circle, while the line continues to pass through some fixed point that is equidistant from all the points on the circle, sweeps out a *circular cone*; every nondegenerate planar cross-section of a circular cone, called a *conic section*, is either an ellipse, a hyperbola, or a parabola. The **tangent surface** of a space curve is the surface swept by the tangent to the curve. A plane, which itself is not developable, is a degenerate instance of each of the three types of developable surfaces. Developable surfaces belong to a larger class of surfaces, called *ruled surfaces*. At every point on a **ruled surface**, it is possible to draw a straight line, or *ruling*, on the surface. There exist ruled surfaces that are not developable—for instance, the hyperboloid of one sheet illustrated in Figure 4.1 (can you show that this surface is ruled?).

As we did for polygonal planar surfaces, let us first look at the line-labeling work in the tradition of Huffman [Huffman 1971], and then at some of the nonlabeling work. Nonlabeling approaches have received greater attention in the case of nonplanar surfaces than they have for planar surfaces, perhaps owing to the relative richness of the domain of nonplanar surfaces.

4.2.1 Line Labeling

As Huffman [Huffman 1971] noted, the critical difference between labeling line drawings of planar and nonplanar surfaces is that, for nonplanar surfaces, a line need not have the same label along its entire length. Turner [Turner 1974] attempted to extend the Huffman–Clowes–Waltz junction dictionary for trihedral-vertex polyhedra to opaque solids with "smooth" faces, each face solely comprising either planar, parabolic, hyperbolic, or elliptic points, and further bounded by discontinuous–surface-normal edges. A general viewpoint was assumed, and shadow boundaries were allowed. In addition, several other assumptions about the viewpoint, background, illumination, and corners were made. Unlike Huffman's junction catalog for trihedral vertices, it is unclear whether Turner's catalog is complete for its domain. Since his pioneering work, Huffman [Huffman 1976] has examined the behavior of developable surfaces near creases and apices of cones, which he claims are natural generalizations of edges and vertices of piecewise planar surfaces, respectively. Other authors ([Shapira and Freeman 1978], [Chakravarty 1979], [Lee, Haralick, and Zhang 1985]) have attempted to categorize junctions for scenes comprising opaque solids with quadric and planar faces, each face bounded by discontinuous–surface-normal edges. It is assumed here that every vertex in the scene is at the intersection of exactly three edges, the viewpoint is general, and that no limb passes through a vertex. Further, surface-reflectance and illumination discontinuities are disallowed. See [Malik 1987] for a detailed critique of this and related work.

Malik [Malik 1987] attempts a systematic derivation of a junction catalog for scenes comprising opaque solids bounded by C^3 surface patches, each patch bounded by discontinuous–surface-normal edges. He bases his analysis on tangent-plane approximations to the faces of an object where these faces touch a vertex of the object, then applying the techniques developed for polyhedra by Huffman [Huffman 1971] and by Mackworth [Mackworth 1973]. For Malik's approach to succeed, it is important that every surface patch (bounded by discontinuous–surface-normal edges) have a unique tangent plane at a vertex, a characteristic not true at apices of cones, which are disallowed by Malik's domain. Orthographic projection and a general viewpoint are assumed by Malik, and surface-reflectance and illumination discontinuities are disallowed. Further, as the results of Whitney [Whitney 1955] described in Appendix A4.1 at the end of the chapter are invoked, Malik also assumes implicitly that the configuration of the line drawing is stable under perturbation of the projected surface. However, as we shall see, this last assumption is unnecessary.

4.2.2 Nonlabeling Constraints

As in the case of polygonal planar surfaces, constraints other than line labeling have also been sought for less restricted domains. Binford [Binford 1981] presented a series of assumptions that he argued should be invoked in the absence of evidence to the contrary. Some of these assumptions are unstated assumptions in previous treatments. Three typical examples of his assumptions follow:

1. At a T-junction—that is, at a junction where a line (the stem) terminates on a noncotangent C^1 line (the top)—the stem is no nearer than the top. In other words, the stem of a T-junction is either at the same distance as the top, or it is farther away than the top.
2. Scene curves that project onto noncotangent lines meeting at junctions other than T-junctions are concurrent in space—that is, they meet at a common point in space.
3. A junction formed by two cotangent lines (which Binford implicitly assumes have different curvatures at the junction) is the projection of a limb touching a discontinuous–surface-normal edge in space.

All Binford's assumptions hinge on the general-viewpoint assumption. In addition, Binford assumes a **general source position**; that is, he assumes that the perturbation of the illumination sources would not affect the configuration of the line drawing. Binford uses the latter assumption to derive constraints that are based on the boundaries of cast shadows. Binford's work was subsequently extended by Lowe and Binford [Lowe and Binford 1985], who list numerous three-dimensional inferences that can be drawn from two-dimensional line drawings. Examples of these inferences are provided in Figure 4.12. The strength of each inference depends inversely on the size of the locus of camera viewpoints—and of illumination-source positions, if relevant—under which the inference is violated, in comparison to the full range of camera viewpoints (or of illumination-source positions). The work of Binford and Lowe does not explicitly list any restrictions on the nature of the allowed scene.

The importance of T-junctions in images has long been recognized. As far back as 1866, Helmholtz had observed that an occluding edge in an image has a continuous tangent where it meets an occluded edge, and that this observation "will generally enable us to decide which is which" (see pp. 283–284, [Helmholtz 1910], English translation). Since then, several authors have claimed that a T-junction implies the occlusion in space of the junction's stem by its top. Whereas this claim is valid for Huffman's trihedral-vertex polyhedral domain, it is not valid in general. The T-junction assumption of Binford described previously—namely, that the stem of a T-junction is either as far away as the top (and hence, unoccluded), or farther away than the top (and hence, occluded)—is different from and more accurate than this claim.

Most of the work discussed thus far has sought to impose, with varying success, necessary and sufficient geometric constraints on the scene based on its line drawing. In a different spirit, some authors (e.g., [Barrow and Tenenbaum 1981b], [Brady and Yuille 1984]) have proposed the extremization of certain heuristic functions as a method of quantitative surface recovery. These attempts have been characterized by their search for global principles applicable to arbitrary environments, and their resort to psychological justification. One typical attempt [Brady and Yuille 1984] recommends that a closed contour be interpreted as the planar surface whose ratio of area to square of perimeter is maximum. The justification for this criterion is provided in part by the claim that humans interpret ellipses as tilted circular discs; further, the authors show that this criterion leads to the interpretation of skewed symmetries as planar bilateral symmetries. Recourse to heuristics may indeed be necessary to duplicate human performance. However, in the view of this author, heuristics should be resorted to only near the exhaustion of mathematical constraints—a situation that is remote at present.

Inference Under General Viewpoint	Violation
 Collinearity in 2-D ⇒ Collinearity in 3-D	Collinear points in 2-D are coplanar in 3-D, and are viewed from within common plane.
 Common termination of two or more noncotangent lines in 2-D ⇒ Common termination in 3-D	Common terminations in 2-D are collinear in 3-D, and are viewed from along common straight line.
 Common intersection of three or more noncotangent straight lines (perhaps virtual) in 2-D ⇒ Common intersection in 3-D (perhaps at ∞)	Points along the straight lines (perhaps virtual) at common intersection in 2-D are collinear in 3-D, and are viewed from along common straight line.
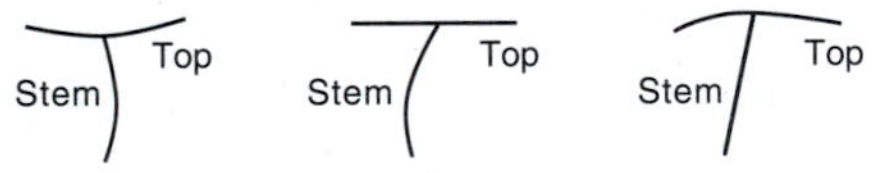 Stem Top Stem Top Stem Top *T-Junctions* Termination in 2-D of one line (*stem*) at another noncotangent line with a continuous tangent (*top*) ⇒ Stem is no closer than the top in 3-D	Points of contact in 2-D are viewed from along a straight line in 3-D that passes through the termination of the stem and a point on the top, all such 3-D lines constituting a cone (or a plane).

Figure 4.12 Inferences that can be drawn from particular line-drawing configurations under the assumption of a general viewpoint. In the figure, 2-D and 3-D refer to two and three dimensions, respectively. The strength of an inference depends inversely on the size of the set of viewpoints under which the inference may be violated. Although the inferences described in the figure are valid for both viewpoint-independent and viewpoint-dependent edges, they are much more difficult to establish when viewpoint-dependent edges are included (e.g., [Nalwa 1988a], [Nalwa 1988b]). A *viewpoint-independent edge* is an edge whose location in three-dimensional space *does not* depend on the viewpoint—for instance, a surface-normal discontinuity. A *viewpoint-dependent edge* is an edge whose location in three-dimensional space *does* depend on the viewpoint—for instance, a depth discontinuity in space across which the surface normal varies continuously (see Figure 3.3). (After [Binford 1981] and [Lowe and Binford 1985].)

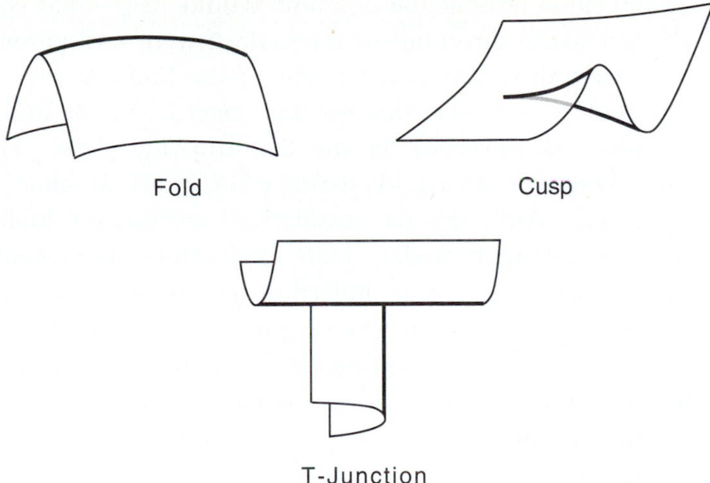

Figure 4.13 The canonical singularities of the projection of a C^3 (i.e., thrice continuously differentiable) surface under general viewpoint: fold, cusp, and T-junction. The projection of a surface is said to be *singular* wherever the projection direction is tangent to the surface; then, the *canonical singularities* of the projection of a surface are the simplest surface configurations and their projections to which all instances of singular projection can be reduced without any loss of generality. At a *fold*, the surface folds over to form a continuous-surface-normal depth discontinuity—*limb*, for short. At a *cusp*, the projection of the limb would cusp—that is, it would undergo a 180° reversal in direction—if the surface were transparent: For an opaque surface, however, only one branch of the cusp is visible in the line drawing, and this branch just terminates freely. Note that it is only the projection of a limb that may cusp, and not the limb itself in space. At a *T-junction*, an opaque fold partially occludes another fold.

In an influential paper, Koenderink and van Doorn [Koenderink and van Doorn 1976] apply certain powerful results from differential topology to line-drawing interpretation. Unlike other work discussed here, their work assumes a mobile observer (camera). Further, as their work is based on Whitney's results [Whitney 1955] (see Appendix A4.1), it concerns itself only with the interior of C^3 surface patches and assumes that the configuration of the line drawing is stable under perturbation of both the viewpoint and the projected surface. The requirement of stability under perturbation of the viewed surface, which is awkward owing to its difficulty of verification, is, as we shall soon see, unnecessary. The authors suggest that the topological structure of limbs in line drawings be described with respect to convex and concave *folds*, *cusps*, and T-junctions. As illustrated in Figure 4.13, **folds** are the interiors of limbs—places where the surface folds over with respect to the observer—and **cusps** are the nonjunction terminations of limbs. The line drawing at a nonjunction termination of a limb would cusp—that is, it would undergo a 180° reversal in direction—if the surface were transparent. Cusps occur where the viewing direction is tangent to the limb on the surface in space. It is important to note here that the limb itself is smooth and does not cusp in space; only its projection in the line drawing does. Finally, **T-junctions** occur whenever one fold partially occludes another. Opaque surfaces are assumed. Although the qualitative structure of limbs in line drawings is usually invariant under small exploratory movements of the viewpoint, on occasion cusps and inflection points may be created or annihilated. Koenderink and van Doorn provide an inventory of such "events," which they show to reveal second-order properties of the surface local to the limbs. Although the authors assume orthographic projection in their analysis, they claim that similar arguments could be provided for perspective projection.

In two related papers directed toward an audience of perceptual psychologists, Koenderink and van Doorn ([Koenderink and van Doorn 1982], [Koenderink 1984b]) elaborate on some of the ideas contained within [Koenderink and van Doorn 1976]. In particular, they show that a surface is elliptic wherever its limb in a line drawing is convex with respect to the object, hyperbolic wherever its limb is concave, and parabolic wherever the curvature of its limb is zero [Koenderink 1984b]; both orthographic and perspective projection are considered. Figure 4.14 illustrates this result. The figure also illustrates that nonjunction terminations of limbs in line drawings are always concave with respect to the object [Koenderink and van Doorn 1982]; in other words, cusps may occur in line drawings only within hyperbolic surface regions.

In a paper similar in spirit to Koenderink and van Doorn's work, Nalwa [Nalwa 1988a] seeks to establish a mathematical framework for line-drawing interpretation under the following assumptions: The imaging geometry is well approximated by perspective or orthographic projection, the viewpoint is general, the world comprises opaque piecewise C^3 surfaces, and finally, continuous-surface-normal depth discontinuities are the only viewpoint-dependent edges. A **piecewise C^3 surface** is defined to comprise finitely many compact C^3 patches, each patch extendible to a C^3 surface and bounded by a finite curve comprising finitely many C^3 segments—these segments are neither required to be viewpoint-independent edges, nor required to be known a priori. Nalwa's domain encompasses all previously invoked (or implicitly assumed) domains. Further, this domain allows all viewpoint-independent edges, including shadow boundaries and surface markings. Within the proposed framework, Nalwa establishes that

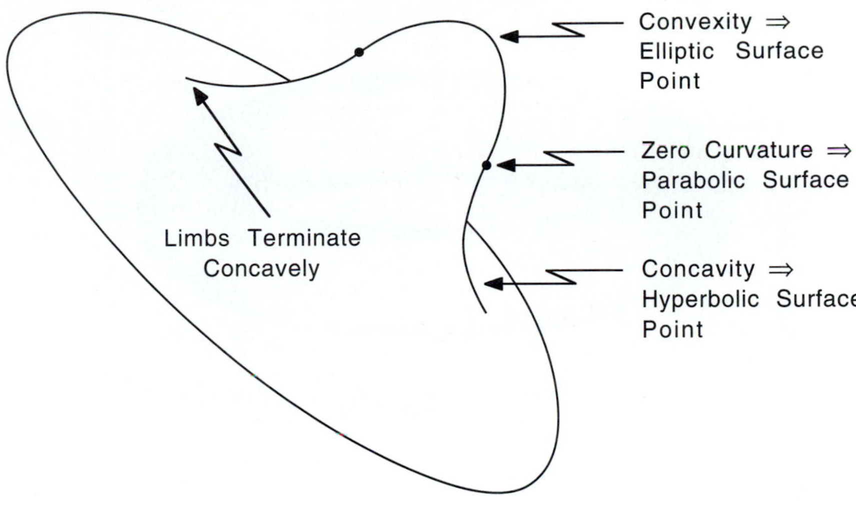

Figure 4.14 The qualitative relationship between the curvature of a limb in a line drawing and the shape of the surface in the vicinity of the limb in space. A C^3 surface is elliptic in space wherever its limb in a line drawing is convex with respect to the object; it is hyperbolic, wherever its limb is concave; it is parabolic, wherever the curvature of its limb is zero. The figure illustrates these assertions with a bell-shaped protrusion from a surface. The figure also illustrates that nonjunction terminations of limbs in line drawings of C^3 surfaces are always concave with respect to the object, which is equivalent to the assertion that cusp singularities of projection can occur only within hyperbolic surface regions. (After [Koenderink 1984b] and [Koenderink and van Doorn 1982].)

orthographic and perspective projections of piecewise C^3 surfaces are excellent mappings in the sense of Whitney [Whitney 1955] explained in Appendix A4.1 at the end of the chapter. The physical significance of this result is that every local singularity of the projection of a C^3 surface belongs to one of two canonical classes: folds and cusps. By a *singularity of projection* is meant an instance of projection in which the direction of projection is tangent to at least one surface in space, and by a *local* singularity of projection is meant an instance in which the direction of projection is tangent to a single surface at a single location. Both folds and cusps were described earlier in this section. The excellent-mapping result is of fundamental importance. It rules out, for instance, the possibility (under general viewpoint) of viewing a planar point from within its plane, or of viewing a parabolic point from along its axis of zero curvature. It is the singularities of projection that constitute the class of viewpoint-dependent edges that we are

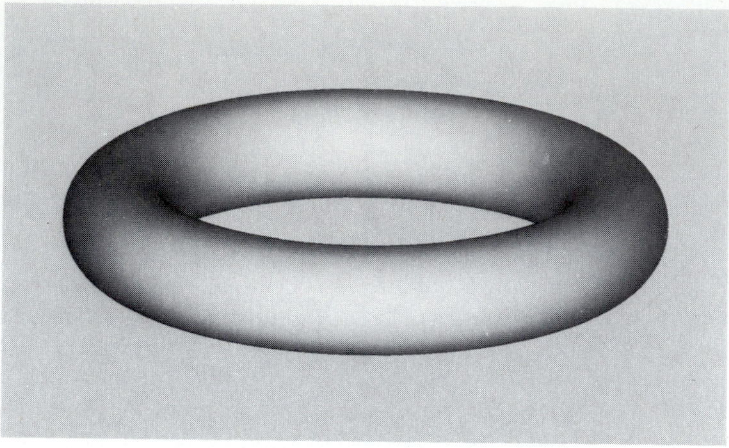

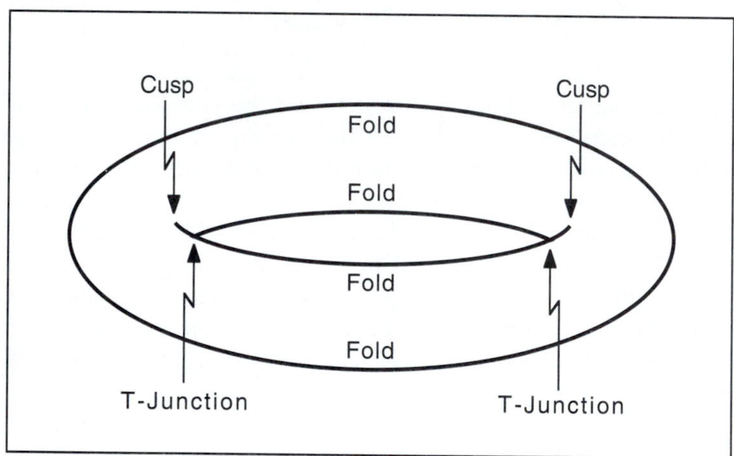

Figure 4.15 Oblique view of a torus exhibiting folds, cusps, and T-junctions. Folds, cusps, and T-junctions are the canonical singularities of the projection of a C^3 surface under general viewpoint (see Figure 4.13). A *torus* is a (doughnut-shaped) surface that we can generate by revolving a circle about a straight line that lies within the plane of the circle but that does not intersect the circle. In the figure, a synthetic image of a torus is shown above its line drawing.

considering here. The loci of the instances of singular projection in a line drawing are C^3 curves, these curves possibly with cusps whose only one branch is visible—assuming that the cusp is otherwise unoccluded. In addition to the two canonical local singularities, there is also the T-junction, which is formed by the partial occlusion of one fold by another fold. All three types of singularities are illustrated in Figure 4.15, which shows an oblique view of a torus along with its line drawing. The excellent-mapping

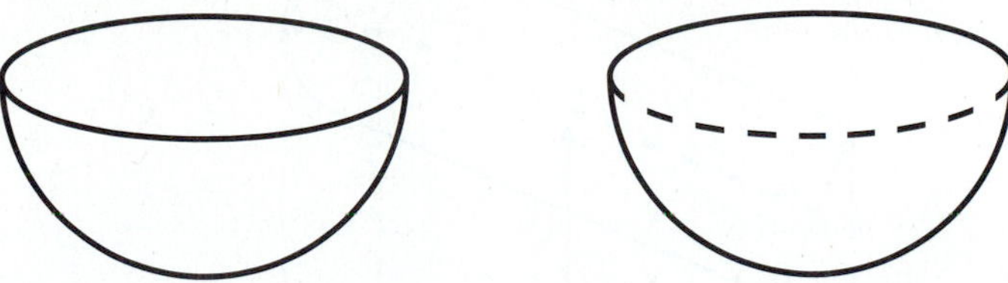

Figure 4.16 Two views of a hemisphere illustrating two types of nonocclusion junctions that can be formed between viewpoint-independent and viewpoint-dependent edges in a line drawing. At every nonocclusion junction of viewpoint-independent and viewpoint-dependent edges in a line drawing of a piecewise C^3 surface that is viewed under general viewpoint, the viewpoint-independent edge and the viewpoint-dependent edge are cotangent at the junction, but they have different curvatures there. Loosely speaking, a *piecewise C^3 surface* is a surface that can be divided into a finite number of surface patches, each of which is C^3 (i.e., thrice continuously differentiable) in its interior. A *nonocclusion junction* between edges in a line drawing is a junction that is not caused by the partial occlusion in space of an edge by the surface adjoining another edge—all junctions due to occlusion appear as T-junctions in the line drawing. Recall that a viewpoint-independent edge in a line drawing is an edge whose location in three-dimensional space is independent of the viewpoint, and that a viewpoint-dependent edge in a line drawing is an edge whose location in three-dimensional space depends on the viewpoint. Here, as elsewhere in this book, the only viewpoint-dependent edges that we are considering are limbs, which are are depth discontinuities in three-dimensional space across which the surface normal varies continuously.

result just described makes all of Koenderink and van Doorn's work on line-drawing interpretation valid within Nalwa's framework. In particular, this result renders unnecessary the assumption of the stability of the line drawing under perturbation of the viewed surface, an assumption that is unverifiable by a remote observer.

Having characterized viewpoint-dependent edges as comprising folds and cusps, Nalwa [Nalwa 1988a] goes on to show that viewpoint-independent and viewpoint-dependent edges in line drawings are always cotangent at their nonocclusion junctions, but have different curvatures there. Figure 4.16 furnishes a straightforward illustration of this assertion; see Figure 4.1 for a more contrived example. Although similar observations had been made before, this work seems the first to provide a complete proof. Nalwa claims that every nonocclusion junction involving a viewpoint-dependent edge in a line drawing comprises either two or three cotangent lines—no more. Finally, a viewpoint-independent edge in a line drawing is

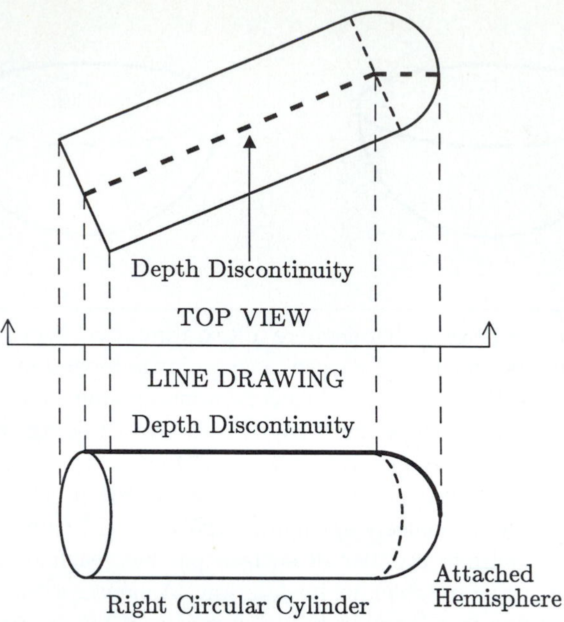

Figure 4.17 The implication of a second-order discontinuity along a limb in a line drawing with regard to the surface on which the limb resides in space. A second-order discontinuity in a curve (or a surface) is a discontinuity in the curvature of the curve (or the surface). A second-order discontinuity along a limb in a line drawing of a piecewise C^3 surface viewed under general viewpoint corresponds to a second-order discontinuity in the surface in space. This correspondence is illustrated here with the line drawing of a circular cylinder that is capped by a hemisphere. The top view of the object is shown in addition to the line drawing to highlight that where the limb exhibits a curvature discontinuity in the line drawing, it exhibits a tangent discontinuity in space, this tangent discontinuity residing at a curvature discontinuity in the surface. (From [Nalwa 1988a] with permission.)

C^3 if and only if the edge is C^3 in space: In particular, first-, second-, and third-order discontinuities in a viewpoint-independent edge in a line drawing correspond to discontinuities of the same order in the edge in space. On the other hand, a viewpoint-dependent edge in a line drawing is C^3 if and only if the surface on which it lies in space is C^3 along the edge: In particular, second- and third-order discontinuities in a viewpoint-dependent edge in a line drawing correspond to discontinuities of the same order in the surface in space; see Figure 4.17 for an illustration of this phenomenon. A noteworthy feature of Nalwa's work is that all results are first derived for orthographic projection, and then extended to perspective projection by the application of a simple projective mapping.

In a related paper, Nalwa [Nalwa 1988b] establishes a few specific results within the preceding mathematical framework. He shows that straight lines and conic sections (i.e., ellipses, hyperbolas, and parabolas) in line drawings are necessarily projections of edges in space that are also straight lines and conic sections, respectively. Such edges are exclusively viewpoint independent or viewpoint dependent all along their lengths. Viewpoint-dependent edges that project onto straight lines can be locally described by developable surfaces (i.e., by cylinders, cones, and tangent surfaces). Viewpoint-dependent edges that project onto conic sections can be locally described by nondevelopable quadric surfaces (i.e., by ellipsoids, hyperboloids, and paraboloids), each such surface with four degrees of freedom. All the results apply to both continuous and fragmented curves. As before, they were first derived for orthographic projection, and then extended to perspective projection by a simple projective mapping. In a sequel, Nalwa [Nalwa 1989a] describes various line-drawing cues whose presence in a bilaterally symmetric (i.e., mirror symmetric) line drawing obtained under orthographic projection indicates that the viewed object is locally a surface of revolution in the neighborhood of the projected edges.

4.3 Discussion

Although line-drawing interpretation is a seductive intellectual pursuit, and, for the most part, a relatively fluent human ability, most of the constraints derived thus far have found limited practical use. This limited usefulness, however, does not imply that the constraints are of no scientific value—only that their practicality remains to be established. The principal hindrance to the application of line-labeling constraints has been the unreliability of edge detection at junctions—the assumption of edgel detectors that the underlying edgel is isolated within the operator's span is clearly violated in the vicinity of junctions. Although this unreliability may conceivably be surmounted in images of polyhedra by the extrapolation of straight lines that best fit the edgel data away from junctions, there is no easy way out in more general settings. For nonplanar surfaces, the accurate localization of free-standing (i.e., nonjunction) terminations of limbs in line drawings is also an issue, as cusps by their very nature "fade" into the surface, as is evident from Figure 4.15. A further impediment to the application of results for nonplanar surfaces is their frequent need for accurate tangents and curvatures. It is worth pointing out here that, to the best of this author's knowledge, none of the work on line-drawing interpretation to this point has addressed in any substantial fashion the issue of the robustness of results to noise.

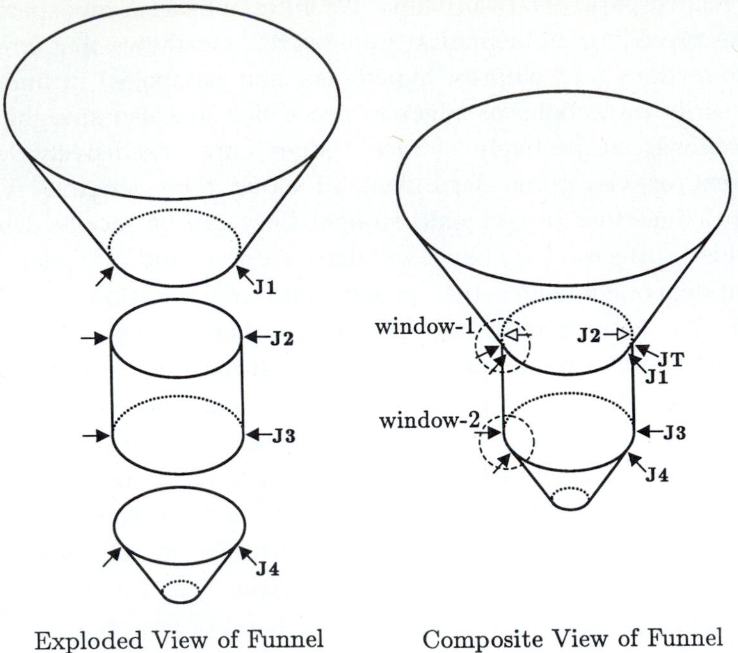

Figure 4.18 Genesis of junctions that are seemingly not due to the partial occlusion of an edge in space, even though these junctions involve noncotangent viewpoint-dependent lines in the line drawing. Nonocclusion junctions involving noncotangent viewpoint-dependent lines are ruled out mathematically in line drawings of piecewise C^3 surfaces viewed under general viewpoint. Whereas, at first sight, the funnel on the right seems to exhibit a nonocclusion junction between noncotangent viewpoint-dependent lines within each of window-1 and window-2, a closer examination of the individual components of the funnel reveals that window-1 contains an occlusion T-junction, and that the lines in window-2 are all cotangent. The actual junctions in the figure are indicated by arrows. (From [Nalwa 1988a] with permission.)

In conclusion, it is instructive to go over an example provided by Nalwa [Nalwa 1988a] that illustrates how the strict satisfaction of a line-drawing result may require a level of resolution that is, for all practical purposes, unaccomplishable. Consider the line drawing of a funnel shown on the right in Figure 4.18. At first sight, it may seem that each of window-1 and window-2 contains a nonocclusion junction comprising one viewpoint-independent edge and two noncotangent viewpoint-dependent edges. This apparent violation of the result that viewpoint-dependent edges may not participate in nonocclusion junctions involving noncotangent lines is a direct consequence of insufficient resolution. To verify this assertion, consider the three quadric surfaces that constitute the funnel. These surfaces are shown on the left in Figure 4.18. Junctions J1, J2, J3, and J4 are easily identified as being formed by cotangent viewpoint-independent and viewpoint-dependent lines. When we bring the three surfaces together, junction J2 is occluded and a new junction is formed by the partial occlusion of the cylinder by the upper cone. In the figure, this T-junction is identified as JT. Junctions J1, J3, and J4 remain visible in the composite view. Thus, it is apparent that window-1, in fact, contains two separate junctions: a nonocclusion junction between a viewpoint-independent edge and a viewpoint-dependent edge, and an occlusion junction between two viewpoint-dependent edges. Window-2, on the other hand, contains two separate nonocclusion junctions, each junction between a viewpoint-independent edge and a viewpoint-dependent edge. Identification of the separate junctions within either of the two windows is clearly rather demanding, making it seem that viewpoint-dependent edges in the line drawing are participating in nonocclusion junctions formed by noncotangent lines.

A4.1 Whitney's Results in the Context of Line Drawings

For those readers with the necessary mathematical background in advanced calculus, it is worth discussing some of the details of Whitney's seminal paper [Whitney 1955]. First, note that if we parameterize a surface s by the coordinates x and y, say $z = s(x, y)$, and the image plane onto which the surface is projected by the coordinates u and v, then we can consider the projection of the surface to be a mapping from the x–y plane onto the u–v plane.

Consider a C^3 mapping f from an open set S in the x–y plane to the u–v plane. The determinant of the **Jacobian** matrix at a point p is, by definition, $J(p) \triangleq u_x v_y - u_y v_x$, where the subscripts denote partial derivatives. We say that p is a **regular point** or a **critical point** according as $J(p) \neq 0$ or $J(p) = 0$, respectively. The image of a critical point is said to be a **critical value**. A point in the u–v plane whose preimage does not contain any critical point is said to be a **regular value**. If $J(p) \neq 0$ or $\nabla J(p) = \sqrt{J_x^2 + J_y^2} \neq 0$ then p is called a **good point**. If every point of S is good then f is said to be **good** in S.

If f is good in S, then it follows from the implicit function theorem (see [Spivak 1965]) that the critical points of f form C^2 curves in S. Such curves are called **general folds** of f. Let f be good and assume a general fold Q through some critical point p. Then p is called a **fold point** if the image of the tangent vector to Q at p is nonzero. It is called a **cusp point** if the image of the tangent vector to Q at p is zero but is becoming nonzero at a nonzero rate as we move away from p on Q. It follows from this definition that cusp points are isolated. If p is a regular, fold, or cusp point, then p is said to be an **excellent point** of f (assumed good). The mapping f is said to be **excellent** if every point of S is excellent—that is, if every critical point of S is either a fold point or a cusp point.

Now, what Whitney [Whitney 1955] establishes is that, arbitrarily near any mapping f_o, there is an excellent mapping f. However, if the two mappings are to have the same topological nature of folds and cusps, then f must approximate not only f_o, but also f_o's partial derivatives of up to third order. Hence, f_o must be at least C^3 if f is to preserve its folds and cusps. It is always possible to choose an analytic f that approximates f_o and f_o's derivatives arbitrarily well. Whitney goes on to describe canonical parameterizations of folds and cusps.

Recall here that f in the current context of line-drawing formation encompasses both the geometry of the surface and that of its projection. In connection with line-drawing interpretation, especially by a mobile observer, you should find the survey of singularities of systems of rays by Arnol'd [Arnol'd 1983] useful.

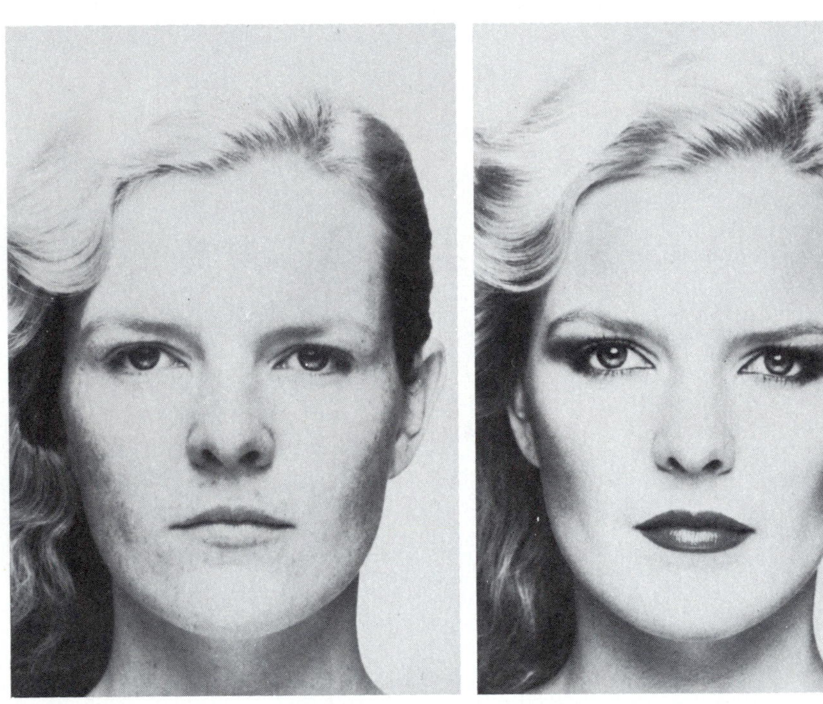

Figure 5.1 Photographs of a model with and without makeup illustrating how the shading of a surface may dramatically affect our perception of the surface's shape. *Shading*—that is, variation in the brightness of a surface—plays an important role in our perception of surface shape. On the left is a photograph of a model without makeup; on the right is a photograph of the same model with makeup. The photographs demonstrate how the skillful application of makeup does more than just alter surface texture: It creates highlights and shadows that manipulate our perception of surface shape. When a surface whose reflective properties are taken to be uniform has these properties altered, the perceived shape of the surface changes [Horn 1975]. (Photographs, courtesy Merle Norman Cosmetics, Bellanca Avenue, Los Angeles.)

Chapter 5

Shading

In Chapter 4, we were concerned with understanding discontinuities in the image intensity. In this chapter, we shall examine shape recovery from continuous intensity variations. Continuous intensity variations are better known as **shading**. We all know well that our perception of the shape of a surface depends on the shading of the surface; facial makeup, for instance, as in Figure 5.1, often exploits this dependence of perceived shape on shading.

Quantitative shape-from-shading methods in computer vision have been developed primarily by Horn and his colleagues. The treatment here will to a large extent be based on [Horn 1977]. A coherent description of this and related work is to be found in [Horn 1986] and [Horn 1990]. The significance of Horn's work, as is true of Huffman's line-drawing analysis [Huffman 1971], lies not so much in its direct practical applicability, or lack of it, but rather in its concern for the science of image formation. Quantitative

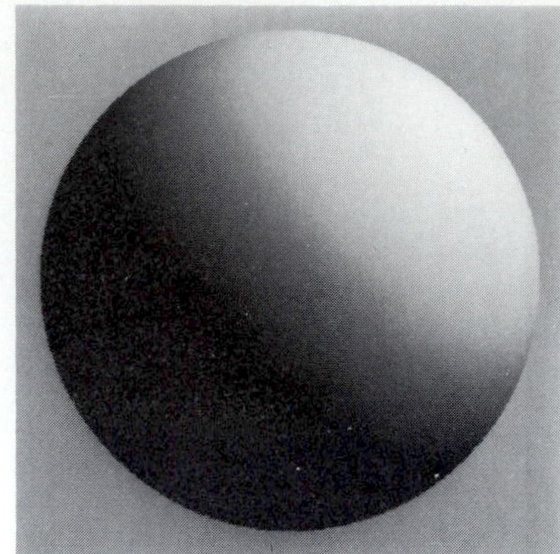

Figure 5.2 Shading as a cue to surface shape. The shading of an image region affects the perceived three-dimensional shape of the region. In contrast to the circular image region on the left, which has a constant intensity and is perceived to be a flat disc, the circular image region on the right has a varying intensity and is perceived to be a sphere. (After [Gibson 1950].)

approaches to shape from shading will be considered first, and then, an interesting qualitative observation by Koenderink and van Doorn [Koenderink and van Doorn 1980] will be described.

The significance of shading as a cue to surface shape is demonstrated easily by Figure 5.2. The circle on the left, which has a uniform intensity in its interior, is perceived to be a flat disc; in contrast, the circle on the right, which has a varying intensity in its interior, is perceived to be a sphere. Although in either case the image contour across which the magnitude of the image brightness changes abruptly is just a circle, in the image on the left, this circle is perceived to be a viewpoint-independent edge, whereas in the image on the right, this circle is perceived to be an apparent contour. (See Chapter 4 for a characterization of edges.)

Although shading is indeed a cue to three-dimensional shape, it is the line drawing of a shaded pattern that seems to play a central role in the interpretation of the shaded pattern by humans [Barrow and Tenenbaum 1981b]. This phenomenon is demonstrated convincingly by Figure 5.3 from [Ramachandran 1988]. Even though both shaded regions in the figure exhibit qualitatively similar variations in intensity (up to a displacement), the upper region is perceived to comprise three cylinders lit from above, whereas the lower region appears to be a corrugated surface lit from one side—either from the left, or from the right, depending on the perceived peaks and

Figure 5.3 The shape of the boundary of a shaded image region as a factor in the three-dimensional interpretation of the region by humans. The three-dimensional interpretation of a shaded image area by humans is influenced strongly by the shape of the area's boundary. Although both the shaded regions in the image exhibit qualitatively similar variations in intensity, the region on top is perceived to comprise three cylinders, whereas the region at the bottom appears corrugated. (From [Ramachandran 1988] with permission.)

troughs. Barrow and Tenenbaum [Barrow and Tenenbaum 1981b] describe an informal experiment demonstrating that, whereas the direction of the shading gradient has an important qualitative effect on the perceived shape, the exact magnitude of this gradient is of little importance.

5.1 Quantitative Shape Recovery

In this section, we shall examine methods of quantitative shape recovery from image shading. Let us restrict ourselves to orthographic projection. Orthographic projection, as explained in Section 2.1.2, closely models the imaging geometry if and only if the viewed object is both distant from the camera and close to the camera's optical axis—that is, if and only if α, the angle subtended by individual object points at the camera's optical center with respect to the camera's optical axis, is, in effect, 0. But if α is 0, then the $\cos^4\alpha$ term in the fundamental radiometric relation derived in Section 2.2 will be 1, and, hence, the image irradiance will be equal to the scene radiance in the direction of the viewer up to a constant factor. Note, however, that the orthographic-projection assumption is not necessary to remove the $\cos^4\alpha$ dependence of the image irradiance, which we could remove by simply calibrating the camera (see Section 2.2); we invoke the orthographic-projection assumption here in addition to simplify the analysis that follows considerably. At any rate, to understand the connection between the image irradiance and the surface shape, what we must determine is the relationship between the surface geometry and the scene radiance in the direction of the viewer. Before we analyze this relationship, let us pause to consider a particularly useful representation for the orientation of a vector.

5.1.1 Gradient Space

The orientation of a vector in three-dimensional space has two degrees of freedom. For instance, if we consider the set of all the unit vectors directed from the center of a unit sphere to the sphere's surface, every orientation corresponds to some point on the unit sphere, and each such point has two degrees of freedom (e.g., longitude and latitude). Now, suppose that we are interested in only those orientations on a unit sphere that span a particular hemisphere—say, that span the $z < 0$ hemisphere. Then, we can represent the orientation of any vector $[\alpha \;\; \beta \;\; \gamma]$ by (p, q), where $[p \;\; q \;\; -1] = [-\alpha/\gamma \;\; -\beta/\gamma \;\; -1]$. That is, as illustrated in Figure 5.4, we can represent the orientation of any vector with a negative z-component by (p, q), where $(p, q, -1)$ is the intersection of the vector with the $z = -1$ plane when the vector is positioned at the origin, and is extended if necessary. The $z = -1$ plane, when it is spanned as described here by the (p, q) coordinates that represent the orientations of vectors with a negative z-component, is called the **gradient space** (for reasons that we shall examine shortly).

If we assume that the orthographic projection of an imaged surface is along the negative-z direction, then the gradient space is adequate to represent the orientation of every surface normal at a visible point (assuming opaque surfaces). Note, however, that the orientations of surface normals along limbs (i.e., along continuous–surface-normal depth discontinuities) would be represented by points at infinity in various directions in gradient space; when such a representation at infinity poses a problem, we must take recourse to alternate representations of surface-normal orientation.

Finally, let us examine the origin of the term *gradient space*. If the imaged surface is denoted by $z = f(x, y)$, then its surface normal will be in the direction $\pm[\partial f/\partial x \;\; \partial f/\partial y \;\; -1]$, the sign distinguishing between the inward surface normal and the outward surface normal. You can verify this observation easily by noting that the surface normal must be orthogonal to

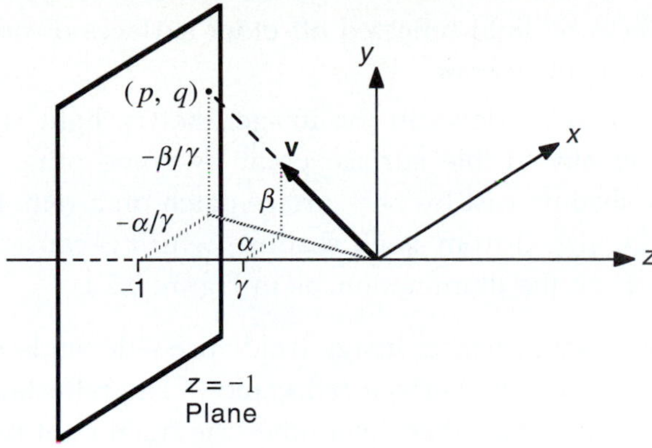

Figure 5.4 Gradient space. The gradient-space representation of the orientation of a vector $\mathbf{v}$ is given by the (x, y) coordinates (p, q) of the intersection of the vector with the $z=-1$ plane when the vector is positioned at the origin, and is extended if necessary; only vectors with a negative z-component can be represented in this fashion. If $\mathbf{v} = [\alpha \;\; \beta \;\; \gamma]$, then $(p, q) = (-\alpha/\gamma\,, \;\; -\beta/\gamma)$. The space of all (p, q) coordinates in this context is called the *gradient space.*

each of the two surface vectors $[1 \;\; 0 \;\; \partial f/\partial x]$ and $[0 \;\; 1 \;\; \partial f/\partial y]$, and, hence, the surface normal must lie along the cross-product of these two vectors. It thus follows that the (p, q) coordinates of the surface-normal orientation, assuming that this orientation has a negative z-component, are simply $(\partial f/\partial x, \; \partial f/\partial y)$, and the name *gradient space* comes from $[\partial f/\partial x \;\; \partial f/\partial y]$ being the gradient of the surface $z = f(x, y)$. On a historical note, although the term *gradient space* was first coined by Mackworth in 1973 [Mackworth 1973] in the context of polyhedral line-drawing interpretation, the (p, q) representation of surface normals was prevalent in geophysics well before 1973 (e.g., [Smith 1967]).

5.1.2 Reflectance Map

Let us now return to the central topic of this chapter: shape from shading. As we discussed, we seek to relate the image irradiance—or, equivalently, under our assumption of orthographic projection, the scene radiance—to the surface geometry. Without any loss of generality, let the orthographic-projection direction be the negative-z direction (i.e., (0, 0) in gradient space). Further, let us assume that the scene illumination is a function of only direction, and not of position. This assumption incorporates three subassumptions:

1. The illumination sources are distant from the imaged surfaces.

2. **Secondary illumination** is not significant; that is, the illumination of imaged surfaces by light reflected off other surfaces or other parts of the same surface is not a factor.
3. There are no cast shadows in the image; that is, light is not obstructed from reaching any visible surface point by some other remote surface point(s). (A shadow cast by one surface patch on a remote surface patch is to be distinguished from a self shadow, which is caused by the surface facing away from the illumination, as in Figure 5.2.)

Scene radiance—and, hence, image irradiance—depends not only on the illumination, but also on the surface reflectance. The **reflectance** of a surface is the property of the surface that determines the fraction of the light incident on the surface that is reflected in a particular direction. In general, the reflectance is a function of the specific directions of reflection and illumination relative to the surface; each of these directions can be specified in spherical polar coordinates by two angles, the angle between the direction and the surface normal, and the angle between the direction and some fixed orientation in the surface tangent plane. The reflectance of many surfaces, however, is invariant at each point under rotation of the surface about the surface normal at the point; that is, for any given set of illumination and viewing conditions, the radiance of many surfaces remains unchanged at a point as the surface is rotated about the surface normal at the point. In addition to its dependence on the directions of illumination and viewing, the reflectance of a surface also depends on a scale factor, called the surface's *albedo*. The **albedo** of a surface is the the fraction of the light incident on the surface that is reflected over all directions; that is, the albedo is the ratio of the total reflected illumination to the total incident illumination.

Let us assume here a constant-albedo surface whose reflectance is rotationally invariant at each point under rotation of the surface about the surface normal at the point. Then, under the previously described assumption of the position independence of the illumination and viewing directions, the image irradiance of the surface at a point will depend only on the surface normal at the point. This dependence is expressed in the **image-irradiance equation**:

$$Irrad(x, y) \;=\; Ref(p(x,y),\, q(x,y)),$$

where *Irrad* is the image irradiance, *Ref* is the **reflectance map**, (x, y) are the image coordinates, and (p, q) are the gradient-space coordinates of the corresponding surface normal. For convenience, both sides of the image-irradiance equation are normalized to have a maximum value of 1; the image intensity, of course, cannot be negative. The terms *image intensity* and *image irradiance* are used interchangeably here, and both are assumed to be

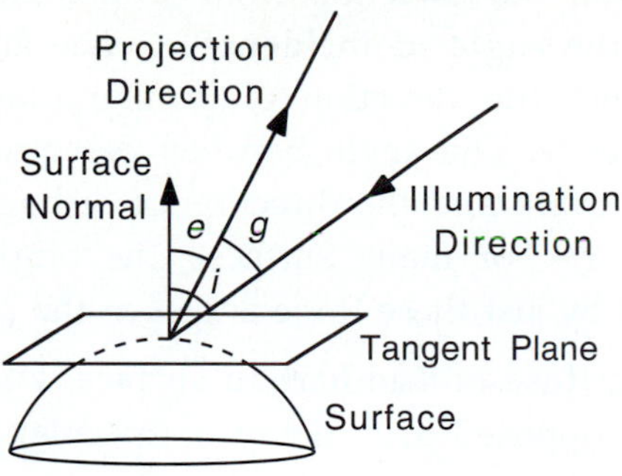

Figure 5.5 The incidence, emittance, and phase angles, i, e, and g, respectively. The *angle of incidence* of a particular ray of light that is incident on a surface is the angle between the surface normal at the point of incidence and the direction from which the ray is incident. The *angle of emittance* of a particular ray of light that is emitted by a surface is the angle between this ray and the surface normal at the point of emittance. Finally, the *phase angle* is the angle between the direction from which a particular ray of light is incident at a surface point and the direction in which a particular ray of light is emitted at the point of incidence as a result. Note that, at any surface point, a given incident ray and a resulting emitted ray together need not share a common plane with the surface normal; that is, the incidence, emittance, and phase angles at a surface point need not be all coplanar. The brightness of a surface is determined by the rays emitted by the surface toward the camera, or the viewer. A *Lambertian* or *diffuse surface*, which is an idealization of a matte surface, has the property that it appears equally bright from all directions; when such a surface is illuminated from a single direction, its brightness is proportional to $\cos i$. A *specular surface* is a mirror surface, which ideally has the property that it reflects every incident ray only in the single direction for which $i = e$ and $i + e = g$.

continuously defined over the image plane. Irrevocable degradations introduced in the course of sensing the image irradiance (Section 2.3) are assumed to be unimportant as far as smooth shading is concerned.

The reflectance map provides a normalized intensity for each surface orientation (p, q). This map is necessarily many-to-one; that is, several different surface orientations may map to the same image intensity. Hence, even in a carefully calibrated environment, each value of image intensity only constrains the corresponding surface normal to some isobrightness contour in gradient space. $Ref(p, q)$ encodes both the light-source distribution and the surface reflectance characteristics. However, it is independent of the way in which the imaged surfaces are configured.

Let us now explore some typical reflectance maps. To keep the analysis simple, let us assume a single distant point-light-source. Then, the reflection geometry is as illustrated in Figure 5.5. The angle between the outward surface normal and the direction from which the light is incident on the surface is called the **angle of incidence**, *i*. The angle between the outward surface normal and the direction of orthographic projection is called the **angle of emittance**, *e*. The angle between the direction from which light is incident on the surface and the direction of orthographic projection is called the **phase angle**, *g*. For many surfaces, the brightness of the surface at a point is governed by just these three angles at the point.

A perfectly **diffuse** or **Lambertian surface**, which is an idealization of a matte surface (as opposed to a glossy or specular surface), has the property that its radiance depends on only the illumination, and not the viewing direction. That is, each point on the surface appears equally bright from all directions. Its brightness depends on only the amount of light incident per unit area, which is proportional to the cosine of the incident angle for a single distant point-light-source. Let us consider one such surface. Let us further assume that the direction of the incident light is given by the vector $[\alpha_s\ \beta_s\ \gamma_s]$, or, equivalently, that light is incident *from* the direction $-[\alpha_s\ \beta_s\ \gamma_s]$. The latter vector may or may not have a gradient-space representation depending on whether the surface is lit from the front or the back. At any rate, the reflectance map is simply

$$\begin{aligned} Ref(p,\, q) \;&=\; \cos i \;=\; \frac{-[\alpha_s\ \beta_s\ \gamma_s]}{\|[\alpha_s\ \beta_s\ \gamma_s]\|} \cdot \frac{[p\ \ q\ \ -1]}{\|[p\ \ q\ \ -1]\|} \\ &=\; \frac{-(\alpha_s p + \beta_s q - \gamma_s)}{\sqrt{\alpha_s^2 + \beta_s^2 + \gamma_s^2}\ \sqrt{p^2 + q^2 + 1}}\,. \end{aligned}$$

By equating this expression to a constant in the range $(0\ \ 1)$, we see that every isobrightness contour in gradient space is a conic section. We can confirm that the isobrightness contours in gradient space are conic sections alternately by noting that all the surface normals that lead to the same image intensity are normal to a single circular cone in space, this cone with its axis along the illumination direction and its vertex at the origin. The intersection of each such cone with the $z=-1$ plane gives us an isobrightness contour in gradient space—this intersection, of course, is a conic section.

Figure 5.6 illustrates the family of isobrightness contours of the reflectance map of a perfectly diffuse surface illuminated in the direction $[\alpha_s\ \beta_s\ \gamma_s] = -[1\ 0.5\ -1]$; a synthetic image of a Lambertian sphere with the same illumination is shown alongside. When a scene is illuminated from up front as in Figure 5.6, it is convenient to express the negative incident direction (i.e., the direction from which the scene is illuminated) in gradient-

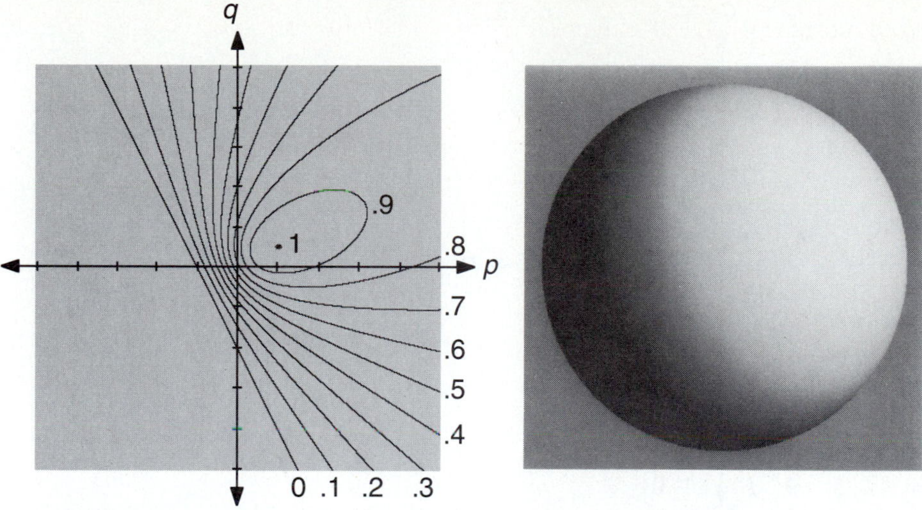

Figure 5.6 The reflectance map. The *reflectance map* of any particular type of surface is a two-dimensional plot over gradient space of the normalized image intensity of the surface as a function of its surface-normal orientation. The existence of a reflectance map of a surface implies that the image intensity of each visible surface point depends only on the orientation of the surface normal at the point. This sole dependence of the image intensity on the surface-normal orientation assumes the following about the imaging geometry and the illumination: orthographic projection, distant illumination, the absence of visible cast shadows, and the absence of secondary illumination (i.e., of illumination not directly from the source but from reflections off surfaces in the scene). On the left is the reflectance map of a Lambertian surface that is illuminated in the direction $-[1\ \ 0.5\ -1]$, and on the right is a synthetic image of a Lambertian sphere that is illuminated in the same direction. The coordinate system of Figure 5.4 is assumed here, with the imaged surface being located in the positive-z half-space and the image being formed on the x–y plane by orthographic projection. The positive x-axis and the positive y-axis, both not shown in the image, are respectively oriented along the directions of the positive p-axis and the positive q-axis in gradient space. The isobrightness contours of a reflectance map of a Lambertian surface are a set of conic sections in gradient space—these conics are nested about the direction *from* which the surface is illuminated when this direction has a negative z-component.

space coordinates: $(p_s,\ q_s) = (-\alpha_s/\gamma_s,\ -\beta_s/\gamma_s)$. Then, it is easily verified that $Ref(p,\ q)$ is maximum (i.e., 1) when $(p,\ q) = (p_s,\ q_s)$. On the other hand, when the illumination is from the back, Ref is maximum for the surface-normal orientation antiparallel to the projection of the incident ray onto the image plane—in gradient space, this particular surface-normal orientation is a "point at infinity." The reflectance map of a Lambertian

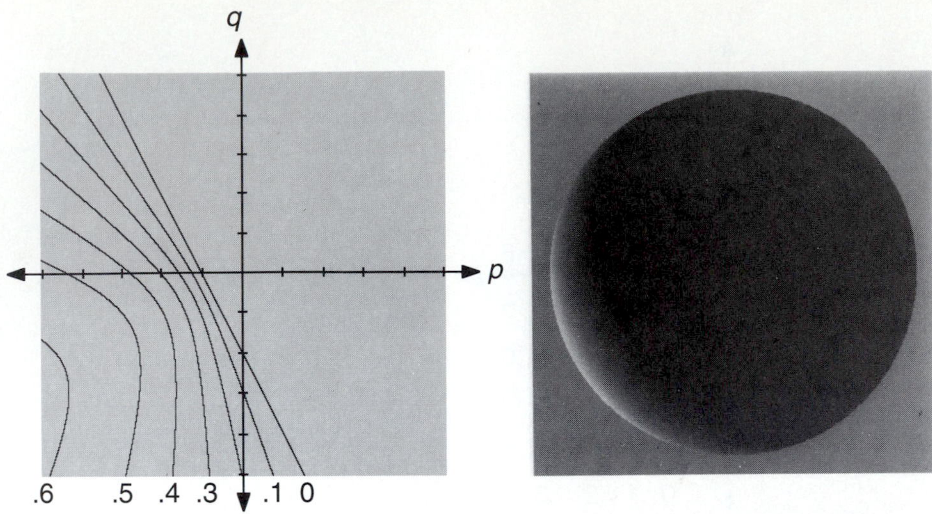

Figure 5.7 The reflectance map of a Lambertian surface that is illuminated in the direction [1 0.5 −1] on the left, and a synthetic image of a Lambertian sphere that is illuminated in the same direction on the right.

surface illuminated in the direction $[\alpha_s \; \beta_s \; \gamma_s] = [1 \; 0.5 \; -1]$ is illustrated by its family of isobrightness contours in Figure 5.7; a synthetic image of a Lambertian sphere with the same illumination is shown alongside. Irrespective of whether the illumination is from the front or the back, the reflectance is minimum (i.e., 0) when $(\alpha_s p + \beta_s q - \gamma_s) \geq 0$; that is, when the angle between the direction from which the scene is lit and the surface normal is greater than 90°. Thus, a straight line in gradient space separates the shadowed-region orientations from the illuminated-region orientations—this line is called the **terminator**. As is both physically and algebraically evident, the only case where there is no terminator (i.e., where none of the visible points are self-shadowed) is where the illumination is from the orthographic-projection direction (i.e., where $(p_s, q_s) = (0, 0)$). A synthetic image under such an illumination condition is illustrated in Figure 5.8—the isobrightness contours here are concentric circles.

No surface is completely matte. Most surfaces, in practice, exhibit a degree of specular or mirrorlike reflection. It is well known that a perfectly **specular surface**—that is, an ideal mirror—reflects light only when $i = e$ and $i + e = g$, where i is the angle of incidence, e is the angle of emittance, and g is the phase angle. Equivalently, an ideal mirror reflects light toward the viewer only when the mirror's surface normal bisects the phase angle, which is the angle between the direction from which the surface is illuminated and the direction from which the surface is viewed. For specular

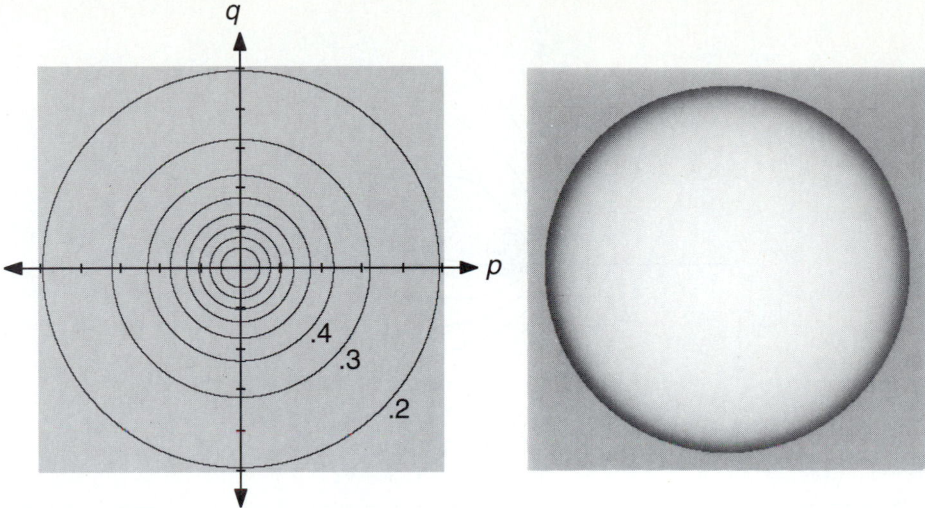

Figure 5.8 The reflectance map of a Lambertian surface that is illuminated in the direction $-[0\ \ 0\ -1]$ on the left, and a synthetic image of a Lambertian sphere that is illuminated in the same direction on the right.

surfaces illuminated by a single distant point-light-source, the radiance in the direction of the viewer is nonzero for only one particular surface orientation. In practice, most surfaces reflect light over a range of directions and exhibit both matte and specular reflective characteristics.[1] A typical reflectance map

1. At a microscopic level, no surface is perfectly smooth. There is always some degree of local statistical variation in the height (and orientation) of the surface, the magnitude of this variation providing a measure of the surface roughness. When the surface roughness is comparable to or less than the wavelength of the incident light, we must use physical optics (i.e., electromagnetic wave theory) to model the surface reflection (see [Beckmann and Spizzichino 1963]). On the other hand, when the surface roughness is significantly greater than the wavelength of the incident light, we can take recourse to geometrical optics, which relies on ray theory, and is as a result, far simpler than physical optics. When geometrical optics is applicable, a widely used surface-reflection model that conforms well with experimental data is the Torrance–Sparrow model [Torrance and Sparrow 1967]. The **Torrance–Sparrow model** is an analytical model for surface reflection that is derived by assuming that the surface comprises small, randomly disposed, mirrorlike facets, each facet providing specular reflection subject to shadowing and masking by adjacent facets. In addition to specular reflection by the facets, the Torrance–Sparrow model also postulates nonspecular surface reflection that is caused by either one or both of multiple reflections between the facets, and internal scattering. A salient characteristic of the Torrance–Sparrow model is the model's successful prediction of the off-specular peak that is exhibited, in practice, by the reflected radiance of a rough surface when such a surface is illuminated at moderate to large angles of incidence. See [Nayar, Ikeuchi, and Kanade 1991a] for a concise review of the Beckmann–Spizzichino and Torrance–Sparrow models of surface reflection.

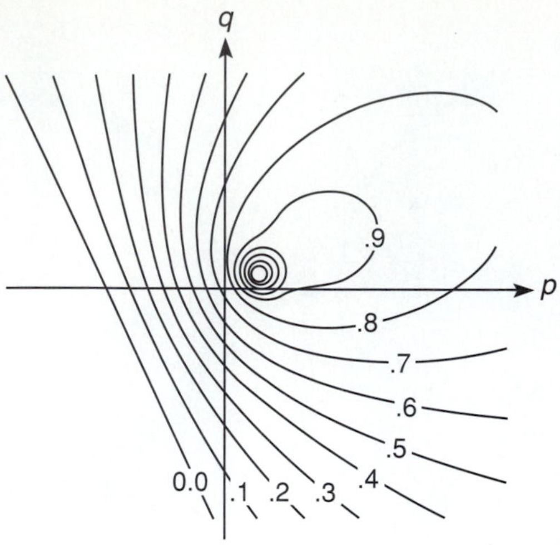

Figure 5.9 The reflectance map of a surface that exhibits both matte and specular reflection, and that is illuminated by a single distant point-light-source. This map is the weighted average of the individual diffuse- and specular-component reflectance maps of some glossy white paint. Whereas the isobrightness contours of the reflectance map of a perfectly diffuse surface that is illuminated from a single direction in front of the surface are a set of conics that are nested about this direction in gradient space, the reflectance map of a perfectly specular surface that is illuminated from a single direction is nonzero for only that surface-normal orientation that bisects the angle between the direction from which the surface is illuminated and the direction from which the surface is viewed. These two competing effects of diffuse and specular reflection are evident in the reflectance map shown. (From [Horn 1977] with permission.)

of one such surface is illustrated in Figure 5.9; Horn [Horn 1977] derived this map by taking the weighted average of the diffuse- and specular-component reflectance maps of some glossy white paint.

We have pursued the analytic determination of reflectance maps primarily for pedagogic reasons. As the scene illumination and surface-reflection properties may, in general, be quite complicated, in practice, reflectance maps are almost always determined experimentally—the orthographic image of a sphere would do the job.

A "Nonintuitive" Image-Intensity Edge

Before we study various methods of shape recovery from image shading, let us pause to consider an example from [Horn 1977] that illustrates the need for a careful analysis of the relationship between the image intensity and surface shape. Consider a trihedral vertex formed by the intersection of three planar surfaces, say A, B, and C, whose surface normals in gradient space are G_A, G_B, and G_C, respectively, as illustrated in Figure 5.10(b). Further,

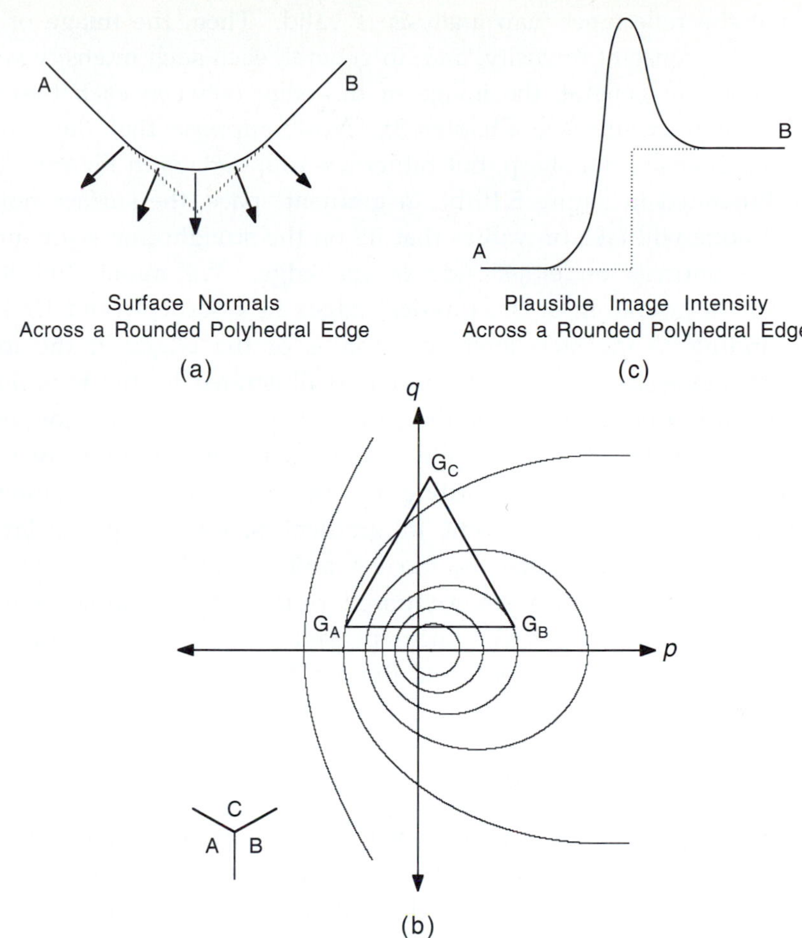

Figure 5.10 The effect of rounding a polyhedral edge on the image intensity across the edge, assuming the applicability of a reflectance map. If we round a polyhedral edge that has a step-shaped intensity profile to begin with, the intensity profile of the edge may or may not simply get rounded: The intensity profile of the edge may end up exhibiting a peaked-step shape. **(a)** The surface normals across a rounded polyhedral edge are positive linear combinations of the normals on either side of the edge; in the figure, the shape of the polyhedral edge prior to rounding is indicated by a dotted line, and the shape of the polyhedral edge after rounding is indicated by a solid line. **(b)** Hence, given a trihedral vertex—say, a vertex formed by faces A, B, and C, whose surface-normal orientations in gradient space are G_A, G_B, and G_C, respectively—the image intensity across an edge at the vertex will, on rounding, vary according to the variation in the reflectance map along the straight-line segment in gradient space that connects the surface-normal orientations of the two faces forming the edge. **(c)** For the reflectance map shown in (b), the effect of rounding the polyhedral edge between the faces A and B on the image of the edge is to transform the edge's step intensity profile, which is shown dotted, into a peaked-step profile, which is shown solid. (After [Horn 1977].)

assume that the reflectance-map analysis is valid. Then, the image of each face will have a constant intensity, and, in general, each such intensity will be different; hence, in general, the image of the edge between each two faces will have a step profile (see Chapter 3). Now, suppose that the physical edges in the scene are not sharp, but rather are rounded, as in Figure 5.10(a). Then, as illustrated in Figure 5.10(b), in gradient space, the surface normals across each edge will take on values that lie on the straight-line segment that connects the normals on either side of the edge. We might "intuitively expect" that the rounding of the physical edges in a scene would lead to a simple rounding of the step intensity profiles of the edges in the image. However, this expectation may not be met, as illustrated by the hypothetical reflectance map superimposed on the gradient-space representation of the trihedral corner in Figure 5.10(b). On rounding, the image-intensity profile across each edge will vary according to the reflectance map along the corresponding straight-line segment in gradient space. In particular, the profile across the edge between the faces A and B will look something like Figure 5.10(c): a step with a superimposed peak. This example is not as contrived as you might think; such peaked edges were reported by Herskovits and Binford [Herskovits and Binford 1970] in their experiments on edge detection in scenes of polyhedra.

5.1.3 Shape Determination

As mentioned earlier, in an environment for which an applicable reflectance map is available, the image intensity constrains the surface normal to an isobrightness curve in gradient space. Each imaged point is thus constrained. Thus far, we have developed only the basic theory underlying such constraints. Let us now investigate how surface shape can be recovered from such constraints in arbitrary reflectance maps. Substantial effort has been devoted to shape recovery since Horn's 1977 formulation. Here, however, we shall consider only the three most prominent approaches: the characteristic-strip method [Horn 1977], the variational approach [Ikeuchi and Horn 1981], and photometric stereo [Woodham 1980].

Characteristic-Strip Method

Horn's **characteristic-strip method** is based on a key observation, illustrated in Figure 5.11(a), that relates the image irradiance to the reflectance map. Given a point in the image and its counterpart in the reflectance map, an infinitesimal step in the image plane in the direction of the gradient of the reflectance map corresponds to an infinitesimal step in gradient space in the direction of the gradient of the image irradiance. Elementary calculus confirms this assertion. First, observe that

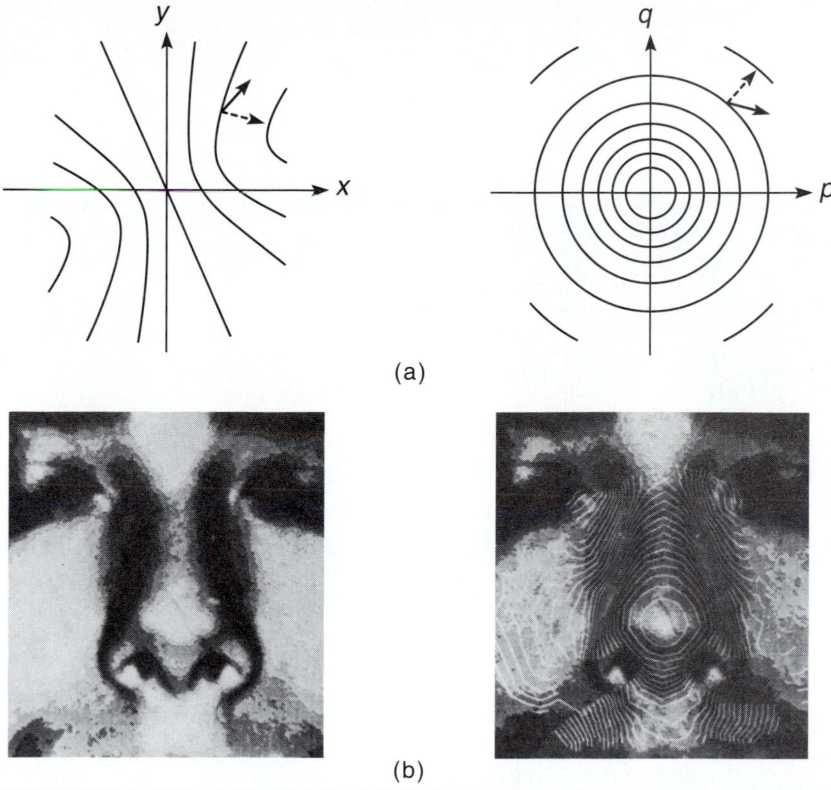

Figure 5.11 The characteristic-strip method of shape from shading. For any given image intensity of a surface point, the reflectance map of the surface constrains the orientation of the surface normal at the point to an isobrightness contour in gradient space. Now, suppose that we have somehow established a one-to-one correspondence between a point in the image plane and a point in gradient space; that is, we have determined the point in gradient space that provides the surface-normal orientation of the image point. Then, we can show that an infinitesimal motion in the image plane in the direction of the steepest descent in the reflectance map corresponds to a motion in gradient space in the direction of the steepest descent in the image intensity. The *characteristic-strip method* of shape from shading uses this observation to "grow" a solution to the shape of an imaged surface, starting from one or more points in the image where the surface-normal orientation is known. **(a)** On the left are the isobrightness contours in an image of a surface, on the right are the corresponding isobrightness contours in the reflectance map of the surface, and superimposed on the two sets of isobrightness contours are vectors that illustrate the described relationship between an infinitesimal motion in the image plane and the corresponding motion in gradient space (from [Horn 1977] with permission). **(b)** On the left is a coarsely quantized image of a human nose, and on the right is the same image with a superimposed elevation contour map that is computed using the characteristic-strip method; the solution to the shape of the nose here is grown from the tip of the nose, where the surface normal points toward the viewer (from [Horn 1986] with permission, © 1986 MIT).

$$dp = \frac{\partial p}{\partial x}\,dx + \frac{\partial p}{\partial y}\,dy\,,$$

$$dq = \frac{\partial q}{\partial x}\,dx + \frac{\partial q}{\partial y}\,dy\,.$$

Using $\dfrac{\partial p}{\partial y} = \dfrac{\partial^2 f}{\partial y\,\partial x} = \dfrac{\partial^2 f}{\partial x\,\partial y} = \dfrac{\partial q}{\partial x}$, where $f(x, y) = z$, we get

$$dp = \frac{\partial p}{\partial x}\,dx + \frac{\partial q}{\partial x}\,dy\,,$$

$$dq = \frac{\partial p}{\partial y}\,dx + \frac{\partial q}{\partial y}\,dy\,.$$

Now, let us assume that we know the surface normal (p, q) at some image point (x, y)—that is, that we have available a boundary condition for the first-order partial differential equation implicit in $Irrad(x, y) = Ref(p, q) = Ref(\partial f/\partial x,\ \partial f/\partial y)$. Then, an infinitesimal step in the image plane in the direction of the gradient of Ref is given by

$$dx = \frac{\partial Ref}{\partial p}\,ds \quad \text{and} \quad dy = \frac{\partial Ref}{\partial q}\,ds\,.$$

Substitution in the earlier equations easily yields the desired result:

$$dp = \left(\frac{\partial Ref}{\partial p}\frac{\partial p}{\partial x} + \frac{\partial Ref}{\partial q}\frac{\partial q}{\partial x}\right) ds = \frac{\partial Irrad}{\partial x}\,ds\,,$$

$$dq = \left(\frac{\partial Ref}{\partial p}\frac{\partial p}{\partial y} + \frac{\partial Ref}{\partial q}\frac{\partial q}{\partial y}\right) ds = \frac{\partial Irrad}{\partial y}\,ds\,.$$

It is thus clear that a step in the image plane in the direction of the gradient of Ref, $\vec{\nabla} Ref = [\,\partial Ref/\partial p \quad \partial Ref/\partial q\,]$, corresponds to a step in gradient space in the direction of the gradient of $Irrad$, $\vec{\nabla} Irrad = [\,\partial Irrad/\partial x \quad \partial Irrad/\partial y\,]$. This observation suggests that, starting at any image point where the surface normal is known, we grow a solution step by step by proceeding along these conjugate directions. We could thus obtain the surface normals along a curve in the image plane, and, subsequently, we could integrate along this curve to determine its spatial trajectory up to a constant spatial displacement along the direction of orthographic projection. This spatial curve is called a *characteristic curve*; along with its surface-normal assignment, this spatial curve is called a *characteristic strip*; the projection of this spatial curve onto the image plane is called a *base characteristic*.

Possible boundary conditions (initial values) for the development of characteristic strips are provided by singular points in the image intensity, and by intensity edges in the image that correspond to limbs in space. By a *singular point in the image intensity* is meant an image point where the image intensity assumes a (maximum) value that is unique to a single point in gradient space. Along a limb—that is, along a continuous-surface-normal depth discontinuity in space—the surface normal in space is parallel to the edge normal in the image (under our assumption of orthographic projection). Figure 5.11(b) illustrates the result of using a singular point in an image to grow a solution to the shape of a human nose. The use of limbs as a boundary condition has been explored by Ikeuchi and Horn [Ikeuchi and Horn 1981], who seek to overcome the overriding problem with the characteristic-strip method—cumulative error buildup owing to the integral nature of this method—by an approach that is described next. Of course, before we can use a limb in an image as a boundary condition, we must identify the limb. In this connection, it is useful to observe that, in general, on elliptic and hyperbolic diffuse surface patches, the isobrightness contours in the image are tangent to the limbs on which these contours terminate; in contrast, the image isobrightness contours are transverse to other image-intensity edges [Rieger 1990]. (This observation is closely related to the characterization of nonocclusion image junctions between viewpoint-independent and viewpoint-dependent edges in Section 4.2.2; the comments about the detectability of such junctions in Section 4.3 are also pertinent.)

Variational Methods

Over and above its problem with cumulative error buildup, the characteristic-strip method has the drawback that it does not enforce integrability on its solution for $p(x, y)$ and $q(x, y)$. That is, if we were to integrate $\{p(x, y)\, dx + q(x, y)\, dy\}$ along some closed image contour to determine the latter's variation in depth, there would be no guarantee that the computed spatial trajectory would be closed. Equivalently, there need not exist any function $z = f(x, y)$ such that $p(x, y) = \partial f(x, y)/\partial x$ and $q(x, y) = \partial f(x, y)/\partial y$, and, therefore, $dz = \{p(x, y)\, dx + q(x, y)\, dy\}$. One approach to overcome both cumulative error buildup and the lack of integrability is to solve a modification of the original problem. We could, for instance, determine the $p(x, y)$, $q(x, y)$, and $f(x, y)$ that minimize

$$\iint \Bigg\{ [\, Irrad(x, y) - Ref(p, q)\,]^2 + \lambda \left[\left(\frac{\partial p(x, y)}{\partial x}\right)^2 + \left(\frac{\partial p(x, y)}{\partial y}\right)^2 + \left(\frac{\partial q(x, y)}{\partial x}\right)^2 + \left(\frac{\partial q(x, y)}{\partial y}\right)^2 \right] + \mu \left[\left(\frac{\partial f(x, y)}{\partial x} - p(x, y)\right)^2 + \left(\frac{\partial f(x, y)}{\partial y} - q(x, y)\right)^2 \right] \Bigg\}\, dx\, dy$$

[Horn 1990]. The first term here comes from the image-irradiance equation; the second term is a smoothing term that discourages solutions for $p(x, y)$ and $q(x, y)$ from having large first derivatives; the third term encourages integrability. The parameters λ and μ control the relative weights of the three terms. The minimization of the preceding expression is a problem of the calculus of variations; hence, this approach is called a **variational approach** to shape from shading. The **calculus of variations** is a branch of mathematics that is concerned with the extremization of **functionals**, a term used to describe functions that vary over the space of functions (see [Horn 1986] and the references therein); one instance of a functional is the length of the curve $y = f(x)$ (within some interval) as a function of f. Ikeuchi and Horn [Ikeuchi and Horn 1981] were the first authors to suggest a variational approach to shape from shading, and Horn and Brooks [Horn and Brooks 1986] were the first authors to address the question of integrability.

Horn [Horn 1990] provides a unified and comprehensive treatment of various variational formulations. Lee [Lee 1988] investigates questions of the existence and uniqueness of solutions, and of the convergence of iterative solution methods. As Horn [Horn 1990] points out, the problem of shape from shading is heavily underconstrained if we choose to ignore the issue of integrability. However, note that the variational approach is not the only approach to address the question of integrability; see [Frankot and Chellappa 1988] and [Simchony, Chellappa, and Shao 1990] for alternate approaches.

In the double integral sought to be minimized in the preceding variational formulation, in addition to the term that encourages an integrable solution, there is a regularizing smoothness term, which is included to help avoid problems of instability in the iterative solution method. (See Footnote 3 in Section 3.1.2 for a description of regularization.) In this context, Dupuis and Oliensis [Dupuis and Oliensis 1992] argue that, if we take full advantage of the constraints that are imposed on shape from shading by singular points in the image intensity, then we can successfully pursue a variational approach to shape from shading without taking recourse to regularization. In particular, Dupuis and Oliensis analyze and experimentally demonstrate a variational approach that does not use regularization and that recovers the shape of a Lambertian surface from its image directly, without first computing the surface normals.

Photometric Stereo

Thus far, we have examined only single-image methods to recover surface orientation from image shading. An alternative is to use multiple images, each image taken from the same viewing direction, but under a different illumination condition that leads to a different reflectance map. This method,

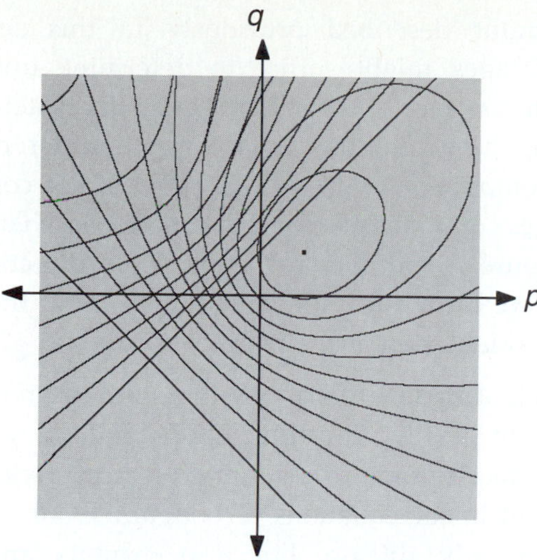

Figure 5.12 Photometric stereo. Different illumination conditions lead to different reflectance maps for the same surface. Two such reflectance maps are shown superimposed. Given the image intensity of a surface point under a particular illumination condition, the reflectance map of the surface under that illumination condition constrains the surface-normal orientation at the image point to a particular isobrightness contour in gradient space. Thus, given multiple images of a surface point, each image acquired under a different illumination condition, the multiple reflectance maps of the surface under the various illumination conditions constrain the surface-normal orientation at the surface point to the intersection of multiple isobrightness contours in gradient space. A method that recovers the shape of a surface by using multiple illumination conditions as described to determine the surface-normal orientations at various image points is called *photometric stereo.*

called **photometric stereo**, was first proposed by Woodham [Woodham 1980]. The underlying principle is simple. A single reflectance map constrains the surface-normal orientation of an image point to an isobrightness contour in gradient space; a different reflectance map would constrain the surface-normal orientation at the same point to a different isobrightness contour; as the surface-normal orientation is unique at each point, it must lie at the intersection of all its constraining isobrightness contours in gradient space. For instance, in Figure 5.12, which shows two superimposed reflectance maps, each surface-normal orientation would be constrained to the intersection of two gradient-space isobrightness contours, one in each reflectance map. In most cases, three different illumination conditions will uniquely constrain the surface-normal orientation at a visible surface point to a single point in gradient space; this point is at the intersection of three isobrightness contours in gradient space. (However, if we invoke the integrability constraint described previously in this section, two images instead of three images might suffice to determine uniquely the surface-normal orientation at each point [Onn and Bruckstein 1990].) We are implicitly assuming here that the surface point under consideration has a diffuse reflective component, and that this point is not completely shadowed in any of the images. If a surface point is completely shadowed in an image, or if it exhibits purely specular reflection in a direction other than the viewing direction, we cannot use the image intensity at the point to constrain the surface-normal orientation at the point to a curve in gradient space.

For a completely diffuse surface (possibly with unknown reflectance) that is illuminated individually in three independent (known) directions, determining the surface-normal orientation at a point reduces to solving a set of three independent linear equations [Woodham 1980]. If the reflectance of the surface is not only diffuse, but also exhibits an additive specular component—perhaps unknown, but with localized contributions to the individual reflectance maps—then illumination in a fourth direction can provide an approximate solution to the surface-normal orientation at a point via linear equations once again [Coleman and Jain 1982]. Nayar, Ikeuchi, and Kanade [Nayar, Ikeuchi, and Kanade 1990] adopt a different strategy to photometric stereo: They assume a functional form for the surface reflectance, which is taken to be unknown a priori and possibly varying over the surface, and then use several extended illumination sources to estimate both the shape and the reflectance of the surface.

Finally, it is worth mentioning that, although photometric stereo has thus far found use only where carefully controlled illumination of an unchanging scene is possible, it is not necessary that the scene be stationary. Multiple images can be acquired simultaneously through the use of multiple illuminations that are separable by color [Woodham 1980].

5.2 Qualitative Shape Recovery

Let us now examine briefly an interesting observation by Koenderink and van Doorn [Koenderink and van Doorn 1980] that pertains to qualitative shape recovery from image shading. Although the precise mathematical formulation of this observation requires the use of the Gauss map, which we shall discuss in Chapter 9, it is possible to elucidate the underlying principle by invoking some elementary differential geometry. If you are unfamiliar with differential geometry (e.g., [Lipschutz 1969]), you may skip this section.

Let us assume orthographic projection once again. Let us further assume a single distant light source, and ignore secondary illumination and cast

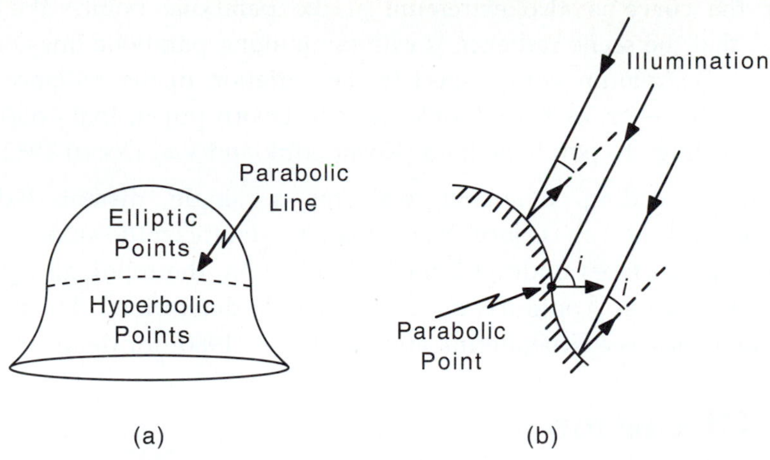

Figure 5.13 Variation in the brightness of a Lambertian surface across a parabolic line that separates elliptic and hyperbolic regions on the surface. Consider a parabolic line (i.e., a line comprising parabolic points) that separates elliptic and hyperbolic regions (i.e., regions comprising elliptic and hyperbolic points, respectively) on a Lambertian surface that is illuminated from a single direction. Along every surface curve across this parabolic line, the brightness of the surface will assume either a local maximum or a local minimum at the parabolic line. **(a)** A parabolic line that separates elliptic and hyperbolic regions on a Lambertian surface. **(b)** A section of the surface across the parabolic line illustrating that the angle of incidence is extremum at the line; hence, so is the surface brightness, which for a Lambertian surface is proportional to the cosine of the angle of incidence. (After [Koenderink and van Doorn 1982].)

shadows. If we now consider a Lambertian surface, as indicated in Section 5.1.2, the scene radiance will simply be the cosine of the incident angle up to a constant multiplicative factor. Hence, it is the incident angle that we need to examine.

A parabolic line on a "generic" surface (assumed sufficiently smooth) separates elliptic points from hyperbolic points, as on the surface in Figure 5.13(a). Consider a point on one such line; more precisely, consider the intersection of the surface at such a point with a plane containing the surface normal and the zero-curvature principal direction. For a "generic" surface, this intersection curve will have an inflection at the parabolic point—that is, it will undergo a curvature sign change at the parabolic point. Now, if we use the well-known fact that the normal to this intersection curve in the immediate vicinity of the parabolic point is also normal to the surface, then, as illustrated in Figure 5.13(b), we can conclude that the incident angle along the curve is extremum at the parabolic point. Hence, the scene radiance along the curve is also extremum at the parabolic point. We have thus shown that the scene radiance is extremum along parabolic lines of "generic" surfaces—extremum with respect to the variation in the radiance across the parabolic line—or, as Koenderink and van Doorn put it, that "highlights and shadows cling" to parabolic lines [Koenderink and van Doorn 1982].

The preceding treatment was for a single distant light source. Koenderink and van Doorn argue that, for (sufficiently smooth "generic") Lambertian surfaces under arbitrary illumination, the topological structure of the isobrightness contours on a surface is determined by the surface's parabolic lines; see [Koenderink and van Doorn 1980] for details.

5.3 Discussion

Whereas the practical applicability of line-drawing analyses is hindered by the limitations on what may be observed reliably and accurately in an image, the practical applicability of shape from shading is limited by assumptions about the scene. Let us go over the principal assumptions that underlie the application of reflectance maps once again: surfaces with constant albedo whose reflectance at any point is rotationally invariant under rotation of the surface about its surface normal at that point, orthographic projection, distant and calibrated illumination sources, absence of cast shadows from the image, and the insignificance of secondary illumination in the imaged scene. Of these assumptions, it is the last that is the Achilles' heel of shape from shading. Perspective projection and nondistant illumination sources do not pose an insurmountable problem in a carefully modeled environment [Horn 1975]. We can avoid cast shadows in images of arbitrary shapes if we have control over the environment—for instance, by placing all the light sources close to the viewer. As far as secondary illumination—also known as *interreflection*—is concerned, tangible progress has been reported by Nayar, Ikeuchi, and Kanade [Nayar, Ikeuchi, and Kanade 1991b], who use an interreflection model proposed by Koenderink and van Doorn [Koenderink and van Doorn 1983] to provide an iterative procedure for computing the shapes of Lambertian surfaces that have only visible surface elements contributing to their interreflections. Starting with an initial shape estimate, perhaps obtained through photometric stereo, Nayar, Ikeuchi, and Kanade iteratively first use the current shape estimate to compute the interreflections, and then use these interreflections in turn to update the shape.

Of course, if a particular surface is not imaged at all, there is no way we can take into account its contribution to secondary illumination by examining the image alone. In a carefully controlled experimental study, Forsyth and

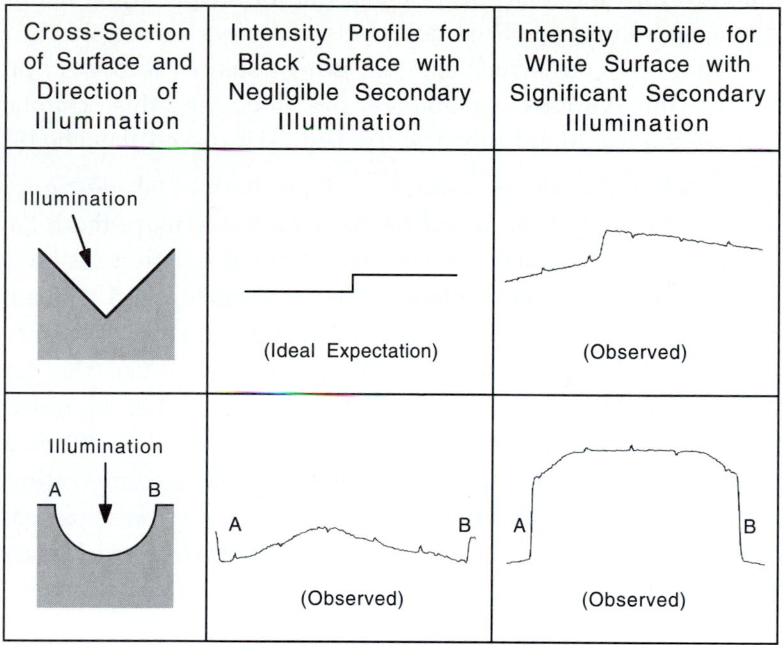

Cross-Section of Surface and Direction of Illumination
Intensity Profile for Black Surface with Negligible Secondary Illumination
Intensity Profile for White Surface with Significant Secondary Illumination
Illumination
(Ideal Expectation)
(Observed)
Illumination
A
B
A
B
(Observed)
A
B
(Observed)

Figure 5.14 The effect of secondary illumination on the image of a surface. The *secondary illumination* of a surface—that is, the illumination of a surface by light that is reflected either off the surface itself, or off other surfaces in the scene—may substantially alter the image of the surface. Illustrated here is the effect of secondary illumination on the images of two matte surfaces, each of which exhibits translational invariance orthogonal to its cross-section shown. On the left are the cross-sections of the surfaces, and the relative directions of illumination; in the center are the corresponding intensity profiles for black surfaces that exhibit negligible secondary illumination; on the right are the intensity profiles observed when the surfaces are white, and, hence, secondary illumination is substantial. (The experimental plots are all from [Forsyth and Zisserman 1991] with permission, © 1991 IEEE.)

Zisserman [Forsyth and Zisserman 1991] demonstrate that, in practice, secondary illumination is often substantial. Based on this observation, they argue cogently that, in a practical sense, accurate numerical shape from shading is unlikely to succeed in nonsynthetic environments with complex shapes. If anything, they argue, their experiments confirm the primacy of edges (especially step edges), which, although sparse unlike shading, exhibit a reliable, robust, and tractable correlation to surface shape. Figure 5.14 illustrates the effect of secondary illumination on two matte surfaces exhibiting translational invariance orthogonal to the cross-sections shown. It may eventually turn out that the primary role of shape from shading in an uncontrolled environment will be not as a stand-alone process, but rather as a process that is complementary to other shape recovery processes. Evidently, of the various techniques described in this chapter, only photometric stereo has found practical use (e.g., [Horn and Ikeuchi 1984]).

Finally, although almost all the quantitative shape-from-shading techniques thus far have been based on the reflectance map, there have been other approaches. For instance, as we saw in our discussion on photometric stereo, Nayar, Ikeuchi, and Kanade [Nayar, Ikeuchi, and Kanade 1990] assume a functional form for the surface reflectance to recover surface shape. Also, Healey and Binford [Healey and Binford 1988] use the Torrance–Sparrow reflection model (see Footnote 1 in Section 5.1.2) to recover local shape from just specular image features. In the absence of a reflectance map, shading analysis would clearly be facilitated by the decomposition of the reflected light into its diffuse and specular components; examinations of the spectral composition of the reflected light [Klinker, Shafer, and Kanade 1988], and of its polarization [Wolff and Boult 1991], have been shown to be helpful in this connection.

Figure 6.1 *The Visual Cliff,* by William Vandivert, 1960. This photograph of a Siamese kitten peering over a checkered cliff demonstrates how variation in the image characteristics of a spatial texture may affect our perception of the depth and layout of the texture in space. The kitten in the photograph is on a ledge, with its tail protruding over a shallow drop. (A similar photograph by the same photographer first appeared on the cover of *Scientific American,* April 1960.)

Chapter 6

Texture

As the photograph in Figure 6.1 confirms, texture plays a significant role in our perception of the shapes of surfaces and their layout in space. In Chapter 5, we examined several methods of shape recovery from image shading. Let us now turn our attention to the use of image textural variation to recover surface shape.

Before we address the difficult question of what is texture, let us adopt the standard practice and consider several photographs of textures from Brodatz's classic album of textures [Brodatz 1966]. In Figure 6.2(a) and Figure 6.2(b) are photographs of two natural textures, water and pebbles, respectively. In Figure 6.2(c) and Figure 6.2(d) are photographs of two human-made textures, raffia weave and brick wall, respectively.

Conceptually, the principal characteristic of a texture is the repetition of a basic pattern. That having been said, several clarifications are immediately called for. As is clear from the photographs in Figure 6.2, the structure of the

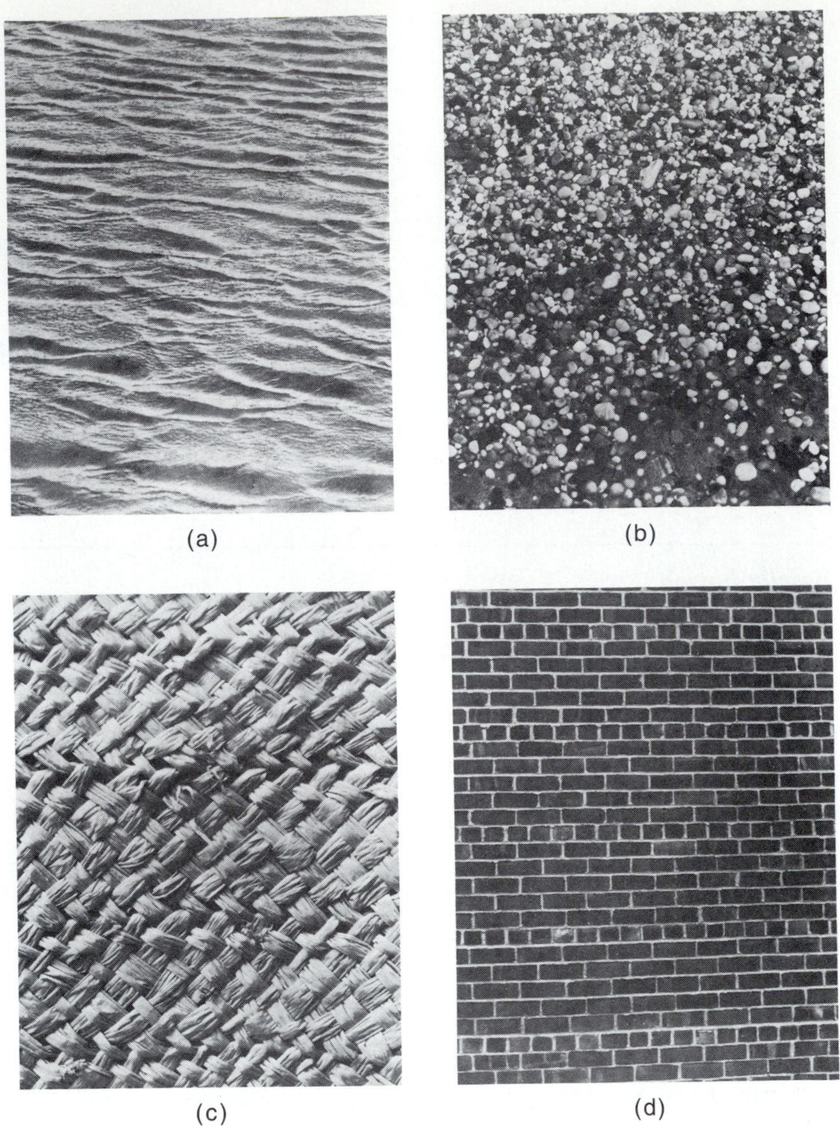

Figure 6.2 Our richly textured visual world. **(a)** Water. **(b)** Beach pebbles. **(c)** Raffia weave. **(d)** Brick wall. (From [Brodatz 1966] with permission.)

basic pattern may not be deterministic, but rather only statistical, and the repetition of the basic pattern may neither be regular nor deterministic, but rather only statistically regular (e.g., uniformly distributed). Furthermore, as is evident from Figure 6.1, the images of the various instances of the basic repetitive textural pattern in space may not all be identical: These images may be related by geometric distortions. As we shall soon see, it is these distortions that make texture useful for shape recovery.

As Julesz [Julesz 1975], among others, has pointed out, texture is a nonlocal property: It is a property that is characteristic of a region much larger than the size of the basic repetitive textural pattern. On close scrutiny, the structure of a texture that leads to the texture's textural quality becomes significant in its own right—as, for instance, might the individual blades of grass, or the individual waves on the surface of water. Pertinent here is Attneave's view that, for humans, texture is the abstraction of certain statistical homogeneities from a portion of the visual field that contains a quantity of information grossly in excess of the observer's perceptual capacity (p. 188, [Attneave 1954]).

The preceding characterization of texture might strike you as fuzzy; it should. However, this fuzziness should not surprise you as it is precisely our inability to formalize the notion of texture that is at the heart of the difficulties we face in pursuing the two main aspects of image textural analysis: texture discrimination, and the use of texture to recover shape. Let us now study both these aspects of image textural analysis in turn.

6.1 Discrimination

The first step in image textural analysis is the discrimination of different textures. The various approaches can be categorized broadly as statistical or structural. The books by Levine [Levine 1985] and by Ballard and Brown [Ballard and Brown 1982] contain extensive treatments of both approaches; see the book by Pratt [Pratt 1991] for an extensive treatment of statistical approaches. If you have a greater interest in the topic, you should in addition look at Haralick's extensive survey [Haralick 1979], and at Nevatia's book [Nevatia 1982].

Before we discuss various statistical and structural approaches to image-texture discrimination, consider that a perfectly "featureless" surface can be regarded as the most elementary spatial texture—the degenerate case. Images of such surfaces were the focus of Chapter 5. Even "featureless" surfaces, of course, have microstructures that determine their reflectance properties. However, these reflectance properties are, for all practical purposes, uniform (or smoothly varying) over the surface and do not lead to a discernible visual texture. This observation raises an interesting point mentioned earlier: Texture is a scale-dependent phenomenon. Its manifestation requires that a large number of textural primitives be encompassed by the observation, but not so many that the sensor resolution does not permit the discernment of individual elements. When we say that a surface is smooth, what we usually mean is that the surface texture is imperceptible to our sense of vision—or to our sense of touch.

6.1.1 Statistical Methods

Statistical methods of texture discrimination are best suited to images of those textures that have statistical underlying causes. Most natural textures fall in this category. The simplest statistical approach to texture discrimination is to compare the statistics of the gray levels of image pixels. More sophisticated methods compute and compare the statistics of image features such as image-intensity edges.

One way to discriminate between different image textures is to compare their **first-order gray-level statistics**. By *first order* is meant the statistics of single pixels, in contrast to the statistics of pixel pairs, triples, and so forth. All conceivable first-order statistical measures of an image texture are determined by the image texture's gray-level histogram, whose normalization yields the single-pixel gray-level discrete probability density function. We could either compare the normalized gray-level histograms of image textures themselves, or use various derived measures, such as the mean, the median, or the variance. The fundamental limitation of all first-order measures is their insensitivity to pixel permutations; for instance, a black-and-white checkerboard pattern has the same first-order gray-level statistics as does an image whose left half is completely black and whose right half is completely white.

The most obvious way to overcome this shortcoming of first-order statistics is to use higher-order statistics. In fact, it would suffice to use **second-order gray-level statistics**: the combined statistics of the gray levels of pairs of pixels in which each two pixels in a pair have a fixed relative position. For instance, in a binary image, we could compute the probability of finding a white pixel with a black left-neighbor. All second-order gray-level statistical measures are specified completely by the following joint probability:

$$P(l,\ m,\ \Delta i,\ \Delta j) \;=\; \text{probability}\{\, I(i,\ j) = l \;\text{ and }\; I(i+\Delta i,\ j+\Delta j) = m \,\},$$

where I is the image intensity and $(i,\ j)$ is the position of an arbitrary pixel in the image. In other words, $P(l,\ m,\ \Delta i,\ \Delta j)$ is the probability that an arbitrary pixel indexed by $(i,\ j)$ has the gray level l, while the pixel indexed by $(i+\Delta i,\ j+\Delta j)$ has the gray level m. This function is four-dimensional: If the total number of gray levels that a pixel in the image might assume is g, then, for each value of $(\Delta i,\ \Delta j)$, P will be a two-dimensional discrete function that is conveniently represented as a $g \times g$ matrix whose $(l,\ m)$ entry is $P(l,\ m,\ \Delta i,\ \Delta j)$. We can derive every such matrix, as illustrated next by an example, by normalizing the corresponding two-dimensional pixel-pair gray-level histogram, which too is conveniently represented as a matrix.

Let the image be the 5×5 matrix $\mathbf{I}$ with pixels $I(i, j)$, where i is the row index of $\mathbf{I}$ increasing from top to bottom, and j is the column index of $\mathbf{I}$ increasing from left to right. Let the gray levels that an image pixel may assume be 0, 1, 2, and 3. Further, let $\mathbf{H}$ be the gray-level histogram matrix for pairs of pixels that are spaced a specific $(\Delta i, \Delta j)$ apart; let the individual entries of $\mathbf{H}$ be denoted by $H(l, m)$, where l is the row index of $\mathbf{H}$ increasing from top to bottom, and m is the column index of $\mathbf{H}$ increasing from left to right, both l and m varying from 0 to 3. Each entry $H(l, m)$ of the histogram matrix $\mathbf{H}$ for a specific $(\Delta i, \Delta j)$, is the total number of pairs of pixels that, for an arbitrary (i, j), satisfy $I(i, j) = l$ and $I(i+\Delta i, j+\Delta j) = m$ simultaneously. That is, $H(l, m)$ is the total number of image locations (i, j) for which the pixel at location (i, j) has the gray level l, while the pixel at location $(i+\Delta i, j+\Delta j)$ has the gray level m. The joint probability $P(l, m, \Delta i, \Delta j)$ here is simply $H(l, m) \,/\, \Sigma_{l=0}^{3} \Sigma_{m=0}^{3} H(l, m)$. Now, to be specific, suppose that we let $(\Delta i, \Delta j) = (0, 1)$, and that we let the image

$$\mathbf{I} = \begin{bmatrix} 0 & 1 & 2 & 3 & 1 \\ 2 & 1 & 3 & 1 & 1 \\ 0 & 0 & 2 & 2 & 1 \\ 1 & 2 & 0 & 3 & 1 \\ 0 & 0 & 0 & 0 & 3 \end{bmatrix}; \qquad \text{then,} \qquad \mathbf{H} = \begin{bmatrix} 4 & 1 & 1 & 2 \\ 0 & 1 & 2 & 1 \\ 1 & 2 & 1 & 1 \\ 0 & 3 & 0 & 0 \end{bmatrix}$$

and $P(l, m, 0, 1) = H(l, m) \,/\, 20$.

It is generally assumed that only pixels that are located close to one another in the image are correlated; as a result, second-order statistics are generally computed for only small Δi and Δj. Observe that, unlike the single-pixel gray-level probabilities, the joint pixel-pair gray-level probabilities are sensitive to the choice of the i- and j-axes in the image. Consequently, a direct comparison of the joint gray-level probabilities of image textures is likely to classify textures that are rotated versions of one another as different. For purposes of texture classification, it is frequently assumed that we need not distinguish between $P(l, m, \Delta i, \Delta j)$ and $P(m, l, \Delta i, \Delta j)$; that is, that we need not distinguish between which of two pixels that are spaced $(\Delta i, \Delta j)$ apart has the gray level l, and which has the gray level m. Hence, comparisons between textures are often based on the textures' **co-occurrence matrices** that are symmetric matrices defined as follows: $\mathbf{C} \triangleq \mathbf{H} + \mathbf{H}^{\mathrm{T}}$, where $\mathbf{C}$ is the co-occurrence matrix and $\mathbf{H}$ is the histogram matrix, both defined for a specific $(\Delta i, \Delta j)$, and $\mathbf{H}^{\mathrm{T}}$ is the transpose of $\mathbf{H}$. Equivalently, each entry of the co-occurrence matrix $\mathbf{C}$ is $C(l, m) = C(m, l) = H(l, m) + H(m, l)$. A variety of statistical measures derived from co-occurrence matrices have been proposed in the literature (see

[Haralick 1979]). It seems that Julesz was the first to propose the use of gray-level co-occurrence statistics for texture discrimination [Julesz 1962]. Several researchers have since pursued such an approach (e.g., [Haralick, Shanmugam, and Dinstein 1973]). It is likely that these efforts have, at least in part, been encouraged by the well-known conjecture by Julesz that humans cannot distinguish between textures that have the same gray-level co-occurrence statistics. This conjecture is now known to be false (see [Julesz 1981] for details).

We could possibly also use the gray-level autocorrelation function, or, equivalently, the power spectrum, to classify an image texture; both rotate with the image, but are invariant under its displacement. The **autocorrelation** of a real-valued function $I(i, j)$ is $I(i, j) * I(-i, -j)$, where $*$ denotes convolution. The **power spectrum** of $I(i, j)$ is the square of the magnitude of its Fourier transform (see Appendix A2.1); equivalently, it can be shown that the power spectrum of a function is the Fourier transform of its autocorrelation function (e.g., see [Bracewell 1978]). The power spectrum of an image captures not only the frequency content of the image, but also the image's directionality, as explained next. If the Fourier domain is parameterized by polar coordinates, high frequencies (i.e., rapid variations) in the image manifest themselves at large radii in the Fourier domain, and low frequencies (i.e., slow variations) in the image manifest themselves at small radii in the Fourier domain; the direction of variation in the image manifests itself in the polar angle in the Fourier domain. Periodicity in an image texture leads to peaks in the image texture's power spectrum, the radial polar coordinate of a peak determining the period of repetition, and the angular polar coordinate determining the direction of repetition. Thus, we see that we can classify image textures by first dividing the Fourier domain into independent sets of angular and radial bins as illustrated in Figure 6.3, and then identifying those bins within which most of the signal power of the image texture is concentrated. Such a strategy, which seems to have originated with Lendaris and Stanley [Lendaris and Stanley 1970], was subsequently adopted by Bajcsy [Bajcsy 1973]. In a related approach, Laws [Laws 1980] suggested convolving the image with a set of masks to compute directly various frequency-sensitive energy measures. Bovik, Clark, and Geisler [Bovik, Clark, and Geisler 1990] refined Lendaris and Stanley's original proposal substantially to demonstrate successful texture segmentation in a variety of images, each image containing a pair of image textures.

All the statistical texture-discrimination methods that we have discussed thus far have been image-intensity based. Hence, each of these methods is

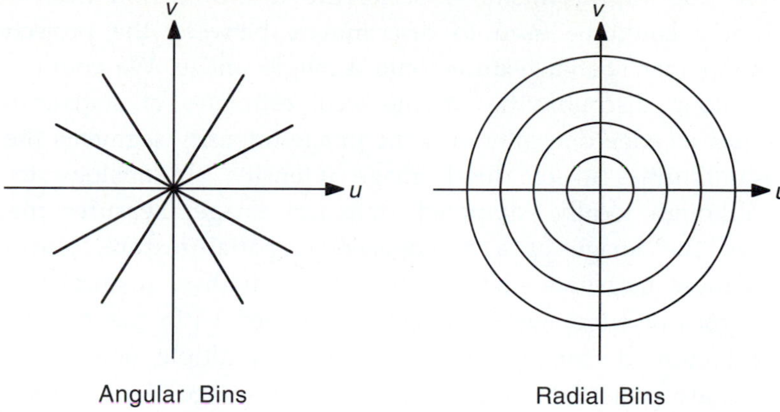

Figure 6.3 Angular and radial bins in the Fourier domain. Angular and radial bins in the Fourier domain capture the directionality and the rapidity of fluctuation of an image texture, respectively. Any image pattern can be mapped uniquely onto the Fourier domain by the Fourier transform. Loosely speaking, the *Fourier transform* decomposes a signal into sinusoidal waves, the frequency of each sinusoid (given by $\sqrt{u^2 + v^2}$ in the figure) indexing the rapidity of change, and the orientation of each sinusoid (given by $\tan^{-1}(v/u)$ in the figure) indexing the direction of change. (After [Lendaris and Stanley 1970].)

sensitive to gray-level transformations. An alternative strategy is to compute the statistics of image features such as image-intensity edges (e.g., [Davis, Johns, and Aggarwal 1979], [Vistnes 1989]). Other strategies in the literature include the use of image-texture models such as Markov random fields (e.g., [Hassner and Sklansky 1980], [Cross and Jain 1983], [Derin and Elliott 1987], [Cohen and Cooper 1987]) and fractals (e.g., [Pentland 1984], [Keller, Chen, and Crownover 1989]). (See Section 3.3.3 for a brief description of Markov random fields; see the end of this section for a description of fractals.)

Statistical texture-discrimination methods have found use almost exclusively in aerial images—for instance, to classify terrain in LANDSAT satellite images [Weszka, Dyer, and Rosenfeld 1976]. Such methods are designed primarily for homogeneous image textures (i.e., for image textures whose image properties do not vary over the image), rather than for images of homogeneous spatial textures (i.e., for images of spatial textures whose properties in space do not vary with spatial position). Spatially homogeneous textures, as we shall soon see, may exhibit systematic textural variations in the image as a result of projective distortion. In general, it is only when the spatial texture is planar, and the projection geometry orthographic, that homogeneity in space implies homogeneity in the image.

In principle, the various methods of texture discrimination that we have discussed here could be used to discriminate between the projections of multiple nonplanar spatial textures onto a single image: We could segment the image along discontinuities in the local estimates of statistical image measures, just as edge detection over the image intensity segments the image along discontinuities in the local image intensity. In analogy to image shading, although locally computed statistical image measures may vary greatly over the image of a homogeneous spatial texture, abrupt local changes in these measures signify either one or both of textural transitions and other types of edges we discussed in Chapter 3. In practice, however, competent texture discrimination in images of multiple nonplanar spatial textures that are projected perspectively onto the image plane remains to be demonstrated.

Fractals

Before we move on to structural methods of texture discrimination, let us pause to consider a class of interesting mathematical textures that seem to be ubiquitous nowadays: fractals. The engaging book by Mandelbrot [Mandelbrot 1983] provides an excellent introduction to fractals. **Fractals** are geometric shapes that exhibit self-similarity. That is, they are shapes that can be subdivided recursively into smaller nonoverlapping parts such that each part is a scaled-down version of the whole—either in a deterministic sense, or in a statistical sense; in practice, of course, there is an upper bound on the number of recursions over which self-similarity can be exhibited. Equivalently, fractals can be defined as shapes that can be generated by the recursive application of a "subdivision" scheme—this scheme, either deterministic, or statistical. If we can generate a fractal by recursively "subdividing" a geometric shape into N self-similar nonoverlapping shapes, each shape with a scale-down factor of r, then the *dimension of the fractal* is, by definition, $\log(N)/\log(1/r)$. This notion of fractional dimension is not incompatible with our notion that curves have dimension 1, surfaces have dimension 2, and so on; for example, the fractal dimension of a planar checkered pattern is easily computed to be 2. An example here should elucidate the various concepts.

Consider Figure 6.4. Let us start with a straight-line segment, called the *initiator*. From there on, let us "subdivide" recursively each straight-line segment using the rule illustrated immediately below the initiator in the figure; this rule is called the *generator*. Within a few steps of the recursion, we end up with a deterministic fractal "curve." The "roughness" of this "curve" is indexed by the latter's fractal dimension, which is $\log(6)/\log(4) \approx 1.3$. We could similarly generate variously textured fractal

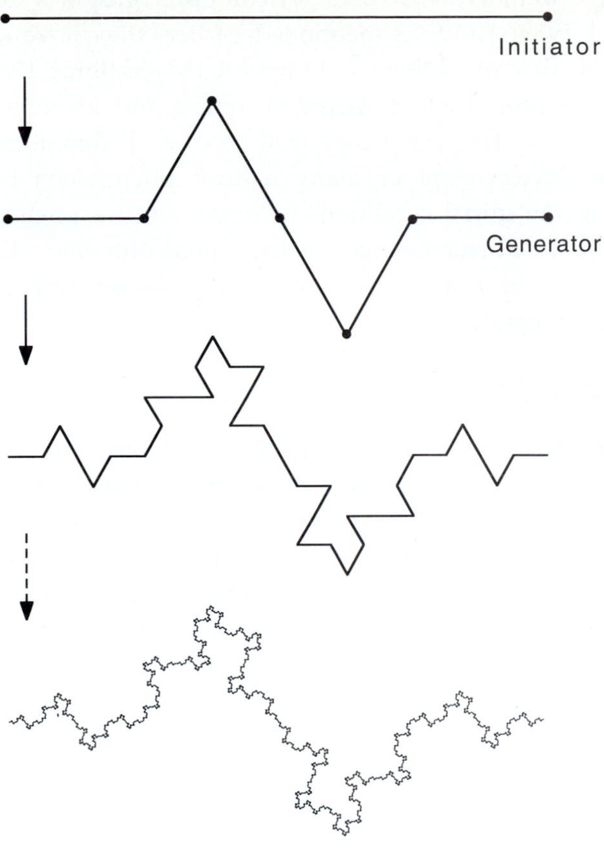

Figure 6.4 Fractals. *Fractals* are shapes that exhibit recursive self-similarity: Every fractal can be recursively subdivided into smaller nonoverlapping shapes, each of which is a scaled-down version of the whole, either in a deterministic sense, or in a statistical sense. Equivalently, fractals are shapes that, in principle, can be generated by the recursive "subdivision" of a geometric shape, called the *initiator*, into a number of self-similar nonoverlapping shapes according to some fixed rule, called the *generator*. A deterministic fractal is generated here by starting with a straight-line initiator and recursively applying to it the illustrated one-dimensional generator. If at each step of the (perhaps hypothetical) generation of a fractal, a shape is replaced by N self-similar nonoverlapping shapes, each of which is r times the size of the shape it replaces, then the *dimension of the fractal* is, by definition, said to be $\log(N)/\log(1/r)$. By this definition, the dimension of the fractal illustrated here is $\log(6)/\log(4) \approx 1.3$.

"surfaces" and "volumes" by recursively "subdividing" surfaces and volumes, respectively. Choosing the generator (and possibly also the initiator) to be nondeterministic would result in statistically self-similar shapes. Clearly, the number of possibilities is unlimited.

Fractals have found extensive use in computer graphics (e.g., [Musgrave and Mandelbrot 1989]), and, as mentioned earlier, they have also been used for image-texture discrimination. Mandelbrot [Mandelbrot 1983] claims that several natural textures, such as mountain reliefs and wave patterns, exhibit fractal characteristics. This claim may well be true. It definitely does not run contrary to the development of many natural phenomena being unstable: Small changes in the initial conditions of many natural phenomena, such as the weather, lead to drastic changes in their final outcome. It is easily seen that the generation of fractals is also unstable—with respect to both the initiator, and the generator.

6.1.2 Structural Methods

Structural methods of texture discrimination are best suited to images of those textures that have deterministic underlying causes. Most human-made textures fall in this category. In general, the structure of an image texture may be fairly difficult to discern or describe. Consequently, discrimination of image textures on the basis of the structures of the textures is, in general, more involved than that on the basis of the statistics of the textures. Hence, structural discrimination is pursued infrequently in practice. Clearly, textures that have identical structures, also have identical statistical properties of all orders. In this sense, statistical texture discrimination can be viewed as a convenient low-order approximation to structural discrimination. However, as statistical discrimination is applicable in many instances in which structural discrimination is not, statistical discrimination is more general. Hence, we shall keep our discussion of structural discrimination brief.

Structural texture discrimination is frequently based on the hypothesis that the textures comprise distinct identifiable **texels**, an abbreviation for *texture elements*, that are arranged in regular repetitive patterns. Each texture is sought to be characterized by a texel and its placement rules. Owing to the geometric distortion introduced by perspective projection, an image texel may be characterizable only up to certain invariant properties, rather than by an exact quantitative description. For example, if a three-dimensional texture were formed by the regular arrangement of identical circles on a surface, the image texels would be characterizable only as ellipses with varying major and minor axes and orientations (see Figure 6.6).

Zucker [Zucker 1976b] has proposed that structural texture description be modeled as a two-step process: first, the generation of "unobservable, highly regular ideal textures," and then, the introduction of "distortions" to yield observable textures. For instance, the first step might be the generation of a square planar grid, and the next, the generation of the perspective

Figure 6.5 An Escher-inspired pattern with two of several possible candidate *texels* (an abbreviation for *texture elements*). On repetition, each of the two candidate texels shown can be made to cover the illustrated pattern completely. An alternative to the choices of texels shown is a texel that is either completely black or completely white—such a choice assumes that the pattern comprises a foreground residing on a background of the opposite color. (Escher was a famous graphic artist whose work has received considerable attention in both art and psychology—we saw an example of his work, *Belvedere*, in Figure 1.6.)

projection of the grid. Although this two-step process is a reasonable model for many image textures with deterministic causes, it does not provide any help with the basic problems of texel identification and the determination of the texel placement rules. Further, as pointed out by Zucker, every texture has an equivalence class of structural descriptions. That is, as illustrated by the Escher-inspired pattern in Figure 6.5, it is possible to describe a texture by more than one choice of texels and accompanying placement rules.

One of the few implementations of a structural texture analyzer has been provided by Vilnrotter, Nevatia, and Price [Vilnrotter, Nevatia, and Price 1986]. Their approach is first to detect edges, and then to use the edge co-occurrence statistics to guide the extraction of texels; subsequently, the placement rules are determined. The authors claim that this technique is applicable to both regular and nondeterministic textures.

The extended discussion on structural texture description in [Ballard and Brown 1982] is used as a pretext here to conclude this section simply with the observation that, in practice, even textures that are deterministic by design necessarily exhibit statistical variations that may need to be modeled. Of course, often a texture is neither completely deterministic nor completely statistical by the very nature of its formation. For example, consider the texture we form by throwing pennies onto a horizontal planar surface. Whereas the underlying texture-forming elements here are deterministic, their placement is random. If we ignore the thickness of the pennies, this particular spatial texture happens to be well described by the so-called bombing model, which assumes a mosaic formed by the random placement of patterns ("bombs") within a plane [Ahuja and Rosenfeld 1981].

6.2 Shape Recovery

Variation in the image characteristics of a texture has been long recognized as a cue to surface shape. Ever since Gibson's classic *The Perception of the Visual World* [Gibson 1950], image textural variation as a cue to shape has been the subject of several investigations. Figure 6.6 provides a simple example of image textural variation in which a particular distribution of ellipses of various shapes and sizes suggests a receding corrugated surface in space. Note that the caveat for shape from shading, which was illustrated in Figure 5.3, applies equally well to shape from texture: Even though textural variation in an image is indeed a cue to three-dimensional surface shape, it is often the boundary of an image region that plays a central role in the region's three-dimensional interpretation by humans.

The principle that facilitates the recovery of shape from image texture is perspective projection, or some approximation to it. First, we shall study recovery under perspective projection, and then, that under orthographic projection. All the analyses, and the ensuing recovery methods, are based on the premise that the spatial texture resides on a physical surface in space. In practice, spatial textures are rarely confined to physical surfaces in space. What we have often is a fuzzy hypothetical surface that is defined by the texture itself—as, for instance, in the case of a ceiling of fleecy clouds in the

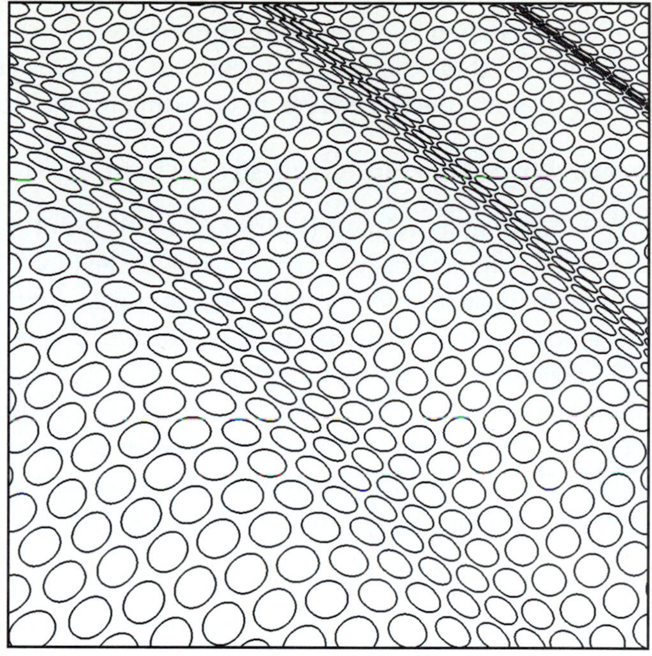

Figure 6.6 Image textural variation as a cue to three-dimensional shape. Variation in the image properties of a spatial texture often is a cue to three-dimensional shape. The illustrated distribution of ellipses of various shapes and sizes suggests a receding corrugated surface in space.

sky. In such cases, then, it shall be understood implicitly that what we are seeking to recover is this hypothetical, and only roughly defined, surface.

Invoking the assumption that the spatial texture resides on a surface in space entails more than just assuming that the spatial texture defines a (perhaps hypothetical and fuzzy) surface in space. It also entails the assumption that, from the standpoint of projection onto the image plane, the spatial texture is without relief [Stevens 1981]; that is, from the standpoint of projection, the texture is essentially two-dimensional in three-dimensional space, analogous to a printed pattern on a textile. Such an assumption precludes, for instance, three-dimensional spatial textures such as those constituted by tall blades of grass, or by roughly spherical pebbles on a beach. When viewed obliquely, three-dimensional textures not only distort quite differently from surface textures—spheres, for instance, project onto circles under orthographic projection irrespective of the projection direction—but also are subject to local self-occlusion. For instance, each individual sphere constituting a three-dimensional texture may partially occlude some of its neighbors, with the result that the fraction of a sphere that is visible under projection is different for different spheres. Thus, we see that the projections of three-dimensional textures are substantially more difficult to analyze than are the projections of two-dimensional textures.

6.2.1 Recovery Under Perspective Projection

As is evident from both Figure 6.1 and Figure 6.6, depth is not the only factor that determines the characteristics of an image texture vis-à-vis the characteristics of the spatial texture: Surface orientation also plays a role. A simple analysis elucidates the relationship. Consider an infinitesimal vector $[\Delta x_o \;\; \Delta y_o \;\; \Delta z_o]$ positioned at the point (x_o, y_o, z_o) in three-dimensional space. Let the center of perspective projection be at $(0, 0, 0)$, and let the image plane x_i–y_i be the plane $z = f$; this geometry is the same geometry as in Section 2.1.1. Then, it follows easily that the image of the infinitesimal vector is a vector in the image plane from $(fx_o/z_o, \;\; fy_o/z_o)$ to

$$\left(f(x_o + \Delta x_o)\,/\,(z_o + \Delta z_o)\,, \quad f(y_o + \Delta y_o)\,/\,(z_o + \Delta z_o)\right).$$

Pulling out the common factor (f/z_o), we can express the image vector as

$$\frac{f}{z_o}\left[\{(x_o + \Delta x_o)\,(1 - \frac{\Delta z_o}{z_o}) - x_o\} \quad \{(y_o + \Delta y_o)\,(1 - \frac{\Delta z_o}{z_o}) - y_o\}\right].$$

Now, if we assume $(\Delta z_o/z_o) \ll 1$, this image vector is approximately

$$\frac{f}{z_o}\left[\{\Delta x_o - \frac{x_o}{z_o}\Delta z_o\} \quad \{\Delta y_o - \frac{y_o}{z_o}\Delta z_o\}\right],$$

which is clearly a fairly complicated expression. Let us consider two special cases. First, let $\Delta z_o = 0$; that is, let the object vector be confined to a plane parallel to the image plane. Then, we see that the image vector is simply $(f/z_o)\,[\Delta x_o \;\; \Delta y_o]$; that is, the object is **scaled** by the factor (f/z_o). Now, assume that $\Delta z_o \neq 0$, but $\Delta x_o = \Delta y_o = 0$—that is, that the object vector is parallel to the optical axis (the *z*-axis here). Then, the image vector is $-(f/z_o^2)\,[x_o \;\; y_o]\,\Delta z_o$; in this case, the object is said to be **foreshortened** by the factor $(f/z_o)\left(\sqrt{x_o^2 + y_o^2}\,/\,z_o\right)$. Figure 6.7 illustrates the geometry of instances of scaling and foreshortening under perspective projection; see Figure 6.1 for manifestations of such instances in a photograph. The term *foreshortening* is used to describe the projective distortion of surfaces and lines that are not parallel to the image plane. It indicates that the dimension parallel to the optical axis—that is, the fore–aft dimension—is compressed relative to the frontal dimension. This assertion is, of course, strictly valid only when $\sqrt{x_o^2 + y_o^2} < z_o$.

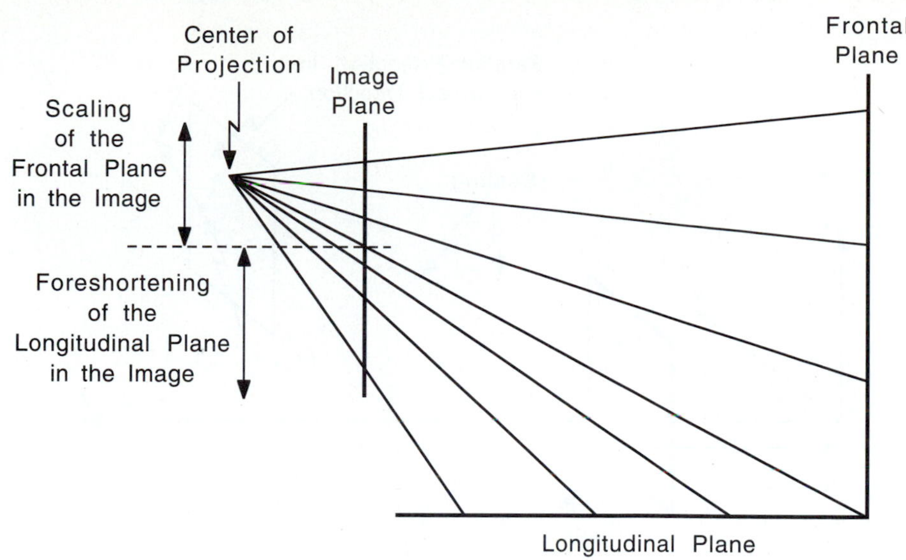

Figure 6.7 Scaling and foreshortening under perspective projection. The term *foreshortening* describes the deformation of lines and surfaces that are not parallel to the image plane under projection onto this plane. Whereas the term *scaling* indicates that the proportions of the object are maintained, the term *foreshortening* implies that the fore–aft dimensions of the object are compressed relative to its frontal dimensions. Strictly speaking, perspective projection leads to foreshortening in this sense only when the object lies within that 90° circular cone whose vertex is at the center of projection and whose axis is orthogonal to the image plane. The figure illustrates the geometry of instances of scaling and foreshortening that occur under perspective projection in the photograph in Figure 6.1. (After [Gibson 1950].)

What can we deduce from this simple analysis? Not only do changes in the characteristics of a texture under perspective projection depend on both depth and surface orientation, but also these changes are anisotropic; that is, at any point on a textured surface in space, these changes are different along different surface directions. That an isotropic scene texture may project onto an anisotropic image texture is immediately evident from the observation that the perspective projection of a circle is, in general, an ellipse. (It is worth pointing out here that, as far back as circa 300 B.C., Euclid had pursued a nonquantitative analysis of the variation among the angles subtended at the center of projection by the diameters of a (tilted) circle (pp. 365–367, [Euclid c. 300 B.C.], English translation).)

Recall the argument in Section 2.1.3 that, when an object is small relative to its average distance from the center of projection, perspective projection

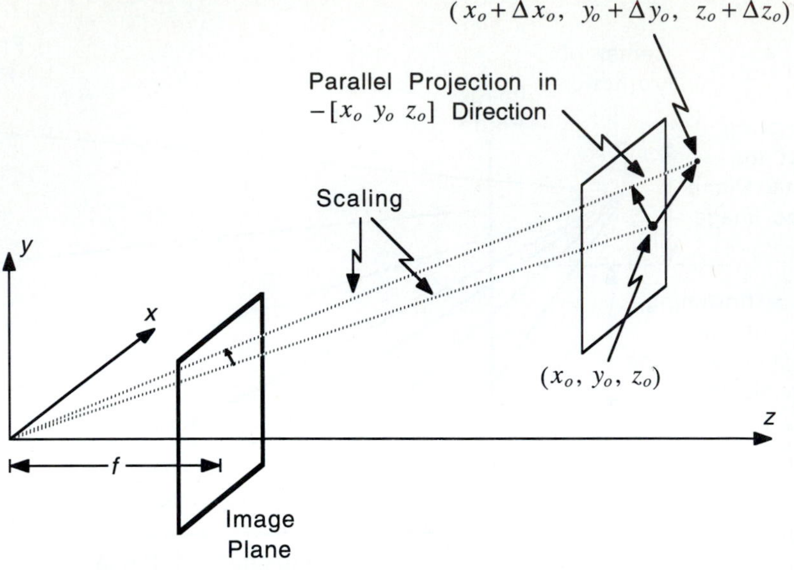

Figure 6.8 Paraperspective projection. *Paraperspective projection*—illustrated here for an infinitesimal vector—describes the approximation of perspective projection by parallel projection in the "average direction" of perspective projection, followed by scaling.

can be approximated by parallel projection up to a scale factor. Figure 6.8 illustrates this so-called paraperspective-projection geometry for an infinitesimal object vector. As paraperspective projection is a linear transform in three-dimensional space, it is a useful local approximation to perspective projection. Bear in mind, however, that each paraperspective approximation is valid only within a region that is small with respect to the viewing distance. In particular, every such region has a different paraperspective approximation—both the parallel projection direction and the scale factor depend on object position. With these qualifications in mind, let us apply the paraperspective approximation to perspective projection.

Let us consider a variety of **shape-from-texel** methods that are all based on the distortion of individual texels (i.e., texture elements). Suppose that a spatial surface texture comprises identifiable nonoverlapping texels, each texel with an identical area that is small enough for two conditions to be met:

1. The texel can be considered planar; that is, the orientation of the surface normal over the texel's area can be considered constant.
2. Paraperspective projection can be used to approximate the imaging geometry of the texel.

Then, if (x_o, y_o, z_o) is the position of a texel in the paraperspective-projection geometry of Figure 6.8, **n** is the texel's unit surface normal, A is the texel's area in space, and A' is the texel's area in the image, it can easily be verified that the area of the spatial texel projected orthographically in the direction of perspective projection is the following:

$$A \ \mathbf{n} \cdot \frac{-[\,x_o \ y_o \ z_o\,]}{\sqrt{x_o^2 + y_o^2 + z_o^2}} \ = \ \{A'\,(z_o/f)^2\} \ [\,0 \ \ 0 \ \ 1\,] \cdot \frac{[\,x_o \ y_o \ z_o\,]}{\sqrt{x_o^2 + y_o^2 + z_o^2}} \ .$$

This expression follows from three observations:

1. Orthographic projection foreshortens a planar area by the cosine of the angle between the area's surface normal and the direction of projection.
2. Both the original texel and its parallel projection in the direction of perspective projection have identical orthographic projections in the direction of perspective projection.
3. Under paraperspective projection, the parallel projection of the texel in the direction of perspective projection is a scaled version of its final image, the scale factor being (z_o/f).

Rearranging the preceding expression, we get

$$A' \ = \ -\frac{f^2}{z_o^3} \ \mathbf{n} \cdot [\,x_o \ \ y_o \ \ z_o\,] \ A\,.$$

Ohta, Maenobu, and Sakai [Ohta, Maenobu, and Sakai 1981] proposed the use of this relationship to estimate surface normals from triples of coplanar texels, assuming that the area A of the texel in space is not known a priori. Aloimonos and Swain [Aloimonos and Swain 1988] extended this work to recover nonplanar surfaces, providing experimental results for their algorithm on images of some simple shapes (e.g., cylinder, bottle) that were first painted black and then covered with synthetic circular texels.

Like most authors, both Ohta, Maenobu, and Sakai, and Aloimonos and Swain, essentially sidestep the issue of detecting texels in images, demonstrating their algorithms only on images of synthetic patterns. In contrast, Blostein and Ahuja [Blostein and Ahuja 1989] develop an algorithm that integrates the identification of image texels from among various candidates in the image, with the recovery of the orientation of the surface underlying the texels in space, this surface assumed to be planar. Blostein and Ahuja too base their surface recovery on the previously described relationship between the area of a texel in an image and its area in space. Blostein and Ahuja model candidate image texels, each of which they assume has an identical but unknown area in space, as image regions that are relatively bright or dark compared to their surround, and that exhibit a small gray-level variation relative to neighborhood image regions of the same size.

They represent each such region by a union of overlapping circular discs, the larger discs capturing the rough shape of the image texel, and the smaller discs capturing the details of the image texel (cf. the symmetric axis transform in Section 9.2.2). This work stands out—not only with respect to other work on shape from texture, but also with respect to other work in computer vision as a whole—for the number and variety of images on which the authors demonstrate their algorithm. Blostein and Ahuja provide estimates of image texels, along with an estimate for the orientation of the underlying spatial surface, which is assumed to be planar, for images of natural textures that range from an audience in a movie theater, to a field of sunflowers, to bathers on the Ganges. In most instances, at least one of their two estimates of the surface orientation—one estimate based on the hypothesis that the image texels are brighter than their background, and the other estimate based on the hypothesis that the image texels are darker than their background—appears subjectively plausible. A few sample results from this work are illustrated in Figure 6.9.

It was indicated in Section 2.1.1 that perspective-projection rays are conveniently represented by their intersections with a unit sphere centered at the center of projection. A unit spherical imaging surface rids us of the three unnecessary degrees of freedom needed for the position and orientation of a projection plane. Although spherical projection seems the most natural choice for computer vision, planar-perspective analysis is often preferred owing to our familiarity with planar geometry. (You are referred to [Gans 1973] for a collection of several useful well-known facts pertaining to spherical geometry.) Note that analysis under spherical projection does not require the physical existence of a spherical imaging surface: It is analytically straightforward to go from planar perspective to spherical perspective, and then back.

Ikeuchi [Ikeuchi 1984] makes a strong case in favor of texture analysis under spherical perspective projection in preference to that under planar perspective projection. He observes that, in spherical projection, the projection direction is always orthogonal to the image surface, as is true of orthographic projection. Consequently, the projective distortion is determined by only the relationship of the texel to the center of projection—both by the texel's relative position and by the texel's orientation relative to the projection direction. In particular, the projective distortion does not depend on the position of the projection on the imaging surface. If the assumptions detailed earlier for paraperspective approximation are satisfied here, the image sphere can be locally approximated by its tangent plane. Then, it is clear that spherical perspective projection onto a unit sphere can

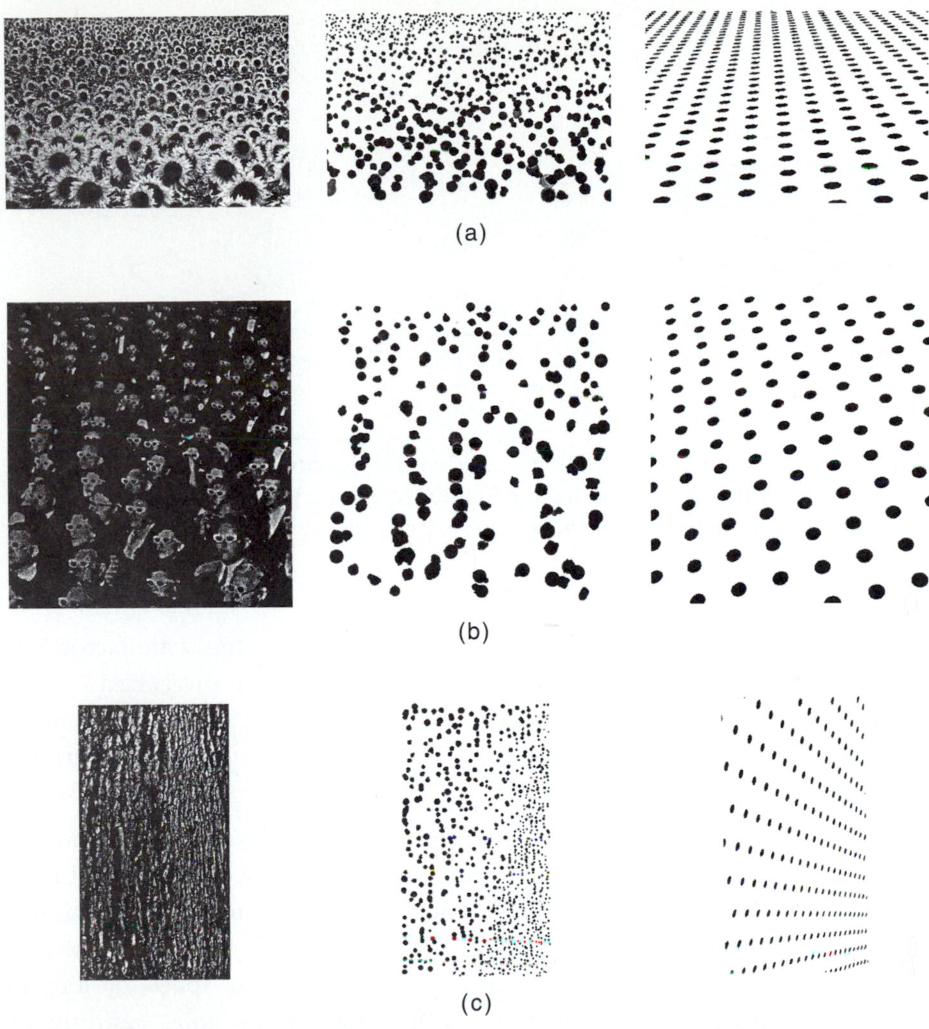

Figure 6.9 Results of an integrated approach to the identification of image texels from among various candidates, and the simultaneous recovery of the orientation of the (perhaps hypothetical) surface that underlies the texels in space. The surface underlying the texels in space is assumed to be planar here. Each image texel is modeled here as a region that has a relatively uniform intensity that is different from the surrounding intensity, and each such image texel is represented as a union of overlapping circular discs of varying sizes. On the left is the original image; in the middle are the image texels that are identified in the image; on the right is a synthetic image that illustrates the estimated surface orientation by simulating the perspective distortion of identical circular texels that reside on a planar surface in space. **(a)** Sunflowers. **(b)** Audience at a three-dimensional movie. **(c)** Tree trunk. (From [Blostein and Ahuja 1989] with permission, © 1989 IEEE.)

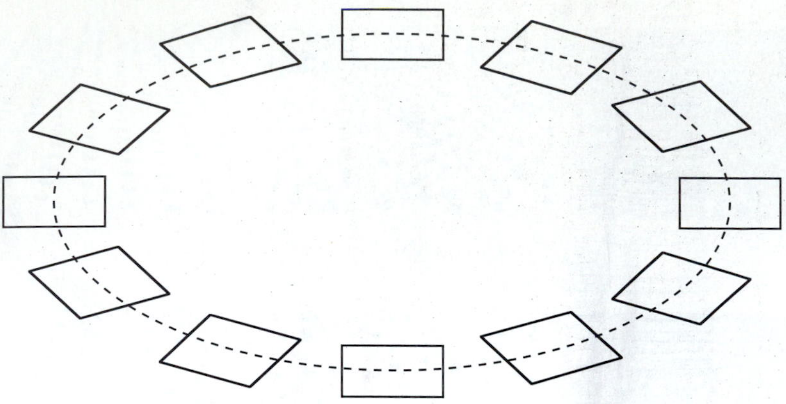

Figure 6.10 Orthographic projections of identical squares that are rotated with respect to one another in a plane inclined at 60° to the image plane. Notice that the orthographic projections of the rotated squares are not mere rotations of one another. (After [Ikeuchi 1984].)

be locally approximated by orthographic projection up to the scale factor $1/d$, where d is the distance of the object from the center of projection. Thus, recourse to spherical projection instead of planar projection leads to local orthographic-projection approximations, rather than to local parallel-projection approximations.

Ikeuchi [Ikeuchi 1984] invokes the local orthographic approximation to spherical projection described in the preceding paragraph to recover surface shape from the images of identifiable nonoverlapping texels with known spatial shape. He proposes a projection distortion measure that is based on the projections $\mathbf{p}_1$ and $\mathbf{p}_2$ of two orthogonal vectors in space of lengths l_1 and l_2, respectively, these spatially orthogonal vector pairs residing on the texels and assumed to be identifiable in the image. For instance, with square spatial texels, we could use the sides of the projected parallelogram for this purpose. The proposed projection distortion measure is $\| (\mathbf{p}_1/l_1) \times (\mathbf{p}_2/l_2) \| \;/\; [\| \mathbf{p}_1/l_1 \|^2 + \| \mathbf{p}_2/l_2 \|^2]$. This measure is shown to be equal to $(\cos\omega)/(1 + \cos^2\omega)$, where ω is the angle between the projection direction and the surface normal. Note that the measure varies neither under rotation of the texel about its surface normal, nor under translation of the texel along the projection direction. In contrast, the texel image itself, in general, changes shape when the texel is rotated about its surface normal. Figure 6.10 illustrates this change in shape for a square. The preceding dependence of the distortion measure on the angle between the surface normal and the projection direction quite naturally leads to constraint curves

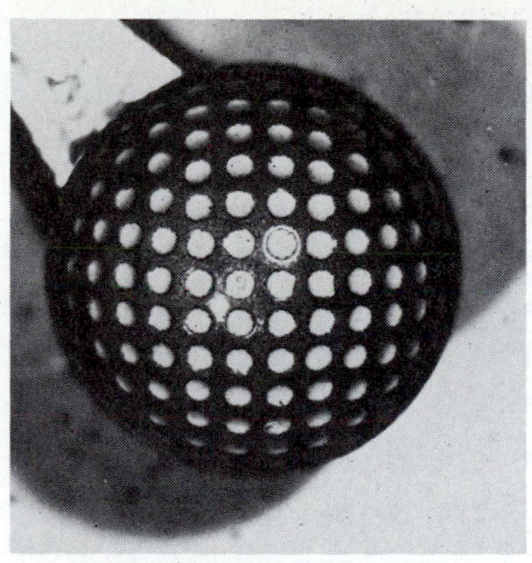

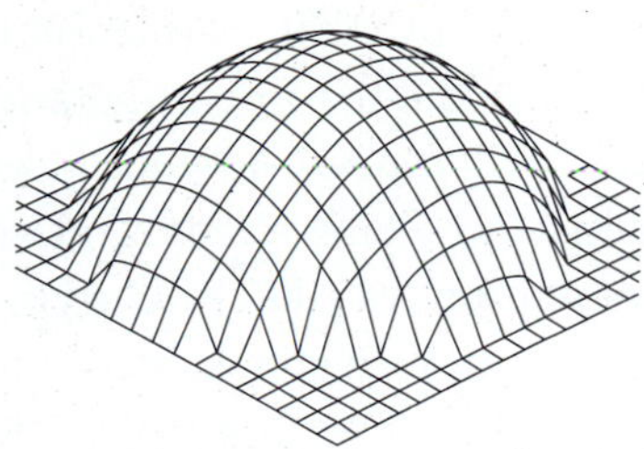

Figure 6.11 The shape of a golf ball recovered from the projective distortion of circular texels on the ball in space. On the left is an image of a golf ball that is covered with identical circular texels in space. On the right is the ball's shape recovered from the projective distortion of the texels on the ball. (From [Ikeuchi 1984] with permission.)

in surface-normal–orientation space. Although such curves are analogous to gradient-space reflectance-map curves in shape-from-shading analysis, it is important to note that a different set of curves applies to every projection direction here, as would be the case with shape from shading if we considered perspective projection instead of orthographic projection. Ikeuchi goes on to present an algorithm for surface recovery from surface-normal constraint curves; boundary conditions provided by continuous–surface-normal depth discontinuities are invoked (see Section 5.1.3). Figure 6.11 illustrates the performance of this algorithm on an image of a golf ball covered with circular texels.

The works of Ohta, Maenobu, and Sakai, and other authors, described in this section invoke just a few of the constraints that are possible under the assumption of identifiable nonoverlapping texels that are (possibly randomly) distributed over some surface. Another constraint that we might fruitfully employ, for instance, is that of skewed symmetry arising from the orthographic projection of bilaterally symmetric texels (see Section 4.1.2). Kender has proposed a general framework for such constraints, suggesting the use of the so-called normalized texture-property map, which for a particular image textural property provides the corresponding scene textural property as a function of surface orientation ([Kender 1980], [Kender and Kanade 1980]). For instance, given the area of an image texel, such a map would provide access to the possible texel areas in the scene as a function of surface orientation. In this fashion, each texel of a particular type and with a particular image property can be used to generate its own image–scene relationships. If we can further relate the properties of different individual texels in space—for instance, that they are coplanar and have the same area (as assumed by Ohta, Maenobu, and Sakai [Ohta, Maenobu, and Sakai 1981])—then the feasible orientations that the underlying surface may assume in space will reduce, in most cases, to a few. Relating texels in this way constrains the scene, enough relations leading to a complete determination of the orientation of the underlying surface. In the event that a sufficient number of such relations between texels are not available a priori, we could perhaps seek out surface orientations that favor regularity, homogeneity, and symmetry of texture elements in space under the premise that indications of such properties in the image are not accidental.

Our discussion thus far has been confined to textures comprising identifiable nonoverlapping texels. As we saw in Section 6.1, many natural textures do not fit such a characterization. Although the basic principles of shape recovery from such textures remain as described earlier, we may no longer use deterministic metrics—we must take recourse to statistical measures. Ever since Gibson's 1950 book [Gibson 1950], numerous authors have stated repeatedly that what we need to measure are variations in **texture density**. As was the case with shape-from-texel analysis, it is once again necessary to make assumptions about the spatial texture. Different assumptions yield different results, the validity of one implying the validity of the other. One assumption that has been invoked in the literature is **textural isotropy** in space: The properties of the texture at any point on the surface on which the texture resides in space are (statistically) the same in every surface direction. From Brodatz's textures illustrated in Figure 6.2, it would seem that such an assumption is often invalid. Another common assumption—one that is perhaps more tenable—is **textural homogeneity** in space: The (perhaps anisotropic) properties of the texture are the same at every point where the texture exists in space. Kanatani and Chou [Kanatani and Chou 1989], among other authors, adopt this assumption in the tradition of Gibson [Gibson 1950]. In addition to textural homogeneity, they also assume that the projection is perspective, and that "appropriate" image preprocessing provides a texture composed of dots "without area" and line segments "without width." The highlight of this work is that it does not require explicit image-texture density computations; rather, it requires only that the rule for density computation be available. The authors claim that this lack of dependence on explicit texture-density computations circumvents the requirement of other approaches that the image-texture density vary smoothly. However, they demonstrate their approach on only a few relatively simple synthetic examples.

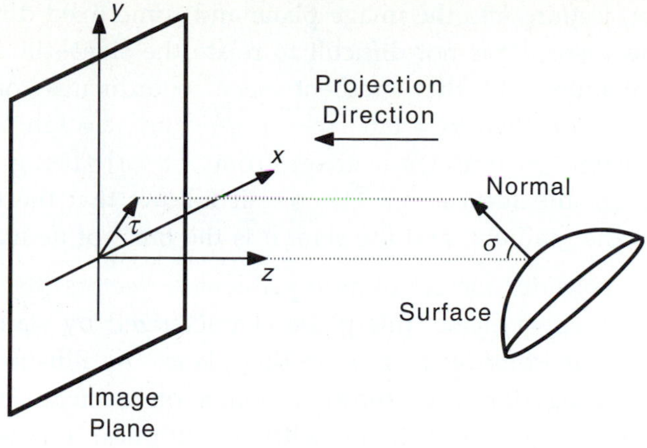

Figure 6.12 The slant σ and tilt τ of a surface. The *slant* of a surface at any point is the angle between the surface normal at the point and the direction of orthographic projection onto the image plane. The *tilt* of a surface at any point is the angle between the orthographic projection of the surface normal at the point onto the image plane and some fixed direction in the image plane. Equivalently, the slant and tilt of a surface at any point are the spherical polar coordinates of the surface-normal orientation at the point in a spherical coordinate frame whose polar axis is directed orthogonally toward the image plane. These definitions are independent of whether or not the surface is, in fact, projected orthographically onto the image plane.

6.2.2 Recovery Under Orthographic Projection

Thus far, we have restricted our attention to texel distortion under perspective projection (and its local approximations). When orthographic projection is an acceptable global approximation to perspective projection (see Section 2.1.2), the analysis becomes exceedingly simple. Let us now consider orthographic projection.

Recall the gradient-space representation for surface-normal orientation introduced in our discussion on shape from shading (in Section 5.1.1). In gradient space, the orientation of any vector with a component along the orthographic-projection direction, say the negative z-axis, is given by $(p,\ q)$, where $[p \quad q \quad -1]$ is the intersection of the $z=-1$ plane with the vector positioned at the origin and extended if necessary (see Figure 5.4). It is now convenient to introduce yet another representation, the slant–tilt representation, which specifies the orientation of a surface normal by two angles, **slant** (σ) and **tilt** (τ), both of which are illustrated in Figure 6.12; see, for instance, [Witkin 1981]. Slant is the angle between the normal and the orthographic-projection direction, and tilt is the angle between the normal's orthographic projection onto the image plane and some fixed direction in this plane—say, the x-axis. It is not difficult to relate the slant–tilt and gradient-space representations: If the gradient-space coordinates of a vector's orientation are (p, q), then $\sigma = \tan^{-1}\sqrt{p^2 + q^2}$ and $\tau = \tan^{-1}(q/p)$. Recall here that the name *gradient space* arises from $[p \;\; q]$ being the gradient $[\partial f/\partial x \;\; \partial f/\partial y]$ of the surface $z = f(x, y)$. It follows that the tilt τ is along the direction of the gradient, and the slant σ is the $\tan^{-1}$ of its magnitude.

Let us now consider the set of all equal-length vectors that are confined to some surface tangent plane, this plane characterized by slant–tilt σ_n–τ_n. Equivalently, we can consider a circle in this plane. As illustrated in Figure 6.13(a), parallel projection rays through points on a circle sweep out an elliptic cylinder—that is, a cylinder with an elliptical cross-section. The orthographic projection of a circle is, of course, that elliptical cross-section of such a cylinder that is orthogonal to the axis of the cylinder. The easiest way to convince yourself that the orthographic projection of a circle is an ellipse is to observe that all that orthographic projection does to any figure in a plane is to compress the figure uniformly along the direction of the plane's steepest descent with respect to the image plane. The direction of the steepest descent of a plane is the same as the direction of the gradient of the plane; hence, this direction is the same as the direction of the tilt τ_n of the plane. The dimensions of the planar figure that are orthogonal to the direction of the steepest descent of the figure's plane are parallel to the projection plane, and, hence, these dimensions remain unchanged under orthographic projection. Now, as any planar curve that is a second-order polynomial in x and y remains a second-order polynomial in x and y under uniform compression of the curve along any direction in the curve's plane, and every second-order polynomial in x and y with a closed trajectory is an ellipse (or a circle), we have the result that the orthographic projection of a circle is an ellipse. The major axis of the ellipse has the length of the diameter of the circle, and the minor axis of the ellipse has the length of the circle's diameter compressed by the cosine of the angle between the plane of the figure and the projection plane. But as this angle is the same as the angle between the surface normals to the two planes—and, hence, it is the same as the slant σ_n—the compression factor is simply $\cos\sigma_n$. Thus, we see that the direction of maximum foreshortening in the image plane is along the surface-normal tilt direction, and the magnitude of this foreshortening is the cosine of the surface-normal slant. Two comments are in order here, both comments illustrated in Figure 6.13(b). First, the surface-normal tilt is determined only up to a 180° ambiguity; this ambiguity is characteristic of orthographic projection—recall the ambiguous Necker cube in Figure 4.2. Second, for an

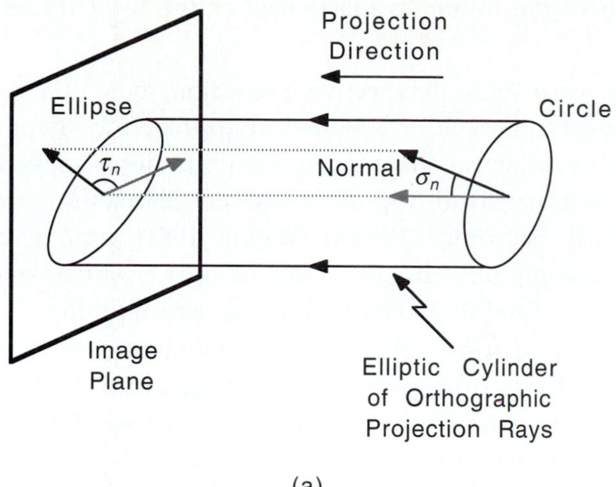

(a)

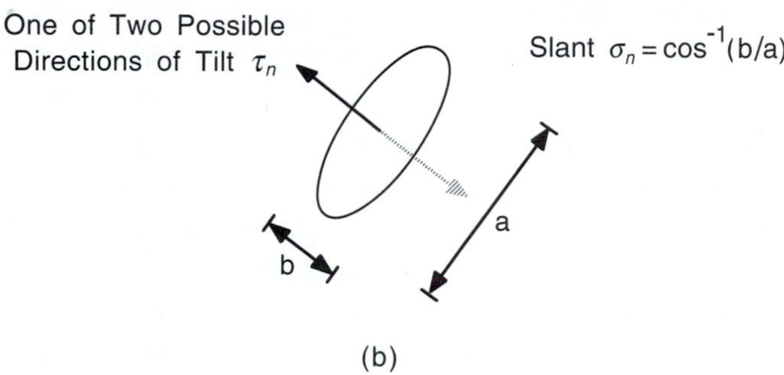

(b)

Figure 6.13 Recovery of the slant σ_n and tilt τ_n of a textured surface from the orthographic projection of that surface. The anisotropic (i.e., direction-dependent) distortion of surface texture under orthographic projection facilitates the recovery of the slant and tilt of a textured surface: The tilt of the surface is determined up to a 180° ambiguity by the direction in the image plane in which the surface texture undergoes maximum compression under projection, and the slant of the surface is determined by the extent of this compression. This relationship between the slant and tilt of a surface and the distortion of surface texture under orthographic projection is illustrated here with a circle. **(a)** Parallel rays that are oriented in the direction of orthographic projection and that pass through points on a circle sweep out an elliptic cylinder, whose elliptical intersection with the image plane yields the orthographic projection of the circle. **(b)** The direction of the tilt of the circle is along the minor axis of the elliptical projection of the circle, and the slant of the circle is the inverse cosine of the ratio of the minor to major axis of the elliptical projection of the circle.

isotropic texel—that is, for a circular texel—the maximum foreshortening is simply the ratio of the minor to major axis of the texel under orthographic projection.

As was the case with perspective projection, here too we can pursue either a texel-based approach or a statistical approach to shape recovery. As we saw in our discussion on shape from texture under perspective projection, when we pursue a statistical approach, one possible assumption is that the texture is spatially isotropic. Witkin [Witkin 1981], among other authors, adopts such an assumption. In particular, he carries out a Bayesian analysis (see Footnote 7 in Section 3.3.3) under the assumptions of orthographic projection and that a priori all surface orientations are equally likely, all edge-tangent directions of the texture on a surface are equally likely, and that the edge-element orientations on a surface are independent of one another and of the surface orientation. He seeks to assign to an image texture that spatial surface orientation that would tend to imply an isotropic distribution of the texture's edgel orientations on a surface in space. This proposal leads, for instance, to the interpretation of ellipses as slanted circles. As was illustrated in Figure 6.13(b), there is an ambiguity of tilt—the global sign of the depth gradient was set manually by Witkin in his experiments. The appeal of Witkin's work lies in his careful analysis; the work's shortcoming, as noted by Witkin, lies in his assumptions. For instance, as is evident from Brodatz's textures in Figure 6.2, one assumption that is often suspect is that the distribution of the texture's edgel orientations in space is isotropic. Two other works that, in the tradition of Witkin, invoke this isotropy assumption are [Kanatani 1984] and [Blake and Marinos 1990]. The former is a deterministic proposal that is based on counting the number of intersections of the texture's edges with variously oriented lines across the image, whereas the latter seeks to extend Witkin's approach.

6.3 Discussion

Clearly, much work lies ahead in the analysis of image textures. None of the research to this point has confronted the combined problems of texture discrimination and shape from texture in their generality: the recovery of the shapes of multiple nonplanar textured surfaces in space from their simultaneous perspective projections onto a single image. General solutions to the two central problems in image-texture analysis—discrimination and shape recovery—remain largely elusive for natural textures even when each of these problems is considered in isolation. Almost all the work on image-texture analysis to this point has been restricted to one of two scenarios:

1. The discrimination between planar spatial textures that are, for all practical purposes, viewed orthographically, as in satellite imagery
2. The recovery of surface shape from single isolated image textures under various highly simplifying assumptions, such as a planar textured surface in space, or a surface texture comprising identical spatial texels whose shapes are known a priori

The key to shape recovery lies in accurate models of spatial textures, these models accompanied by observable image metrics. It is plausible that progress in image-texture analysis has been hindered by the overambitiousness of the various projects: exact surface recovery from insufficient world knowledge, rather than just approximate recovery. Based on their extensive experiments with images of natural textures (see Figure 6.9), Blostein and Ahuja [Blostein and Ahuja 1989] argue that the significant variability that is characteristic of natural textures precludes the exact recovery of the surface orientation underlying such textures: The best we can hope for is coarse judgments of surface orientation.

The reasons for the limited success of image-texture analysis may have much to do with the physical limitations of digital images. Now, although a spatial texture might ideally exhibit certain characteristic intensity variations on the image plane, the ability of a digital image to capture these variations depends on their rapidity of fluctuation relative to the sampling interval of the digital image (as explained in Section 2.3.1). Thus, we see that the nature of the digital image of a spatial texture depends not only on the geometry of image formation, but also on the density of the texture in the image relative to the interpixel spacing. In particular, as a spatial texture recedes from a camera, or as it is viewed at increasingly oblique angles, the digital image of the texture will eventually begin to exhibit systematic and substantial sampling artifacts.

Even when we are unable to derive accurate numerical estimates for the surface orientation based on image textural variation, we may be in a position to impose tangible nonmetric constraints on the scene based on such variation. Figure 6.14 illustrates two relatively simple but powerful constraints that we may be able to impose on the scene in the presence of discontinuities in a quantifiable image textural characteristic, such as image-texture density. If we assume that the particular textural characteristic that is discontinuous in the image varies continuously over the imaged surface(s) in space, then we can deduce spatial depth discontinuities and surface-normal discontinuities, respectively, from zeroth-order and first-order discontinuities in the image textural characteristic. As illustrated in Figure 6.14, under this

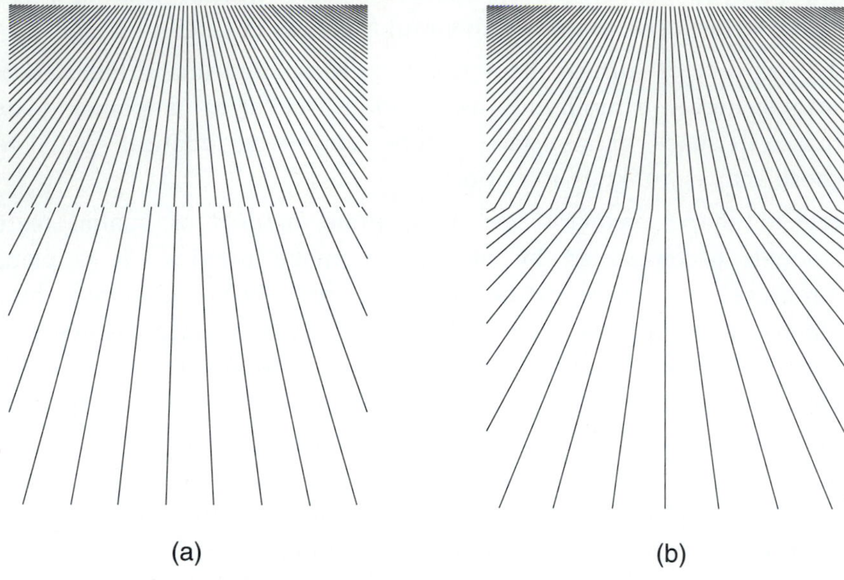

Figure 6.14 Three-dimensional implications of discontinuities in the image characteristics of a spatial texture. Discontinuities in the image characteristics of a spatial texture indicate surface discontinuities in space, assuming that these texture characteristics vary continuously over the imaged surface(s) in space. **(a)** A zeroth-order discontinuity in an image property of a texture—that is, a discontinuity in the magnitude of an image-texture property such as image-texture density—indicates a depth discontinuity in space. **(b)** A first-order discontinuity in an image property of a texture—that is, a discontinuity in the gradient of an image-texture property such as image-texture density—indicates a surface-normal discontinuity in space. (From [Gibson 1950] with permission. Copyright © 1977, 1950 by Houghton Mifflin Company.)

assumption, a spatial depth discontinuity could manifest itself in the image as a zeroth-order discontinuity in the image-texture density, and a surface-normal discontinuity could manifest itself in the image as a first-order discontinuity in the image-texture density [Gibson 1950].

Finally, for those of you who might be tempted to believe that shading is simply an instance of image textural variation, it is pointed out that the two are fundamentally different. For instance, whereas the image irradiance depends on the scene illumination, the image-texture density is independent of the scene illumination. Further, whereas the image irradiance depends only on the orientation of the surface, and not on the distance of the surface from the camera, the image-texture density depends on both, as illustrated in Figure 6.14.

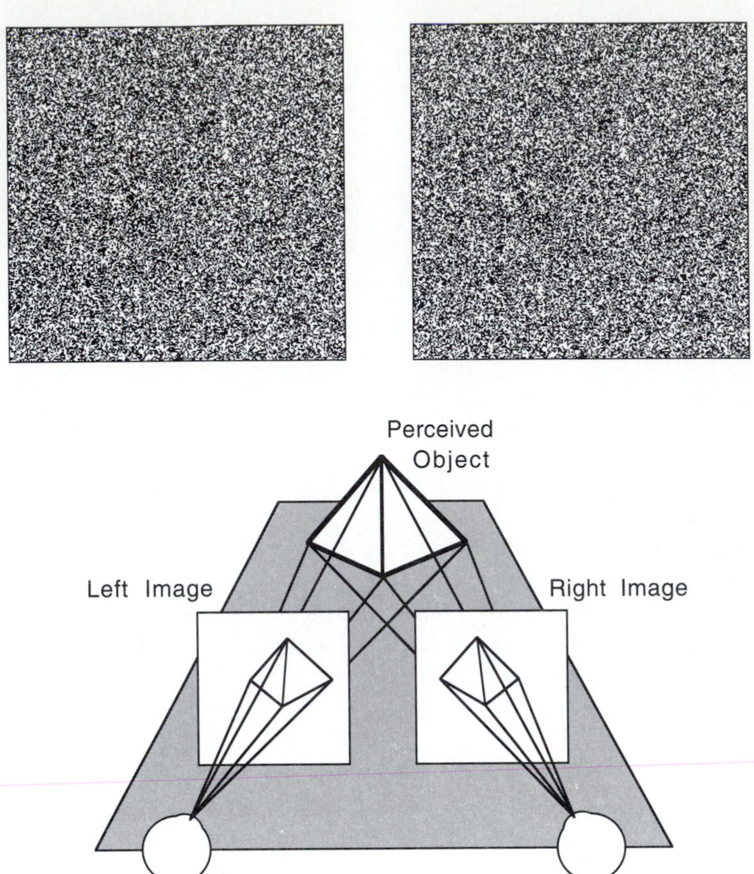

Figure 7.1 Stereo. Multiple images of a three-dimensional scene, each image acquired from a different viewpoint in space, facilitate the recovery of the three-dimensional structure of the scene in a process known as *stereo.* Whereas each of the two binary random-dot images on top lacks monocular coherence and structure, when we view the two images together stereoscopically as illustrated below, we see a + partially occluding a □, both floating above a background. Mental fusion of the two disparate images—the left image viewed by the left eye, and the right image viewed by the right eye—may require considerable effort on the part of some observers, and may not be possible for others. You might find the following suggestion helpful in fusing the two images: First, place a thin opaque partition (e.g., a piece of cardboard) between the two images to restrict each eye's view to a single image, and then try to stare continuously at a single central point in one image until a single coherent image emerges from the two disparate views. (Pairs of stereo images—*stereograms,* for short—in which each image comprises random dots, as here, were first devised by Julesz in 1960 [Julesz 1960]; the illustrated schematic for stereoscopic viewing is after [Gibson 1950].)

Chapter 7

Stereo

Stereo—from *stereós*, Greek for solid—is a broad term indicating the involvement of three-dimensional space. However, the use of the term *stereo* in computer vision, as in human vision, has traditionally been restricted to the recovery of a three-dimensional scene from multiple images of the scene. Our focus in this chapter shall be on the recovery of a scene from a pair of images of the scene, each image acquired from a different viewpoint. Previously, in Chapter 1, we saw how the human visual pathways from the two eyes to the brain are configured to make stereoscopic depth perception possible in humans. Figure 7.1 outlines an experiment designed to heighten your awareness of your stereo vision if you possess such vision. You are encouraged to attempt this experiment, especially if you have never attempted such an experiment before: The delight you will experience on performing the experiment successfully will more than compensate you for the frustration you might experience along the way.

With the exception of photometric stereo (Section 5.1.3), all the three-dimensional constraint-generation techniques that we have discussed thus far employ single-image cues—for example, image textural variation. Shape recovery using single-image cues typically depends on the propagation of constraints across image regions—as, for instance, in the characteristic-strip shape-from-shading method (Section 5.1.3). In contrast, stereo methods are more local and direct; hence, they hold the potential for greater robustness.

As we saw at length in Chapter 2, image formation depends on several geometric and radiometric parameters. We can vary any or several of these parameters to generate multiple images. Of course, three-dimensional recovery might be more feasible under certain variations than it is under others. Also, certain parametric variations might be easier to accomplish and to control accurately than are others. A method employing variation of scene illumination—photometric stereo—was outlined in Section 5.1.3. Although this technique seems fairly reliable and accurate where the reflectance-map analysis is valid and carefully controlled variation of the lighting is possible, its applicability in more general settings is limited. Another parameter that might be varied to generate multiple images is the location of the object plane that is in focus. We can accomplish such a variation easily by varying either the focal length of the lens, or the distance of the image plane from the optical center of the lens. We saw in Figure 2.12 how an object point's not being in focus affects that point's image. Clearly, a (possibly predicted) camera setting that brings a particular point into focus provides an estimate for that point's spatial position via the lens law. Like photometric stereo, **defocus stereo** has thus far been demonstrated only in carefully controlled laboratory settings (see [Nayar and Nakagawa 1990]; see also [Krotkov 1987]).

By far the most widely investigated stereo technique employs the variation of camera position—let us call this technique **geometric stereo**. In the absence of any qualification, the term *stereo* invariably refers to geometric stereo. Although attention has largely been devoted to image pairs generated by two individual cameras, we can conceive of a single camera capturing images while undergoing displacement (and possibly also rotation) in a static environment, or of the use of more than two cameras (e.g., [Ito and Ishii 1986], [Yachida 1986]). For purposes of exposition, let us assume two cameras with known planar-perspective-projection geometric models.

Whereas the theoretical basis for geometric stereo is straightforward, the implementation of geometric stereo is a nontrivial enterprise. The latter requires that we establish correspondence between points in one image with points in the other image such that each of two matched points is the image of the same point in space. Let us first discuss the theory that underlies geometric stereo, and then consider various approaches to the correspondence problem. (See [Faugeras 1989] and [Dhond and Aggarwal 1989] for more detailed reviews with different emphases from the one here.)

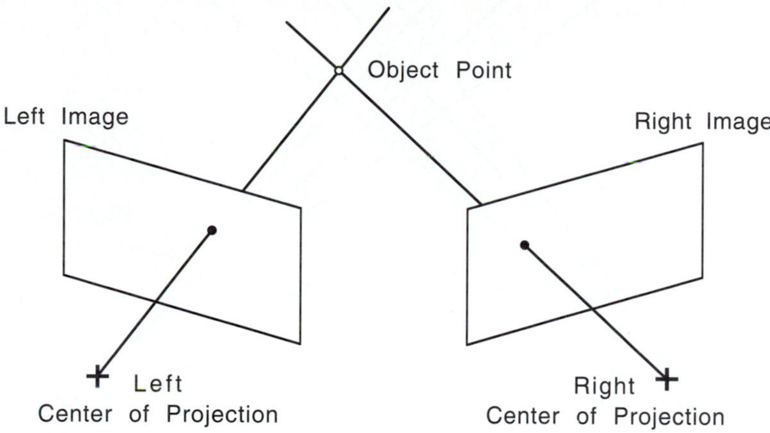

Figure 7.2 Triangulation. Geometric stereo is based on triangulation. Given a single image, the three-dimensional location of any visible object point is restricted to the straight line that passes through the center of projection and the image of the object point; more specifically, the three-dimensional location of the object point is restricted to only that portion of this straight line that extends outward from the image. Consequently, with two independent images, we can locate the three-dimensional position of any object point that is visible in both images to be at the intersection of two straight lines. The determination of the position of an object point in this fashion—by finding the intersection of two straight lines—is called *triangulation*. As is clear from the figure, the recovery of the scene position of an object point through triangulation requires that we match the image location of the object point in one image to the location of the object point in the other image. The process of establishing such matches between points in a pair of images is called *correspondence establishment*.

7.1 Theoretical Basis

The principle that underlies geometric stereo is **triangulation**. As illustrated in Figure 7.2, under the assumption of perspective projection, each image point is the projection of some point along the ray through the image point and its center of projection—actually, along only that portion of this ray that extends outward from the image point. If the corresponding point in the other image is known, then the object point must also lie on the corresponding ray through that point. Hence, the object point must lie at the intersection of the two rays; the determination of this intersection is called *triangulation*. We are assuming here that every image point is the perspective projection of an object point, and that each image point has at most a single unique matching point in the other image; this assumption excludes transparent objects from the scene.

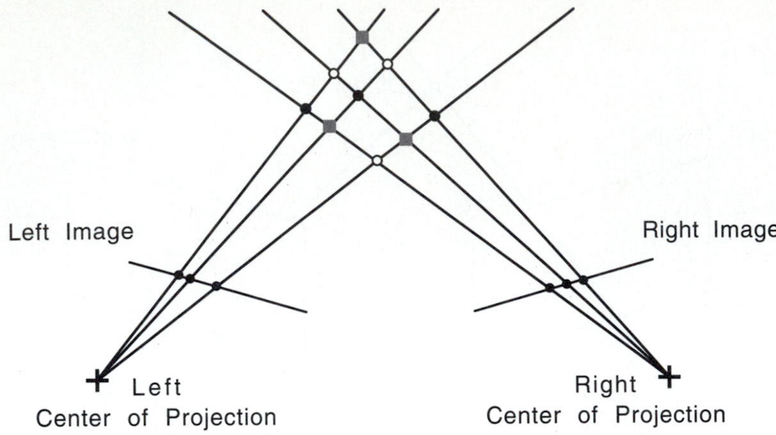

Figure 7.3 The implication of ambiguous correspondence between image points with regard to scene recovery through triangulation. The determination of the three-dimensional locations of scene points through triangulation requires that we establish *correspondence* between individual points in the two images such that each point in a pair of matched points is the image of the same object point. As illustrated, when the correspondence between multiple points in two images is ambiguous, triangulation may lead to several different consistent interpretations of the scene. (After [Julesz 1971].)

The practical difficulty with geometric stereo is the establishment of **correspondence**—that is, the pairing up of points in the two images such that each point in a pair of points is the image of the same point in space. As illustrated in Figure 7.3, ambiguous correspondence between points in the two images may lead to several different consistent interpretations of the scene. However, as we shall see in Section 7.2, such local ambiguities often can be resolved at a global level. The problem of correspondence establishment is further confounded by the fact that, in general, some points in each image will have no corresponding points in the other image. There are two reasons for this absence of corresponding points. First, clearly the two cameras will have different fields of view. Second, as illustrated in Figure 7.4, objects in the scene may occlude differently in the two images.

You might suspect that the establishment of correspondence requires that an entire image be searched for every point in the other image. Fortunately, such a two-dimensional search is unnecessary because of a simple but powerful constraint: the **epipolar constraint**. As illustrated in Figure 7.5, given an image point, its corresponding point in the other image is constrained to lie on the straight line that is the projection of the line through the given image point and its center of projection—actually, it is constrained

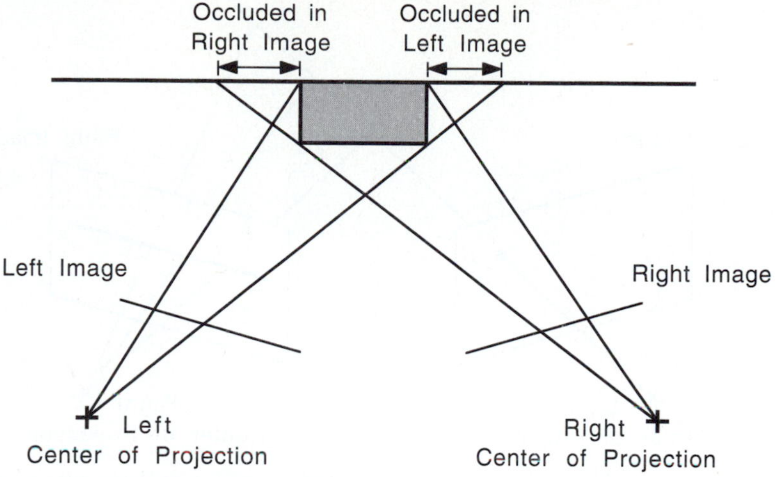

Figure 7.4 Occlusion as an impediment to stereo. Occlusion is a viewpoint-dependent phenomenon: Points in the scene that are visible from one viewpoint may not be visible from another viewpoint. The spatial positions of points that are visible from a single viewpoint cannot be recovered through triangulation.

to lie on the projection of only that portion of this line that extends outward from the given image point, rather than on the projection of the whole line. It is useful to introduce some terminology here. Consider Figure 7.6. The line connecting the two centers of projection is called the **baseline**. A plane through the baseline is termed an **epipolar plane**. Any such plane will, in general, intersect the two image planes along straight lines—these straight lines are called **epipolar lines**. Clearly, any point on an epipolar line has its corresponding image, if any, on the corresponding epipolar line—this restriction is called the *epipolar constraint*. (It seems that Keating, Wolf, and Scarpace [Keating, Wolf, and Scarpace 1975] were the first to describe the epipolar constraint explicitly; however, this constraint had been used earlier implicitly—for example, by Levine, O'Handley, and Yagi [Levine, O'Handley, and Yagi 1973].) Restricting correspondence search to conjugate epipolar lines results in a tremendous computational saving over and above the increase in the likelihood of obtaining correct matches. In general, the epipolar lines in each image converge toward the intersection of the image plane with the baseline—such an intersection is called an **epipole**. For computational convenience, the two image planes are often chosen to be coplanar and parallel to their baseline. Such an arrangement of image planes can be accomplished either physically, or, more conveniently, through analytic transformations. At any rate, when the stereo images are, in effect,

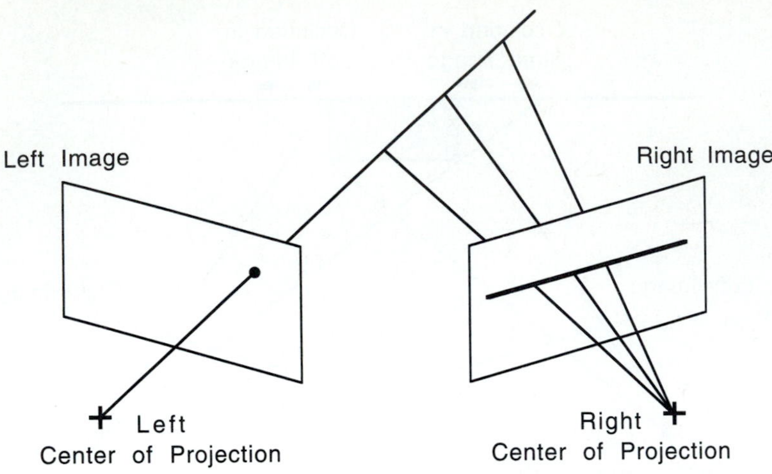

Figure 7.5 Restriction on the image location of the conjugate of a point in one image in another image. The *conjugate*, if any, of a point in one image in another image is the point in the second image that has the same preimage as the point in the first image. In other words, each point in a pair of conjugate image points is the image of the same object point. As illustrated, given a point in one image, its conjugate in another image is restricted to the straight line that is the projection of the straight line through the given image point and its center of projection. More specifically, the conjugate of the given point is restricted to the projection of only that portion of this straight line that extends outward from the image containing the given point.

coplanar and parallel to their baseline, the images are said to be **rectified**. Epipolar lines in rectified stereo images are parallel, and conjugate epipolar lines in rectified stereo images are collinear. Another term that is encountered frequently is **disparity**. Whereas *disparity*, in general, refers to the differences between conjugate image points (or other image features) in any of a number of respects, in the absence of any qualification, *disparity* usually denotes the displacement between conjugate image points when the two images are first rectified, and then overlaid such that their epipolar lines and centers of projection coincide.

Before we move on, note that, as the distance between the two centers of projection is increased, the angle between the corresponding projection rays through any given object point will also increase. For this reason, geometric stereo in which the distance between the two centers of projection is large is called **wide-angle stereo**, and geometric stereo in which the distance between the two centers of projection is small is called **narrow-angle stereo**. Wide-angle stereo provides more precise estimates for the three-dimensional

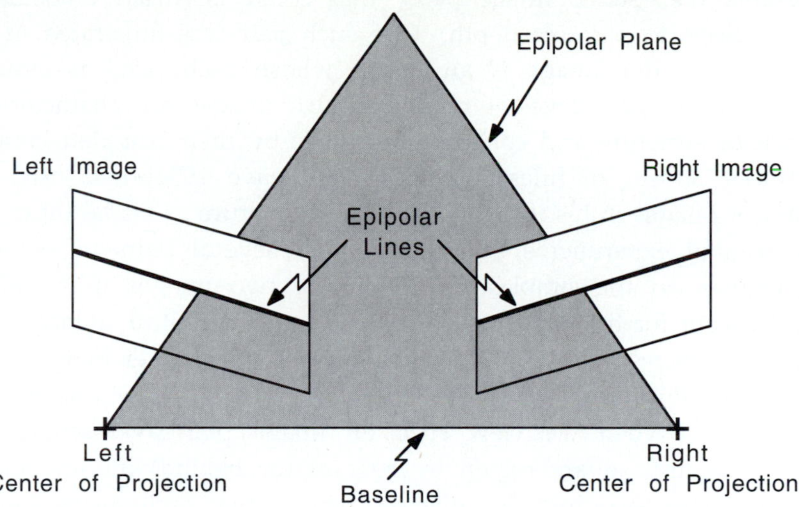

Figure 7.6 The epipolar geometry. Suppose that we have two image planes, each image plane with a different center of projection. Then, each of the possibly two images of every object point that lies within a particular plane passing through the two centers of projection is restricted to the intersection of this plane with the image plane. A plane that passes through the two centers of projection is called an *epipolar plane*, and the two straight-line intersections of an epipolar plane with the two image planes are called *conjugate (or corresponding) epipolar lines*. As is clear from the figure, conjugate epipolar lines exhibit the following important property: The conjugate, if any, of a point on one epipolar line is restricted to the corresponding epipolar line in the other image.

positions of scene points than does narrow-angle stereo. However, wide-angle stereo is disadvantageous with respect to narrow-angle stereo in at least two respects:

1. It is more difficult to establish correspondence between image points when wide-angle stereo is used.
2. In wide-angle stereo, there is likely to be less overlap between the two fields of view.

Random-Dot Stereograms

The epipolar constraint notwithstanding, you might wonder whether binocular depth perception can proceed without monocular interpretation. That is, is it possible to deduce depth variations from a pair of stereo images without first interpreting each image individually? The answer is yes. In a series of innovative experiments, Julesz [Julesz 1960] devised random-dot

stereograms (i.e., stereo image pairs) that could be fused binocularly by human subjects to perceive depth. One such pair was illustrated in Figure 7.1. A **random-dot image** is an image whose each pixel is assigned a (possibly binary) gray level at random. Such images are characterized by their lack of structure and coherence—that is, by their complete monocular randomness. (Prior to Julesz, Attneave [Attneave 1954] had used binary random-dot images in his investigation into the nature of visual information.) In his original experiments, Julesz generated several pairs of random-dot stereo images, in the simplest of which the two images in a pair were identical except for the horizontal displacement of a central square region in one image with respect to the matching region in the other image—the gap ensuing from this displacement (in one of the two images) was filled with random dots. When we view such an image pair stereoscopically, we perceive a central square region in front of (or behind) its surround; this perception, when acquired, is quite distinct, despite each image's apparent complete monocular randomness. Julesz provides an extensive account of this and related work in [Julesz 1971]. Since the original demonstration of Julesz, several more sophisticated random-dot stereograms have been devised; the books by Julesz [Julesz 1971] and Frisby [Frisby 1980] provide a fair variety.

Successful stereoscopic fusion of random-dot images by humans does not indicate that binocular stereopsis precedes monocular interpretation in humans, much less that machine stereo should follow this route. What it does reveal is that binocular depth perception is possible in the absence of monocular cues. However, as noted by Julesz [Julesz 1960], the presence of monocular structure in stereo images greatly speeds up human binocular depth perception. Also, as pointed out by Binford [Binford 1984], our ability to perceive depth from random-dot stereograms is weak, and is limited to the perception of relatively simple surface configurations.

Camera Calibration for Geometric Stereo

For geometric stereo to be possible, it is necessary that we have geometric models of the cameras. Our discussion thus far has been premised on the availability of the perspective-projection model of each camera. We studied how such a model of a camera might be derived in Section 2.1.4. Let us now briefly revisit the problem of camera calibration in the specific context of geometric stereo.

Often, the intrinsic parameters of a camera are known a priori, perhaps due to a priori camera calibration (see Section 2.1.4). Then, to specify the geometric model of the camera, we need only to determine the six degrees of freedom associated with the camera's orientation and position. As far as geometric stereo is concerned, it may be sufficient (and possible) to determine only the orientation and position of one camera with respect to the other; such a determination would allow us to compute the spatial positions of the imaged scene points with respect to the camera pair. We can, of course, determine the orientation and position of one camera with respect to another by simply calibrating each camera individually based on the image positions of six or more points, each point with a known position in space; typically, stereo calibration is pursued in this fashion using a known calibration object (see Section 2.1.4, and, in addition, [Faugeras and Toscani 1986]). However, although the use of a calibration object may be the preferred route to stereo calibration, such a route is neither always possible nor convenient—as, for instance, in a stereo system in which a single camera undergoes (an unknown, or inaccurately known) displacement in an unknown environment, capturing images at multiple camera locations.

We may have no choice but to calibrate a stereo system by establishing correspondence between individual points in the two images such that each point in a pair of matched points is the image of the same object point (whose spatial location is unknown a priori). Under such circumstances, we can argue easily, as we will in Chapter 8, that the distance between the two camera positions cannot be determined: Only the direction of relative displacement between the two cameras can be determined. We are then left with just five determinable degrees of freedom: three for the orientation of one camera with respect to the other, and two for the direction of displacement between the two cameras. A variety of solutions to these five degrees of freedom have been proposed in the literature. It has been known for some time that an iterative solution to the five degrees of freedom requires at least five pairs of corresponding points. However, considerations of robustness demand that many more points be used; see, for instance, [Gennery 1977]. Longuet-Higgins [Longuet-Higgins 1981] has shown that, barring the case where all the points in the scene lie on a quadric surface that passes through the two viewpoints [Longuet-Higgins 1984b], eight point pairs determine a set of simultaneous linear equations that provide a unique closed-form solution to the five degrees of freedom (see also [Longuet-Higgins 1988]). Faugeras, Lustman, and Toscani [Faugeras, Lustman, and Toscani 1987] modified this approach to derive a more robust closed-form solution that accommodates a larger set of noisy data. Tsai and Huang [Tsai and Huang 1984] arrived at the Longuet-Higgins eight-point result independently, showing in addition that (barring degenerate cases) seven point pairs are sufficient to guarantee uniqueness. Subsequently, Zhuang [Zhuang 1989] proposed a simplification to the eight-point approach, and Weng, Huang, and Ahuja [Weng, Huang, and Ahuja 1989] modified the eight-point approach to make it more robust to noisy data, and then pursued its error analysis.

Although the eight-point approach and its variants provide convenient closed-form solutions to the five determinable degrees of freedom that relate the orientations and positions of two cameras, these approaches only partially exploit the constraints that are imposed on the solution by the data. When the data are noiseless, the constraints that remain unused by the eight-point approach are consistent with the constraints that are enforced, and, hence, the underutilization of constraints is not an issue. However, when the data are noisy, this underutilization is a concern. When the data are noisy, one possible strategy is to use the eight-point approach to determine a tentative solution that serves as a starting point for an iterative numerical solution to the complete set of constraints that are imposed on the solution by the data.

7.2 Correspondence Establishment

With the background of Section 7.1, let us now turn our attention to correspondence establishment. The issues here are what to match, how to select candidate matches, and how to determine the goodness of a match. We established in Section 7.1 that correspondence search can be restricted to conjugate epipolar lines. Let us now consider how search along such lines may proceed. One set of techniques is based on matching image intensities, and the other is based on matching intensity edges. We shall not discuss the large number of locally cooperative and parallel mechanisms that have been proposed in the literature specifically for the establishment of correspondence between random-dot stereo images; see, for instance, [Julesz 1971], [Dev 1975], [Marr and Poggio 1976], and [Marroquin, Mitter, and Poggio 1987].

7.2.1 Intensity-Based Methods

A straightforward approach to establishing correspondence along conjugate epipolar lines is to match points on the basis of their image intensities. Such a strategy, of course, assumes that scene points have the same intensity in each image. As is evident from our discussion of shading in Chapter 5, such an assumption is, in general, strictly accurate for only perfectly matte surfaces. (It is of passing interest to note here that humans are capable of stereoscopically fusing binary-image pairs in which one of the two images has undergone contrast reversal in that its blacks and whites have been interchanged [Helmholtz 1910]. The perceived three-dimensional surface, then, appears lustrous, a lustrous surface providing a plausible explanation for a sudden change in the image intensity between two viewpoints.)

As several points along each epipolar line may have closely matching intensities, establishing correspondence by matching intensities on a point-by-point basis is clearly not feasible. We must instead minimize some measure of similarity between the intensity patterns exhibited by image regions. These regions could be small image windows, whole epipolar lines, or even complete images. Two conceivable measures of similarity are the sum of squared differences and the cross-correlation. If we represent the two images by $I_l(m, n)$ and $I_r(m, n)$, then the **sum of squared differences** between the two images over a region R can be defined as

$$SSD(\Delta m, \Delta n) \triangleq \sum_{i,j \in R}\sum [I_l(i, j) - I_r(i-\Delta m, j-\Delta n)]^2 ,$$

where $(\Delta m, \Delta n)$ is the disparity between the image locations of the two matched regions. The **cross-correlation** can be defined as

$$CC(\Delta m, \Delta n) \triangleq \sum_{i,j \in R}\sum I_l(i, j)\, I_r(i-\Delta m, j-\Delta n) .$$

Variations of these definitions include computing weighted sums rather than just plain sums, and, in the case of the cross-correlation, normalizing the sum by the product of the root-mean-square intensities of each of the two matched regions. It is the cross-correlation that is used most often as a matching index as it has the advantage of simply scaling under constant scaling of either of the two image's gray levels—in the event that the cross-correlation is normalized, it scales by unity.

When we choose to match image regions that are not localized—for instance, complete epipolar lines—we must warp the two images to accommodate variations in disparity between the positions of conjugate points. This disparity, of course, depends on the spatial position of the imaged scene point. The warping of each image must, in general, be allowed to be discontinuous as the viewed scene, and hence the image disparity, is discontinuous across scene depth discontinuities. As illustrated in Figure 7.4, occlusion causes certain regions in each image to have no conjugate region in the other image. A more fundamental concern in this signal-matching approach is that conjugate points along corresponding epipolar lines may not have the same order in each image. Conjugate points do not have the same order in the two images whenever, as illustrated in Figure 7.7, one object point is imaged from either side of another imaged object point.

Localized image matching generally proceeds as follows. One considers a small window centered at an image point on some epipolar line, and finds the closest matching image window along the conjugate epipolar line—the center of this window may be chosen as the conjugate point. It is assumed

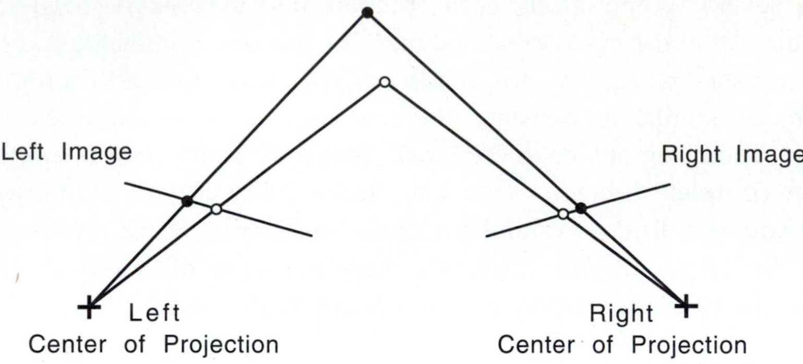

Figure 7.7 Violation of the monotonic-ordering assumption. The *monotonic-ordering assumption* is this: Conjugate image points along corresponding epipolar lines have the same order in each image. As illustrated, the monotonic-ordering assumption is violated whenever an object point is imaged from either side of another imaged object point that lies within the same epipolar plane as the first point.

here, of course, that scene points have matching intensity neighborhoods in the two images. Even if we assume perfectly matte surfaces, this assumption may be violated in the vicinity of scene depth discontinuities, and also in regions with widely disparate foreshortening in the two images. Almost all proposals for intensity-based correspondence seek to match small image windows on the basis of these windows' cross-correlation. For an approach that uses sum of squared differences, see [Matthies, Kanade, and Szeliski 1989]. Irrespective of the similarity index that is used, the success of intensity-based matching depends on whether the image window in one image exhibits a distinctive structure that occurs infrequently along the conjugate epipolar line in the other image. Thus, we see that intensity-based methods are best suited to textured image regions that exhibit comparable foreshortening in the two images.

An important issue in area-based matching is the size of the window. Too small a window may not capture enough image structure, and may be too noise sensitive, thus resulting in many false matches. Too large a window, on the other hand, may lead to a violation of the assumption that conjugate points have matching intensity neighborhoods; such a violation, as we just saw, may arise from either radiometric or geometric differences in the formation of the two images. In addition, too large a window may lead to an unacceptable loss of resolution of scene detail. In a pioneering correlation-based approach, Levine, O'Handley, and Yagi [Levine, O'Handley, and Yagi 1973] suggested the use of an **adaptive matching window** whose dimension along the epipolar line at any image location depends inversely on the variance of the intensity there, the underlying idea being to choose the smallest window adequate for matching. In another adaptive approach, Kanade and Okutomi [Kanade and Okutomi 1991] proposed that the size and shape of the matching window be chosen adaptively on the basis of a local evaluation of the variation in both the intensity and the (previously estimated) disparity. The idea here is that, irrespective of the intensity fluctuations within a window, if the underlying variation in disparity over the window is large—a large variation in disparity is likely, for instance, if the window spans an occluding edge—then a single estimate for the disparity based on matching the whole window is likely to be erroneous. Kanade and Okutomi propose starting out with an initial disparity estimate that is computed over the image using a window with an invariant shape and size, and then refining this estimate iteratively using an adaptive window. They have implemented an algorithm that uses rectangular matching windows with variable dimensions. Figure 7.8 illustrates the performance of this algorithm on noisy synthetic image data. For purposes of comparison, also shown in the figure are the corresponding results for fixed-size square windows: As one would expect, increasing the window size decreases the noisiness of the computed disparities, but at the expense of smoothing across discontinuities. An adaptive window, of course, seeks to smoothen the noise without smoothing sharp variations in disparity. Figure 7.9 illustrates the performance of Kanade and Okutomi's algorithm on a stereo image pair of a laboratory setup of a "town scene."

Related to the adaptive approaches described here is the correlation-based approach of Mori, Kidode, and Asada [Mori, Kidode, and Asada 1973] that seeks to overcome ambiguity in matching by first using large windows to establish "global" correspondences, and then using these correspondences to delimit the range of search for smaller windows that provide "local" correspondences. The authors also propose an iterative prediction-correction method that corrects for matching inaccuracies caused by viewpoint-dependent foreshortening by using each complete depth-map estimate to take into account this foreshortening in the (re)matching (until convergence). Further, they suggest that large depth discontinuities are infrequent (in the domain under consideration: cartography), and, hence, that a depth-continuity constraint be used to exploit high-confidence matches along edges.

The correlation-based stereo system built by Moravec ([Moravec 1977], [Moravec 1979]) is well known for its innovative design. It was incorporated into a mobile robot called the *Stanford Cart*. At each pause of the Cart, a single camera slid from left to right taking nine pictures at precisely

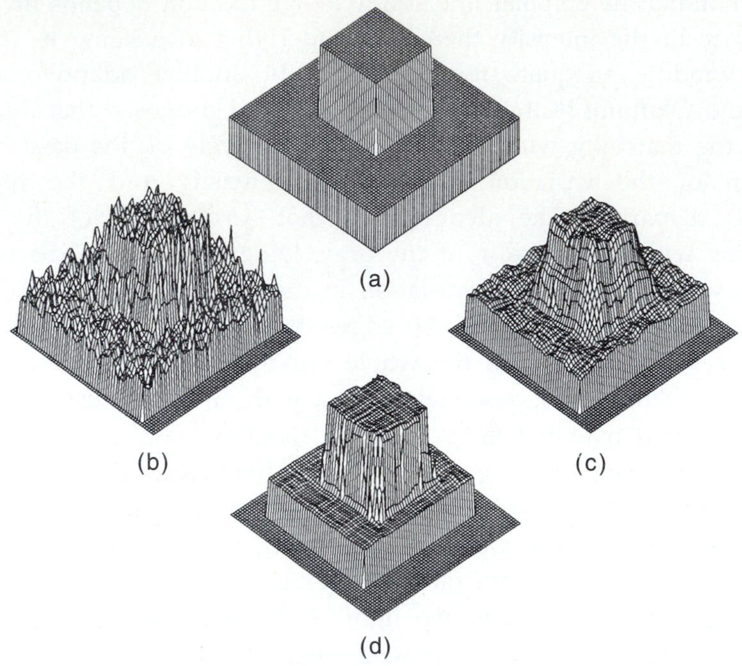

Figure 7.8 Intensity-based correspondence establishment using an adaptive matching window. We may establish correspondence between points in a pair of stereo images by matching the intensity patterns within image windows of a particular shape and size that are centered at points along conjugate epipolar lines. As the size of the matching window is increased, the matching becomes less sensitive both to image noise, and to actual variations in the image intensity. Whereas loss of sensitivity to image noise is desirable, loss of sensitivity to actual image-intensity variations is undesirable as it causes discontinuities in the depth of the scene, which lead to discontinuities in the disparity between the image positions of conjugate points, to get smoothed under recovery. Ideally, we would like to suppress the effects of image noise without smoothing out sharp variations in the image disparity. Toward this end, we can adapt the shape and size of the matching window locally in an iterative fashion, basing each adaptation on the preceding estimate of the local variation in the disparity between the image positions of conjugate points: The smaller the local variation in disparity, the larger we can make the matching window. Illustrated here are the disparities that are computed between two synthetic stereo images, first using two invariant windows, and then using an adaptive window. **(a)** Original disparity pattern underlying a pair of 128×128 synthetic stereo images, each image corrupted by additive i.i.d. zero-mean Gaussian noise. **(b)** Disparities computed using a 3×3 invariant window. **(c)** Disparities computed using a 7×7 invariant window. **(d)** Disparities computed using an adaptive rectangular window with variable dimensions. The image disparities in each of (b), (c), and (d) are established over only that part of the image over which the matching window used can be accommodated within each of the stereo images. (From [Kanade and Okutomi 1991] with permission, © 1991 IEEE.)

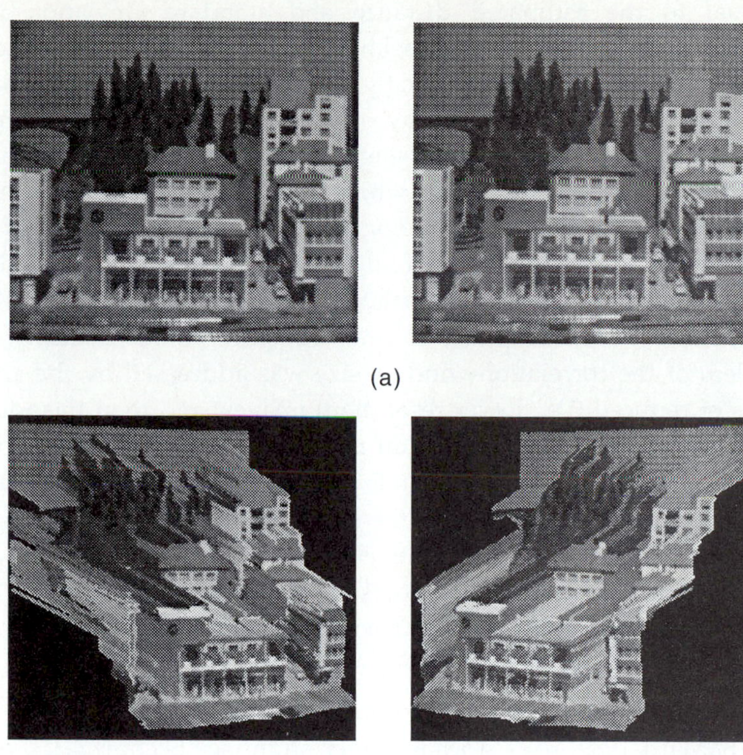

(a)

(b)

Figure 7.9 Scene recovered from a pair of stereo images using an adaptive rectangular intensity-matching window to establish correspondence. Illustrated are a pair of stereo images, and the three-dimensional scene recovered from these images using an adaptive rectangular intensity-matching window with variable dimensions to establish correspondence between image points along conjugate epipolar lines. **(a)** Stereo image pair, obtained under vertical camera displacement, of a laboratory setup of a "town scene" (256×256). **(b)** Two perspective views of the recovered scene illustrating the scene depths that are computed by first establishing correspondence between image points, and then triangulating the spatial positions of the scene points. (From [Kanade and Okutomi 1991] with permission, © 1991 IEEE.)

controlled intervals—this arrangement was termed *slider stereo*. The slide of the camera was parallel to the horizontal axis of the image-coordinate system. This direction of slide made image rectification unnecessary, the epipolar lines simply being the horizontal rows of the digital images. Nine images furnish 36 stereo pairs. Stereo pairs with a longer baseline provide greater accuracy while posing greater difficulty in correspondence establishment. The 36 possible stereo pairings give up to 36 estimates for the position of each image feature. Each such estimate was modeled as a normal curve with mean equal to the estimated distance and standard deviation inversely proportional to the length of the baseline. (The term *normal* when applied to a probability distribution, as implicitly done here, refers to the Gaussian.) These estimates were weighted by the correlation of their underlying matches, and then combined into a single final estimate. The image features sought to be matched were chosen where an "interest measure" was locally maximum, the "interest measure" being the minimum of the sum of squared differences between the intensities of adjacent pixels in each of four directions (horizontal, vertical, and two diagonals) within a square window. Moravec's interest operator essentially seeks to find cornerlike image-intensity features. The problem of the correlation-window size was addressed by the generation of a series of reduced (i.e., lower resolution) images, and then the adoption of a **hierarchical coarse-to-fine-resolution matching** strategy for correspondence search along narrow horizontal bands containing conjugate epipolar lines. The reduced-image matches restrict the search in the zoomed-in images, thus making possible the use of relatively small windows in the original (unreduced) images. Hierarchical coarse-to-fine-resolution matching reduces not only ambiguity in matching, but also computation.

Since Moravec [Moravec 1977], several authors have adopted a multiresolution approach to correspondence establishment. For instance, Barnard [Barnard 1989] uses stochastic relaxation (see Section 3.3.3) to pursue hierarchical coarse-to-fine-resolution matching to obtain a "dense" disparity map satisfying the following two constraints: one, the matched points have "similar" image intensities, and, two, the map vary "as slowly as possible." The matching index used here is the sum of squared differences between the intensities of the matched points in the two images after each image has been convolved with the Laplacian of a Gaussian. This index is applied to the whole image at once with the disparity being allowed to vary over the image, rather than to small subregions of it with fixed disparity. Various phases of Barnard's approach as applied to a stereo image pair of an outdoor scene are illustrated in Figure 7.10.

As indicated earlier, Moravec [Moravec 1979] modeled the error in each estimate of a scene point by a Gaussian curve with standard deviation inversely proportional to the length of the baseline. In itself, a one-dimensional error model is valid for the estimated position of a scene point when the point's exact location in one image is known. (Camera-calibration errors are disregarded here.) However, such a model is inappropriate when the image of the scene point can be located only approximately in each image—that is, when there is an uncertainty in the exact location of each conjugate feature. Now, it is clear from Figure 7.3 that an uncertainty in the locations of two conjugate image points to within some intervals along conjugate epipolar lines maps onto an uncertainty in the location of the scene point to within a quadrilateral in space. Analogously, a two-dimensional uncertainty in the positions of conjugate image points maps onto a three-dimensional uncertainty in the position of the estimated scene point. If we model the image errors by two-dimensional probability distributions, the spatial error is given by a three-dimensional probability distribution. Note that the three-dimensional probability distribution depends not only on the shapes of the two-dimensional distributions, but also on the latter distributions' locations in the images. In a study that illustrates the importance of careful error modeling, Matthies and Shafer [Matthies and Shafer 1987] model the three-dimensional stereo localization error by a Gaussian distribution with ellipsoidal constant-probability contours. They show that this error model leads to substantially more accurate final estimates than does the following less sophisticated error model: a three-dimensional Gaussian with spherical constant-probability contours.

Barnard and Thompson [Barnard and Thompson 1980] propose a stereo technique that uses Moravec's interest operator to obtain candidate image features for matching, but that does not use the epipolar constraint, thus obviating the need for a priori camera calibration. Their strategy proceeds roughly as follows. First, the interest operator is applied independently to each image, and candidate features for matching are selected. Next, an initial set of possible matches is constructed for each feature in one image with all the features within some radius in the other image. Each of these matches is assigned a likelihood based on the cross-correlation between the subimages surrounding the features. Then, these likelihoods are refined iteratively (10 times) on the basis of a measure of local consistency (continuity in disparity) between neighboring matches. This iterative refinement, which provides the final matches, is a locally cooperative and parallel process (i.e., relaxation) of the type proposed for random-dot stereo pairs. The constraint on local continuity in disparity is, of course, not valid across depth discontinuities; although this invalidity was noted by Barnard and Thompson, it was not modeled.

Intensity-based approaches to correspondence establishment commonly enforce consistency (continuity in disparity) between neighboring matches in either one or both of two ways:

1. They proceed with the matching from a coarse resolution to a fine resolution, using the result at a particular resolution as a starting point for the matching at the next finer resolution.
2. They optimize an objective function that imposes a penalty for the lack of smoothness in the disparity computed over the image.

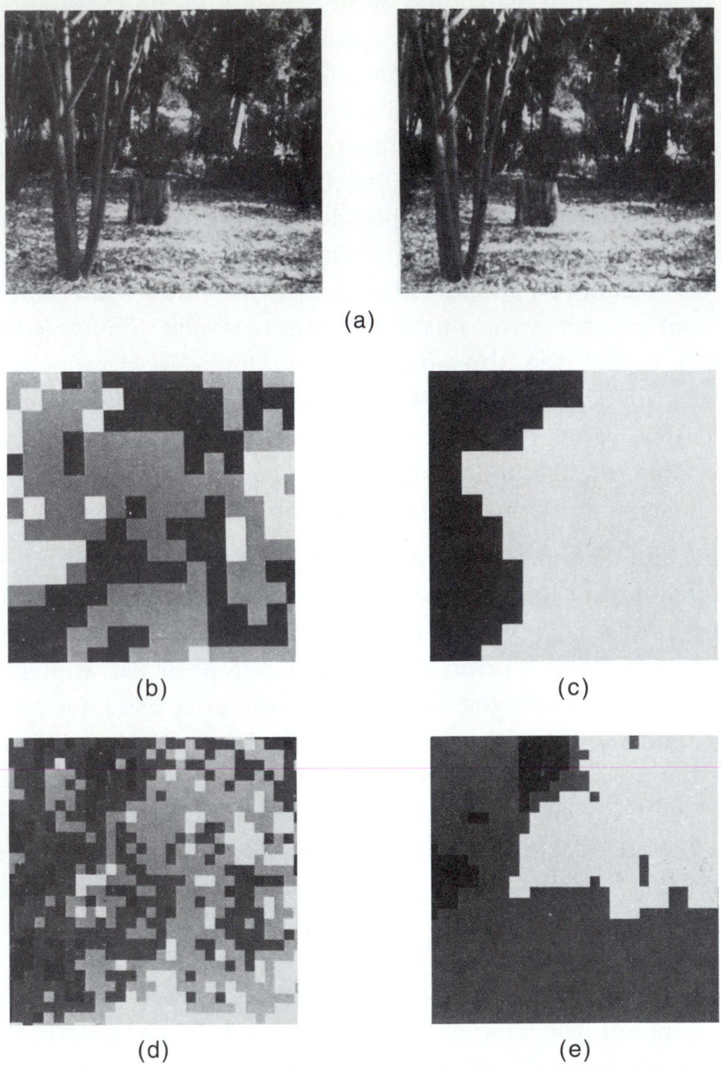

Figure 7.10 Stochastic relaxation as a tool for correspondence establishment. We can use stochastic relaxation to establish correspondence between points in a pair of stereo images by iteratively optimizing an objective function that measures all at once the goodness of match between each two pixels that are postulated to form a conjugate pair. (Recall that stochastic relaxation is a computational strategy that simulates annealing to optimize an objective function; annealing is a physical process by which we can drive certain substances to their low-energy highly regular states by first raising the temperature of the substance, and then gradually lowering the temperature in a carefully controlled fashion.) Now, in a pair of stereo images that is acquired by cameras that have identical geometrical parameters and coplanar image planes, the disparity between the image positions of any two conjugate points is inversely proportional to the depth of the scene point that projects onto the

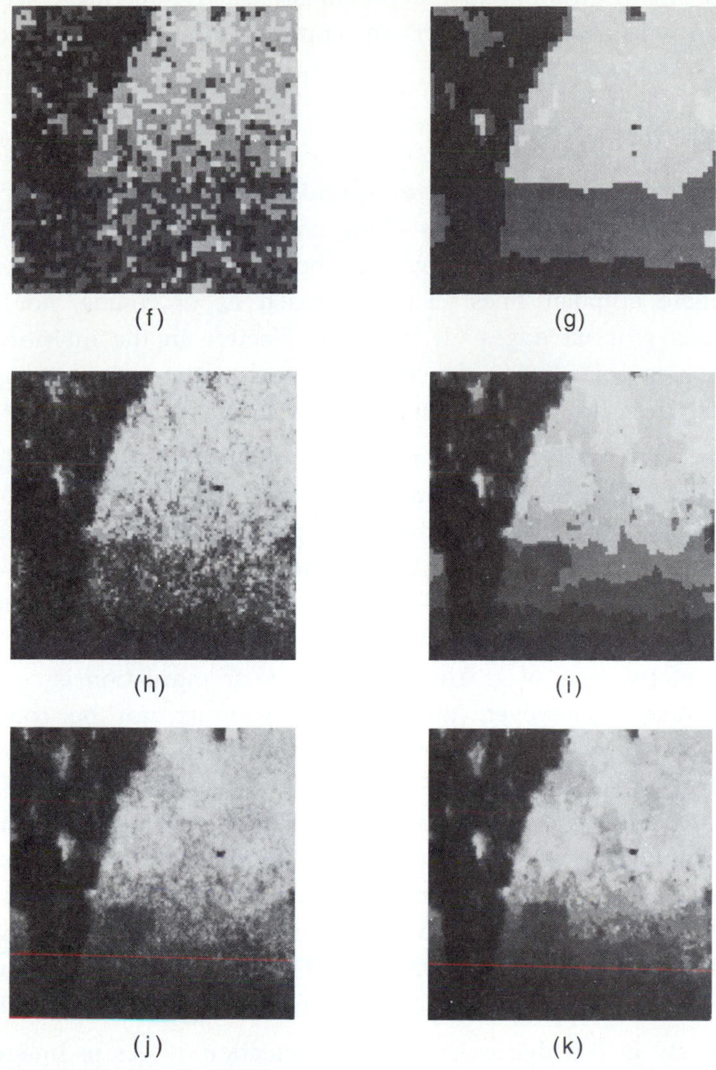

two conjugate points. Illustrated here is the computation of image disparity in one such pair of stereo images by hierarchical coarse-to-fine-resolution intensity-based matching that uses stochastic relaxation at each resolution to refine the matching of the previous resolution. **(a)** Stereo image pair of an outdoor scene (256×256). **(b)** 16×16 disparity image at the initial stage of stochastic relaxation—high intensity indicates a low disparity between the image positions of conjugate pixels, and low intensity indicates a high disparity. **(c)** 16×16 disparity image at the final stage of stochastic relaxation. **(d)** Initial 32×32 disparity image. **(e)** Final 32×32 disparity image. **(f)** Initial 64×64 disparity image. **(g)** Final 64×64 disparity image. **(h)** Initial 128×128 disparity image. **(i)** Final 128×128 disparity image. **(j)** Initial 256×256 disparity image. **(k)** Final 256×256 disparity image. (From [Barnard 1989] with permission.)

In this context, in addition to the previously cited references, see [Witkin, Terzopoulos, and Kass 1987] for an approach that employs both these techniques simultaneously.

7.2.2 Edge-Based Methods

An alternative to establishing correspondence between image points by matching image-intensity patterns along conjugate epipolar lines is first to detect edges, and then to seek matches between these edges' intersections with conjugate epipolar lines. This approach is, of course, not useful in image regions without edges. It is also ineffective in the interior of edges that lie along epipolar lines. Hence, edge-based methods for correspondence establishment are often used in conjunction with intensity-based methods.

Edge-based matching assumes viewpoint-independent edges (see Chapter 4). In principle, this assumption, whose need is evident from Figure 7.11, is less restrictive than is the assumption underlying intensity-based matching: viewpoint-independent image intensities. As illustrated in Figure 7.11, the position of a continuous–surface-normal depth discontinuity, which is one type of viewpoint-dependent edge, cannot be recovered from the intersection of two sets of grazing rays; simple triangulation is conceptually inadequate here. (However, this inadequacy must not be construed to indicate that such viewpoint-dependent edges are less amenable to recovery from multiple images than are viewpoint-independent edges. On the contrary, as each image provides a cone of directions tangent to the surface along a continuous–surface-normal depth discontinuity, sufficiently many images would allow us to reconstruct the imaged surface along such an edge. In contrast, surfaces adjoining a viewpoint-independent edge cannot be recovered from any number of images of the edge. Recall the discussion on viewpoint-independent and viewpoint-dependent edges in Chapter 4.)

As we saw in our discussion of edge detection, edges in images can be localized fairly accurately. Consequently, edge-based depth recovery through triangulation can be fairly accurate too. Further, edges provide the simple but powerful **edge-continuity constraint** that is immensely useful in noisy images: If the intersection of an edge with an epipolar line in one image matches some intersection of an edge with the conjugate epipolar line in another image, then all other (existing) intersections of these two edges with conjugate epipolar lines must also match. This constraint hinges on the general-viewpoint assumption, which we discussed at length in Chapter 4, as it assumes that the continuity of an edge in an image implies the continuity of the edge's preimage in space.

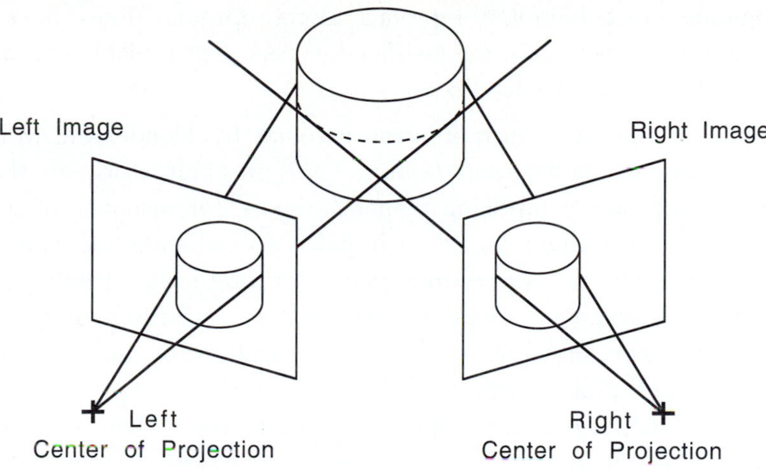

Figure 7.11 Edge-based correspondence establishment, and its limitation with respect to scene recovery through triangulation. An alternative to establishing correspondence between image points along conjugate epipolar lines by matching the intensity patterns within image windows centered at these points is to establish correspondence by matching image-intensity edges where they intersect conjugate epipolar lines. Whereas intensity-based matching assumes that the image intensity of each visible scene point is the same in each image, edge-based matching assumes that the scene position of an image-intensity edge does not depend on the viewpoint—that is, that image-intensity edges that match have identical locations in space. As illustrated, edge-based three-dimensional scene recovery through simple triangulation is conceptually inadequate for continuous–surface-normal depth discontinuities as the spatial locations of such discontinuities depend on the position of the camera.

Although the edge-continuity constraint is the most widely used, a number of other constraints and heuristics have been proposed in the literature. Arnold and Binford [Arnold and Binford 1980] show that a (uniformly) randomly oriented edge in space is likely to have a small angular disparity in a rectified stereo image pair—the smaller the baseline, the stronger the likelihood. It must be emphasized that this observation can serve only as a heuristic because, for any given imaging configuration, the angular disparity between the two images of a spatial edge is large for a whole variety of spatial configurations of the edge; for instance, the angular disparity is likely to be large when the spatial edge has an orientation close to either line of sight. As the strength of this heuristic depends on the spatial position of the edge, we should use this heuristic, if at all, with a dependence on positional disparity. Another heuristic proposed by Arnold and Binford is that conjugate edge-delimited intervals along epipolar lines have closely matching lengths; once again the justification was probabilistic, and a smaller baseline results in a higher likelihood.

The edge-continuity constraint was invoked by Henderson, Miller, and Grosch [Henderson, Miller, and Grosch 1979] in their work on the stereo reconstruction of sites comprising planar surfaces, for instance, of buildings. They used edge matching along each pair of conjugate epipolar lines to restrict search along the succeeding pair. Although the strictly sequential nature of this matching exploits the continuity constraint to propagate correct matches, it is also susceptible to the propagation of incorrect matches. Henderson, Miller, and Grosch used dynamic programming[1] to optimize an intensity-based metric relating conjugate epipolar lines. Their approach leads to the matching of both edge crossings and points in the intervening intervals. (Note that, although a planar occluding surface is determined completely by the spatial positions of any two noncollinear occluding edges that belong to the surface, the spatial position of an occluding edge provides no assistance in determining the spatial position of an occluded surface that adjoins the edge in the image—hence, the need for an intensity-based metric here.) Although dynamic programming results in a considerable computational saving over exhaustive search, its application here requires that conjugate points along corresponding epipolar lines have the same order in each image—this requirement, called the **monotonic-ordering assumption**, was invoked at least as far back as 1973 by Levine, O'Handley, and Yagi [Levine, O'Handley, and Yagi 1973]. As illustrated in Figure 7.7, the monotonic-ordering assumption is violated whenever an object point is imaged from either side of another imaged object point. Also, as is clear from the figure, the likelihood of the violation of the assumption decreases as the depth of the scene relative to the separation between the two cameras increases.

The monotonic-ordering assumption was also invoked by Baker and Binford [Baker and Binford 1981] to use dynamic programming to match edge crossings along epipolar lines. The authors used various edge features, such as side intensities, contrast, and orientation, to define the matching

---

1. **Dynamic programming** [Bellman and Dreyfus 1962] is the following technique for designing efficient algorithms: Subdivide a problem recursively into smaller subproblems that may need to be solved in the future, solving each subproblem—proceeding from the smaller ones to the larger ones—and storing the solutions in a table that can be looked up as and when the need arises. For an introduction to dynamic programming, see [Aho, Hopcroft, and Ullman 1983].

metric. Unlike in the work of Henderson, Miller, and Grosch, attention was not limited to planar surfaces. A coarse-to-fine-resolution strategy was used to reduce high-resolution search. Because an occluding edge belongs to only one of the two surfaces adjoining it in the image, each edge was treated as a doublet with a left and a right component—in case of occlusion, the component on the occluded side does not have any matching half-edge in the other image. Although Baker and Binford did invoke the edge-continuity constraint, this constraint's full power was not exploited in that it was used only to prune nonconforming matches after each pair of conjugate epipolar lines had been processed independently. In particular, the advantage of using the continuity constraint during search along conjugate epipolar lines was sacrificed for parallelism. Finally, an intensity-based metric was used to establish correspondence between nonedge points bounded by matched half-edges along conjugate epipolar lines.

Ohta and Kanade [Ohta and Kanade 1985] adopt a computationally more expensive but potentially higher-performance edge-matching strategy than that of Baker and Binford. They use dynamic programming to simultaneously match edge-delimited intervals along both conjugate epipolar lines and consecutive epipolar lines, the matching metric in the latter case imposing the edge-continuity constraint. Once again, the monotonic–edge-ordering assumption is invoked. In addition, it is required that a connected edge not cross an epipolar line more than once, and that two connected edges not cross each other; these requirements can be enforced during the edgel-aggregation process.

An alternative to matching edge crossings along conjugate epipolar lines while enforcing the continuity constraint between consecutive lines is to match extended edge segments. This alternative enforces the continuity constraint automatically. Such an approach has been pursued by, among others, Medioni and Nevatia [Medioni and Nevatia 1985], who match linear edge segments on the basis of their endpoints, contrasts, and orientations. Ayache and Faverjon [Ayache and Faverjon 1987] also pursue a linear-edge-segment matching strategy to provide a fairly impressive set of results for office scenes. They first describe each image by a graph of straight-line edge segments, and then use these graphs to encourage simultaneously similar positional disparities for all neighboring edges, the underlying heuristic being that edge proximity in an image is more often than not an indication of proximity in space. (See [Horaud and Skordas 1989] for a different approach to stereo correspondence that also uses linear-edge-segment graphs.) A novel feature of Ayache and Faverjon's image-acquisition process is the 45° inclination of the baseline with respect to the horizontal; they argue that human-made scenes have a preponderance of horizontal and vertical edges, and, hence, that this inclination of the baseline reduces the likelihood of edges being imaged along epipolar lines.

Binford [Binford 1984] has argued that, from a computational-complexity point of view, it is advantageous to use higher-order image features (e.g., extended edges, junctions, areas) and monocular interpretation to establish stereo correspondence. Such an approach has not been pursued widely primarily due to the limitations of current edge-detection and image-segmentation techniques. However, Lim [Lim 1987] has demonstrated one such strategy for blocks-world scenes.

Among the other well-known proposals for stereo correspondence is the Marr–Poggio theory of human stereopsis [Marr and Poggio 1979]. The initial proposal entailed coarse-to-fine-resolution matching of edges detected at the zero-crossings of the second directional derivatives. Later, however, the Marr–Hildreth operator was used to detect edges instead [Grimson 1981]. A strong case for such an approach was based primarily on its performance on random-dot stereograms. Random-dot images, of course, have no monocular cues, and none were exploited by the Marr–Poggio–Grimson model of human stereopsis. Mayhew and Frisby [Mayhew and Frisby 1981] have since reported psychophysical experiments suggesting that spatial edge continuity is an important underlying principle in human stereopsis.

7.3 Discussion

Of the various shape-recovery techniques that we have discussed thus far, geometric stereo, in general, has been the most effective. This relative effectiveness of geometric stereo should come as no surprise: The underlying principle is simple, and depth computations are direct. Note, however, that geometric stereo, at best, provides depth estimates at only those image points that are locally distinguishable along epipolar lines (e.g., edge crossings). The distribution of such points in an image is, in general, sparse and irregular in untextured environments. Hence, several authors have suggested various interpolation schemes to estimate depths at intervening points (e.g., [Terzopoulos 1983], [Grimson 1984], [Blake and Zisserman 1987], [Szeliski 1990a]); see [Szeliski 1990b] and [Wolberg 1990] for reviews. All such schemes seek to determine the imaged surface uniquely by restricting the class of admissible solutions severely—for example, to models of thin elastic membranes or plates.

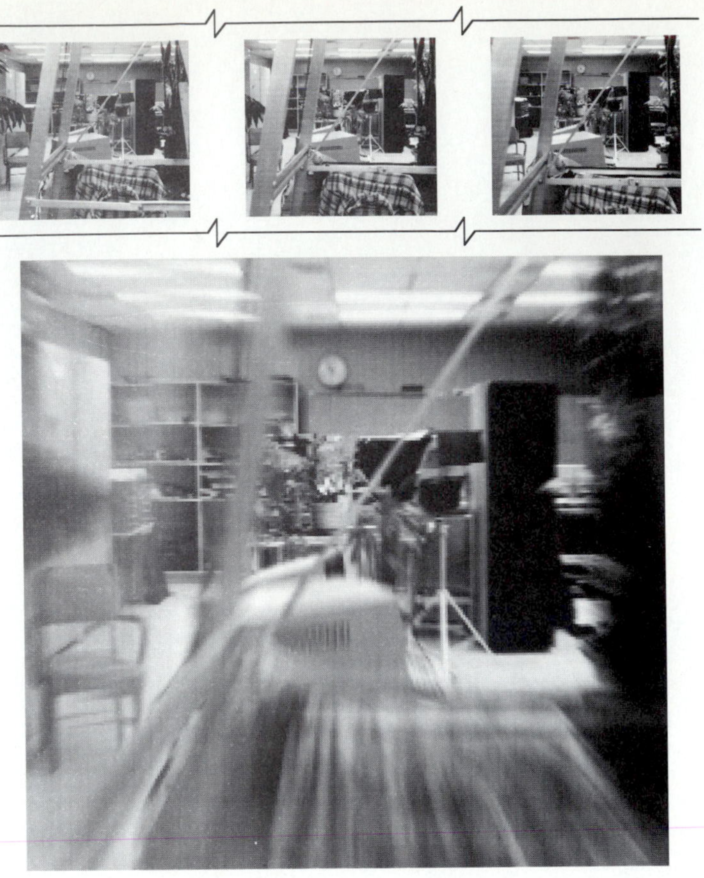

Figure 8.1 Information available to a moving observer. The continuous stream of images available to an observer who is in motion with respect to the environment provides the observer with information not only about the observer's motion relative to the environment, but also about the depths of the observed scene points. Consider the illustrated sequence of images, which was acquired by a forward-moving camera: The superimposed sequence is shown below three of its individual frames. Whereas points in the scene that are either distant from the observer, or along the observer's direction of translation, remain relatively clear under translation of the observer—that is, the image positions of such points remain relatively unchanged under translation of the observer—other points appear to move radially outward from the observer's point of approach in the image. In general, the magnitude of the image motion of a scene point increases both with a decrease in the distance of the point from the observer, and with an increase in the angle between the direction in which the scene point lies and the direction in which the observer is translating. The notion of *motion parallax*—that of the apparent relative motion between objects that are stationary with respect to one another and at different depths along a common line of sight of an observer who is in motion with respect to the objects—was first outlined by Euclid in his treatise *Optics*, circa 300 B.C. (Image sequence, courtesy SRI International.)

Chapter 8

Motion

To this point, we have restricted ourselves to visual perception by a stationary observer. Let us now explore the recovery of a three-dimensional scene from multiple images of the scene, these images captured by a camera that is in motion with respect to the scene. That the recovery of a scene from multiple images of the scene captured by a single moving camera is partially feasible should come as no surprise. Most of us have experienced the feeling of racing through the starry skies—past stars at varying distances from us—while watching science-fiction movies that have stars moving radially outward from our supposed point of approach. A graphic illustration of precisely this phenomenon is provided in Figure 8.1. At the top, in Figure 8.1, are three image frames from a sequence of images that is captured by a camera moving toward the point at the center of images; at the bottom, is the image that results when we superimpose the individual images in the captured sequence.

Barring geometric and photometric stereo, our focus thus far has been on the recovery of a three-dimensional scene from a single two-dimensional image of the scene. The difference in dimensionality between the scene and its image made it necessary for us to invoke several assumptions about the world and the observer. For instance, in line-drawing interpretation, we assumed that the observer has a general viewpoint, and in our analysis of shape from shading, we assumed the applicability of, and the a priori knowledge of, a reflectance map. It is clear that an arbitrary three-dimensional scene cannot be recovered from a single two-dimensional projection of the scene; see, for instance, Figure 4.3.

Image capture under camera motion that includes camera translation provides the image data with an extra dimension: the dimension of a varying viewpoint. For the sake of discussion, let us assume throughout this chapter that the camera has a constant velocity and that the camera is capturing images at equal time intervals. Then, the additional dimension that the camera motion imparts to the image data can equivalently be described as a *temporal dimension*. We thus have intensity variation over the image plane and over time, as illustrated in Figure 8.2. Let us call this three-dimensional image-intensity variation a **spatiotemporal** variation in the image intensity, where *spatio* in *spatiotemporal* refers to the two dimensions of a single image frame, and *temporal* refers to the time axis over which the image evolves. If we now assume that the scene comprises surfaces that are both temporally unchanging and stationary with respect to one another, then, under relative motion between the camera and the scene, the dimension of the image data will match the dimension of the scene. The third dimension imparted to the image data by the relative motion between the camera and the scene can be expected to make the recovery of the scene easier: At any rate, this additional dimension cannot make the recovery of the scene more difficult as we are always at liberty to restrict ourselves to a single image frame.

Shape recovery using time-varying imagery is, in a sense, a generalization of geometric stereo. The underlying principle is the same: Every scene point lies on all its projection rays, and, hence, multiple identifiable rays from a scene point determine the spatial position of the point. However, there is one major difference between three-dimensional recovery through stereo (using a calibrated multicamera system) and that through motion. The use of time-varying imagery to recover shape requires that the relative motion between the camera and the world be determined. That such a determination is partially feasible should come as no surprise. As we already discussed, most of us have experienced the feeling of racing through the starry skies while watching science-fiction-movie sequences that have stars moving radially outward from our supposed point of approach.

Figure 8.2 Spatiotemporal image data block. It is clear that an arbitrary three-dimensional scene cannot be recovered from a single two-dimensional image of the scene; see, for instance, Figure 4.3. We can impart an additional dimension to the image data by acquiring a sequence of images, rather than a single image, while moving the camera relative to the scene. Such an additional dimension is labeled the time axis in the illustrated oblique view of a three-dimensional stack of images, each image in the stack acquired in sequence by a forward-moving camera; the sequence of images stacked here is a superset of the superimposed sequence in Figure 8.1. The stack of images shown may be described as a *spatiotemporal image data block*, where *spatio* in *spatiotemporal* refers to the two dimensions of a single image, and *temporal* refers to the time axis over which the image evolves. (After [Bolles, Baker, and Marimont 1987]. Image sequence, courtesy SRI International.)

Figure 8.3, from Gibson's classic *The Perception of the Visual World* [Gibson 1950], illustrates this phenomenon by simulating the dynamics of the view of a pilot in straight-ahead level flight on an overcast day. Figure 8.3, which is obtained through the perspective projection of a scene onto a plane perpendicular to the flight path of the pilot, has superimposed on it vectors that represent the instantaneous image velocities of the projected scene points. These vectors, which are the projections of the motions of scene points relative to the observer, constitute the observer's so-called **motion field**, around which much of our attention in this chapter shall center.

Although Helmholtz is generally credited with first recording the importance of the evolution of the perspective view of a mobile observer to the observer's ability to estimate scene depth (e.g., pp. 267–268, [Boring 1942]), more than 2000 years earlier Euclid had outlined the concept of motion parallax, noting that, "When objects move at equal speed, those more

Figure 8.3 The motion field. Illustrated is the motion field of a pilot looking straight ahead in level flight on an overcast day. The *motion field* of a camera, or an observer, that is in motion with respect to the scene it is imaging is an assignment of vectors to image points in which each vector represents the image motion of the corresponding scene point. When a camera translates, without rotating, all the image motion vectors radiate outward from (or in toward) a single image point called the *focus of expansion* (or *contraction*). This point is located where the camera's direction of translation intersects the imaging surface. Under camera translation, the magnitude of the image motion of a scene point depends inversely on the distance of the point from the camera, and it depends directly on the sine of the angle between the direction in which the scene point lies and the direction in which the camera is translating; see Figure 8.4 for an explanation. (From [Gibson 1950] with permission. Copyright © 1977, 1950 by Houghton Mifflin Company.)

remote seem to move more slowly" (pp. 370–371, [Euclid c. 300 B.C.], English translation). In particular, Euclid established that, if two objects that are located at different positions along a single ray originating at the point of observation undergo identical motions perpendicular to the ray, then the object that is farther away sweeps out a smaller angle at the point of observation than does the object that is closer to the point of observation. More recently, Helmholtz observed,

> In walking along, the objects that are at rest by the wayside stay behind us; that is, they appear to glide past us in our field of view in the opposite direction to that in which we are advancing. More distant objects do the same way, only more slowly, while very remote bodies like the stars maintain their permanent positions in the field of view, provided the direction of the head and body keep in the same directions. Evidently, under these circumstances, the apparent angular velocities of

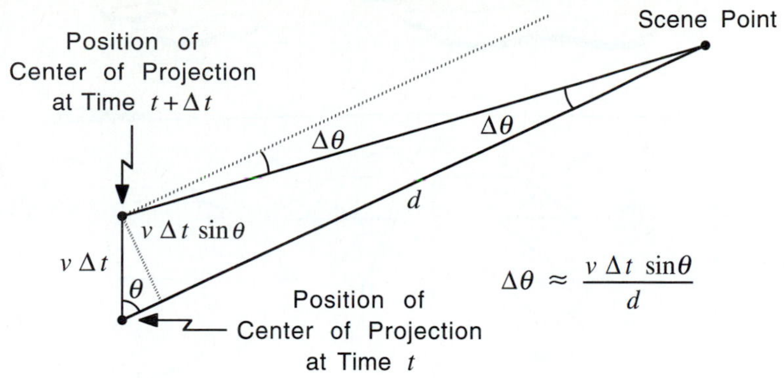

Figure 8.4 The evolving orientation of a ray from a translating center of projection toward a fixed scene point. The incremental change $\Delta\theta$, undergone in time Δt, by the orientation θ of a ray that continues to originate at a translating center of projection and to pass through a fixed scene point is approximately the following: $(v\ \Delta t\ \sin\theta)/d$, where θ is the angle between the ray and the direction of translation, v is the speed with which the center of projection is translating, and d is the distance of the scene point from the center of projection. Thus, we see that, under camera translation, the magnitude of the image motion of a scene point depends inversely on the distance of the point from the camera, and it depends directly on the sine of the angle between the direction in which the scene point lies and the direction in which the camera is translating.

> objects in the field of view will be inversely proportional to their real distances away; and, consequently, safe conclusions can be drawn as to the real distance of the body from its apparent angular velocity. (p. 295, [Helmholtz 1910], English translation)

Helmholtz's observation—that the angular velocity of a translating observer's line of sight to a fixed scene point is inversely proportional to the distance of the point from the observer—needs to be qualified. As pointed out by Gibson, Olum, and Rosenblatt [Gibson, Olum, and Rosenblatt 1955], this velocity is also proportional to the sine of the angle between the observer's line of sight and the observer's direction of translation. Let us derive the expression for the angular speed of a ray that originates at a translating center of projection and continues to pass through a fixed scene point, as illustrated in Figure 8.4. Let θ be the angle between the direction of translation of the center of projection and a ray from the center of projection toward the fixed scene point; let d be the distance of the scene point from the center of projection; let v be the speed with which the center of projection is translating. Then, it easily follows from Figure 8.4 that the angular speed of the ray from the center of projection to the scene point is $v \sin\theta / d$. Thus, we

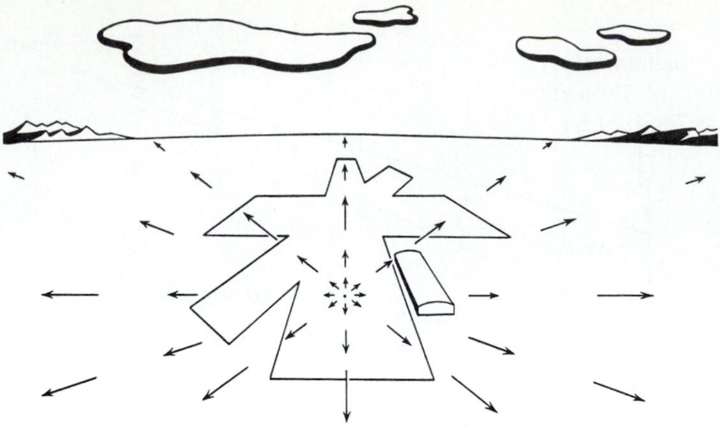

Figure 8.5 The motion field of a pilot looking straight ahead in the direction of motion while approaching a fixed point on a landing strip. (From [Gibson 1950] with permission. Copyright © 1977, 1950 by Houghton Mifflin Company.)

see that, given the direction of translational motion of a camera, and the magnitudes of the angular velocities of projection rays through fixed scene points, the distances of these points from the camera can be recovered up to the scale factor v. Given a calibrated translating camera, it is straightforward to determine the angular velocities of projection rays from their image-plane velocities. Now, if we assume that the image-plane velocities are determinable, then the question that remains is, how do we determine the direction of camera translation?

In the simple case of purely translational camera motion that we are considering currently, the direction of camera translation is along the projection ray through that image point from which, or toward which, all the image motion vectors radiate [Gibson 1950]. The point of the divergence, or the convergence, of all the motion-field vectors is called the **focus of expansion (FOE)**, or the **focus of contraction (FOC)**, respectively. The divergence of motion-field vectors, as in Figure 8.3, implies forward motion, and the convergence of motion-field vectors implies backward motion. The phenomenon of a radially directed motion field under camera translation is easily confirmed by directly considering the evolution of any projection ray through a fixed scene point and a translating center of projection. An alternate way to confirm this phenomenon is to take the trajectory of camera translation to define the baseline for geometric stereo (see Section 7.1); then, every projection of a fixed scene point must translate along an epipolar line, and all such lines converge at the epipole, termed the *FOE* (or *FOC*) here.

Figure 8.6 The motion field of a pilot looking to the right in level flight. The focus of expansion here is off at infinity to the left of the figure; equivalently, the focus of contraction is off at infinity to the right of the figure. (From [Gibson 1950] with permission. Copyright © 1977, 1950 by Houghton Mifflin Company.)

We might be tempted to deduce from Figure 8.3 that the direction of camera translation is equivalently determined by the image point that exhibits a zero image velocity. This deduction is easily seen to be false. As the expression derived in Figure 8.4 indicates, the image velocity vanishes not only in the direction of camera translation, but also in the directions of scene points at infinity. A vivid illustration of this phenomenon is provided in Figure 8.5, where the pilot is assumed to be heading toward a fixed point on a landing strip; the image velocity here is zero not only at the point of approach, but also off along the horizon. In the event that all the image velocity vectors are parallel, as in Figure 8.6, we can easily confirm that the direction of translational motion must be antiparallel to these vectors. This brief discussion of translational camera motion was intended to provide you with some intuition prior to the introduction of a more detailed mathematical analysis of general motion.

Our discussion here shall be restricted to time-invariant scenes. Our goal is to recover both the structure of a time-invariant scene, and the scene's motion relative to the camera, from a sequence of perspectively projected images of the scene. We invoke the **rigid-body assumption** here: Although components of the scene may be in motion, there is no relative motion among these components. The rigid-body assumption is not as limiting as it may first seem: It is individually applicable to each collection of rigid bodies that are undergoing the same motion relative to the camera. In the event that the scene exhibits multiple independent rigid motions, we would need to be able to distinguish between bodies that are undergoing different rigid-body motions; see [Adiv 1985] for one approach to this problem.

Whether the scene moves with respect to the camera, or the camera with respect to the scene, is geometrically one and the same: Motion is always relative. However, the temporally evolving characteristics of the image may well depend on whether it is the scene that moves, or the camera. For instance, in the event that the scene moves not only with respect to the camera but also with respect to the illumination, the shadows will, in general, undergo a spatial motion that is different from the motion of the rest of the scene. Multiple motions in the scene may also arise from specularities—the motion of specularities is, in general, more complicated than that of shadows as specularities depend on the relative directions of viewing, the illumination, and the surface normal (see Chapter 5). In our discussion here, we shall ignore all motions that depend on more than the relative motion between the camera and the scene. Whereas this restriction excludes shadows and specularities, it does not exclude continuous-surface-normal depth discontinuities, which depend on the viewpoint (see Chapter 4) but not on the illumination.

As already indicated, our aim here is to discover the structure and the relative motion of a scene from a sequence of the scene's perspectively projected images. As an aside, in a now-famous set of experiments, Wallach and O'Connell [Wallach and O'Connell 1953] demonstrated that human subjects can perceive the structure and the motion of a wide variety of three-dimensional rigid forms, both solid and wire-edged, when such forms are rotated behind a translucent screen and only their orthographically projected shadows are observed. This phenomenon, termed the *kinetic depth effect*, is witnessed even with some objects whose no single stationary cast shadow is perceived to be three-dimensional. In a similarly inspired set of experiments, Johansson [Johansson 1975] demonstrated that untrained human observers can recognize familiar biological motions in the absence of nonkinetic three-dimensional cues. In one typical experiment, naive subjects were shown a film sequence in which two dancers performed a lively folk dance in the dark, each dancer fitted with 12 small lights attached to the dancer's major joints. The subjects in this experiment were able to tell, in a fraction of a second, that they were witnessing the movements of two people.

With this introduction, we are ready to proceed to the details of motion analysis. First, we shall concern ourselves with estimating the motion field. Then, we shall discuss using the motion field to recover the relative motion and structure of the scene.

We encountered the notion of a motion field previously. Recall that the **motion field** is a vector field, defined over the image, in which each vector assigned to an image point represents the image motion of the scene point that projects onto that image point. The image motions that are represented in a motion field may all be either the instantaneous image velocities or the interframe displacements of the projections of scene points. As we shall see shortly, in general, it is possible to estimate the motion field over the image plane at only sparsely distributed image locations. Our notion of a motion field, as defined here, entails first-order (i.e., straight-line) approximations to the image trajectories of scene points. It is likely that this notion will need to be refined in the not too distant future to include higher-order trajectory information—for instance, to include the curvatures of the image trajectories of scene points.

For perspectives on motion analysis that are quite different from and more detailed than the one presented here, you are referred to [Murray and Buxton 1990] and [Aggarwal and Nandhakumar 1988]. See also [Thompson and Barnard 1981] and [Ullman 1981] for two readable, although slightly dated, reviews.

8.1 Motion-Field Estimation

In this section, we shall discuss the various approaches to motion-field estimation; see [Fleet 1992] for a more extensive review. Owing to the widespread prevalence of digital technology, the images are almost always sampled both over space—the image plane—and over time. Hence, what we typically have available is a temporal sequence of digital images. Whereas a small temporal sampling interval leads to relatively small variations between consecutive image frames, a large interval may result in significant changes between consecutive image frames. To estimate the displacement field in the latter case, we may have no choice but to establish correspondence on the basis of one of the methods described for geometric stereo, except that now we cannot use the epipolar constraint unless we know the camera motion (see Chapter 7).

In connection with motion-field estimation under a large temporal sampling interval, see [Dreschler and Nagel 1982] for a feature-matching approach akin to the approach of [Barnard and Thompson 1980] described in Section 7.2.1. See [Nagel 1983] for an approach that matches second-order variations in the image intensity at gray-level corners. See [Waxman and Wohn 1985] for an interesting idea that entails matching extended image-intensity edges, and then using the deformation of these edges between

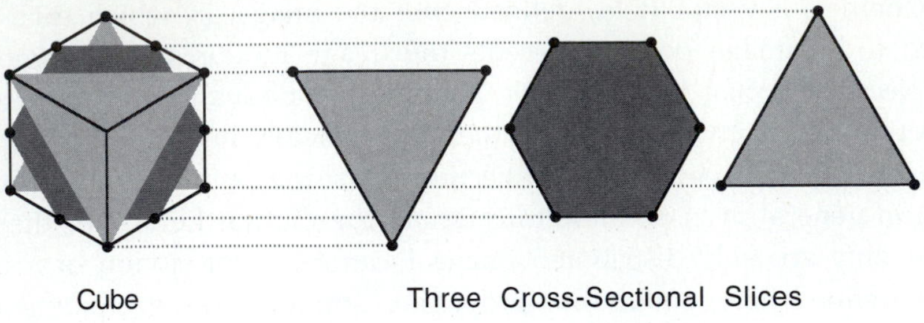

Figure 8.7 Three not-so-familiar two-dimensional vertical slices of a tilted cube illustrating that the structure of a three-dimensional entity is not necessarily apparent from its two-dimensional slices. Suppose, as in Figure 8.2, we consider two dimensions to span the space of a single image frame, and one dimension to span the axis of time over which the image evolves, then the implication here is that the richness of the spatiotemporal structure and coherence of an image entity is often not captured by individual image frames. Consequently, motion-field estimation that is based on the spatiotemporal analysis of image sequences acquired at high temporal sampling rates is more general, and potentially more robust, than is estimation based on pairs of images.

frames to constrain the displacement field. See [Anandan 1989] for a hierarchical coarse-to-fine-resolution approach that seeks to match the image intensities over image windows. Finally, see [Konrad and Dubois 1988] for an intensity-based approach that uses stochastic relaxation to pursue hierarchical coarse-to-fine-resolution Bayesian estimation (both stochastic relaxation and Bayesian estimation are described in Section 3.3.3).

Of greater interest to us than image acquisition under a low temporal sampling rate, is image acquisition under a high temporal sampling rate. A high temporal sampling rate leads to relatively small changes between consecutive image frames in a sequence, and this facilitates the estimation of the instantaneous motion field, whose evolution over a length of time can be used to derive robust estimates for the structure and relative motion of the scene. Even under a high temporal sampling rate, we could, of course, use one of the previously described stereo-correspondence methods to estimate the motion field (e.g., [Nevatia 1976]). However, such methods fail to exploit fully the spatiotemporal coherence of the three-dimensional image data; that is, they fail to take full advantage of the coherence exhibited by the image data jointly over the two dimensions of the image plane and over the single dimension of time (see Figure 8.2). Consider Figure 8.7; it shows a familiar three-dimensional solid, a tilted cube, alongside its three not-so-familiar two-dimensional slices. Now, if we consider each slice of the cube to constitute a single image frame as in Figure 8.2, then it is clear that sudden unexpected changes among consecutive members of a temporal image sequence could render stereo-correspondence methods ineffective even when these sudden changes are systematic and spatiotemporally coherent. We shall have further opportunity to appreciate the significance of spatiotemporal coherence to motion-field estimation. As was the case with edge detection, and for the same reason—namely, to improve the resolution of subsequent processing—in motion-field estimation too it is advisable to interpolate the images: over both space and time. Thus, we see that the spatiotemporal analysis of images acquired at a high temporal sampling rate not only facilitates the estimation of the motion field, but also provides the motion-field estimates with a greater generality and a potentially higher resolution than does the discrete-frame analysis of images. Hence, we shall limit ourselves here to motion-field estimation on the basis of the spatiotemporal analysis of image sequences that are acquired at high temporal sampling rates.

As already indicated, the spatiotemporal interpolation of an image sequence could lead to an improvement in the resolution of spatial and temporal detail in subsequent processing. Although explicit spatiotemporal interpolation has yet to be reported in the computer-vision literature, it is of interest to note that, in the physiological literature, Barlow [Barlow 1979] has speculated that spatiotemporal interpolation is performed explicitly by the human visual cortex prior to any other processing. Also of interest here is that, in the psychological literature, Gibson [Gibson 1979] has provided epistemological arguments for what essentially amounts to spatiotemporal processing by the human visual system.

Two fundamental criteria for distinguishing among the various techniques for motion-field estimation are the following:

1. What image properties of the scene are assumed to be preserved under relative motion between the camera and the scene—that is, what image properties, when tracked over time, are assumed to yield the image motions of scene points
2. What is the mechanism used to infer the image motions of scene points, to the extent possible, under the assumption of criterion 1—that is, what is the method of tracking the image properties of the scene that are assumed to be preserved in criterion 1

With respect to the image properties of the scene that are assumed to be preserved under relative motion between the camera and the scene, the situation is somewhat analogous to the situation we encountered in geometric stereo: Broadly speaking, we may assume either that the image intensity is preserved, or that the image-intensity edges are preserved. Let us call a motion field that is estimated under the assumption that the image intensity is preserved **intensity flow**. Let us call a motion field that is estimated under the assumption that the image-intensity edges are preserved **edge flow**. Owing to its widely varying usage, let us avoid the term *optical flow* altogether. The intensity-flow and edge-flow approaches to motion-field estimation are respectively analogous to the intensity-based and edge-based methods of correspondence establishment in geometric stereo (Chapter 7). However, there is the key difference that in motion-field estimation, unlike in correspondence establishment for calibrated geometric stereo, we do not have the epipolar constraint available a priori. As a result, in motion-field estimation, we must, in general, track the image motions of the image isobrightness contours or of the image-intensity edge contours, depending on whether we are pursuing an intensity-flow approach or an edge-flow approach to motion-field estimation, respectively. Recall that, in calibrated geometric stereo, it suffices to match the image intensities or the image-intensity edge crossings along conjugate epipolar lines.

Motion-field estimation based on the flow of edges in an image, rather than on the flow of image isobrightness contours, has the same arguments in its favor as edge-based stereo correspondence has with respect to intensity-based correspondence. The spatial positions of the preimages of edges are, in general, more likely to be invariant (relative to the surfaces on which they reside) under motions of the camera and the scene, and also under changes in illumination, than are the preimages of isobrightness contours. Even many viewpoint-dependent edges—in particular, all continuous–surface-normal depth discontinuities—can be recovered from their image flow (see Section 7.2.2). A frequent argument in favor of intensity flow over edge flow is that the distribution of edges in an image—and hence, the motion field computed from the flow of these edges—is often sparse. However, Gibson, among other authors, has argued that image-motion analysis presupposes image texture (with its accompanying edges), and that it is scene texture that provides an anchor for space (p. 124, [Gibson 1950]).

As far as implementation is concerned, most approaches to motion-field estimation assume to varying degrees, perhaps implicitly, the preservation of both the image intensity and the image-intensity edges under relative motion between the camera and the scene. As indicated earlier, an alternative to distinguishing between the various techniques for motion-field estimation on the basis of what image properties of the scene they assume to be preserved, is to distinguish between the techniques on the basis of how they track these properties over time to infer the motion field.

One set of techniques to estimate the motion field is based on the **spatiotemporal derivatives** of the image data. Recall that *spatio* in *spatiotemporal* here refers to the two dimensions of a single image, and *temporal* refers to the time axis over which the image evolves (see Figure 8.2). Each technique in this class computes the intensity flow—the image motions of image isobrightness contours, these motions leading to the motion field under the assumption that the image intensities of scene points are strictly preserved over time. Techniques that depend on spatiotemporal differentiation to estimate the motion field assume implicitly that the spatiotemporal variation in the image intensity is continuously differentiable everywhere. We shall study this class of intensity-flow techniques first.

Subsequently, we shall turn our attention to a class of techniques for motion-field estimation that is based on what is best described as local **spatiotemporal coherence**. Each technique in this class assumes, to a varying degree, that either one or both of the image intensity and the image-intensity edges of the scene are preserved over time. What is meant here by *spatiotemporal coherence* is best elucidated by examples. Now, as an image-intensity edge evolves under relative motion between the camera and the scene, the edge sweeps out a coherent structure of one higher dimension than itself in spatiotemporal image space: It sweeps out a spatiotemporal surface across which the image intensity undergoes an abrupt change (see Figure 8.2). Analogously, a locally discriminable image point sweeps out a locally discriminable spatiotemporal image curve, and a constant-intensity image region sweeps out a spatiotemporal constant-intensity image volume. Although we can think of motion-field estimation based on spatiotemporal differentiation as also seeking out spatiotemporally coherent image structures—namely, spatiotemporal image isobrightness surfaces—there is a key distinction between such approaches and those that we are describing here as coherence-based: Coherence-based approaches do not, in general, explicitly require or depend on the spatiotemporal differentiability of the image data. On the contrary, they thrive on the lack of continuity in the image data within individual image frames.

8.1.1 Estimation Based on Spatiotemporal Derivatives

Approaches to motion-field estimation that are based on spatiotemporal differentiation all seek to compute the intensity flow; that is, they all seek to estimate the motion field under the assumption that the image intensities of scene points are preserved over time. Such approaches go back at least to Fennema and Thompson [Fennema and Thompson 1979], who extended an earlier relatively crude proposal by Limb and Murphy [Limb and Murphy 1975]. The most popular current formulation of such techniques, however, originated with Horn and Schunck [Horn and Schunck 1981]. We shall follow these authors' development here.

Let us denote the image intensity by $I(x, y, t)$; as always, for purposes of analysis, it is convenient to work with the spatiotemporal continuum underlying the sequence of digital images. Further, let us assume that the image intensity is the scene radiance times a constant—either because of a small field of view, or due to calibrated compensation (see Section 2.2)—and that the image intensity is continuously differentiable over the image plane and time. Finally, let us also assume that the scene radiance of every visible surface point in the direction of the camera is invariant under the specific motions of the camera and the imaged surfaces. This last assumption is quite restrictive, as we shall discuss toward the end of this section. Differentiating $I(x, y, t)$ with respect to t gives

$$\frac{dI}{dt} = \frac{\partial I}{\partial x}\frac{dx}{dt} + \frac{\partial I}{\partial y}\frac{dy}{dt} + \frac{\partial I}{\partial t}.$$

Now, because the image intensity of each visible scene point is unchanging over time under our assumptions, we can equate this expression to zero to obtain a constraint on the image motion of a scene point. Denoting the image-intensity gradient $[\partial I/\partial x \quad \partial I/\partial y]$ by $\mathbf{G}$, and the image velocity $[dx/dt \quad dy/dt]$ by $\mathbf{v}$, this constraint is

$$\mathbf{v} \cdot \frac{\mathbf{G}}{\|\mathbf{G}\|} = -\frac{\partial I}{\partial t} \Big/ \sqrt{(\partial I/\partial x)^2 + (\partial I/\partial y)^2}\,.$$

This equation is fundamental to intensity-flow calculations—let us call it the **intensity-flow equation**. (Note that, although the intensity-flow equation is exact under our assumptions, when the derivatives in this equation are implemented as finite differences between the intensities of adjacent pixels, the equation implicitly invokes a first-order Taylor-series approximation to the spatiotemporal variation in the image intensity.)

The intensity-flow equation provides an expression for the component of the image velocity in the direction of the image-intensity gradient at the image of a scene point. Equivalently, as illustrated in Figure 8.8, the intensity-flow equation provides the component of the image velocity orthogonal to the image isobrightness contour through the image point. Note that, as $\|\mathbf{G}\| = 0$ within constant-intensity image regions, the intensity-flow equation is degenerate within such regions, and, as a result, it does not constrain the image velocity within constant-intensity image regions. Further, even where the equation does constrain the image velocity, it tells us nothing about the component of the image velocity perpendicular to the direction of the image-intensity gradient. That is, the intensity-flow equation

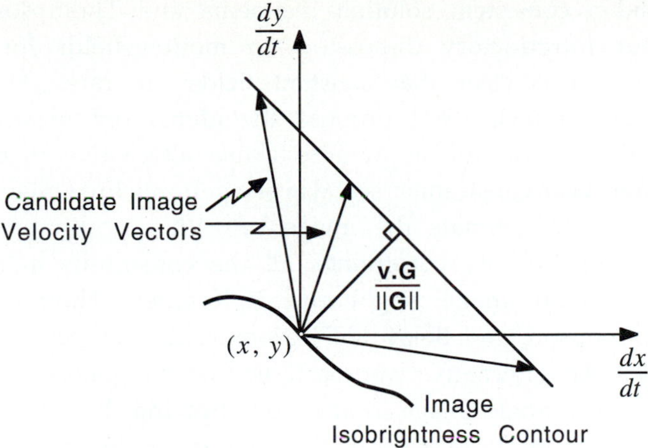

Figure 8.8 Intensity flow. *Intensity flow* describes an estimate of the motion field—that is, of the image motions of scene points—under the assumption that the image intensities of scene points are unchanging over time. Intensity-flow analysis provides a linear constraint between the x- and y-components of the image velocity of a scene point. If we denote the image coordinates of a scene point by (x, y), the image velocity of the scene point by $\mathbf{v} = [dx/dt \;\; dy/dt]$, and the gradient of the image intensity at (x, y) by $\mathbf{G} = [\partial I/\partial x \;\; \partial I/\partial y]$, then the constraint at (x, y) is $dI/dt = \mathbf{v} \cdot \mathbf{G} + \partial I/\partial t = 0$. This constraint specifies only that component of the image velocity that is along the direction of the image-intensity gradient, or, equivalently, that is orthogonal to the image isobrightness contour through the image point: It tells us nothing about the component of the image velocity that is tangent to the image isobrightness contour through the image point.

tells us nothing about the component of the image velocity in the direction tangent to the isobrightness contour through the image point. This indeterminacy is one manifestation of the so-called **aperture problem**, which we shall discuss at greater length in Section 8.1.2. The connotation of the term *aperture problem* here is that the indeterminacy in the image velocity of a scene point is the result of our restricting our attention to within a local image window surrounding the image point.

As illustrated in Figure 8.8, the expression for the image-velocity component in the direction of the image-intensity gradient provided by the intensity-flow equation can alternatively be viewed as a linear constraint between the x- and y-components of the image velocity at the image point. Several proposals to integrate such local constraints on the image velocities into a globally consistent solution for the image velocities everywhere can be found in the literature. In the event that the image velocity is constant over an image region, we can employ a Hough-transform type approach (see

Section 3.2) to find a consistent solution [Fennema and Thompson 1979]; however, from our introductory discussion on motion fields for purely translational motion, it is clear that constant fields are rare. Horn and Schunck [Horn and Schunck 1981] propose the global optimization of a motion-field smoothness criterion as a more viable alternative to derive a global solution from local constraints; see also [Nagel and Enkelmann 1986]. Another possibility is to estimate the image velocities locally by solving groups of linear image-velocity constraints, all the constraints in a group generated within a small image neighborhood; Kearney, Thompson, and Boley [Kearney, Thompson, and Boley 1987] examine the sources of error in such an approach. An alternative approach is first to generate multiple velocity constraints at a single image location by applying the intensity-flow equation to the image at multiple scales at the same image location, and then to assume that the image velocities at the different scales are consistent. Finally, we can adopt the strategy of not estimating the image velocities explicitly at all, but instead of directly estimating the relative motion and structure of the scene from the linear image-velocity constraints. Such direct methods are feasible only under restricted conditions such as the following: known scene depths, planar surface patches, quadratic surface patches, pure rotational motion, and pure translational motion (see [Horn and Weldon 1988]). The first proposal for a direct method originated with Aloimonos and Brown [Aloimonos and Brown 1984]; subsequent proposals include [Negahdaripour and Horn 1987] and [Horn and Weldon 1988].

As indicated earlier, the spatiotemporal-differentiation approach to motion-field estimation described here has limited applicability. In effect, it estimates the flow of image isobrightness contours, which, in general, is different from the flow of the images of scene points. The principal assumption—that scene radiance in the direction of the camera is time-invariant—holds primarily for Lambertian surfaces under time-invariant irradiance (see Section 5.1.2). Irrespective of the camera motion, this assumption holds, for instance, for Lambertian surfaces that are either translating under homogeneous time-invariant illumination or undergoing arbitrary motion under homogeneous and isotropic time-invariant illumination. Verri and Poggio [Verri and Poggio 1989] provide a detailed analysis of the described intensity-flow approach to motion-field estimation. They argue that, although intensity flow is of limited quantitative applicability, it could provide stable qualitative characteristics of the motion field. An extreme example of the invalidity of the intensity-flow approach is provided by the time-invariant image of a uniform sphere that is rotating under time-invariant illumination while being viewed by a stationary camera [Horn and Schunck 1981].

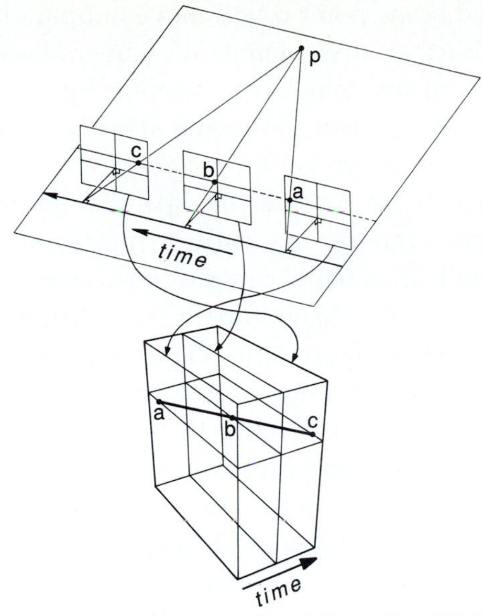

Figure 8.9 Geometry of image acquisition by a camera that is capturing images at equidistant intervals while the camera is translating horizontally in a direction parallel to the camera's image plane. Three positions of the camera's center of projection and its image plane are illustrated, and in each instance, the image position of the scene point p is indicated. The figure illustrates that a fixed scene point sweeps out a straight horizontal trajectory in the spatiotemporal stack of images that are captured by a camera at equidistant intervals while the camera is translating horizontally along a straight line parallel to its image plane. (From [Bolles, Baker, and Marimont 1987] with permission.)

8.1.2 Estimation Based on Spatiotemporal Coherence

Approaches to motion-field estimation that we are describing as based on spatiotemporal coherence apparently originated with Yamamoto [Yamamoto 1981]. Subsequently, several similar investigations were launched; see, for instance, [Adelson and Bergen 1985], [Bolles, Baker, and Marimont 1987], [Heeger 1988], [Baker and Bolles 1989], and [Fleet and Jepson 1990]. Proposals to discover spatiotemporal image coherence range from Fourier analysis to three-dimensional edge detection. We shall not discuss the details of any of the proposals here. Instead, we shall focus on the nature of spatiotemporally coherent image structures.

Let us first consider the simple case of a camera that is translating horizontally with constant velocity in a direction parallel to the camera's image plane, as illustrated in Figure 8.9. The camera is acquiring images at small constant time intervals while it is translating. Now, it is apparent that the image of any fixed scene point p will move antiparallel to the direction of camera translation. Further, if we denote the camera speed by v, the distance of the image plane from the center of projection by f, and the distance of p from the image plane by g, then the image speed s of p is easily seen from similar triangles in Figure 8.9 to be $(v - vg/(f+g)) = vf/(f+g)$, which is a constant. Equivalently, if we consider the spatiotemporal data block that we obtain by stacking the temporal sequence of images as illustrated in Figure 8.9, the image of p will trace out a straight horizontal line whose slope with respect to the time axis has magnitude s. A striking illustration of this phenomenon is provided in Figure 8.10. Figure 8.10(a) shows three frames of a 125-image sequence, and Figure 8.10(b) shows the corresponding spatiotemporal image data block. Notice the straight streaks at the top of the block. Similar straight spatiotemporal edges that correspond to fixed scene points are present within every horizontal slice of the block. One such slice is shown in Figure 8.10(c). Although all unoccluded scene points trace out linear paths, we can distinguish only those that result in intensity edges (or corners) in the image.

Figure 8.11(a) provides a frontal view of the spatiotemporal slice in Figure 8.10(c). An edge within this slice is occluded at any time if and only if the corresponding scene point is occluded in the image at that time. Although the edges in the figure seem predominantly straight, it must be emphasized that a spatiotemporal edge is strictly straight if and only if the corresponding scene point is fixed in space. In particular, a spatiotemporal edge corresponding to a continuous-surface-normal depth discontinuity will be curved; even here, however, the tangent to the spatiotemporal edge determines the instantaneous position of the scene edge point. The spatiotemporal edges would also be curved if the camera motion were not as described previously. Figure 8.11(b) illustrates the effect of linear translation of the camera in a direction not parallel to the camera's image plane, and Figure 8.11(c) illustrates the effect of adding a rotational component to the camera motion.

The example of Figure 8.10 from [Bolles, Baker, and Marimont 1987] was provided to demonstrate the potential of spatiotemporal image analysis. In it, the particularly simple motion of the camera—translation parallel to the image plane—reduced the problem of tracking edge-points to the much easier task of detecting straight edges within planar spatiotemporal slices. (See the original paper for a color-coded display of the resulting pointwise depth estimates.) As we saw in Figure 8.11, for an arbitrary relative motion between the camera and the imaged scene, the spatiotemporal path traced out by the image of a specific scene point need not be linear or even planar.

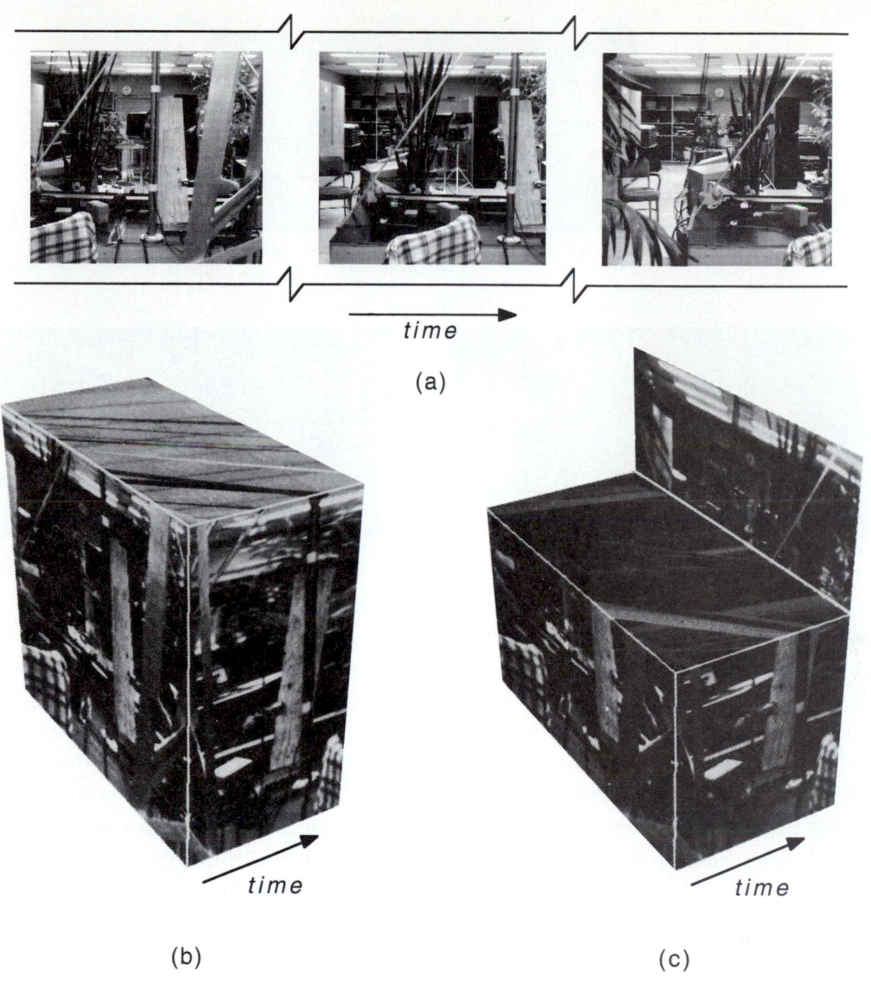

Figure 8.10 Spatiotemporal image data acquired by a camera that is capturing images at equidistant intervals while the camera is translating horizontally (from right to left) in a direction parallel to the camera's image plane. **(a)** Three frames of a 125-image sequence. **(b)** Oblique view of the image sequence in (a) after the sequence has been stacked into a three-dimensional spatiotemporal image data block. **(c)** Same as (b), except now the image data block is horizontally sliced; the top of the last image is shown in conjunction with the bottom of the first image to illustrate the genesis of horizontal spatiotemporal streaks in the image data block. (Adapted from [Bolles, Baker, and Marimont 1987] with permission.)

What is important, then, is not the particular shape of the spatiotemporal image of a scene feature, but rather this image's spatiotemporal coherence; it is this spatiotemporal coherence that makes the "tracking" of the image of a scene feature both simple and robust with respect to noise.

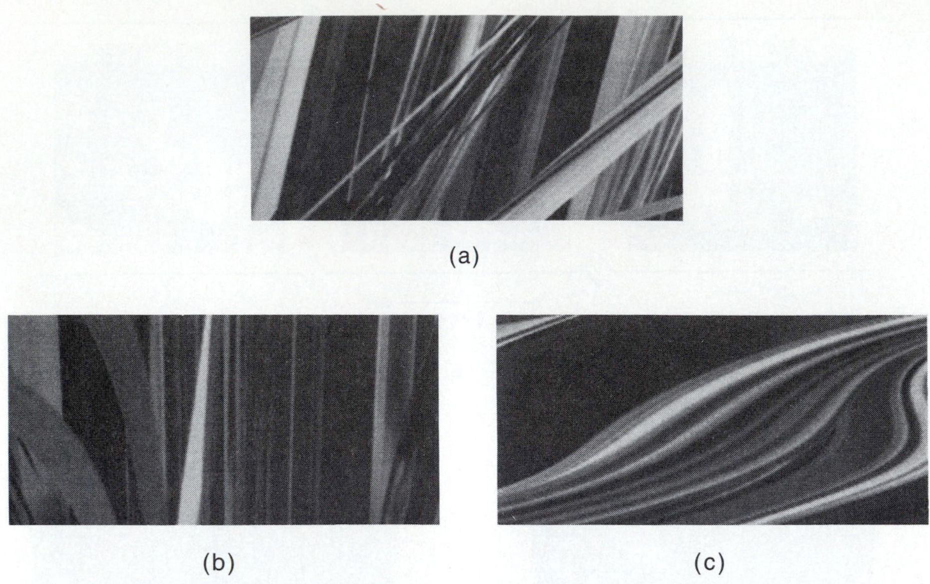

Figure 8.11 Slices of spatiotemporal image data blocks illustrating the image motions of scene points under various camera motions. In each instance, the individual images in the data block from which the slice is taken are captured at equidistant displacements of the camera. **(a)** This horizontal slice from Figure 8.10(c) illustrates the linear (horizontal) spatiotemporal image trajectories of scene points under linear (horizontal) translation of the camera parallel to its image plane. **(b)** This planar slice illustrates the planar, but not necessarily linear, spatiotemporal image trajectories of scene points under linear translation of the camera in a direction not parallel to its image plane—the planar slice here is not horizontal, but rather is oriented to contain the focus of expansion, which sweeps out a straight horizontal trajectory orthogonal to the individual image frames. **(c)** This slice, which is nonplanar in three dimensions, illustrates the nonplanar (and, therefore, nonlinear) spatiotemporal image trajectories of scene points under motion of the camera that includes both linear translation and simultaneous rotation. (From [Bolles, Baker, and Marimont 1987] with permission.)

Now, the spatiotemporal image of a scene point is a coherent structure of one higher dimension: It is a curve. The spatiotemporal image of a scene curve is a surface, and the spatiotemporal image of a scene surface is a volume. Whereas we can easily determine the image velocity of a scene point that maps onto a locally discriminable spatiotemporal image curve by projecting the tangent to this curve (i.e., its time derivative) onto the image plane, the image velocity of a scene point whose spatiotemporal image can be determined only to lie on some discriminable spatiotemporal surface has a one–degree-of-freedom local indeterminacy (assuming unknown camera

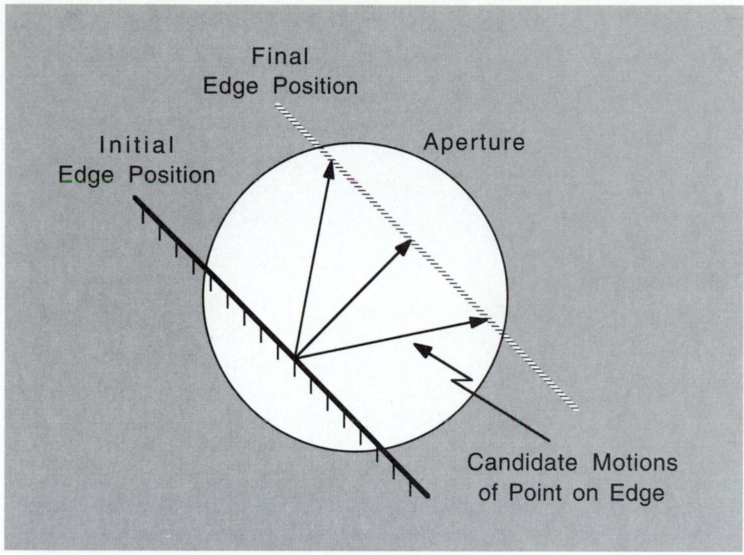

Figure 8.12 Aperture problem for edge flow in an image. *Edge flow* describes an estimate of the motion field that is derived under the assumption that the spatial positions of the preimages of image-intensity edges are independent of the viewpoint of the camera—that is, that the image-intensity edges are all viewpoint-independent. The *aperture problem* for edge flow is the following: In the absence of knowledge of camera motion, when we are looking at a viewpoint-independent edge in an image through an aperture, all we can say about the evolving image position of an indistinguishable point along the edge is that this position continues to lie somewhere along the evolving image of the edge. In the limit, we can locally determine only that component of the image motion of an image-intensity edge that is orthogonal to the edge, and not the component that is tangent to the edge. The aperture problem for edge flow is analogous to the intensity-flow constraint (described in Figure 8.8), which provides only that component of the image velocity that is orthogonal to an image isobrightness contour. (After [Wallach 1976].)

motion). This indeterminacy is a manifestation of the **aperture problem** (which we encountered earlier in Section 8.1.1): In any image, it is locally possible to determine the evolution of a viewpoint-independent edge, but not that of individual indistinguishable points on the edge. In particular, consider Figure 8.12, which is based on the description of a similar phenomenon in the context of human vision by Wallach ([Wallach 1935], [Wallach 1976]); see also p. 28, [Wohlgemuth 1911] in this context. As illustrated in Figure 8.12, in the limit, it is locally possible to determine only that component of the image motion of an edge that is orthogonal to the edge, and not the component that is tangent to the edge. In this connection,

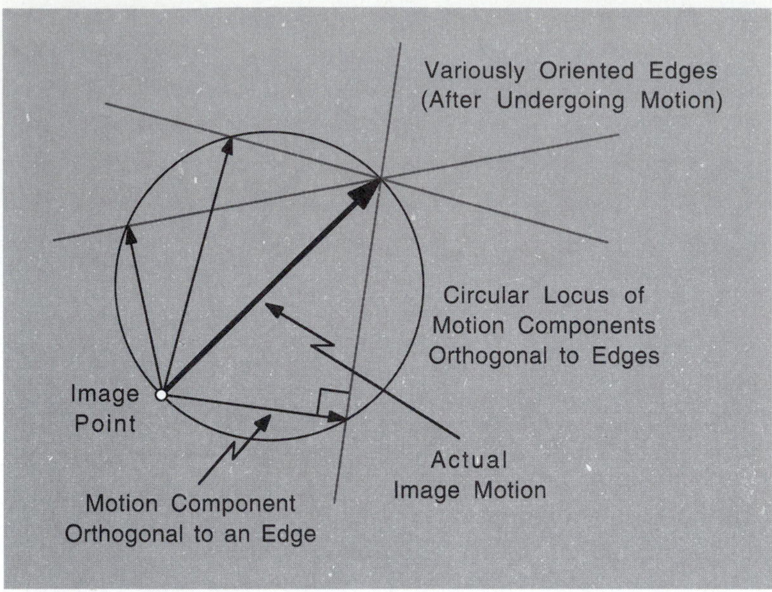

Figure 8.13 Manifestation of the aperture problem for edge flow as a function of the orientation of the edge in the image. For any given image motion of a point that continues to lie on an image-intensity edge, the component of the image motion that is orthogonal to the edge depends on the orientation of the edge. In particular, this component extends from the initial position of the image point to some point on the circle that passes through the initial position and is diametrically spanned by the image motion vector at the given image point. You can confirm this observation easily by noting that, in any triangle whose one side is along a diameter of a circle that circumscribes the triangle, the angle opposite the circle diameter is a right angle. (After [Adelson and Movshon 1982].)

see also Figure 8.13, which illustrates the range of possible component motions orthogonal to an edge in an image as a function of the orientation of the edge, given the actual image motion of the edge. Finally, note that a large maxima in the curvature of an edge in an image, unlike a strict tangent discontinuity along the edge, does not necessarily help us to overcome the aperture problem for edge flow; consider, for instance, the increasingly flat ellipse that is imaged when a circular disc spinning about its axis of rotational symmetry is viewed from an increasingly oblique angle (p. 20, [Murray and Buxton 1990]).

Before we proceed, let us pause to consider the nature of spatiotemporal image surfaces that are swept out by temporally evolving edges in an image. The discussion here relies on Section 4.2.2. First, let us consider viewpoint-independent edges. Now, discontinuities of all orders along a viewpoint-independent edge in space are, in general, preserved under the projection of such an edge (see [Nalwa 1988a] for a low-order proof). Hence, on a viewpoint-independent edge's spatiotemporal image surface, a curve across which the image surface exhibits a discontinuity of a certain order corresponds to a discontinuity of the same order along the viewpoint-independent edge in space. (As a practical matter, this author expects only first- and second-order spatiotemporal surface discontinuities—that is, discontinuities in the orientation and the curvature of the surface—to be detectable.) This correspondence between scene-edge discontinuities and spatiotemporal-surface discontinuities is violated only when the curve across which the spatiotemporal image surface is discontinuous is confined to a constant-time plane; such a curve results from a discontinuity in the motion of the camera relative to the scene. Now, let us consider continuous–surface-normal depth discontinuities—limbs, for short. Along limbs, it is known that surface discontinuities of order greater than 1 in space—that is, discontinuities in the second- and higher-order derivatives of the surface in space—in general, have a one-to-one correspondence with discontinuities of the same order along edges in the image (see [Nalwa 1988a] for a low-order proof). Hence, on a limb's spatiotemporal image surface, a curve across which the image surface exhibits a discontinuity of a certain order (greater than 1) corresponds to a curve traversing the limb in space across which the surface containing the limb exhibits a discontinuity of the same order. Once again, we are disregarding spatiotemporal surface-discontinuity curves that are confined to constant-time planes; any such curve may result either from a discontinuity in the camera motion relative to the scene, or from a curve that lies along a limb in space at a particular time instant and across which the surface containing the limb is discontinuous (in second- or higher-order derivatives). Finally, let us consider nonocclusion junctions between viewpoint-independent edges and limbs in the scene. As the projection of such a junction, in general, produces a second-order discontinuity along the edge in the image (possibly with a simultaneous cusp) [Nalwa 1988a], the spatiotemporal image of the junction is a second-order surface-discontinuity curve (possibly with a simultaneous surface cusp along its length). The remarks of this paragraph would benefit from increased precision and formality: The aim here has been simply to provide some intuition for the structure of spatiotemporal image surfaces that are swept out by temporally evolving edges in an image.

The edge-flow aperture problem has received the attention of several researchers. Some authors have proposed smoothness criteria to derive globally consistent solutions for the motion field from edge flow; see, for instance, [Hildreth 1984] and [Yuille and Grzywacz 1989]. Others have investigated conditions that result in the inherent global ambiguity of the motion field (e.g., [Bergholm 1989]). It seems that, in most practical situations, we could resolve this problem as follows. First, detect spatiotemporal discontinuous–surface-normal curves, and possibly also free-floating spatiotemporal curves; the latter would be produced by isolated distinguishable point objects. Disregard curves that either are confined to constant-time planes or lie along surface T-junctions; surface T-junctions may result from occlusion T-junctions between scene edges (see Chapter 4). The remaining spatiotemporal curves are projections of specific scene points. In each case, the instantaneous image velocity is given by the projection of the tangent to the spatiotemporal curve—that is, by the projection of the curve's time derivative—onto the image plane. As we shall see in Section 8.2.3, the image velocities at sufficiently many points (in principle, more than six) uniquely determine the (relative) velocity of the camera. Once the camera velocity is thus computed, we are effectively rid of the aperture problem along all edge segments that are not coplanar with the instantaneous camera translational velocity vector; this observation follows easily from a generalization of the epipolar constraint for geometric stereo (see Section 7.1). Let us call this strategy the **bootstrap approach** to motion-field estimation.

8.2 Motion-Field Analysis

Motion-field analysis has a rich tradition dating at least as far back as Helmholtz. More recently, Gibson has been the principal driving force. Although much of the effort has focused on human vision, the same geometric principles are applicable to machine vision. We examined some of the contributions of Helmholtz and Gibson earlier in this chapter. What is truly remarkable is the realization since the very beginning that it is the angular velocities of projection rays that carry all the information, and that image velocities are simply accidents of the projection surface. (As in motion-field estimation, the focus of this section is on velocity fields, rather than on large interframe displacement fields; determining the (relative) camera motion in the latter case is essentially the same as stereo camera calibration (see Section 7.1).)

Although we may wish to pursue motion-field analysis on a perspective-projection plane because of the physical shape of the imaging surface, we must keep in mind that the associated dependence of the image on camera orientation is simply a nuisance. Rotating the camera about its center of projection distorts the image without contributing any new information about that part of the scene that remains visible. It is often more convenient to work with projection onto a sphere (say of unit radius) centered at the center of projection (see Section 2.1.1). Although spherical projection provides a completely unbiased representation of the manifold of projection rays, note that, irrespective of the projection surface, the angular velocity of a ray is only partially specified by the ray's image velocity considered in isolation. In particular, the component of the angular velocity that specifies the rotation about the ray itself is not reflected in the corresponding image velocity (see also [Prazdny 1983]).

Let us first invoke spherical perspective projection to understand the basic concepts that underlie motion-field analysis. Then, let us use planar perspective projection to examine how we may use the motion field to determine the relative camera motion and scene structure. As indicated earlier, we shall restrict our attention throughout to single-rigid-body motions. Finally, we shall consider a few uniqueness results pertaining to the conclusions we can draw from a motion field.

8.2.1 Basic Concepts

We are all familiar with accomplishing an arbitrary rigid-body motion relative to a coordinate frame by first rotating the object about the origin of the coordinate frame, and then translating the object—or vice versa. Let us assume, without any loss of generality, that the origin is at the center of projection. Now, there is the well-known **Euler's theorem** pertaining to rotation about a point (p. 2, [Whittaker 1937]): Any arbitrary rotation of a rigid body about a point can be accomplished by a rotation about a unique line through the point. It follows from this theorem that any rigid-body (relative) motion (or velocity) can be decomposed into two three–degree-of-freedom components: translation, and rotation about a line through the center of projection. This decomposition is unique with respect to the direction and magnitude of translation, and with respect to the axis of rotation through the center of projection and the magnitude of rotation modulo 2π. The degrees of freedom for rotation are, of course, independent of the representation of the rotation: Rotation about a point has one degree of freedom per rotation about each of three orthogonal axes through the point; the equivalent rotation about a line through the point has two degrees of freedom for the orientation of the line, and one degree of freedom for rotation about the line.

Although the preceding representations for rigid-body motion are all we need for our discussion here, there are situations in which they are not the most convenient. An elegant and useful alternative is suggested by **Chasles' theorem** [Roth 1984] (see also [Whittaker 1937]): Any arbitrary motion of a rigid body can be achieved by a single rotation about a unique axis combined with a unique translation parallel to that axis. It follows that every rigid-body motion can be represented as a **screw motion**. The unique rotation axis, which also provides the translation direction, is called the **screw axis** and accounts for four degrees of freedom. Of the remaining two degrees of freedom, one is for rotation about the screw axis, and the other is for translation parallel to the screw axis.

Translational- and Rotational-Component Motion Fields

The feasibility of the decomposition of any given motion into a pure translation and a pure rotation about a line through the center of projection implies that any motion field can be viewed as the vector sum of two fields: the motion field for the translational component of the given motion, and that for the rotational component. Hence, to understand the relation of the motion field to the relative camera motion and scene structure, it suffices to examine the individual motion fields for just pure translation and pure rotation about a line through the center of projection. Let us do so now.

We have already familiarized ourselves with motion fields for pure translation. We explicitly derived the dependence of the angular velocity of a projection ray on the location of the scene point. In addition, we argued that on a planar projection surface all the image motion vectors either point away from or toward a single image point called the *focus of expansion* or the *focus of contraction*, respectively. This point may possibly be off at infinity in some direction. It is the focus of expansion or contraction alone that determines the direction of translation, as illustrated beautifully in Figure 8.14 (taken from [Gibson 1950]): If we consider a spherical projection surface that is centered at a translating observer, the motion field for all of surrounding space will radiate outward from the intersection of the sphere with the direction of translation, and will flow into the diametrically opposite pole. The orientation of the observer (camera) defines only the field of view, and not the motion field itself. Whereas, as we saw earlier, the length of any flow vector depends on the distance of the corresponding scene point (and also on the orientation of the projection ray relative to the direction of translation), its orientation is independent of the scene. Figure 8.15(a) illustrates a typical translational-motion field under projection onto a hemispherical surface centered at the center of projection.

In sharp contrast to a translational-motion field, a rotational-motion field depends only on the (relative) rotational motion of the camera and not on the structure of the scene. Hence, a rotational-motion field provides no information about the scene structure. Whereas translational fields are "polar" under spherical projection, rotational fields are "axial" about the axis of rotational motion through the center of projection—that is, they flow in

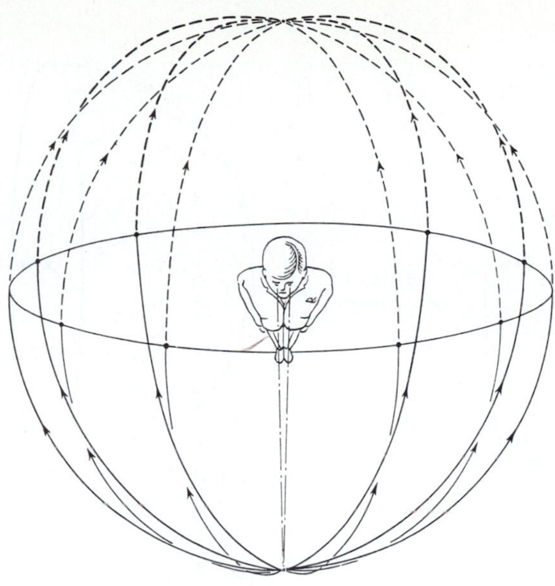

Figure 8.14 The flow pattern of the motion field of a forward-moving observer, this pattern represented on a spherical imaging surface centered at the observer. On a spherical imaging surface that is centered at a translating observer, all the motion-field vectors radiate outward from that point on the spherical imaging surface toward which the observer is translating, and they radiate inward toward the diametrically opposite point. (From [Gibson 1950] with permission. Copyright © 1977, 1950 by Houghton Mifflin Company.)

circles about this axis. Figure 8.15(b) illustrates a typical rotational-motion field under projection onto a hemispherical surface centered at the center of projection. The magnitude of a rotational field along any flow circle is a constant proportional to the radius of the circle. We can derive the described characteristics of a rotational-motion field easily by observing that any rotational motion of the camera about an axis through the center of projection simply induces an identically opposite rotation of the image with respect to the spherical projection surface. Whereas a polar translational-motion field obtained under spherical projection maps onto a centrally radiating motion field for planar perspective projection, an axial rotational field maps onto a nested-conic field. That is, as is clear from the geometry, the motion field for pure rotation under planar perspective projection is tangent to the set of nested conics that lie at the intersection of the projection plane with the concentric circular cones having vertices at the center of projection and axes along the axis of rotation.

That an arbitrary motion field can be analyzed as the sum of a translational field and a rotational field has been well known for some time.

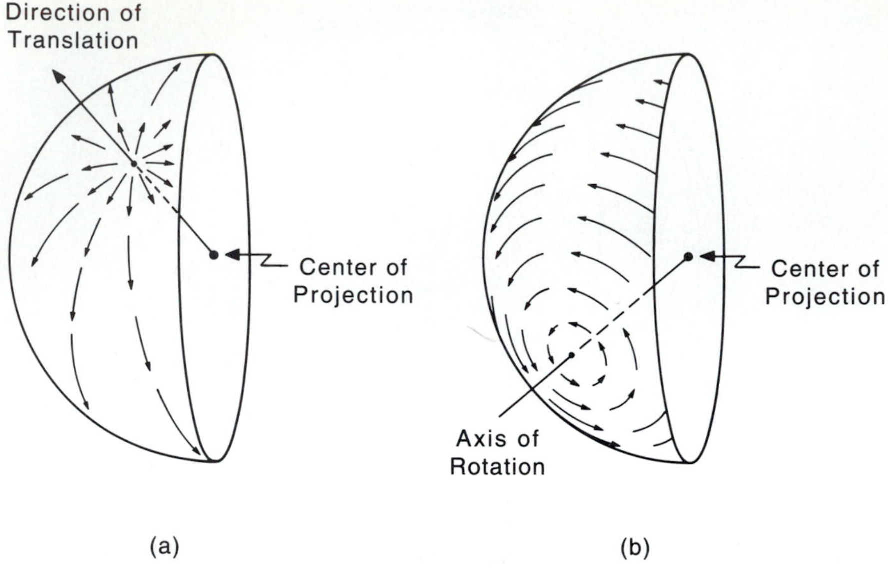

Figure 8.15 Translational- and rotational-component motion fields. Any arbitrary motion of a camera (observer) relative to a single rigid body can be uniquely decomposed into two component motions: translation, and rotation about an axis through the camera's (observer's) center of projection. The net motion field on any projection surface is the sum of the individual fields induced by these component motions: It is the sum of the *translational-component motion field* and of the *rotational-component motion field*. Note that, whereas the translational-component motion field depends on both the camera translation and the scene geometry, the rotational-component motion field depends only on the camera rotation, and not on the scene. As a result, it is only the translational-component motion field that is useful in determining scene structure. A typical translational-component motion field and a typical rotational-component motion field are illustrated, each field on a hemispherical projection surface that is centered at the center of projection. **(a)** Polar field for camera translation. **(b)** Axial field for camera rotation about an axis through the center of projection. Strictly speaking, the vectors constituting the (instantaneous) component fields are tangent to the image trajectories of scene points shown. (After [Longuet-Higgins and Prazdny 1980].)

Nakayama and Loomis [Nakayama and Loomis 1974] derived explicit expressions for the component fields under spherical projection. Subsequently, Longuet-Higgins and Prazdny [Longuet-Higgins and Prazdny 1980] addressed the all-important inverse question: How can we decompose an arbitrary motion field into a pure rotational field and a pure translational field? Such a decomposition is clearly useful: The component fields, as we just saw, have a simple structure and are almost trivial to analyze. Let us make this decomposition, then, the next item on our agenda.

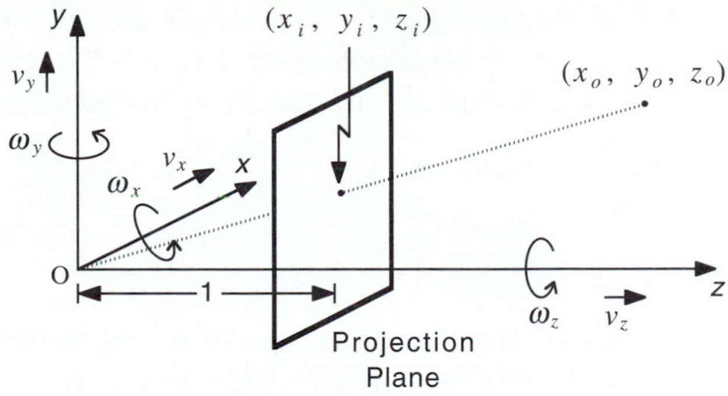

Figure 8.16 Geometry for the analysis of the motion field on a plane onto which the scene is projected perspectively. In the figure, the velocity of the camera relative to the scene is represented by the velocity's translational and rotational components along each of the *x*-, *y*-, and *z*-axes. The translational components of the velocity along the *x*-, *y*-, and *z*-axes are denoted by v_x, v_y, and v_z, respectively; the rotational components of the velocity along the *x*-, *y*-, and *z*-axes are denoted by ω_x, ω_y, and ω_z, respectively.

8.2.2 Analytical Formulation

Although the conceptual simplicity of spherical projection has led several authors to pursue motion-field analysis on the sphere (e.g., [Nakayama and Loomis 1974], [Yen and Huang 1983], and effectively also [Koenderink and van Doorn 1975]), most have preferred analytical formulations on the image plane, perhaps prompted in part by our familiarity with planar geometry, and in part by considerations of ease of implementation. The latter work is followed here, especially the development of Longuet-Higgins and Prazdny [Longuet-Higgins and Prazdny 1980].

Without any loss of generality, let us assume a coordinate frame attached rigidly to the camera, with the origin at the center of perspective projection and the *z*-axis orthogonal to the image plane, as illustrated in Figure 8.16. Further, let us assume the camera to be in motion relative to the single-rigid-body imaged scene with translational velocity **v** and rotational velocity **ω** about the origin; equivalently, we can assume the single rigid body to be in motion with respect to the camera with relative translational velocity −**v** and rotational velocity −**ω**. The direction of **ω** gives the orientation of the line through the origin about which the rotation occurs, and the magnitude of **ω** gives the rate of rotation. Equivalently, as illustrated in Figure 8.16, the *x*-, *y*-, and *z*-components of **ω** specify the rotational velocities about the *x*-, *y*-, and *z*-axes, respectively, just as the *x*-, *y*-, and *z*-components of **v** specify the translational velocities along these axes. Now, the total instantaneous (relative) velocity of any scene point is given by $-(\mathbf{v} + \boldsymbol{\omega} \times \mathbf{p})$, where $\mathbf{p}$ is the position vector of the point. If we denote $\mathbf{p}$ by $[x_o \;\; y_o \;\; z_o]$, then we can express the components of the instantaneous velocity of the scene point as

$$\dot{x}_o = -v_x - \omega_y z_o + \omega_z y_o,$$

$$\dot{y}_o = -v_y - \omega_z x_o + \omega_x z_o,$$

$$\dot{z}_o = -v_z - \omega_x y_o + \omega_y x_o,$$

where subscripts on v and ω denote components of $\mathbf{v}$ and $\boldsymbol{\omega}$, respectively, and a dot above a variable denotes the variable's time derivative.

If for convenience, and without any loss of generality, we assume that the distance of the image plane from the origin is 1, then the image coordinates of the scene point under consideration are given by $x_i = x_o/z_o$ and $y_i = y_o/z_o$. Differentiating, substituting, and simplifying, we finally arrive at the following expressions for the image velocity:

$$\dot{x}_i = t_x + r_x,$$

$$\dot{y}_i = t_y + r_y,$$

where

$$t_x = (-v_x + v_z x_i) / z_o,$$

$$t_y = (-v_y + v_z y_i) / z_o,$$

$$r_x = \omega_x x_i y_i - \omega_y (1 + x_i^2) + \omega_z y_i,$$

$$r_y = \omega_x (1 + y_i^2) - \omega_y x_i y_i - \omega_z x_i.$$

The image velocity field $[\dot{x}_i \;\; \dot{y}_i]$ is expressed here as the sum of two fields: a translational field $[t_x \;\; t_y]$, and a rotational field $[r_x \;\; r_y]$. Several important observations follow easily. First, as we argued geometrically in Section 8.2.1, only the translational component of the image velocity depends on the spatial position of the scene point; the rotational component depends on just the image position (x_i, y_i). Second, the image velocity field is invariant under equal scaling of all the position vectors $\mathbf{p}$ and the translational velocity vector $\mathbf{v}$. This invariance too is geometrically obvious: As is evident from Figure 8.17, such a scaling leaves the orientations and angular velocities of all projection rays unchanged. It follows that we can determine the (relative) motion and scene structure only up to a scale factor. Finally, we can verify easily that the translational-motion field is radial with respect to the image point $(v_x/v_z, \; v_y/v_z)$, which lies at the intersection of the image plane with a line parallel to the direction of translation through the center of projection.

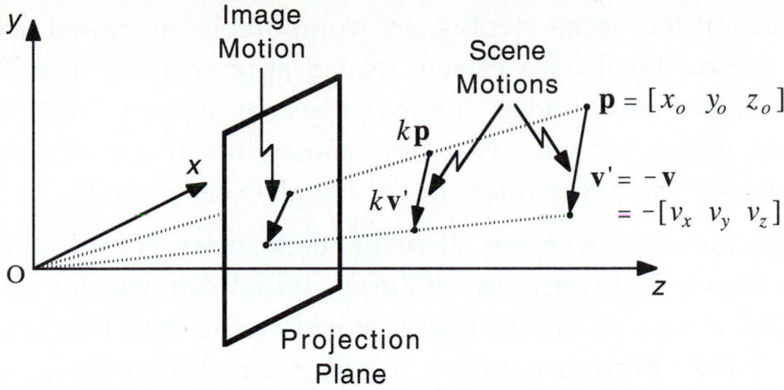

Figure 8.17 Indeterminacy in the magnitude of both the relative translation of a camera and the structure of the scene the camera is imaging, given the motion field of the camera. The component of a motion field that is due to camera translation is invariant under equal scaling of the translational-motion vector $\mathbf{v}$, and of all the scene position vectors $\mathbf{p}$. As the component of a motion field that is due to camera rotation does not depend on $\mathbf{p}$ or $\mathbf{v}$ at all, a single camera allows us to determine the relative translation and structure of a scene only up to a scale factor, which is denoted by k in the figure.

As indicated earlier, and as is obvious from the preceding equations, once the motion field has been decomposed into its translational and rotational components, establishing the scene structure (up to a scale factor) is trivial. Hence, this decomposition has been the subject of extensive research. However, a practical and robust solution remains elusive. In principle, we can accomplish the desired decomposition by determining the (relative) rotational velocity $\boldsymbol{\omega}$, among other possibilities.

As the (relative) rotational velocity determines the rotational component of any given velocity field completely, this velocity also determines the translational component of the given velocity field. But, as we saw earlier, all the vectors in a translational field must either point in toward, or out from, a single point in the image. Prazdny [Prazdny 1981] uses this observation to propose estimating the (relative) rotational-velocity parameters by minimizing the deviation of the implied translational component of the motion field from a radial one. As indicated earlier, once the rotational velocity is known, the rest is easy (see also [Prazdny 1983]). An alternative approach is to iterate over the direction of translation, minimizing the least-squares error between the given image velocities and those compatible with the postulated direction of translation. As the expressions for the image velocity (derived earlier in this section) are linear in the rotational-velocity parameters and the reciprocal of the scene depth, at each step of the iteration, the least-squares-error estimates for the rotational-velocity parameters and the reciprocals of the scene depths are computable in closed form. (See [Heeger and Jepson 1990] for a closely related approach; see also [Bruss and Horn 1983].) Note that under single-rigid-body motion, each additional image velocity vector provides two new constraints while introducing just one new unknown, the z-coordinate of the imaged scene point.

Rather than iterate over the direction of translation, we might try to estimate this direction directly (or obtain an initial estimate for it) from the motion parallax across occluding edges, as explained next [Longuet-Higgins and Prazdny 1980]. **Motion parallax** describes the relative image motion of objects that are stationary with respect to one another and at different depths along a common line of sight. Now, as we saw earlier, the rotational-velocity component of the motion field at any image point does not depend on the scene; neither does the direction of the translational component. Further, barring the focus of expansion (or contraction), both the rotational component and the direction of the translational component vary smoothly over the image. In contrast, the magnitude of the translational component of the motion field not only depends on the scene but is also discontinuous across occluding edges, the difference in magnitude at an image point depending on the scene depths across the edge and also on the location of the point in the image with respect to the focus of expansion (or contraction). Hence, in principle, the difference in the image velocity vectors across any occluding edge will point away from (or toward) the focus of expansion (or contraction). Thus, multiple such difference vectors—in theory, two that are independent—will determine the direction of translation. Such an approach, of course, requires reliable estimates for the image velocities across occluding edges, such estimates being feasible only when we are able to anchor space on the occluded and occluding surfaces—perhaps, onto texture, or some other viewpoint-independent surface feature. Such an anchoring of space is not always feasible.

Nelson and Aloimonos [Nelson and Aloimonos 1988] argue that, rather than trying to determine all the motion parameters simultaneously, it is computationally more viable to estimate the relative velocity of the camera by independently computing each of its three rotational-velocity components along three mutually orthogonal axes. They show that, if we consider motion-field vectors located along a great circle on a spherical projection surface, then the components of these vectors tangent to the great circle will depend on only the following two motions: translation parallel to the plane of the circle, and rotation about an axis orthogonal to the plane of the circle. (Recall that a great circle on a sphere is any circle that is centered at the center of the sphere.) This observation suggests three independent one-parameter iterations, each one-parameter iteration determining a single rotational-velocity component—and also the direction of the accompanying translational-velocity component—on the basis of the motion field along one of three mutually orthogonal great circles. This author has concerns about the robustness of such an approach.

Finally, several authors have approached the structure-from-motion problem theoretically by assuming the availability of a twice continuously differentiable motion field for a twice continuously differentiable imaged surface. Various approaches have been proposed in this context to perform the local determination of (relative) velocity (up to the scale factor mentioned earlier); see, for instance, [Longuet-Higgins and Prazdny 1980], [Waxman and Ullman 1985], and [Subbarao 1988]. In a similar vein, Koenderink and van Doorn [Koenderink and van Doorn 1975] had earlier described various differential invariants (i.e., coordinate-free properties) of the motion field that provide information about the orientation and shape of the imaged surface. From the foregoing discussion on motion-field estimation, it would seem that the assumption of the availability of a twice continuously differentiable motion field is rather demanding, if not untenable. Further, velocity estimation based on local differential analysis is inherently susceptible to noise. Consequently, nondifferential least-squares approaches of the type described earlier are generally regarded as more promising.

8.2.3 Uniqueness of Deductions

Two fundamental concerns in any problem-solving enterprise are **existence** and **uniqueness**. Does a solution exist? Is the solution unique? Whenever we address an inverse problem of the type *given* y *and* f *such that* $y = \mathrm{f}(x)$, *find* x, we must not only seek to find an x that is **sufficient** to produce y, but also determine whether the found x is **necessary** to produce y. These issues are of both theoretical and practical significance over and above questions of the robustness and stability of solution methods. Although we might be tempted to believe that the existence of a solution is not a concern in "physical problems," this belief is ill-founded. Whereas a problem itself may have a solution, the mathematical formulation of the problem need not have any solution, perhaps due to inadequate modeling or invalid assumptions.

Let us now examine the most prominent results pertaining to the uniqueness of the (relative) camera motion and scene structure—both, up to a scale factor, of course—that can be recovered from a motion field. These results have been derived both for image displacement fields, and for image velocity fields; we already encountered a few results applicable to displacement fields in the context of stereo camera calibration in Section 7.1.

Not surprisingly, there is a close correspondence between the two sets of results. After all, velocity fields are just scaled displacement fields in the limit.

Hay [Hay 1966] was apparently the first author to show that, if attention is restricted to planar imaged surfaces, the displacement field, in general, has two interpretations for (relative) motion, and hence also for the orientation of the imaged surface. Tsai, Huang, and Zhu [Tsai, Huang, and Zhu 1982] rederived this result, providing a procedure for computing the solutions. Longuet-Higgins [Longuet-Higgins 1984a] extended the analysis to velocity fields, showing that a unique solution is geometrically guaranteed whenever some imaged points lie in the observer's front half-space and some in the rear, both front and rear being defined with respect to the direction of (relative) translational motion.

What if the imaged surface is not restricted to be a plane? Tsai and Huang [Tsai and Huang 1984] have established that the displacement field for seven scene points uniquely determines the (relative) motion of the camera, provided that neither of the two centers of projection (for the two imaging configurations) and these scene points lie on a quadric cone or a pair of planes. Longuet-Higgins [Longuet-Higgins 1984b] derived the closely related result that the displacement field for eight scene points uniquely determines the relative motion of the camera, provided that these scene points and the two centers of projection do not lie on a quadric surface. Note that both the results provide only sufficient conditions for uniqueness; they do not provide necessary conditions. Although it has been known for some time that we need the displacement field for at least five scene points to determine the relative motion of the camera, it has been shown only recently that even if we disregard degenerate configurations, the displacement field for five scene points may lead to as many as 10 solutions [Faugeras and Maybank 1990]. The question of whether the displacement field for six points is sufficient to guarantee uniqueness, barring degenerate cases, has not been settled.

Maybank [Maybank 1985] established the following important uniqueness results for velocity fields: If the field is ambiguous, then the imaged surface must be a quadric; an ambiguous field that can be generated by a planar surface has at most two interpretations, and such a field cannot be generated by a nonplanar surface; finally, any ambiguous field has at most three interpretations. Horn [Horn 1987] has further shown that the only imaged surfaces that may result in ambiguous velocity fields are, in fact, certain hyperboloids of one sheet (including their degenerate forms) that contain the center of projection (cf. [Longuet-Higgins 1984b]). Longuet-

Higgins [Longuet-Higgins 1988] extended Maybank's results to displacement fields, proving the following:

1. If any interpretation of a displacement field locates a planar imaged surface, then so does every other interpretation.
2. Otherwise, an ambiguous field cannot sustain more than three distinct and physically realizable interpretations, each interpretation locating a quadric imaged surface.

8.3 Discussion

Among the various areas of research in computer vision, image-sequence analysis has undoubtedly seen the most activity over the past several years. It has also provided the most tangible gains. Owing to the extra (temporal) dimension of the data, it is not surprising that motion-based shape recovery is widely seen as holding out more promise than is any other shape recovery technique we have discussed—perhaps, barring stereo—even though this promise is yet to be realized in a robust and practical fashion. In addition to undemonstrated robustness, image-sequence analysis also has the drawback of often imposing unusually large burdens of computation and storage. However, these burdens seem surmountable with special-purpose hardware.

In practice, errors in the estimate of a motion field are inevitable, if for no other reason than the inherent noisiness of images. Such errors are particularly detrimental to the robust recovery of the scene motion and scene structure when either the camera's field of view is small, or the focus of expansion (or contraction) is off to one side of the image. The former condition is conducive to a small range of variation in both the magnitudes and the directions of the image motion vectors constituting the translational-component motion field; the latter condition is conducive to a small range of variation in the directions of the image motion vectors constituting the translational-component motion field. In general, the larger the angular extent of the image (over which the motion field is estimated) about the focus of expansion (or contraction), the more robustly we can estimate the location of the focus of expansion (or contraction). However, even when we have a large field of view about the focus of expansion (or contraction), we are not guaranteed robustness. Also detrimental to robustness is the situation in which the depths of the imaged scene points are large relative to the magnitude of the camera translation—such an imaging geometry leads to the translational-component motion field having small image vectors. (See [Adiv 1989] for an extended discussion on the effect of noisy motion-field estimates on the recovery of the scene motion and scene structure.)

For pedagogical reasons, our treatment of motion-field estimation in this chapter—as of every other estimation problem in this book—has been **deterministic**. That is, we have proceeded with estimation under the assumption that what we are seeking is a single "correct" estimate for each motion-field vector. Given that motion-field estimation is an error-prone enterprise, and that, in our scheme of things, the motion field is simply an intermediate result to be used to derive the scene motion and scene structure, it is advantageous to seek **probabilistic**, rather than deterministic, estimates of the motion field. That is, it is advantageous to seek, at each image point, not a single unique motion-field vector, but rather a set of variously oriented vectors, each vector in the set providing an estimate of the image-motion component along the orientation of the vector, and each vector assigned a confidence level, or probability, or error measure. An approach closely related to this approach has been pursued by Anandan [Anandan 1989], among other authors. In principle, a probabilistic model subsumes a deterministic model: We may assign to every probabilistic vector that conforms to a deterministic estimate a confidence level of 1, and to every nonconforming probabilistic vector a confidence level of 0. More generally, in a uniform-intensity image region, we may assign to the image-motion estimate in every direction a low confidence; along a straight edge in an image, we may assign to the image-motion estimate orthogonal to the edge a high confidence, but that parallel to the edge a low confidence (such an assignment is the probabilistic formulation of the aperture problem); at a locally discriminable image point, we may assign to the image-motion estimate in every direction a high confidence. Thus, it is clear that, by allowing us to represent both uncertainty and ambiguity, a probabilistic motion-field estimate provides us with a more complete representation of the information in an image sequence than does a deterministic estimate.

Owing both to the inherent noisiness of images, and to explicit mistakes in motion-field estimation, estimates of scene structure derived from different motion-field estimates computed over different sets of images in a sequence will, in general, differ. These differences point to a more general problem: the modeling of errors in each motion-field estimate, and the analysis of the propagation of these errors through succeeding computations. We are well advised here to take recourse to the well-established discipline of estimation theory (e.g., see [Kailath 1981] for an introduction). We can reconcile differences between multiple noisy estimates of the depth of a scene point to produce a more robust and accurate final estimate of the depth—for instance, by using Kalman filtering (e.g., [Broida and Chellappa 1986], [Ayache and Faugeras 1988], [Matthies, Kanade, and Szeliski 1989]).

As we saw in Figure 8.17, motion-based image analysis facilitates the recovery of the world only up to a scale factor. This ambiguity, of course, would go away if we were to use multiple cameras to provide stereo. In this connection, see, for instance, [Waxman and Duncan 1986] and [Balasubramanyam and Snyder 1991] in the context of computer vision, and [Regan and Beverley 1979] in the context of human vision. In addition to removing the indeterminacy of a scale factor, simultaneously acquired stereo images also simplify considerably the recovery of the structure and motion of a scene that exhibits multiple independent motions relative to the camera. Perhaps, then, motion-based image analysis with multiple cameras to provide stereo will turn out to be the primary scene-recovery technique in computer vision, with the other methods filling in the gaps.

Finally, note that image-motion analysis has been pursued not only under perspective projection as we discussed in this chapter, but also under orthographic projection (e.g., [Debrunner and Ahuja 1990], [Tomasi and Kanade 1992]). In particular, Tomasi and Kanade [Tomasi and Kanade 1992] report encouraging experimental results that they obtain using telephoto lenses to view distant scenes. Each such distant scene is required to have a small range of depth compared to the distance of the scene from the camera; this requirement, as explained in Section 2.1.2, ensures that the imaging geometry is well approximated by orthographic projection up to a scale factor. Then, the approach of Tomasi and Kanade entails camera translation that is largely orthogonal to the viewing direction—and, on the whole, significant compared to the distance between the camera and the viewed scene—accompanied by camera rotation that ensures that the camera continues to point toward the viewed distant scene. What is recovered from the image sequence, then, is the rotation of the camera and the shape of the viewed scene.

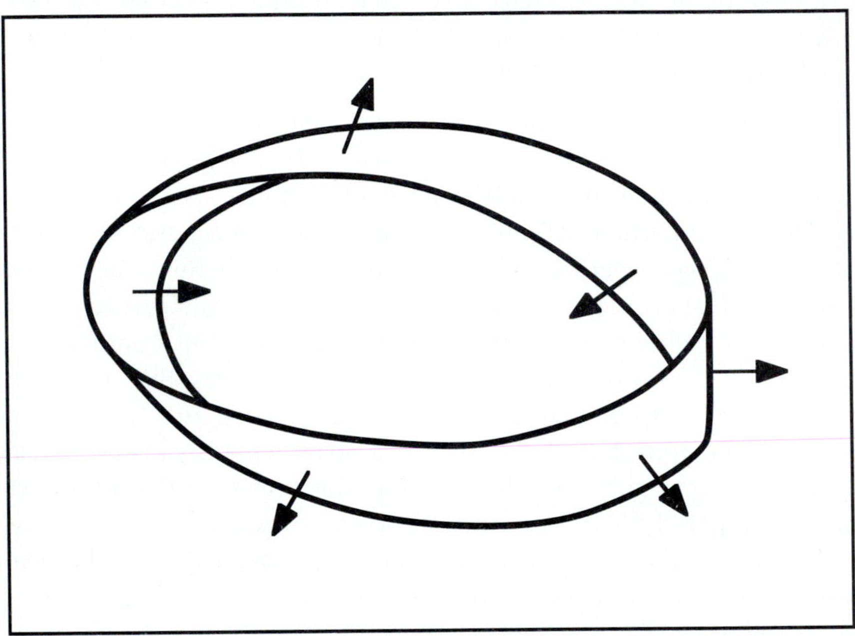

Figure 9.1 The Möbius strip. The Möbius strip is a remarkable surface. We can model the *Möbius strip* by taking a strip of paper, giving the strip half a twist, and then gluing its ends together. The Möbius strip is the classical example of a *nonorientable, or one-sided, surface*. On a one-sided surface, we can "walk" from one side of the surface at any point, to the other side at the same point, without ever crossing the boundary of the surface. If two wheels of a machine are connected by a belt that has the shape of a Möbius strip, the belt will wear out equally on both sides—this application has been patented by the Goodrich Company. If a Möbius strip is cut all along its center line, it will remain in one piece but become two-sided. You are encouraged to construct a Möbius strip to verify both this assertion, and the one-sidedness of the strip. (The one-sidedness of the Möbius strip was discovered independently, and almost simultaneously, in 1858, by two mathematicians, Möbius and Listing.)

Chapter 9

Shape Representation

To reason about an entity, we must first represent the entity, or at least represent relevant aspects of it. This assertion is true of humans, and, more clearly, of machines. Representation is a key issue in several domains: artificial intelligence, computer-aided design, computer-aided manufacturing, computer graphics, computer vision, and robotics, to name a few. Although the entities we seek to represent may be quite diverse—for instance, surfaces, physical laws, beliefs, spatiotemporal events, knowledge—certain features are shared by all good representations. Let us first discuss the generically desirable attributes of a representation, and then examine six popular shape-representation strategies in this light. By a *shape* in three dimensions is meant a volume, or, more generally, a surface. Whereas every volume is bounded by a surface, not every surface bounds a volume. Not only may a surface not enclose a volume, but the surface may not even be extendible to another surface that encloses a volume. An example of a surface that cannot be extended to enclose a volume is the well-known Möbius strip, which is illustrated in Figure 9.1. The Möbius strip is the classical example of a one-sided surface—a surface on which we can "walk" from one side of the surface at any point, to the other side at the same point, without ever crossing the boundary of the surface.

As we go about our everyday lives, we continually invoke representations—representations for everything around us, their interrelationships, and for all else we may seek to reason about or discuss. This process is so spontaneous that we often fail to distinguish among an entity, its abstraction, and its representation. These distinctions, however, are important: They confront us whenever we attempt to represent any entity explicitly.

Consider a simple example. Suppose we wish to represent some **object**—say, a spherical ball. Although a sphere can at best only approximate the shape of a physical object, for the range of applications of interest to us, a sphere might offer an adequate **abstraction** of the object. Strictly speaking, it is the abstraction of an object, rather than the physical object itself, that is or can be represented. As for the **representation** of a sphere, various alternatives suggest themselves, each alternative with its own advantages and disadvantages. These alternatives include $x^2 + y^2 + z^2 = r_o^2$ in a Cartesian coordinate frame, and $r = r_o$ in a spherical coordinate frame, the origin in each case being located at the center of the sphere.

Abstract mathematical models play a pivotal role in the representation of physical entities. An example by Requicha elucidates this role:

> Consider the strings '125' and 'CXXV'. Everybody knows that such strings represent the "same thing," but what is it that they represent? We could say that they represent physical entities such as collections of pebbles, but it is more reasonable to say simply that they represent natural numbers, which are abstract mathematical entities that model those aspects of reality relevant to counting. It is the existence of underlying abstract models—natural numbers—that allows us to study mathematically, without recourse to physical experiments, the properties of decimal and Roman representations, (pp. 439–440, [Requicha 1980])

and the aspects of reality they represent.

Here, we shall use the context of shape representation to examine the principles that guide the design and evaluation of representations. We shall not pay any attention to what might be an appropriate level of abstraction for a particular application. We shall first study the generically desirable attributes of a representation; then, we shall examine several different shape-representation strategies in this light.

9.1 Desirable Attributes

Ideally, there are several characteristics we would like a representation to exhibit. Clearly, the representation must be **sufficient** for the task for which it is intended—the representation must be sufficient both in the breadth of its domain, and in the access it provides to information about the represented entity. However, sufficiency is not enough. We would like a representation that, in addition to having a wide domain, is unique, generative, local, stable, and convenient for the particular task at hand. Let us examine each of these characteristics in turn.

A representation is said to have a **wide domain** if it can represent a large class of entities adequately.

A representation is said to be **unique** if every distinct member of its domain has a single distinct representation. A weaker requirement is that the representation be **unambiguous**: An entity may have multiple representations, but no two distinct entities can have a common representation.

The unambiguity of a representation does not imply that we can, in practice, recover a represented entity from its particular representation. Hence, even when a representation is unambiguous, we may in addition require that the representation be **generative**—that is, that it be capable of directly generating the represented entity. Practical and robust recovery procedures are important even when we do not intend to use them explicitly. The existence of such recovery procedures allows us to interpret meaningfully similarities and differences in representation space, and it further suggests nonarbitrary matching criteria in that space.

A representation is said to be **local** if nonintersecting components of the represented entity have independent representations. The localness of a representation implies that the representation is **additive**—that is, that the simultaneous representation of two independent entities is the sum of their representations. Note that, as nonintersecting entities need not be independent—as, for instance, nonintersecting surface patches that are either connected or coplanar—additivity is a weaker condition than localness. When a representation is local, it is often easy to modify the particular representation of an entity under change in that entity—such ease of modification is a desirable property of a representation in its own right.

A representation is said to be **stable** if small perturbations in the represented entity do not induce large changes in the representation of the entity. It is important to note that the terms *small* and *large* here are meaningful only in the context of specific metrics in the domain and the range of the representation.[1] Although stability and localness often go hand in hand, neither implies the other. Of all the concepts that we have discussed thus far in this section, stability is the most subtle. Hence, let us pause for a moment to consider the following illustration of this concept in the specific context of shape representation. To index the stability of a surface representation scheme, we could introduce a small bump (or dimple) on a surface, and then measure the resulting changes in the representation of the surface—the smallness of the bump introduced here could be measured by the size of the smallest sphere that encompasses all the ensuing surface changes.

With reference to metrics in the domain and the range of a representation, note that, for a metric in representation space to be a candidate index for measuring the similarities and differences between represented entities, it is clearly necessary that the metric be stable vis-à-vis some meaningful metric in the domain of the representation. However, stability is not sufficient: The metric must, in addition, be sensitive (i.e., responsive) to significant changes in the represented entity. Clearly, the existence and formulation of stable, and yet not insensitive, meaningful pairs of metrics—one metric in the domain of the representation, and the other in its range—is of considerable importance.

A representation may exhibit all the characteristics that we have discussed thus far, and yet not be **convenient** for the task at hand. Several factors go into determining the convenience of a representation—for instance, the ease with which we can use the representation to represent an entity, the access the representation provides to information about the represented entity, and the ease with which the particular representation of an entity can be manipulated toward accomplishing a particular task. It is important to note that a particular representation may be suitable for one task, and yet completely inappropriate for another.

---

1. We can formally define **stability** as follows:

> Consider u and z as elements of metric spaces U and F with metrics $\rho_U(u_1, u_2)$ for $u_1, u_2 \in U$ and $\rho_F(z_1, z_2)$ for $z_1, z_2 \in F$. . . . The problem of determining the solution $z = R(u)$ in the space F from the initial data $u \in U$ is said to be **stable on the spaces** (F, U) if, for every positive number ε, there exists a positive number $\delta(\varepsilon)$ such that the inequality $\rho_U(u_1, u_2) \le \delta(\varepsilon)$ implies $\rho_F(z_1, z_2) \le \varepsilon$, where $z_1 = R(u_1)$ and $z_2 = R(u_2)$. . . . (p. 7, [Tikhonov and Arsenin 1977])

Consider shape representation. Whereas tactile exploration and manipulation require the accessibility of first- and second-order surface properties, these properties are relatively unimportant for robot path-planning. For visual tasks, what is important is

> the ease with which we can recognize an object as essentially similar to another we have seen before, or the ease with which we can identify that objects with distinct differences have important similarities (a child and an adult, or a man and a woman). This is one basis for generalization. A representation is intended to express low-level knowledge about shape, that is, class knowledge about familiar shapes, and to serve as a basis for approximation of shape, and conjecture about missing information, for example, the hidden half of objects. The primary criterion is not the simplicity of inference from visual data, although that is important. There are representations which are simple to obtain; arrays of intensity values, polynomial coefficients, Fourier or Hadamard transforms. For these representations to be useful in understanding complex scenes, they must be embedded in systems which use knowledge to accomplish segmentation of a scene into objects, and which make a separation of variables to represent similarities and differences rather than lumping all variables together in a distance measure. No single theory or representation will solve the problems of understanding a visual scene or the general problems of intelligence. The choice of representations depends on the task; special cases and privileged knowledge will always be important. (p. 1, [Binford 1971])

9.2 Popular Strategies

There exists in computer vision and computer graphics, a large body of work devoted to shape representation; see the references in [Requicha 1980] and [Besl and Jain 1985]. By and large, the various representation schemes can be classified as either surface-based or volumetric. Clearly, volumetric schemes are less general in that they can represent only closed (i.e., boundaryless) surfaces. Surface patches can be represented by volumetric schemes only if these patches are first closed; for instance, a visible surface patch can be represented as a part of that cone that the patch defines with the center of projection of the imaging device. As what we perceive are surfaces and not volumes, surface-based schemes are, in general, better suited for use with partial information. At times, however, volumetric schemes can be more convenient—for example, in representing the free (i.e., unoccupied) space surrounding a mobile robot. Also, volumetric schemes may provide more immediate access to global relationships. For example, the three-dimensional spatial proximity of points that are far apart on a surface may be more readily apparent from a volumetric description than it is from a surface-based description—as, for instance, in the case of spatially close points on either side of a large thin sheet.

An obvious way to describe a surface is by a collection of simple approximating patches—for example, planar, quadric, or other low-order–polynomial surface patches—each patch perhaps exhibiting continuous derivatives of up to some order at its seams. This strategy is popular in computer graphics. Such an approach has been pursued in computer vision among others by Faugeras and his coauthors [Faugeras et al. 1984]. Similarly, volumes can be described as combinations of primitive volumes, such as cubes and tetrahedra. The most popular scheme describes a volume as a collection of cubes organized in a data structure called an *oct-tree*; see [Chen and Huang 1988]. Although such techniques are convenient for certain tasks, they are ill-suited for other applications such as object recognition and manipulation. Nevertheless, owing to their immense popularity, let us review one of them here: parametric bicubic patches.

Rather than represent an object directly, as with parametric bicubic patches, we could instead represent a convenient transformation of the object. We shall consider several alternatives here. It is important that we bear in mind that the end products of these transformations themselves need to be represented, and are in this sense not user-ready. The characteristics of the final representation vis-à-vis the represented entity, of course, depend irrevocably on the nature of the transformation invoked.

Following our discussion of parametric bicubic patches (Section 9.2.1), we shall consider five other influential approaches to shape representation. One of them is volumetric: symmetric axis transform (Section 9.2.2). Two are surface-based: differential-geometric (Section 9.2.4) and Gaussian-image representations (Section 9.2.5). One can be used in either fashion: generalized cylinders (Section 9.2.3). The last one is an interesting nonmetric approach that catalogs the distinct topological structures of all the possible views of the object: visual potential (Section 9.2.6). In each case, we shall consider the problem of representing the particularly simple shape illustrated in Figure 9.2: a hemisphere fused to the top of a circular cylinder that has the same radius as the hemisphere.

Whereas all the representations we shall consider here are deterministic, in practice, we might want to represent the uncertainties in shape that result from the uncertainties in measurement, perhaps by incorporating these uncertainties into the parameters of the representation (e.g., [Ayache and

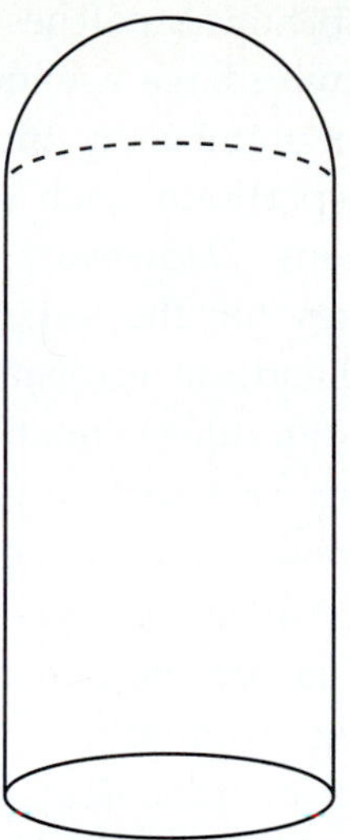

Figure 9.2 A simple object—a hemisphere fused to the top of a circular cylinder—whose shape we shall represent employing various strategies.

Faugeras 1988], [Ikeuchi and Kanade 1988]). In addition, we might also want to represent a shape at varying levels of detail. In this connection, Koenderink and van Doorn [Koenderink and van Doorn 1986] have proposed the *theory of dynamic shape*, which suggests that a three-dimensional shape be uniquely embedded in a morphogenetic (i.e., hypothetically evolutionary) sequence, with resolution being the parameter along the sequence.

9.2.1 Parametric Bicubic Patches

Parametric bicubic patches are a popular tool for describing surfaces in computer graphics; see [Foley and van Dam 1982]. The strategy in this approach to shape representation is to segment the surface into a set of patches, and then to approximate each patch by a parametric bicubic patch such that continuity in position and surface normal across patch boundaries is preserved. A **parametric bicubic patch** is represented by three equations, one equation for each of the x, y, and z Cartesian coordinates: If u and v denote the surface parameters, then the expression for each coordinate takes the bicubic form $\Sigma_{i=0}^{3} \Sigma_{j=0}^{3} c_{ij}\, u^i\, v^j$, where c_{ij} are the coefficients.

As for representing the object in Figure 9.2, whereas the planar surface can be represented exactly, the cylindrical and spherical surfaces must be segmented, and then each segment approximated by a bicubic patch—the finer we make the segmentation, the more accurate we can make the approximating bicubic patches. This exercise is not carried out here.

Individual parametric bicubic patches cannot represent surface discontinuities, but they otherwise have a wide domain. Although they are unambiguous, surface representation using them need not be unique: Most surfaces admit more than one partition, each segment in turn admitting one or more bicubic approximations. However, this representation is clearly generative, each pair of values for the surface parameters determining a surface point. On the other hand, an error-minimizing approximation of a surface by a set of bicubic (or any other) equations is not local. First, because the representation of every part of a surface patch depends on the shape of the rest of the patch. Second, because representations of the various individual patches may be interdependent via boundary conditions imposed between adjoining patches. The parametric-bicubic representation, however, like every other surface-fitting approach, is additive. Further, if surface fitting is pursued with the aim of minimizing some error measure based on the minimum Euclidean distance between points on the represented surface and its representation, then the coefficients of the representation will change only marginally under perturbation of the represented surface. In this sense, we may say that the parametric-bicubic representation is stable.

Parametric bicubic patches have found use primarily in computer graphics, where it is sought to generate synthetic images. The parametric polynomial form of each patch facilitates the computation of the patch's derivatives, and, hence, of the patch's shading (see [Foley and van Dam 1982]). On the other hand, the possibility of several equally acceptable bicubic approximations to any given surface makes this representation inappropriate for surface matching.

9.2.2 Symmetric Axis Transform

The **symmetric axis transform (SAT)**, also known as the **Blum transform** or the **medial axis transform**, is a widely cited shape description technique that was first proposed by Blum in 1967 [Blum 1967]. It has since been extended and further developed by several other authors (e.g., [Nackman and Pizer 1985], [Pizer, Oliver, and Bloomberg 1987]). The SAT is described in two dimensions here. Its extension to three dimensions is obvious.

> One formalism for obtaining the SAT uses a circular primitive. Objects are described by the collection of maximal discs, ones which fit inside the object but in no other disc inside the object. The object is the logical union of all of its maximal discs. The description is in two parts: the locus of centers, called the symmetric axis (not unlike a central contour or stick figure) and the radius at each point, called the radius function, *R*. . . .

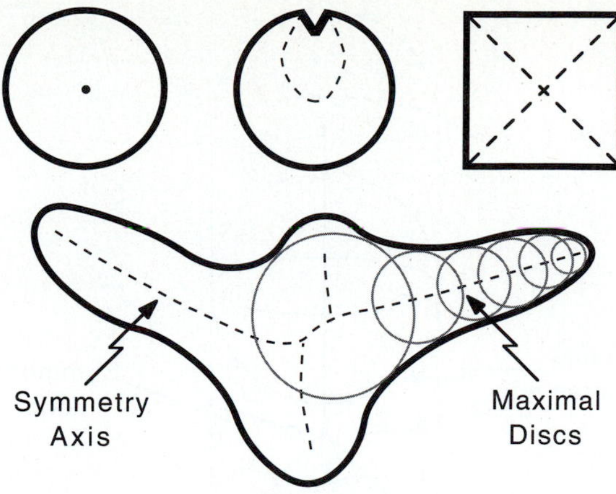

Figure 9.3 "Symmetry axes" of four simple two-dimensional shapes. The *symmetry axis* of an n-dimensional closed shape may be defined as the locus of the centers of the maximal n-spheres that fit inside the shape; the radius of the maximally fitting n-sphere centered at any point of the symmetry axis is specified by the *radius function* of the shape. For $n = 2$, an n-sphere is a disc, and for $n = 3$, an n-sphere is a sphere. Notice in the figure that, whereas the symmetry axis of a circle is a single point at the center of the circle, the symmetry axis of a slightly indented circle is a curve longer than the diameter of the circle.

> An alternative way of describing the axis portion of a symmetric axis transform employs an analogy to a grass fire. Imagine an object whose border is set on fire. The subsequent internal quench points of the fire represent the symmetric axis, the time of quench for unit velocity propagation being the radius function. (p. 167, [Blum and Nagel 1978])

We can easily see that the symmetric axis transform is a straightforward generalization of the Vornoi diagram. The **Vornoi diagram** of a set of points S in a plane is the locus of points in the plane that have more than one nearest neighbor from among members of S. Equivalently, it is a partition of the plane into regions within each of which all points are closer to one member of S than to any other (see [Preparata and Shamos 1985]). Every nonvertex point in the diagram has exactly two nearest neighbors in S, and every nth-order vertex has exactly n nearest neighbors.

Figure 9.3 illustrates the symmetry axes of some simple two-dimensional shapes. The symmetry axis of the object in Figure 9.2 is illustrated in Figure 9.4. It is a circular cone with a straight-line segment extending from its vertex. The radius function is constant along the straight-line segment, and varies linearly down to zero along the straight rulings from the vertex of the cone to its base.

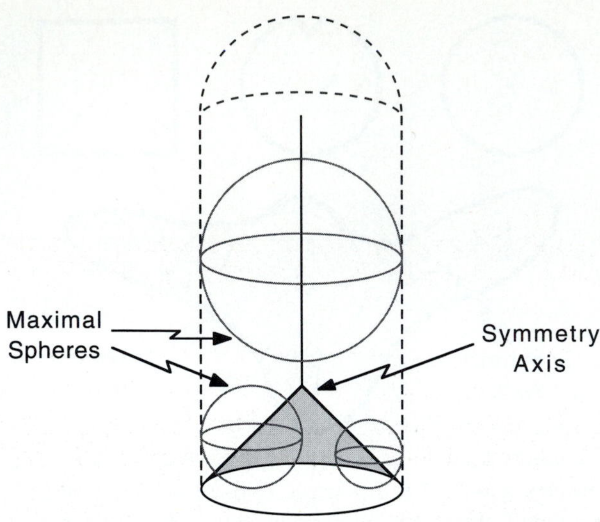

Figure 9.4 The symmetry axis of the object in Figure 9.2. The symmetry axis here is a circular cone with a straight-line segment extending from the vertex of the cone.

Several features are immediately apparent. The SAT is a simple and elegant representation with a wide domain: In two dimensions, its domain comprises all closed (i.e., boundaryless) curves, and, in three dimensions, its domain comprises all closed surfaces. This representation is generative: In three dimensions, any closed surface is simply the envelope of the collection of the maximal spheres that fit inside the surface. The SAT is also unique, but not local: Every maximal sphere represents multiple disjoint points located where the sphere and the surface touch. However, it is additive: The SAT for multiple disjoint closed surfaces is the sum of their individual SATs. On the other hand, as is evident from Figure 9.3, a small change in the shape of a closed surface may drastically affect the surface's symmetry axis. Hence, with respect to a metric in representation space that measures differences between symmetry axes, the SAT is unstable.

The SAT has found limited use—primarily in biological applications (e.g., [Blum and Nagel 1978]). It has not been used extensively perhaps because of its inherent instability described earlier, and also, perhaps, because, in general, it does not offer any advantage in descriptive ease. In three dimensions, the problem of describing the boundary of a volume is reduced to describing the volume's symmetry axis—which, in general, has the same dimension as the volume's boundary—and the accompanying radius function. The SAT derives its appeal from its intuitive interpretation as a "skeleton" with "flesh" added on. Note, however, that the "skeleton" can be fairly nonintuitive if we allow the curvature of the boundary of a shape to vary rapidly, as in the case of the indented disc in Figure 9.3.

9.2.3 Generalized Cylinders

The generalized-cylinder (GC) representation, first proposed by Binford in 1971 [Binford 1971], is perhaps the most popular shape-description method in computer vision today; see [Binford 1987] for a later account of the original proposal, which remains unpublished. Prompted by the SAT, the GC representation aims to parameterize some simple shapes while retaining the intuitive appeal of the "skeleton" and "flesh" of the SAT; unlike in the SAT, however, here the "skeleton" of a three-dimensional shape is restricted to be a space curve. Note that parameterization—which implies a one-to-one correspondence between the domain and the range of a mapping—is not accomplished by the SAT as every point on the symmetry axis of the SAT, along with the value of the radius function at that point, corresponds to more than a single point on the boundary of the represented shape.

We can generate any cylinder by sweeping a cross-section along a straight line, called the cylinder's *axis*. A **generalized cylinder (GC)** generalizes the notion of an ordinary cylinder in two ways: by sweeping the **cross-section** along an arbitrary space curve, called the generalized cylinder's **axis** or **spine**, and by allowing the cross-section to transform (i.e., scale, rotate, and distort) as it is swept, the transformation rule being called the **sweep rule**. For example, we can generate a torus by sweeping a circle along a circle. By this definition, cones are generalized cylinders whose cross-sections are linearly scaled as they are swept along straight spines; hence, generalized cylinders are sometimes also called **generalized cones**. Whereas ordinary cylinders are characterized by translational invariance—that is, their cross-sections are congruent under translation along the axis—generalized cylinders are characterized by what Binford calls "generalized translational invariance" [Binford 1971]: The cross-sections of generalized cylinders are congruent under translation along the spine, this translation accompanied by transformation according to the sweep rule.

A generalized cylinder is specified by its cross-section, sweep rule, and spine. We can represent both surfaces and volumes by appropriately choosing cross-sections that are either curves or surfaces, respectively. Complex shapes can be conceived as part–whole graphs of joined GC primitives. Then, two shapes are similar if they are composed of similar GC primitives that are configured in similar part–whole graphs.

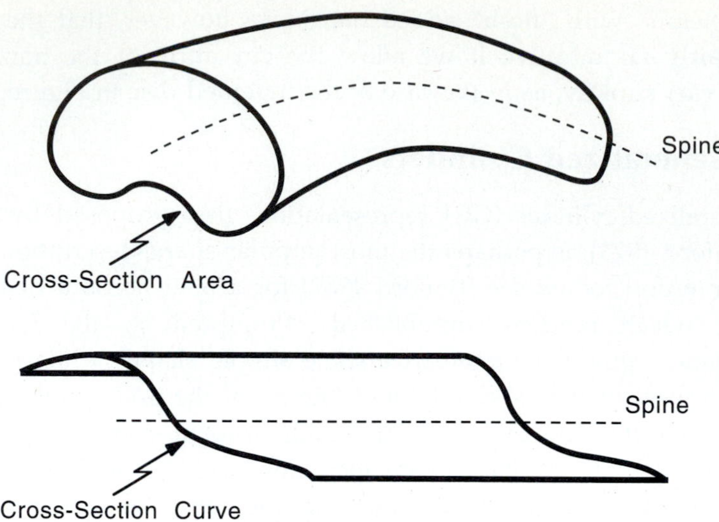

Figure 9.5 Volume and surface generalized-cylinder primitives. We can generate a *generalized cylinder* by sweeping an area or curve along some space curve while allowing the area or curve to transform as it is swept. The area or curve that is swept is called the *cross-section* of the generalized cylinder; the curve along which the area or curve is swept is called the *spine* of the generalized cylinder; the rule according to which the area or curve is transformed while it is swept is called the *sweep rule* of the generalized cylinder.

Figure 9.5 provides instances of volume and surface GC primitives. Figure 9.6 illustrates a GC representation of the object in Figure 9.2. In Figure 9.6, the spine is chosen to be the straight line connecting the center of the base to the top of the hemisphere; the cross-sections are chosen to be orthogonal to the spine, and are all circular discs; the sweep rule is constant along the length of the cylinder, and a quarter-circle for the hemisphere.

Although the GC representation has considerable appeal because of its decomposition of three-dimensional shape-description problems into lower-order problems, and also because of its hierarchical structure, it is clear that the GC-primitive domain is restricted. Whereas shapes that approximately exhibit "generalized translational invariance" are common in human-made environments, in more general settings, GCs can at best provide gross approximations. Further, most shapes to which this description applies admit several spines and cross-sections; that is, unique descriptions are rare. For instance, an ordinary circular cylinder admits as a spine every line parallel to its central axis. However, as the representation is generative—sweeping the cross-section along the spine in accordance with the sweep rule generates the original surface—unambiguity is guaranteed. Although the

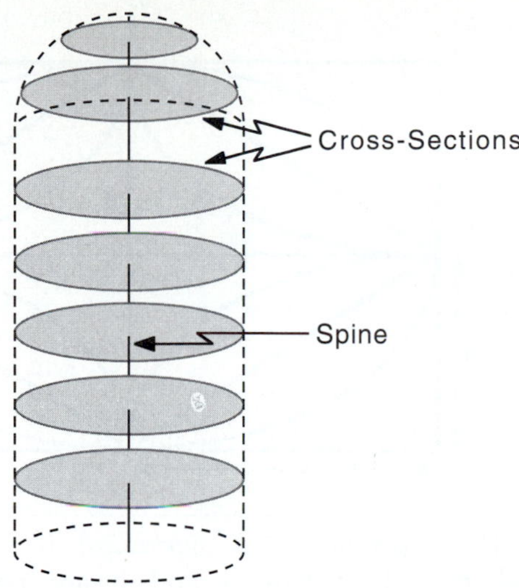

Figure 9.6 The generalized-cylinder representation of the object in Figure 9.2. The spine of the generalized cylinder here is a straight line, and the cross-sections of the generalized cylinder are circular discs.

generalized-cylinder representation is additive, it is not strictly local: Several nonintersecting surface patches may share a common portion of the spine. However, barring sweeps of the cross-section that result in surface self-intersections, this representation can be considered quasi-local in that a change made at a point along a GC primitive does not affect the representation of the GC primitive along the rest of the spine. As far as stability is concerned, a small arbitrary change in the surface is likely to put the shape outside the domain of GCs. In this sense, it is not clear that stability is a meaningful concept here. Of course, if the representation involves finding the closest fitting GC, then this scheme may be termed stable in the same sense as discussed earlier for parametric bicubic patches.

Generalized cylinders, unlike most other representations frequently cited in the computer-vision literature, have been used in working systems (e.g., [Agin and Binford 1976], [Nevatia and Binford 1977], [Brooks 1981])—mainly for object recognition. These systems illustrate many of the difficulties that lie in the path from elegant formalisms to practical implementations. For instance, nonarbitrary hierarchical decomposition of a complex structure into GC primitives is a difficult unsolved problem—easier said than done.

All said and done, GCs are convenient when applicable. The convenience of GCs should come as no surprise as GCs exploit a certain redundancy—namely, "generalized translational invariance." Other types of

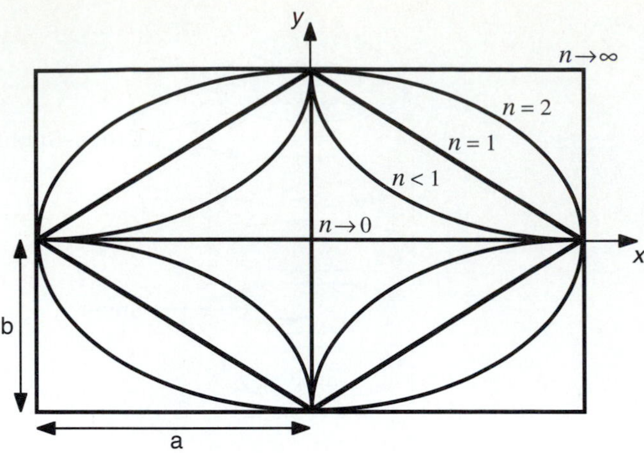

Figure 9.7 The superellipse. A *superellipse* is a curve of the following type: $|x|^n/a^n + |y|^n/b^n = 1$, where a and b are positive constants, and n is a nonnegative exponent. Illustrated are superellipses with exponents ranging from 0 to ∞; for $n = 2$, the superellipse is an ordinary ellipse, and, as $n \to \infty$, the superellipse tends to a rectangle bounding the preceding ellipse.

redundancies that a representation might exploit are planarity and symmetry. For instance, surfaces that exhibit symmetry can be described compactly by their symmetry groups and smallest independent subsurfaces. Specialized techniques provide robustness and performance invariably at the expense of generality—in the context here, at the expense of a wide domain.

Quadrics, Superquadrics, and Hyperquadrics

Surfaces of the algebraic type $\Sigma\,\Sigma\,\Sigma_{i+j+k \leq 2}\, a_{ijk}\, x^i\, y^j\, z^k = 0$, where a_{ijk} are the coefficients, are called **quadrics**. Familiar examples include ellipsoids, hyperboloids, and paraboloids. The other types of quadrics are cones, cylinders, and planes. After suitable rotation and translation, quadrics are seen to be GC primitives with straight spines and quadratic cross-sections and sweep rules. Nondegenerate quadratic curves, also known as *conic sections*, come in three varieties: ellipses, hyperbolas, and parabolas.

A beautiful generalization of an ellipse to a superellipse, first suggested by Piet Hein (see [Gardner 1965]), leads naturally to the notion of superquadratics and **superquadrics**, the latter a subclass of GC primitives that has of late gained popularity. The generalization proposed by Hein was $|x|^n/a^n + |y|^n/b^n = 1$, where a and b are positive constants, and n is a nonnegative exponent. Figure 9.7 illustrates how this curve evolves as n varies between 0 and ∞. (In the original terminology of Hein, for $n < 2$, the curve is a subellipse; for $n = 2$, the curve is an ellipse; and for $n > 2$, the curve is a superellipse. However, the use of *super* as an all-embracing prefix has become prevalent.) Superhyperbolas are defined analogously. Straight spines with superquadratic cross-sections and sweep rules lead us immediately to superquadrics. Superquadrics were introduced to the computer-graphics community by Barr [Barr 1981], and have since been used in computer vision (e.g., [Pentland 1986]).

Hanson [Hanson 1988] has proposed an elegant generalization of superquadrics to what he calls **hyperquadrics**. Although hyperquadrics are not necessarily generalized cylinders, let us avail of this opportunity to examine them. Hanson's proposal is based on the observation that superquadrics provide smooth deformations of their bounding polyhedra. For instance, the superellipsoid $|x/\mathrm{a}|^n + |y/\mathrm{b}|^n + |z/\mathrm{c}|^n = 1$ provides smooth deformations of its bounding cuboid $|x/\mathrm{a}|,\ |y/\mathrm{b}|,\ |z/\mathrm{c}| = 1$. Hanson defines *hyperquadrics* by $\sum_{i=1}^{N} \sigma_i \,|\, a_i x + b_i y + c_i z + d_i \,|^{\gamma_i} = 1$, where $N \geq 3$, $\sigma_i = \pm 1$, and $|\, a_i x + b_i y + c_i z + d_i \,| = 1$ are the bounding planes. This generalization provides a technique to deform arbitrary convex polyhedra smoothly. For instance, we can smoothly deform the octahedron given by $|x|,\ |y|,\ |z|,\ |x + y| = 1$ by varying γ down from ∞ in the equation $|x|^\gamma + |y|^\gamma + |z|^\gamma + |x + y|^\gamma = 1$; $\gamma = 2$ here gives the ellipsoid $2x^2 + 2y^2 + 2xy + z^2 = 1$. Note that, unlike superquadrics, hyperquadrics are not constrained to touch their limiting polyhedra at all. This property of hyperquadrics will probably greatly limit their usefulness.

9.2.4 Differential-Geometric Representations

Unambiguous representations independent of the position and the orientation of the represented entity are clearly desirable. Such representations must necessarily be differential geometric. If you are unfamiliar with differential geometry, you may wish to skip this section. On the other hand, several good introductions are available (e.g., [Lipschutz 1969]), and some of the terminology used in this section is explained in Footnote 2.

Perhaps the simplest example of a differential-geometric representation is the specification of the curvature and torsion of a C^2 curve as functions of the curve's arc-length. Similarly, a C^2 surface could be represented by the coefficients of the surface's first and second fundamental forms for some choice of regular parameterization. The coefficients of the first fundamental form of a surface by themselves determine the arc-lengths, angles, and areas on the surface; the coefficients of the second fundamental form, in conjunction with the coefficients of the first fundamental form, determine the surface curvature in every direction. The various coefficients are not mutually independent: They are related by the Gauss–Weingarten and Mainardi–Codazzi equations. You can find the details in any elementary differential-geometry text (e.g., [Lipschutz 1969], [do Carmo 1976]). Note that both the representations described here are only unambiguous, and not unique. For curves, we must choose the zero arc-length point. For surfaces, assuming sufficient differentiability and the absence of umbilical points, we could conceivably use the lines of curvature as parametric curves with their arc-lengths serving as parameters; once again, the zero arc-length points must be chosen.

Every differential-geometric representation implicitly involves a set of differential equations satisfied by the represented entity. Whereas the domain of a representation is determined by the order of continuity demanded by these equations, unambiguity hinges on their uniqueness of solution. Even when a differential-geometric representation is unambiguous, recovery, if feasible, is subject to cumulative errors and is hence impractical. Consequently, spatial comparisons based on differential-geometric representations, when possible, are inconvenient and unreliable. Further, by their very nature, differential-geometric representations are not strictly local. At the very least, "boundary conditions" need to be propagated. Such representations are also not stable. Although strictly differential-geometric representations are clearly inadequate by themselves as robustness and practicability demand the incorporation of global geometric information, they can be quite useful in conjunction with other representations.

Several differential-geometric representations have been proposed in the computer-vision literature. The use of lines of curvature and asymptotic lines to represent surfaces was suggested by Brady and his coauthors [Brady et al. 1985], and Nalwa [Nalwa 1989b] investigated various unambiguous differential-geometric representations for elliptic and hyperbolic patches parameterized by their surface-normal orientations.

9.2.5 Gaussian-Image Representations

An **orientable surface** (assumed C^1) is a surface that can be continuously assigned a directed unit surface normal at each point. A surface to which such an assignment has been made is said to be **oriented**. The Möbius strip, which was illustrated in Figure 9.1, is the classical example of a nonorientable surface. Intuitively, an orientable surface is one on which we cannot "walk" from one side of the surface to the other side without traversing the boundary of the surface. Clearly, every closed (i.e., boundaryless) surface is orientable. Consequently, every surface patch on the boundary of a volume is orientable; we can orient such patches by assigning to each point the outward surface normal at that point. As every orientable surface can be oriented in only one of two distinct ways, two unoriented but orientable surfaces are the same if and only if an oriented version of one matches one of the two oriented versions of the other.

The **Gauss map** assigns to each point of an oriented surface a point on a unit sphere such that the directed surface normal on the original surface and the outward surface normal on the unit sphere both point in the same direction. The image of the Gauss map of a surface is called the **Gaussian image**, or **spherical image**, of the surface; the unit sphere in the current context is called the **Gaussian sphere**. The Gaussian image of a surface (assumed C^2) has the following salient properties; see [Hilbert and Cohn-Vossen 1952]. The Gauss map is one-to-one in the neighborhood of elliptic and hyperbolic points, and the Gauss map is singular—loosely speaking, locally many-to-one—at parabolic and planar points.[2] Barring degenerate cases, the principal directions are the only surface directions that are parallel to their Gaussian-image directions, and the asymptotic directions are the only surface directions that are perpendicular to their Gaussian-image directions. The Gaussian image of a surface also has the global property that this image is invariant under both translation and scaling of the surface.

---

2. On a C^2 surface (i.e., a twice continuously differentiable surface), the **normal curvature** at a point in any direction (oriented in the tangent plane of the surface) is the curvature at the point of this curve: the curve that lies at the intersection of the surface with the plane containing the surface normal and the direction in which the normal curvature is sought. Barring points where the normal curvature is the same in every direction, there exist at every point on the surface two perpendicular directions, along one of which the normal (signed) curvature is maximum, and along the other of which the normal (signed) curvature is minimum. These directions are called the **principal directions** at the point, and the corresponding normal curvatures are called the **principal curvatures** at the point. At points where the normal curvature is the same in every direction—such points are called **umbilical points**—every direction is a principal direction. At any point, the surface directions (if any) along which the normal curvatures are zero are called the **asymptotic directions** at the point. There are no asymptotic directions at only those surface points at which the two principal curvatures are both nonzero, and they both have the same sign. A surface curve whose tangent at every point is along a principal direction is called a **line of curvature**, and a surface curve whose tangent at every point is along an asymptotic direction is called an **asymptotic line**.

   Every point on a C^2 surface can be classified into one of four types: elliptic, hyperbolic, parabolic, or planar. An **elliptic point** is one where both the principal curvatures are nonzero and have the same sign—that is, where the surface curves the same way in every direction, and it is in this sense locally cup-shaped. A **hyperbolic point** is one where both the principal curvatures are nonzero but have opposite signs—that is, where the surface curves convexly in some directions, and concavely in others, and it is in this sense locally saddle-shaped. A **parabolic point** is one where one of the two principal curvatures is zero and the other is nonzero—that is, where the surface does not curve at all in one direction, but does the same way in every other direction, and it is in this sense locally cylindrical. Finally, a **planar point** is one where both the principal curvatures are zero—that is, where the surface does not curve at all in any direction, and it is in this sense locally planar. Each of these four categories of points on a C^2 surface was illustrated in Figure 4.11. See [Hilbert and Cohn-Vossen 1952] for an intuitive introduction to differential geometry, and [Lipschutz 1969] for an analytical treatment.

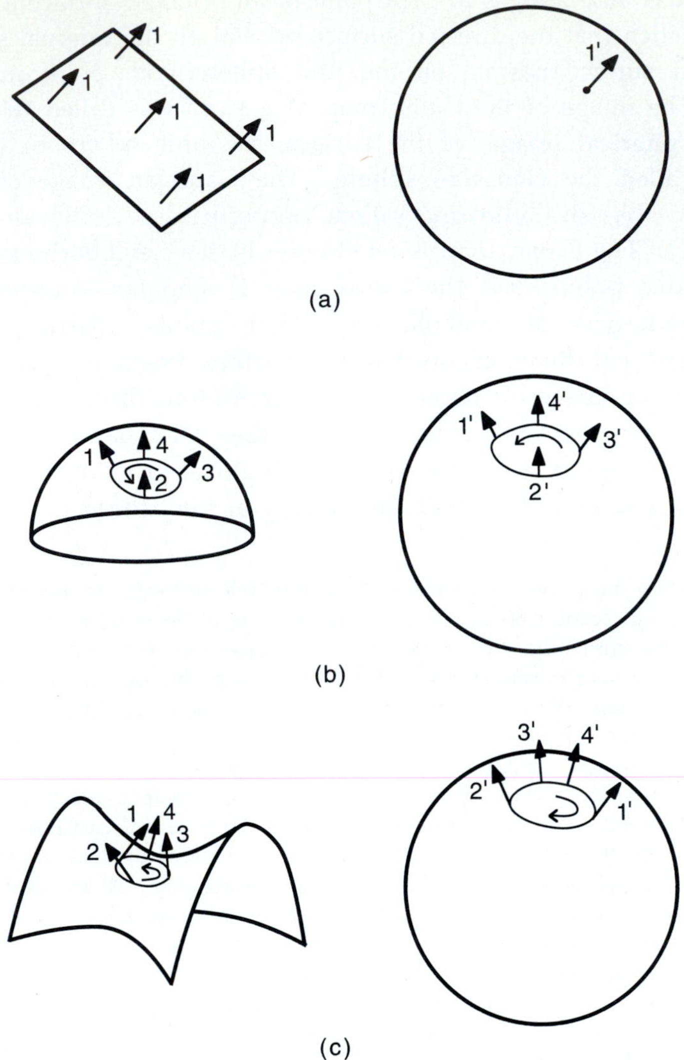

Figure 9.8 The Gaussian image. The *Gaussian image* of a point on a continuously differentiable surface is the point on a unit sphere that has the same surface-normal orientation. The unit sphere in this context is called the *Gaussian sphere*. Illustrated here are the Gaussian images of six typical surfaces. **(a)** Planar patch. **(b)** Elliptic patch. **(c)** Hyperbolic patch. **(d)** Parabolic patch taken from a cylinder. **(e)** Patches with parabolic lines separating elliptic and hyperbolic regions. Planar, elliptic,

Figure 9.8 illustrates several typical Gaussian images. As shown in Figure 9.8(a), the Gaussian image of a plane is just a single point on the Gaussian sphere. Whereas both elliptic and hyperbolic surface patches map onto regions of the Gaussian sphere, rather than onto isolated points, there is

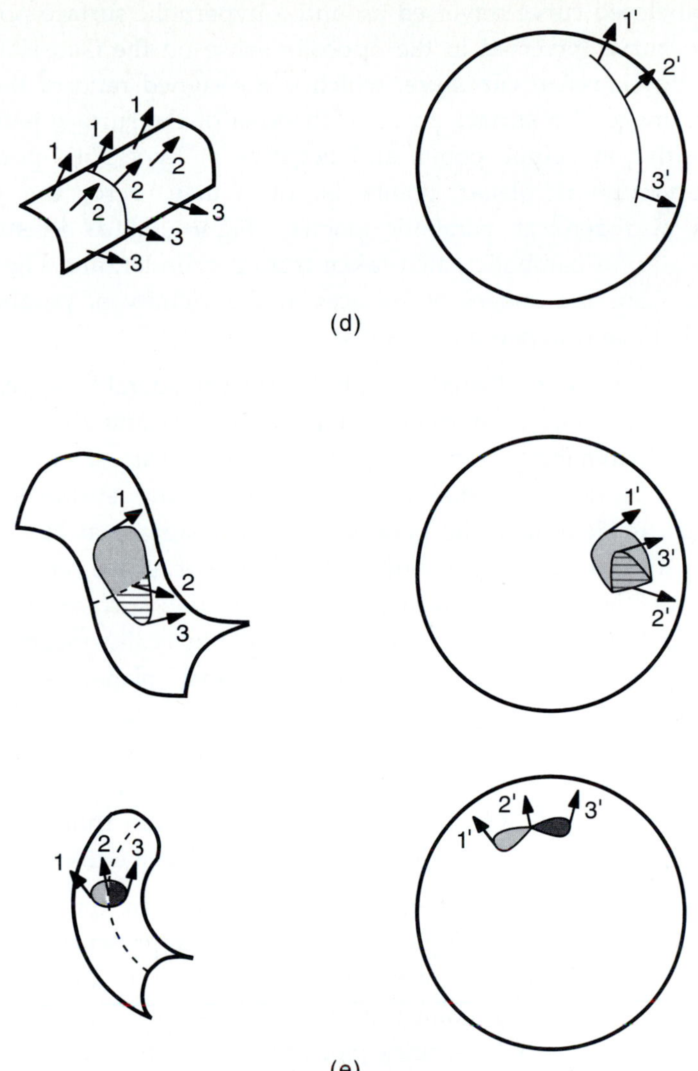

hyperbolic, and parabolic patches are surfaces that respectively comprise planar, elliptic, hyperbolic, and parabolic points; a parabolic line is a line that comprises parabolic points. Loosely speaking, a *planar point* is one where the surface is locally planar, an *elliptic point* is one where the surface is locally cup-shaped, a *hyperbolic point* is one where the surface is locally saddle-shaped, and a *parabolic point* is one where the surface is locally cylindrical.

a key distinction between the Gaussian images of such patches. As illustrated in Figure 9.8(b), the Gaussian image of a small closed curve traversed around an elliptic point on a surface is a closed curve traversed in the same sense on the Gaussian sphere. In contrast, as illustrated in Figure

9.8(c), a small closed curve traversed around a hyperbolic surface point maps onto a closed curve traversed in the opposite sense on the Gaussian sphere. As a result, the **Gaussian curvature**, which is the signed ratio of the area of the Gaussian image of a surface patch to the area of the surface patch in the limit,[3] is positive at elliptic points and negative at hyperbolic points. The Gaussian curvature at planar points is, of course, zero; the Gaussian curvature is also zero at parabolic points. Figure 9.8(d) illustrates the Gaussian image of a parabolic patch taken from a cylinder, and Figure 9.8(e) illustrates the Gaussian images of surfaces in the vicinity of parabolic lines separating elliptic and hyperbolic regions.

Representation on the Gaussian sphere has considerable appeal. Most important, the unit surface normal is a physically meaningful and locally determinable "parameter." In contrast, for instance, if we were to parameterize a surface on the arc-lengths along the surface's lines of curvature, then to determine the parameters of the surface at any point, we would have to evaluate the lengths of a pair of space curves. As a consequence of the physical meaningfulness of the surface normal, the singularities of the Gauss map, if any, are also physically meaningful and nonarbitrary: They correspond to parabolic and planar points. The *singularities of the Gauss map*, which we earlier characterized loosely as instances where the Gauss map is locally many-to-one, are more accurately defined as instances of zero Gaussian curvature. It is worth pointing out here that, for elliptic and hyperbolic surface patches, even though the Gauss map is free of singularities, it is not necessarily globally one-to-one!

With regard to the attractiveness of representation on the Gaussian sphere, we might further argue that such a representation exploits redundancy. Every planar surface patch is represented at an isolated point on the Gaussian sphere, this point indicating the surface-normal orientation of the patch. Every parabolic surface patch is represented along a curve on the Gaussian sphere, each point on this curve representing a straight ruling

---

3. The **Gaussian curvature** of a C^2 surface at any point can equivalently be defined as the product of the surface's principal curvatures at the point. The Gaussian curvature is an intrinsic property of the surface in the following sense: The Gaussian curvature of a surface remains unchanged as the surface is subjected to arbitrary bending, without stretching, where *bending* is defined as any surface deformation that leaves the arc-lengths and angles of all surface curves unaltered. Surfaces that have an identical constant Gaussian curvature everywhere exhibit the remarkable property that any one such surface can be transformed to any other such surface by bending alone. It follows that any surface that comprises only parabolic points—such surfaces are called **developable surfaces**—can be formed by bending a planar patch. See [Hilbert and Cohn-Vossen 1952] for more on the Gaussian curvature.

on the patch. In the neighborhood of elliptic and hyperbolic points, the smaller the Gaussian curvature—and, hence, in a sense, the smaller the local deviation from a plane—the smaller the area of the Gaussian image.

In the absence of symmetries in the Gaussian image of a surface, the orientation of the surface can be deduced from the orientation of the surface's Gaussian image. Thus, representation on the Gaussian sphere can potentially decompose the six–degree-of-freedom surface-matching problem into two much easier three–degree-of-freedom problems: the determination of surface orientation, followed by the relatively easy verification of a spatial match and the determination of surface position. Note, however, that "optimal" solutions to the two matching subproblems do not together constitute an "optimal" solution to the complete problem. But the suboptimal solution could be used as a starting point for an "optimal" search in six-dimensional space; the ensuing computational savings could be tremendous. If the Gaussian image of a surface does exhibit symmetry, but the cardinality of the symmetry group is small, then, once again, the matching problem is potentially decomposable. In general, we could use differential-geometric measures of the surface mapped onto the surface's Gaussian image to help resolve ambiguities in surface orientation. In addition to the potential decomposition of surface matching, representation on the Gaussian sphere also facilitates the computation of line drawings and surface shading.

Extended Gaussian Image

Having established surface representation on the Gaussian sphere to offer certain advantages, we are faced with the question of what information to maintain on the Gaussian image. Clearly, the image of the Gauss map by itself is inadequate: It is too ambiguous. One possibility is to associate with each point of the Gaussian image the inverse of the Gaussian curvature at that point's preimage. Such a representation has been proposed for C^2 closed (i.e., boundaryless) convex (i.e., elliptic everywhere) surfaces and is known as the **extended Gaussian image (EGI)** [Horn 1984]. The theoretical basis for this representation is in Minkowski's theorem—see [Stoker 1969] for a description of this theorem—from which it follows that the EGIs of two C^2 closed convex surfaces are identical if and only if the two surfaces differ by at most a translation. Despite this uniqueness of EGIs, no direct procedure for the recovery of the original surface is known.

The preceding definition of an EGI needs to be modified to accommodate surfaces whose Gauss maps are not one-to-one. First, consider planar and parabolic patches. As the Gaussian curvature is the ratio of the area of the Gaussian image to the area of the original surface in the limit, integrating the

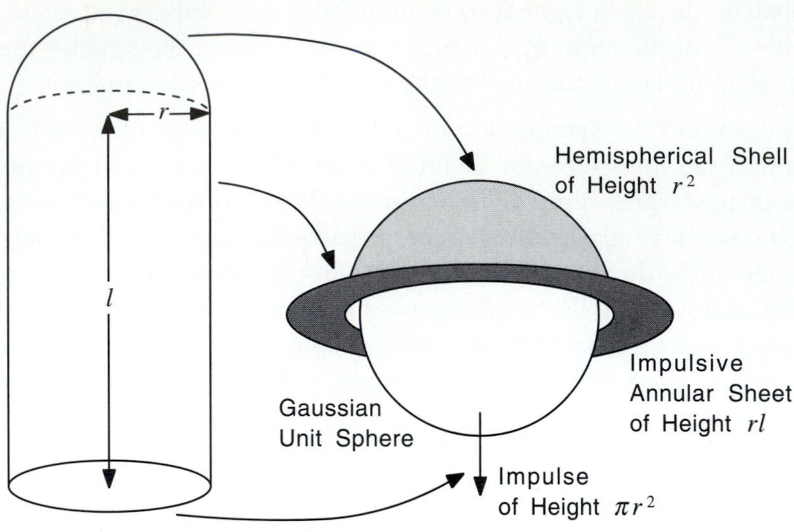

Figure 9.9 The extended Gaussian image of the object in Figure 9.2. The *extended Gaussian image* of a surface is an assignment to each point of a Gaussian sphere onto which the Gaussian image of the surface has been mapped the area of the preimage(s) of the point per unit area of the Gaussian sphere. It follows that the integral of the extended Gaussian image over any region of the Gaussian sphere yields the total area of the surface that maps onto that region of the Gaussian sphere.

inverse of the Gaussian curvature over the Gaussian sphere should give the area of the corresponding surface patch. Hence, we extend Gaussian images of planar and parabolic patches by associating with them impulses whose integrals give the preimage surface areas. At points on the Gaussian sphere whose preimages consist of multiple elliptic and hyperbolic points, we extend the definition of the EGI by associating with each point the sum of the absolute values of the inverse Gaussian curvatures at that point's preimages (see [Horn 1984] for details).

The EGI representation basically assigns to each point on the Gaussian sphere the area of the preimage of that point per unit area of the Gaussian sphere. It follows that, if we integrate the EGI over any region of the Gaussian sphere, we get the total area of the represented object that maps onto that region of the Gaussian sphere. Note that, despite its name, the extended Gaussian image is not a simple extension of the Gaussian image. The Gaussian image, in general, has multiple layers on the Gaussian sphere, whereas what we have here is a single-valued function. The EGI of the object in Figure 9.2 is illustrated in Figure 9.9.

Figure 9.10 Examples of orientable piecewise C^2 surfaces. A C^2 surface is a surface that is twice continuously differentiable, and, loosely speaking, a *piecewise C^2 surface* is a surface that can be divided into a finite number of surface patches, each of which is C^2 in its interior. An *orientable surface* is a surface that can be assigned a directed unit surface normal at each point such that all the surface normals lie on the same side of the surface; a surface to which such an assignment of directed unit surface normals has been made is said to be *oriented*. The Möbius strip, illustrated in Figure 9.1, is the classical example of a nonorientable surface. (From [Nalwa 1989b] with permission.)

Although the domain of EGIs is fairly broad—oriented piecewise C^2 surfaces,[4] examples of which are provided in Figure 9.10—this representation is, in general, neither unique nor unambiguous. For instance, a set of two identical spheres, each sphere with radius r, has the same EGI as does a single sphere with radius $\sqrt{2}\,r$. Horn [Horn 1984] provides an example of a convex object that has the same EGI as a torus. As the EGI representation is ambiguous, it clearly cannot be generative. Although the Gauss map itself is singular and hence nonlocal at only parabolic and planar points, extended Gaussian images are neither local nor additive, except when every surface point has a unique surface-normal orientation. Every surface point, for instance, in every subset of a closed convex surface would have a unique surface-normal orientation. Multiple points with a common surface-normal orientation are represented here as a single entity on the Gaussian sphere. As the EGI is essentially an area-based representation, it is stable under a metric in representation space that computes the integral of squared

4. A **piecewise C^n surface** is defined to comprise finitely many compact C^n patches, each patch extendible to a C^n surface and bounded by a finite curve comprising finitely many C^n segments. By an *oriented piecewise C^n surface* is meant that each of the C^n patches is oriented, and as one crosses over from one C^n patch to an adjoining patch the directed surface normals lie on the same side of the surface.

differences over the Gaussian sphere. In contrast, the Gaussian image itself is not stable because of its insensitivity to scale—that is, because of its lack of distinction between identical shapes of different sizes. The Gaussian image of a molehill is the same as that of a mountain with the same shape!

The principal attractive feature of EGIs is their position independence. As was the case with plain Gaussian images, here too position independence can potentially reduce the six–degree-of-freedom object-matching problem to two much easier three–degree-of-freedom problems: orientation determination, followed by the relatively easy determination of position (assuming a successful match). It seems that Ballard and Sabbah [Ballard and Sabbah 1981] were the first authors to suggest this decomposition. Horn and Ikeuchi have reported experiments that exploit this characteristic of EGIs to accomplish the mechanical manipulation of randomly oriented identical parts [Horn and Ikeuchi 1984].

Support-Function Representation

The fundamental drawback of the EGI representation scheme is this scheme's inherent differential-geometric nature. As a result, the EGI scheme exhibits the limitations that go with differential-geometric representations. Clearly, widespread applicability requires the incorporation of global geometric information. A natural tendency might be to consider the specification of point coordinates. There is at least one problem with this approach: It is unclear what would be represented at many-to-one singular values of the Gauss map. Further, such a specification would depend not only on the origin of the coordinate frame, but also on the frame's orientation. Hence, if we were matching two separate representations, each representation residing on a Gaussian sphere, every time we rotated one sphere with respect to the other sphere, we would have to recompute all the point coordinates.

Nalwa [Nalwa 1989b] has sought to represent oriented piecewise C^2 surfaces on the Gaussian sphere by a scheme that is designed to overcome the limitations of differential-geometric representations. Nalwa proposes that surfaces be represented by their (possibly multilayered) Gaussian images, associating with each point of the image, the value of the support function at that point's preimage. The **support function**, as illustrated in Figure 9.11, is the signed distance of the oriented tangent plane at a surface point from the origin. Basically, under this proposal, each surface is represented by its continuum of oriented tangent planes. (Surface-normal discontinuities and other curves are represented implicitly by their adjoining surfaces.) This representation is called the **support-function representation**. The same representation—along with two other representations on the Gaussian

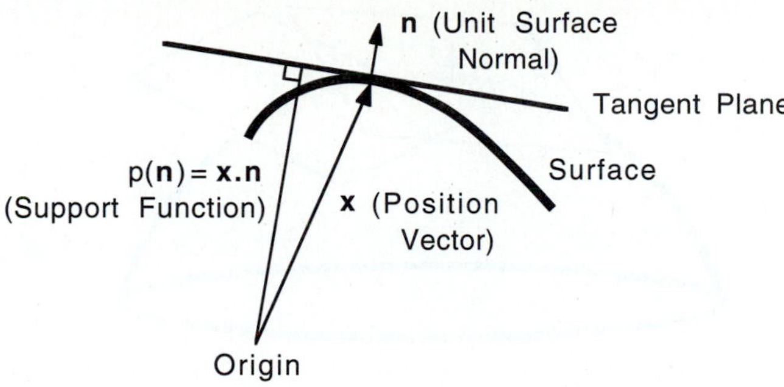

Figure 9.11 The support function. The *support function* provides the signed distance of the oriented tangent plane at a surface point from the origin. The value of the support function at a surface point is the dot product of the following two vectors: the vector from the origin to the surface point, and the oriented unit surface normal at that point. (From [Nalwa 1989b] with permission.)

sphere—was proposed independently earlier for strictly convex objects by Van Hove [Van Hove 1987].

The support-function representation can be shown to be locally generative in that recovery of the original surface from that surface's representation is a local enterprise on the Gaussian sphere [Nalwa 1989b]. A geometrically plausible argument in this regard runs as follows. First, consider elliptic and hyperbolic patches. As illustrated in Figure 9.12, whereas a single oriented tangent plane restricts the surface's point of contact to a plane, two infinitesimally close such planes restrict this point to a line, and three planes determine the point. As for parabolic patches, two infinitesimally close tangent planes determine a straight ruling on the surface. As for planar patches, the tangent plane coincides with the surface. Consequently, this representation is unambiguous. However, it is not unique—it depends on the orientation and position of the represented surface. Owing to its dependence on the existence of just tangent planes, and not on that of surface curvatures, in essence the support-function representation applies to oriented piecewise C^1 surfaces. This representation is additive, but it is strictly local only within elliptic and hyperbolic regions; in parabolic regions, it is only partially local; and, in planar regions, it is not local at all. As the Gaussian image itself is not stable owing to its insensitivity to scale, the support-function representation is unstable under any metric in representation space that does not take into account the relative sizes of the preimages of different regions of the Gaussian image. It cannot

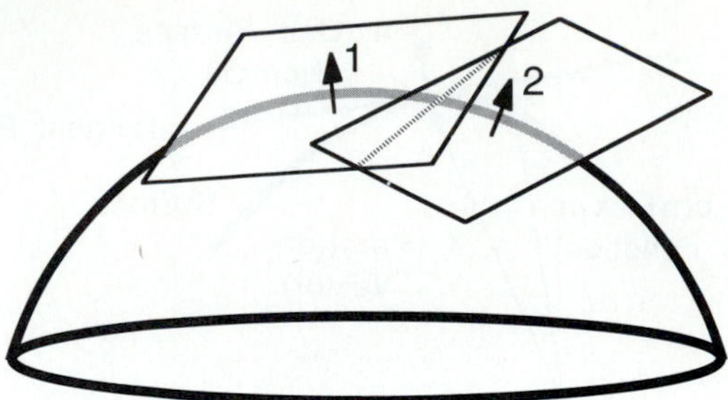

Figure 9.12 Constraints imposed on a surface by its tangent planes. Whereas knowledge of a single oriented tangent plane of a surface restricts the surface's point of contact with the plane to the whole plane, as illustrated, knowledge of two infinitesimally close such planes that are differently oriented restricts the surface's point of contact common to both planes to the straight line at the intersection of the two planes. Analogously, knowledge of three infinitesimally close and differently oriented tangent planes of a surface restricts the surface's point of contact common to all three planes to the single point at the intersection of the three planes.

be overemphasized that all comments pertaining to the stability of various representations are meaningful only in the context of particular metrics in the representation space and its domain. For instance, under an appropriate domain metric that measures differences in surface normal rather than in surface position, the Gauss map would be stable.

The principal disadvantages of the support-function representation reside in the representation's nonlocalness at planar and parabolic points, and in its inability to represent position without the specification of surface normals. These drawbacks are illustrated in Figure 9.13, which provides the representation of the object in Figure 9.2. The origin in the figure is assumed to be at the center of the sphere of which the hemisphere is a part. The surface-normal discontinuity at the base of the cylinder is represented symbolically in the figure by arcs of great circles connecting the Gaussian images of the cylindrical surface and that surface's planar base. Although the support-function representation overcomes the limitations of the extended Gaussian image that stem from the latter's inherent differential-geometric nature by incorporating global geometric information, this relative advantage is gained at a price: the loss of complete position independence. The support-function representation scheme has yet to find any practical application.

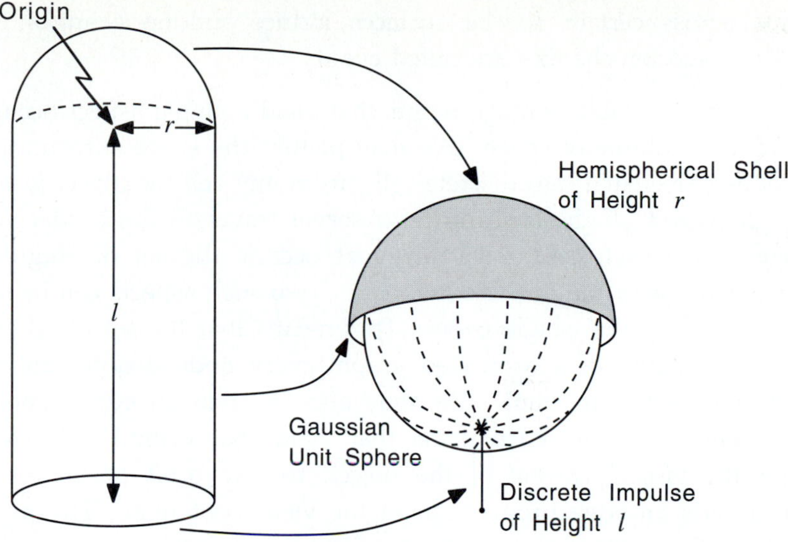

Figure 9.13 The support-function representation of the object in Figure 9.2. The *support-function representation* of a surface is an assignment to each point of the Gaussian image of the surface the value of the support function at the preimage of the point. The dashed arcs on the Gaussian sphere in the figure here symbolically represent the surface-normal discontinuity at the base of the object. As we saw in Figure 9.11, the value of the support function at a surface point is the signed distance of the oriented tangent plane at the surface point from the origin. Hence, wherever on a surface the Gauss map of the surface is many-to-one owing to an unvarying tangent plane—as at planar and parabolic points—the support function is also many-to-one.

9.2.6 Visual Potential

The visual potential of a shape is a nonmetric description quite unlike the other representations we have discussed. The visual potential of an object is characterized by Koenderink and van Doorn [Koenderink and van Doorn 1979] as the catalog of all the possible distinct topologies of the stable singularities of the "motion-parallax shear field" of the object. Although there are many such singularities—including so-called point singularities, which occur where the visual direction is perpendicular to the surface—attention is almost always restricted to just those singularities that constitute line drawings comprising folds, cusps, surface-normal discontinuities, and their junctions. The topological structure of the singularities of a single view of an object is termed an **aspect** of the object. Whereas small motions of almost all viewpoints do not affect an object's aspect, perturbations of viewpoints across certain special surfaces induce sudden changes in the aspect—these sudden changes are called **events**.

> The set of stable vantage points that yield a single aspect occupies a contiguous volume of space. We may picture the space surrounding an object as parcellated into discrete cells, from any cell the object is seen in a single aspect. If the orbit of the observer traverses the border surface between two such cells a visual event occurs: the set of singularities changes in one of the possible manners. Two such aspects can be said to be *connected* by that single event. That means that the set of all aspects has the structure of a connected graph: every node denotes an aspect, every edge a visual event. (We may also say that an edge denotes an equivalence class of space paths that yield that event.) We call this graph the *visual potential* of the object: to any orbit of the observer corresponds an edge progression of the visual potential. The potential contains all possible trains of events.
>
> Thus the visual potential represents in a concise way any visual experience an observer can obtain by looking at the object when traversing any orbit through space. (p. 214, [Koenderink and van Doorn 1979])

Thus, we see that the **visual potential** of an object is a graph in which each node represents an aspect of the object, and each edge represents the possibility of transiting from one aspect to another under motion of the observer. An aspect of an object is the topology that is common to a collection of views of the object, each view from one of a set of contiguous and general viewpoints, where a general viewpoint is as defined in Section 4.1.1. Although the characterization of objects by their topologically distinct two-dimensional projections has historical precedence in computer vision—see, for instance, p. 75, [Turner 1974]—the proposal to relate these distinct topologies through events in a graphlike structure seems to have originated with Koenderink and van Doorn [Koenderink and van Doorn 1979]. Notice, however, the close connection between the visual-potential approach to representing objects and Huffman's analysis of trihedral vertices by dividing observation space into eight octants (see Section 4.1.1).

Figure 9.14 illustrates the visual potential of a tetrahedron. Depending on the viewpoint, one, two, or three faces are visible. Note that events (represented as arcs in the graph) correspond only to traversals of the interiors of border surfaces, better known as *bifurcation surfaces*, and not to traversals of their intersections. Whereas bifurcation surfaces—which, of course, comprise just the nongeneral viewpoints of a static observer—may

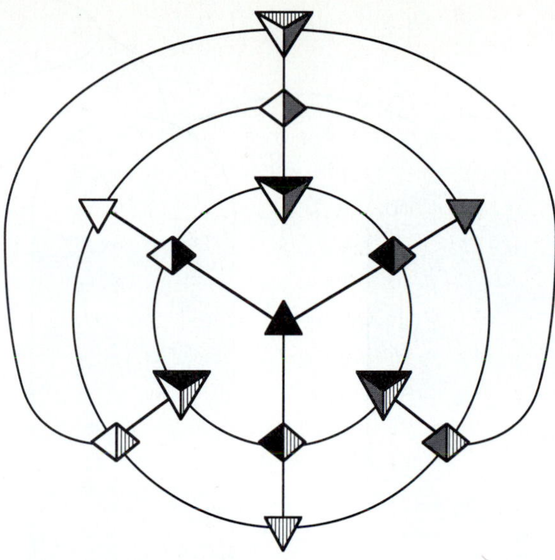

Figure 9.14 The visual potential of a tetrahedron. The *visual potential* of an object is a graph in which each node represents an aspect of the object, and each edge represents the possibility of transiting from one aspect to another under motion of the observer. An *aspect* of an object is, by definition, the topological structure that is common to every view of the object acquired from any of a set of contiguous and general viewpoints. (After [Koenderink and van Doorn 1979].)

intersect the orbit of an observer under "general motion" within their interiors, they cannot do so at their boundaries. Figure 9.15 illustrates the visual potential of the object in Figure 9.2 under perspective projection. Under orthographic projection, with a general viewpoint, we would not see the hemispherical cap or circular base in isolation.

A straightforward extension of the visual-potential representation entails including the parcellation of the view space in the representation, and perhaps also including the transitional degenerate views. This extension of the visual-potential representation was first suggested by Callahan and Weiss [Callahan and Weiss 1985] under orthographic projection; Gigus, Canny, and Seidel [Gigus, Canny, and Seidel 1988] proposed an efficient algorithm to compute such a representation for polyhedral objects. Ikeuchi and Kanade [Ikeuchi and Kanade 1988] have used a representation closely related to the visual potential for some simple recognition tasks. Finally, Rieger [Rieger 1990] has attempted to derive a canonical set of (local) models for the bifurcation surfaces that partition the perspective-view space of closed smooth surfaces.

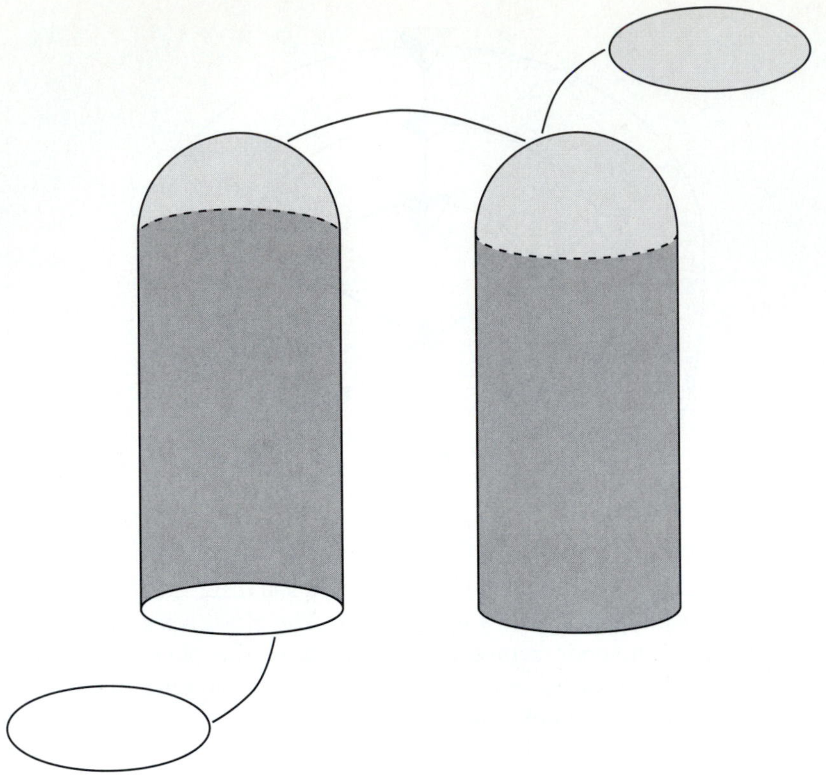

Figure 9.15 The visual potential of the object in Figure 9.2 under perspective projection. (The two elliptical views of the object would be absent under orthographic projection.)

The visual-potential representation is applicable to piecewise C^3 surfaces (see Section 4.2.2). Although we can determine the visual potential of most objects, such a representation can be fairly involved even for relatively simple surface configurations. For instance, the visual potential graph of a tetrahedron has 14 nodes, in contrast to the tetrahedron's straightforward geometric representation, which requires the specification of just four vertices. Due to its sensitivity to occlusion, this representation is neither local nor additive. Clearly, it is not unique or unambiguous. Also, it is not stable in the sense that the introduction of a small bump (or dimple) on a surface could drastically affect the surface's catalog of the topology of stable line drawings; see [Callahan and Weiss 1985] for an example of a sphere with a bump. Because of its topological character, the visual potential is more a classification technique than a representation scheme in the sense of being amenable to surface recovery. The primary reason for its inclusion here is its refreshing originality.

9.3 Discussion

Representation is widely regarded as a central issue in several domains. Although our focus here was on shape representation, we availed of the opportunity to consider issues that span a variety of problem domains. In the context of shape representation, we restricted ourselves to geometric models. In particular, we paid no attention to symbolic descriptions; for example, a man may be described as being large, and as having small round eyes and thinning hair. Even though such descriptions are often subjective, they can be quite useful, either by themselves or in conjunction with geometric descriptions.

> Geometric models are most appropriate for describing specific objects, particularly man-made objects with regular structures. Irregularly shaped objects can also sometimes be modeled usefully by approximate geometric descriptions (e.g., a stick figure of a person, or the envelope of a tree). Symbolic models are appropriate for natural objects (e.g., trees) that are better defined in terms of generic characteristics (e.g., large, green, "leafy") than precise shape. Another advantage of symbolic models is that attributes and relations can be qualified by terms such as "may" and "must" that convey their importance for matching. (p. 592, [Barrow and Tenenbaum 1981a])

The search continues, in computer vision as in other fields, for representations that are simple, elegant, adequate, and convenient. A random sampling of opinion would surely indicate widespread dissatisfaction with existing techniques. The extent of this dissatisfaction is so great that some authors have suggested that explicit representation is both unnecessary and misguided [Brooks 1991]; see [Kirsh 1991] for a refutation of this viewpoint. Perhaps it is only by building systems that we shall discover when explicit representation is necessary, and, then, which one is best suited to a particular task.

Figure 10.1 *Migrant Mother, Nipomo, California*, by Dorothea Lange, 1936. Clearly, there is more to our interpretation of human situations than the mere deduction of geometrical properties. Photographs such as this one evoke our emotions, may they be understanding, sympathy, anguish, hope, or despair. Regardless of where we choose to draw the line between seeing and thinking, undoubtedly both are necessary for successful interaction in a human environment. Evidently, Dorothea Lange, the photographer here, had tacked onto her darkroom door the following variant of a quotation by Francis Bacon (1561–1626) (see p. 6, [Elliott 1966]):

The contemplation of things as they are
Without error or confusion
Without substitution or imposture
Is in itself a nobler thing
Than a whole harvest of invention.

(For the original quotation of Francis Bacon, see p. 115, [Spedding, Ellis, and Heath 1875].) This dictum could well serve as the guiding principle for computer vision. (Photograph, courtesy Library of Congress, Washington, D.C.)

Chapter 10

Conclusion

Reliable, robust, and general-purpose computer vision remains elusive despite the tangible progress we have made in understanding our rich visual world. There, of course, lies a chasm between gaining an understanding of a mapping and being able to invert that mapping—in the context here, between gaining an understanding of the mapping from the world to its images and being able to reconstruct the world from its images. We must bear in mind that, even when we are finally able to reconstruct the world from its images, there will arise situations in which such a recovery would be inadequate. Consider, for instance, the photograph in Figure 10.1; clearly, there is more to the interpretation of this photograph than the mere deduction of the geometrical (and, perhaps, material) properties of the scene the photograph portrays.

The focus of this book was on the science of computational vision, the primary goal being the elucidation of fundamental concepts. Issues of implementation, computational complexity, and system architecture received little or none of our attention. These issues are important no doubt, but clearly an understanding of the physics is primary to, if not a prerequisite for, realizing "intelligent" systems. Which aspects of the science are of practical significance is another matter, and may vary over time. Certain authors have argued that it is necessary to build evolving prototypes to keep the science "relevant"; for instance, Moravec [Moravec 1983] cites biological evolutionary evidence to suggest that autonomous mobility should be the first-level goal of robotics. Although there is some merit to this contention, "relevance" must never be at the expense of science for its own sake: Science, like most intellectual pursuits, is best judged in retrospect.

Among the many topics that did not receive our attention here are model-based object recognition and other high-level tasks that depend on scene recovery. In the view of this author, recognition is a cognitive process, rather than a perceptual one, but other authors would argue otherwise; at any rate, we might wish to realize the capability of object recognition. A typical paradigm for model-based object recognition is illustrated in Figure 10.2. In model-based object recognition, we must be wary of letting prior expectations lead to hallucination—that is, lead to the discovery of instances of models where none exist. In model-based object recognition, as in all exercises in detection, we need to strike a compromise between false negatives (oversight) and false positives (hallucination). A valuable survey of model-based vision is provided by Binford [Binford 1982]; other extensive surveys include [Besl and Jain 1985] and [Chin and Dyer 1986]. For a sampling of work since these surveys, see [Lowe 1987], [Lamdan and Wolfson 1988], [Ikeuchi and Kanade 1988], [Kriegman and Ponce 1990], [Huttenlocher and Ullman 1990], and [Ullman and Basri 1991].

In addition to model-based object recognition, we also neglected color vision, time-of-flight range sensing, industrial applications, and the integration of surface constraints derived from multiple sources. Jarvis [Jarvis 1983] surveys range-finding techniques; Chin and Harlow [Chin and Harlow 1982] survey automated visual inspection. Terzopoulos [Terzopoulos 1988] outlines a proposal for constraint integration; see also [Szeliski 1990b]. The published literature does not seem to contain any comprehensive survey of color vision in the context of computer vision.

As indicated at the outset, our adoption of the system paradigm of Figure 1.13 for the purpose of this book was largely a matter of pedagogical convenience. The basic scientific concepts, of course, remain the same irrespective of how we choose to configure the controls and architecture of a vision system. Of interest here is the book by Mead [Mead 1989] that provides an exciting alternative to traditional computing paradigms; in this book, Mead describes several biologically inspired experiments that use analog VLSI chips each of which incorporates both sensing and computing elements. A related computational paradigm—that too is biologically inspired, and massively parallel and locally cooperative—is connectionism (see [Ballard 1984]).

Also of interest here is the thesis first outlined in the context of human vision by Gibson [Gibson 1979]—and then, in the context of computer vision, by Aloimonos, Weiss, and Bandyopadhyay [Aloimonos, Weiss, and Bandyopadhyay 1988], and by Bajcsy [Bajcsy 1988]—that vision is necessarily

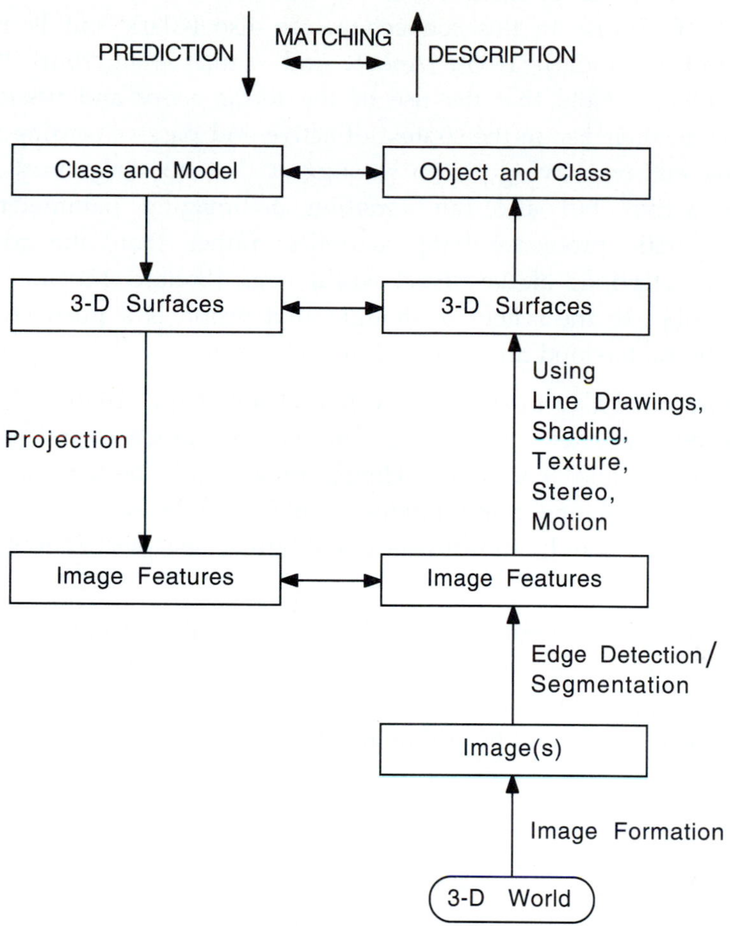

Figure 10.2 A typical paradigm for model-based object recognition. The boxes in the figure denote data, the arrows indicate processes and the direction of data flow, and 3-D is an abbreviation for three-dimensional. On the left, we proceed from classes of objects and their models to descriptions of three-dimensional surfaces and their image projections. This progression from models of objects to their images is called *prediction*. On the right, we start with images that are captured by one or more cameras, and proceed to derive models of objects in the scene. This progression from images of objects to their models is called *description*. The *recognition* of an object in this paradigm entails matching predictions to descriptions at one or several levels. What is missing in the figure is an indication of the all-important control strategy to instantiate models of objects in the prediction process.

an active process, rather than a passive one: that the purposeful variation of geometric and other imaging parameters is essential to the stability and robustness of vision. In this connection, see also [Clark and Ferrier 1988], [Ballard and Ozcandarli 1988], [Abbott and Ahuja 1988], [Burt 1988], and [Krotkov 1987]. (Note that the use of the terms *active* and *passive* here is different from their use in the context of active and passive sensing in Section 1.1.) Some authors have gone on to suggest that not only must computer vision be active, but also the variation of imaging parameters should subserve specific problem-solving activities, rather than aim to generate elaborate descriptions of the visual world (e.g., [Ballard 1991]). This latter view subscribes to the school of thought that vision is a purposive activity that must be understood and pursued in such a role.

Authors have also made the case that accurate quantitative descriptions of the scene are often infeasible given that, in practice, image data are inherently noisy and inaccurate. Hence, they argue, perhaps approximate qualitative error-tolerant computations should precede—and, when adequate for the task at hand, substitute—quantitative analyses [Thompson and Kearney 1986].

The emerging school of thought that visual perception should be automated as an active, purposive, and qualitative process has of late gained considerable momentum. The tenets of this school are outlined in the collection of papers edited by Aloimonos [Aloimonos 1992].

References

Abbott, A. L., and Ahuja, N. 1988. "Surface Reconstruction by Dynamic Integration of Focus, Camera Vergence, and Stereo," in *Proceedings of the Second International Conference on Computer Vision*, Tampa, Florida, December, pp. 532–543.

Adelson, E. H., and Bergen, J. R. 1985. "Spatiotemporal Energy Models for the Perception of Motion," *Journal of the Optical Society of America A*, Vol. 2, No. 2 (February), pp. 284–299.

Adelson, E. H., and Movshon, J. A. 1982. "Phenomenal Coherence of Moving Visual Patterns," *Nature*, Vol. 300, pp. 523–525.

Adiv, G. 1985. "Determining Three-Dimensional Motion and Structure from Optical Flow Generated by Several Moving Objects," *IEEE Transactions on Pattern Analysis and Machine Intelligence*, Vol. PAMI-7, No. 4 (July), pp. 384–401.

Adiv, G. 1989. "Inherent Ambiguities in Recovering 3-D Motion and Structure from a Noisy Flow Field," *IEEE Transactions on Pattern Analysis and Machine Intelligence*, Vol. 11, No. 5 (May), pp. 477–489.

Aggarwal, J. K., and Nandhakumar, N. 1988. "On the Computation of Motion from Sequences of Images—A Review," *Proceedings of the IEEE*, Vol. 76, No. 8 (August), pp. 917–935.

Agin, G. J., and Binford, T. O. 1976. "Computer Description of Curved Objects," *IEEE Transactions on Computers*, Vol. C-25, No. 4 (April), pp. 439–449.

Aho, A. V., Hopcroft, J. E., and Ullman, J. D. 1983. *Data Structures and Algorithms*, Addison-Wesley Publishing Co., Reading, Massachusetts.

Ahuja, N., and Rosenfeld, A. 1981. "Mosaic Models for Textures," *IEEE Transactions on Pattern Analysis and Machine Intelligence*, Vol. PAMI-3, No. 1 (January), pp. 1–11.

Aleksandrov, A. D., Kolmogorov, A. N., and Lavrent'ev, M. A., Eds. 1969. *Mathematics: Its Content, Methods, and Meaning*, Vols. 1, 2, & 3, translated into English from the Russian by S. H. Gould, K. Hirsch, and T. Bartha, MIT Press, Cambridge, Massachusetts.

Aloimonos, Y., Ed. 1992. Special Issue on Purposive, Qualitative, Active Vision, *CVGIP: Image Understanding*, Vol. 56, No. 1 (July).

Aloimonos, J., and Brown, C. M. 1984. "Direct Processing of Curvilinear Sensor Motion from a Sequence of Perspective Images," in *Proceedings of the Workshop on Computer Vision: Representation and Control*, Annapolis, Maryland, April–May, pp. 72–77.

Aloimonos, J., and Swain, M. 1988. "Shape from Patterns: Regularization," *International Journal of Computer Vision*, Vol. 2, pp. 171–187.

Aloimonos, J., Weiss, I., and Bandyopadhyay, A. 1988. "Active Vision," *International Journal of Computer Vision*, Vol. 1, pp. 333–356.

Anandan, P. 1989. "A Computational Framework and an Algorithm for the Measurement of Visual Motion," *International Journal of Computer Vision*, Vol. 2, pp. 283–310.

Andrews, H. C., and Hunt, B. R. 1977. *Digital Image Restoration*, Prentice-Hall, Englewood Cliffs, New Jersey.

Arnol'd, V. I. 1983. "Singularities of Systems of Rays," *Russian Mathematical Surveys*, Vol. 38, No. 2, pp. 87–176.

Arnold, R. D., and Binford, T. O. 1980. "Geometric Constraints in Stereo Vision," in *Proceedings of the Society of Photo-Optical Instrumentation Engineers, SPIE* Vol. 238, San Diego, California, July–August, pp. 281–292.

Attneave, F. 1954. "Some Informational Aspects of Visual Perception," *Psychological Review*, Vol. 61, No. 3, pp. 183–193.

Ayache, N., and Faugeras, O. D. 1988. "Maintaining Representations of the Environment of a Mobile Robot," in *Robotics Research: The Fourth International Symposium*, R. C. Bolles and B. Roth, Eds., MIT Press, Cambridge, Massachusetts, pp. 337–350.

Ayache, N., and Faverjon, B. 1987. "Efficient Registration of Stereo Images by Matching Graph Descriptions of Edge Segments," *International Journal of Computer Vision*, Vol. 1, pp. 107–131.

Babbage, C., and Others 1961. *Charles Babbage: On the Principles and Development of the Calculator*, P. Morrison and E. Morrison, Eds., Dover Publications, New York.

Bajcsy, R. 1973. "Computer Description of Textured Surfaces," in *Proceedings of the Third International Joint Conference on Artificial Intelligence, IJCAI-73*, Stanford, California, August, pp. 572–579.

Bajcsy, R. 1988. "Active Perception," *Proceedings of the IEEE*, Vol. 76, No. 8 (August), pp. 996–1005.

Baker, H. H., and Binford, T. O. 1981. "Depth from Edge and Intensity Based Stereo," in *Proceedings of the Seventh International Joint Conference on Artificial Intelligence, IJCAI-81*, Vancouver, Canada, August, pp. 631–636.

Baker, H. H., and Bolles, R. C. 1989. "Generalizing Epipolar-Plane Image Analysis on the Spatiotemporal Surface," *International Journal of Computer Vision*, Vol. 3, pp. 33–49.

Balasubramanyam, P., and Snyder, M. A. 1991. "The P-Field: A Computational Model for Binocular Motion Processing," in *Proceedings of the IEEE Computer Society Conference on Computer Vision and Pattern Recognition, CVPR'91*, Maui, Hawaii, June, pp. 115–120.

Ballard, D. H. 1981. "Generalizing the Hough Transform to Detect Arbitrary Shapes," *Pattern Recognition*, Vol. 13, No. 2, pp. 111–122.

Ballard, D. H. 1984. "Parameter Nets," *Artificial Intelligence*, Vol. 22, pp. 235–267.

Ballard, D. H. 1991. "Animate Vision," *Artificial Intelligence*, Vol. 48, pp. 57–86.

Ballard, D. H., and Brown, C. M. 1982. *Computer Vision*, Prentice-Hall, Englewood Cliffs, New Jersey.

Ballard, D. H., and Ozcandarli, A. 1988. "Eye Fixation and Early Vision: Kinetic Depth," in *Proceedings of the Second International Conference on Computer Vision*, Tampa, Florida, December, pp. 524–531.

Ballard, D. H., and Sabbah, D. 1981. "On Shapes," in *Proceedings of the Seventh International Joint Conference on Artificial Intelligence, IJCAI-81*, Vancouver, Canada, August, pp. 607–612.

Barlow, H. B. 1979. "Reconstructing the Visual Image in Space and Time," *Nature*, Vol. 279, pp. 189–190.

Barlow, H. B. 1981. "The Ferrier Lecture, 1980: Critical Limiting Factors in the Design of the Eye and Visual Cortex," *Proceedings of the Royal Society of London*, Series B, Vol. 212, pp. 1–34.

Barnard, S. T. 1989. "Stochastic Stereo Matching over Scale," *International Journal of Computer Vision*, Vol. 3, pp. 17–32.

Barnard, S. T., and Thompson, W. B. 1980. "Disparity Analysis of Images," *IEEE Transactions on Pattern Analysis and Machine Intelligence*, Vol. PAMI-2, No. 4 (July), pp. 333–340.

Barr, A. H. 1981. "Superquadrics and Angle-Preserving Transformations," *IEEE Computer Graphics and Applications*, Vol. 1, No. 1 (January), pp. 11–23.

Barrow, H. G., and Popplestone, R. J. 1971. "Relational Descriptions in Picture Processing," in *Machine Intelligence 6*, B. Meltzer and D. Michie, Eds., American Elsevier Publishing Co., New York, pp. 377–396.

Barrow, H. G., and Tenenbaum, J. M. 1978. "Recovering Intrinsic Scene Characteristics from Images," in *Computer Vision Systems*, A. R. Hanson and E. M. Riseman, Eds., Academic Press, New York, pp. 3–26.

Barrow, H. G., and Tenenbaum, J. M. 1981a. "Computational Vision," *Proceedings of the IEEE*, Vol. 69, No. 5 (May), pp. 572–595.

Barrow, H. G., and Tenenbaum, J. M. 1981b. "Interpreting Line Drawings as Three-Dimensional Surfaces," *Artificial Intelligence*, Vol. 17, pp. 75–116.

Beckmann, P., and Spizzichino, A. 1963. *The Scattering of Electromagnetic Waves from Rough Surfaces*, Macmillan Co., New York.

Bellman, R. E., and Dreyfus, S. E. 1962. *Applied Dynamic Programming*, Princeton University Press, Princeton, New Jersey.

Bergholm, F. 1989. "Motion from Flow Along Contours: A Note on Robustness and Ambiguous Cases," *International Journal of Computer Vision*, Vol. 2, pp. 395–415.

Bertero, M., Poggio, T. A., and Torre, V. 1988. "Ill-Posed Problems in Early Vision," *Proceedings of the IEEE*, Vol. 76, No. 8 (August), pp. 869–889.

Besag, J. 1974. "Spatial Interaction and the Statistical Analysis of Lattice Systems," *Journal of the Royal Statistical Society*, Series B, Vol. 36, No. 2, pp. 192–236.

Besag, J. 1986. "On the Statistical Analysis of Dirty Pictures," *Journal of the Royal Statistical Society*, Series B, Vol. 48, No. 3, pp. 259–302.

Besl, P. J., and Jain, R. C. 1985. "Three-Dimensional Object Recognition," *Computing Surveys*, Vol. 17, No. 1 (March), pp. 75–145.

Besl, P. J., and Jain, R. C. 1988. "Segmentation Through Variable-Order Surface Fitting," *IEEE Transactions on Pattern Analysis and Machine Intelligence*, Vol. 10, No. 2 (March), pp. 167–192.

Beveridge, J. R., Griffith, J., Kohler, R. R., Hanson, A. R., and Riseman, E. M. 1989. "Segmenting Images Using Localized Histograms and Region Merging," *International Journal of Computer Vision*, Vol. 2, pp. 311–347.

Binford, T. O. 1971. "Visual Perception by Computer," unpublished paper presented at the IEEE Conference on Decision and Control, Miami Beach, Florida, December.

Binford, T. O. 1981. "Inferring Surfaces from Images," *Artificial Intelligence*, Vol. 17, pp. 205–244.

Binford, T. O. 1982. "Survey of Model-Based Image Analysis Systems," *The International Journal of Robotics Research*, Vol. 1, No. 1 (Spring), pp. 18–64.

Binford, T. O. 1984. "Stereo Vision: Complexity and Constraints," in *Robotics Research: The First International Symposium*, M. Brady and R. Paul, Eds., MIT Press, Cambridge, Massachusetts, pp. 475–487.

Binford, T. O. 1987. "Generalized Cylinder Representation," in *Encyclopedia of Artificial Intelligence*, S. C. Shapiro, Ed., John Wiley & Sons, New York, pp. 321–323.

Blake, A., and Marinos, C. 1990. "Shape from Texture: Estimation, Isotropy and Moments," *Artificial Intelligence*, Vol. 45, pp. 323–380.

Blake, A., and Zisserman, A. 1987. *Visual Reconstruction*, MIT Press, Cambridge, Massachusetts.

Blicher, P. 1984. "Edge Detection and Geometric Methods in Computer Vision," Ph.D. Dissertation, Department of Mathematics, University of California, Berkeley, California.

Blostein, D., and Ahuja, N. 1989. "Shape from Texture: Integrating Texture-Element Extraction and Surface Estimation," *IEEE Transactions on Pattern Analysis and Machine Intelligence*, Vol. 11, No. 12 (December), pp. 1233–1251.

Blum, H. 1967. "A Transformation for Extracting New Descriptors of Shape," in *Models for the Perception of Speech and Visual Form*, W. Wathen-Dunn, Ed., MIT Press, Cambridge, Massachusetts, pp. 362–380.

Blum, H., and Nagel, R. N. 1978. "Shape Description Using Weighted Symmetric Axis Features," *Pattern Recognition*, Vol. 10, No. 3, pp. 167–180.

Bolles, R. C., Baker, H. H., and Marimont, D. H. 1987. "Epipolar-Plane Image Analysis: An Approach to Determining Structure from Motion," *International Journal of Computer Vision*, Vol. 1, pp. 7–55.

Bookstein, F. L. 1979. "Fitting Conic Sections to Scattered Data," *Computer Graphics and Image Processing*, Vol. 9, pp. 56–71.

Boring, E. G. 1930. "A New Ambiguous Figure," *The American Journal of Psychology*, Vol. 42, pp. 444–445.

Boring, E. G. 1942. *Sensation and Perception in the History of Experimental Psychology*, Appleton-Century-Crofts, New York.

Bovik, A. C., Clark, M., and Geisler, W. S. 1990. "Multichannel Texture Analysis Using Localized Spatial Filters," *IEEE Transactions on Pattern Analysis and Machine Intelligence*, Vol. 12, No. 1 (January), pp. 55–73.

Boycott, B. B., and Dowling, J. E. 1969. "Organization of the Primate Retina: Light Microscopy," *Philosophical Transactions of the Royal Society of London*, Series B, Vol. 255, pp. 109–184.

Bracewell, R. N. 1978. *The Fourier Transform and Its Applications*, Second Edition, McGraw-Hill Book Co., New York.

Brady, M. 1982. "Computational Approaches to Image Understanding," *Computing Surveys*, Vol. 14, No. 1 (March), pp. 3–71.

Brady, M., Ponce, J., Yuille, A., and Asada, H. 1985. "Describing Surfaces," *Computer Vision, Graphics, and Image Processing*, Vol. 32, pp. 1–28.

Brady, M., and Yuille, A. 1984. "An Extremum Principle for Shape from Contour," *IEEE Transactions on Pattern Analysis and Machine Intelligence*, Vol. PAMI-6, No. 3 (May), pp. 288–301.

Brice, C. R., and Fennema, C. L. 1970. "Scene Analysis Using Regions," *Artificial Intelligence*, Vol. 1, pp. 205–226.

Brodatz, P. 1966. *Textures: A Photographic Album for Artists and Designers*, Dover Publications, New York.

Broida, T. J., and Chellappa, R. 1986. "Kinematics and Structure of a Rigid Object from a Sequence of Noisy Images," in *Proceedings of the Workshop on Motion: Representation and Analysis*, Charleston, South Carolina, May, pp. 95–100.

Brooks, M. J. 1978. "Rationalizing Edge Detectors," *Computer Graphics and Image Processing*, Vol. 8, pp. 277–285.

Brooks, R. A. 1981. "Symbolic Reasoning Among 3-D Models and 2-D Images," *Artificial Intelligence*, Vol. 17, pp. 285–348.

Brooks, R. A. 1991. "Intelligence Without Representation," *Artificial Intelligence*, Vol. 47, pp. 139–159.

Brown, C. M. 1983. "Inherent Bias and Noise in the Hough Transform," *IEEE Transactions on Pattern Analysis and Machine Intelligence*, Vol. PAMI-5, No. 5 (September), pp. 493–505.

Bruss, A. R., and Horn, B. K. P. 1983. "Passive Navigation," *Computer Vision, Graphics, and Image Processing*, Vol. 21, pp. 3–20.

Burt, P. J. 1988. "Smart Sensing Within a Pyramid Vision Machine," *Proceedings of the IEEE*, Vol. 76, No. 8 (August), pp. 1006–1015.

Burt, P. J., and Adelson, E. H. 1983. "The Laplacian Pyramid as a Compact Image Code," *IEEE Transactions on Communications*, Vol. COM-31, No. 4 (April), pp. 532–540.

Callahan, J., and Weiss, R. 1985. "A Model for Describing Surface Shape," in *Proceedings of the IEEE Computer Society Conference on Computer Vision and Pattern Recognition, CVPR'85*, San Francisco, June, pp. 240–245.

Canny, J. 1986. "A Computational Approach to Edge Detection," *IEEE Transactions on Pattern Analysis and Machine Intelligence*, Vol. PAMI-8, No. 6 (November), pp. 679–698.

Černý, V. 1985. "Thermodynamical Approach to the Traveling Salesman Problem: An Efficient Simulation Algorithm," *Journal of Optimization Theory and Applications*, Vol. 45, No. 1 (January), pp. 41–51.

Chakravarty, I. 1979. "A Generalized Line and Junction Labeling Scheme with Applications to Scene Analysis," *IEEE Transactions on Pattern Analysis and Machine Intelligence*, Vol. PAMI-1, No. 2 (April), pp. 202–205.

Chen, H. H., and Huang, T. S. 1988. "A Survey of Construction and Manipulation of Octrees," *Computer Vision, Graphics, and Image Processing*, Vol. 43, pp. 409–431.

Chin, R. T., and Dyer, C. R. 1986. "Model-Based Recognition in Robot Vision," *Computing Surveys*, Vol. 18, No. 1 (March), pp. 67–108.

Chin, R. T., and Harlow, C. A. 1982. "Automated Visual Inspection: A Survey," *IEEE Transactions on Pattern Analysis and Machine Intelligence*, Vol. PAMI-4, No. 6 (November), pp. 557–573.

Chow, C. K., and Kaneko, T. 1972. "Boundary Detection of Radiographic Images by a Threshold Method," in *Frontiers of Pattern Recognition*, S. Watanabe, Ed., Academic Press, New York, pp. 61–82.

Clark, J. J., and Ferrier, N. J. 1988. "Modal Control of an Attentive Vision System," in *Proceedings of the Second International Conference on Computer Vision*, Tampa, Florida, December, pp. 514–523.

Clowes, M. B. 1971. "On Seeing Things," *Artificial Intelligence*, Vol. 2, pp. 79–116.

Cohen, F. S., and Cooper, D. B. 1987. "Simple Parallel Hierarchical and Relaxation Algorithms for Segmenting Noncausal Markovian Random Fields," *IEEE Transactions on Pattern Analysis and Machine Intelligence*, Vol. PAMI-9, No. 2 (March), pp. 195–219.

Coleman, G. B., and Andrews, H. C. 1979. "Image Segmentation by Clustering," *Proceedings of the IEEE*, Vol. 67, No. 5 (May), pp. 773–785.

Coleman, Jr., E. N., and Jain, R. 1982. "Obtaining 3-Dimensional Shape of Textured and Specular Surfaces Using Four-Source Photometry," *Computer Graphics and Image Processing*, Vol. 18, pp. 309–328.

Cornsweet, T. N. 1970. *Visual Perception*, Academic Press, Orlando, Florida.

Cross, G. R., and Jain, A. K. 1983. "Markov Random Field Texture Models," *IEEE Transactions on Pattern Analysis and Machine Intelligence*, Vol. PAMI-5, No. 1 (January), pp. 25–39.

Davis, L. S., Johns, S. A., and Aggarwal, J. K. 1979. "Texture Analysis Using Generalized Co-Occurrence Matrices," *IEEE Transactions on Pattern Analysis and Machine Intelligence*, Vol. PAMI-1, No. 3 (July), pp. 251–259.

Davis, L. S., and Rosenfeld, A. 1981. "Cooperating Processes for Low-Level Vision: A Survey," *Artificial Intelligence*, Vol. 17, pp. 245–263.

Debrunner, C. H., and Ahuja, N. 1990. "A Direct Data Approximation Based Motion Estimation Algorithm," in *Proceedings of the Tenth International Conference on Pattern Recognition*, Vol. 1, Atlantic City, New Jersey, June, pp. 384–389.

Derin, H., and Elliott, H. 1987. "Modeling and Segmentation of Noisy and Textured Images Using Gibbs Random Fields," *IEEE Transactions on Pattern Analysis and Machine Intelligence*, Vol. PAMI-9, No. 1 (January), pp. 39–55.

Dev, P. 1975. "Perception of Depth Surfaces in Random-Dot Stereograms: A Neural Model," *International Journal of Man–Machine Studies*, Vol. 7, No. 4 (July), pp. 511–528.

Dhond, U. R., and Aggarwal, J. K. 1989. "Structure from Stereo—A Review," *IEEE Transactions on Systems, Man, and Cybernetics*, Vol. 19, No. 6 (November–December), pp. 1489–1510.

do Carmo, M. P. 1976. *Differential Geometry of Curves and Surfaces*, Prentice-Hall, Englewood Cliffs, New Jersey.

Draper, S. W. 1981. "The Use of Gradient and Dual Space in Line-Drawing Interpretation," *Artificial Intelligence*, Vol. 17, pp. 461–508.

Dreschler, L., and Nagel, H.-H. 1982. "Volumetric Model and 3D Trajectory of a Moving Car Derived from Monocular TV Frame Sequences of a Street Scene," *Computer Graphics and Image Processing*, Vol. 20, pp. 199–228.

Duda, R. O., and Hart, P. E. 1972. "Use of the Hough Transformation to Detect Lines and Curves in Pictures," *Communications of the ACM*, Vol. 15, No. 1 (January), pp. 11–15.

Duda, R. O., and Hart, P. E. 1973. *Pattern Classification and Scene Analysis*, John Wiley & Sons, New York.

Dupuis, P., and Oliensis, J. 1992. "Direct Method for Reconstructing Shape from Shading," in *Proceedings of the IEEE Computer Society Conference on Computer Vision and Pattern Recognition, CVPR'92*, Champaign, Illinois, June, pp. 453–458.

Elliott, G. P. 1966. *Dorothea Lange*, Museum of Modern Art, New York.

Ernst, B. 1986. "Escher's Impossible Figure Prints in a New Context," in *M. C. Escher: Art and Science*, H. S. M. Coxeter, M. Emmer, R. Penrose, and M. L. Teuber, Eds., North-Holland (Elsevier Science Publishers), Amsterdam, pp. 125–134.

Euclid c. 300 B.C. *Optics*. English translation from the Greek by H. E. Burton: "The Optics of Euclid," *Journal of the Optical Society of America*, Vol. 35, No. 5 (May 1945), pp. 357–372.

Faugeras, O. D. 1989. "A Few Steps Toward Artificial 3-D Vision," in *Robotics Science*, M. Brady, Ed., MIT Press, Cambridge, Massachusetts, pp. 39–137.

Faugeras, O. D., Hebert, M., Pauchon, E., and Ponce, J. 1984. "Object Representation, Identification, and Positioning from Range Data," in *Robotics Research: The First International Symposium*, M. Brady and R. Paul, Eds., MIT Press, Cambridge, Massachusetts, pp. 425–446.

Faugeras, O. D., Lustman, F., and Toscani, G. 1987. "Motion and Structure from Motion from Point and Line Matches," in *Proceedings of the First International Conference on Computer Vision*, London, June, pp. 25–34.

Faugeras, O. D., and Maybank, S. 1990. "Motion from Point Matches: Multiplicity of Solutions," *International Journal of Computer Vision*, Vol. 4, pp. 225–246.

Faugeras, O. D., and Toscani, G. 1986. "The Calibration Problem for Stereo," in *Proceedings of the IEEE Computer Society Conference on Computer Vision and Pattern Recognition, CVPR'86*, Miami Beach, Florida, June, pp. 15–20.

Feldman, J. A., and Yakimovsky, Y. 1974. "Decision Theory and Artificial Intelligence: I. A Semantics-Based Region Analyzer," *Artificial Intelligence*, Vol. 5, pp. 349–371.

Fennema, C. L., and Thompson, W. B. 1979. "Velocity Determination in Scenes Containing Several Moving Objects," *Computer Graphics and Image Processing*, Vol. 9, pp. 301–315.

Fischler, M. A., and Bolles, R. C. 1981. "Random Sample Consensus: A Paradigm for Model Fitting with Applications to Image Analysis and Automated Cartography," *Communications of the ACM*, Vol. 24, No. 6 (June), pp. 381–395.

Fleet, D. J. 1992. *Measurement of Image Velocity*, Kluwer Academic Publishers, Boston, Massachusetts.

Fleet, D. J., and Jepson, A. D. 1990. "Computation of Component Image Velocity from Local Phase Information," *International Journal of Computer Vision*, Vol. 5, pp. 77–104.

Foley, J. D., and van Dam, A. 1982. *Fundamentals of Interactive Computer Graphics*, Addison-Wesley Publishing Co., Reading, Massachusetts.

Forsyth, D., and Zisserman, A. 1991. "Reflections on Shading," *IEEE Transactions on Pattern Analysis and Machine Intelligence*, Vol. 13, No. 7 (July), pp. 671–679.

Frankot, R. T., and Chellappa, R. 1988. "A Method for Enforcing Integrability in Shape from Shading Algorithms," *IEEE Transactions on Pattern Analysis and Machine Intelligence*, Vol. 10, No. 4 (July), pp. 439–451.

Fraser, J. 1908. "A New Visual Illusion of Direction," *The British Journal of Psychology*, Vol. 2, pp. 307–320.

Frisby, J. P. 1980. *Seeing: Illusion, Brain and Mind*, Oxford University Press, Oxford, U.K.

Ganapathy, S. 1984. "Decomposition of Transformation Matrices for Robot Vision," *Pattern Recognition Letters*, Vol. 2, pp. 401–412.

Gans, D. 1973. *An Introduction to Non-Euclidean Geometry*, Academic Press, New York.

Gardner, M. 1965. "The 'Superellipse': A Curve That Lies Between the Ellipse and the Rectangle," in the Mathematical Games section of *Scientific American*, Vol. 213, No. 3 (September), pp. 222–232.

Geman, S., and Geman, D. 1984. "Stochastic Relaxation, Gibbs Distributions, and the Bayesian Restoration of Images," *IEEE Transactions on Pattern Analysis and Machine Intelligence*, Vol. PAMI-6, No. 6 (November), pp. 721–741.

Geman, D., Geman, S., Graffigne, C., and Dong, P. 1990. "Boundary Detection by Constrained Optimization," *IEEE Transactions on Pattern Analysis and Machine Intelligence*, Vol. 12, No. 7 (July), pp. 609–628.

Gennery, D. B. 1977. "A Stereo Vision System for an Autonomous Vehicle," in *Proceedings of the Fifth International Joint Conference on Artificial Intelligence, IJCAI-77*, Cambridge, Massachusetts, August, pp. 576–582.

Gibson, J. J. 1950. *The Perception of the Visual World*, Houghton Mifflin Co., Boston, Massachusetts.

Gibson, J. J. 1979. *The Ecological Approach to Visual Perception*, Houghton Mifflin Co., Boston, Massachusetts.

Gibson, J. J., Olum, P., and Rosenblatt, F. 1955. "Parallax and Perspective During Aircraft Landings," *The American Journal of Psychology*, Vol. 68, pp. 372–385.

Gigus, Z., Canny, J., and Seidel, R. 1988. "Efficiently Computing and Representing Aspect Graphs of Polyhedral Objects," in *Proceedings of the Second International Conference on Computer Vision*, Tampa, Florida, December, pp. 30–39.

Gillispie, C. C., Ed. 1971. *Dictionary of Scientific Biography*, Vol. 4, Charles Scribner's Sons, New York.

Goodman, J. W. 1968. *Introduction to Fourier Optics*, McGraw-Hill Book Co., New York.

Gregory, R. L. 1965. "Seeing in Depth," *Nature*, Vol. 207, pp. 16–19.

Gregory, R. L. 1978. *Eye and Brain: The Psychology of Seeing*, Third Edition, McGraw-Hill Book Co., New York.

Grimson, W. E. L. 1981. "A Computer Implementation of a Theory of Human Stereo Vision," *Philosophical Transactions of the Royal Society of London*, Series B, Vol. 292, pp. 217–253.

Grimson, W. E. L. 1984. "On the Reconstruction of Visible Surfaces," in *Image Understanding 1984*, S. Ullman and W. Richards, Eds., Ablex Publishing Corp., Norwood, New Jersey, pp. 195–223.

Gupta, J. N., and Wintz, P. A. 1975. "A Boundary Finding Algorithm and Its Applications," *IEEE Transactions on Circuits and Systems*, Vol. CAS-22, No. 4 (April), pp. 351–362.

Hansen, F. R., and Elliott, H. 1982. "Image Segmentation Using Simple Markov Field Models," *Computer Graphics and Image Processing*, Vol. 20, pp. 101–132.

Hanson, A. J. 1988. "Hyperquadrics: Smoothly Deformable Shapes with Convex Polyhedral Bounds," *Computer Vision, Graphics, and Image Processing*, Vol. 44, pp. 191–210.

Hanson, A. R., and Riseman, E. M., Eds. 1978. *Computer Vision Systems*, Academic Press, New York.

Haralick, R. M. 1979. "Statistical and Structural Approaches to Texture," *Proceedings of the IEEE*, Vol. 67, No. 5 (May), pp. 786–804.

Haralick, R. M. 1980. "Edge and Region Analysis for Digital Image Data," *Computer Graphics and Image Processing*, Vol. 12, pp. 60–73.

Haralick, R. M. 1984. "Digital Step Edges from Zero Crossing of Second Directional Derivatives," *IEEE Transactions on Pattern Analysis and Machine Intelligence*, Vol. PAMI-6, No. 1 (January), pp. 58–68.

Haralick, R. M., Shanmugam, K., and Dinstein, I. 1973. "Textural Features for Image Classification," *IEEE Transactions on Systems, Man, and Cybernetics*, Vol. SMC-3, No. 6 (November), pp. 610–621.

Haralick, R. M., and Shapiro, L. G. 1985. "Image Segmentation Techniques," *Computer Vision, Graphics, and Image Processing*, Vol. 29, pp. 100–132.

Hassner, M., and Sklansky, J. 1980. "The Use of Markov Random Fields as Models of Texture," *Computer Graphics and Image Processing*, Vol. 12, pp. 357–370.

Hay, J. C. 1966. "Optical Motions and Space Perception: An Extension of Gibson's Analysis," *Psychological Review*, Vol. 73, No. 6, pp. 550–565.

Healey, G., and Binford, T. O. 1988. "Local Shape from Specularity," *Computer Vision, Graphics, and Image Processing*, Vol. 42, pp. 62–86.

Hecht, E., and Zajac, A. 1974. *Optics*, Addison-Wesley Publishing Co., Reading, Massachusetts.

Heeger, D. J. 1988. "Optical Flow Using Spatiotemporal Filters," *International Journal of Computer Vision*, Vol. 1, pp. 279–302.

Heeger, D. J., and Jepson, A. 1990. "Visual Perception of Three-Dimensional Motion," *Neural Computation*, Vol. 2, pp. 129–137.

Helmholtz, H. von 1909. *Handbuch der Physiologischen Optik*, Third Edition, Vol. 1, Verlag von Leopold Voss, Hamburg, Germany. English translation from the German edited by J. P. C. Southall: *Helmholtz's Treatise on Physiological Optics*, Vol. 1, The Optical Society of America, 1924.

Helmholtz, H. von 1910. *Handbuch der Physiologischen Optik*, Third Edition, Vol. 3, Verlag von Leopold Voss, Hamburg, Germany. English translation from the German edited by J. P. C. Southall: *Helmholtz's Treatise on Physiological Optics*, Vol. 3, The Optical Society of America, 1925.

Helmholtz, H. von 1911. *Handbuch der Physiologischen Optik*, Third Edition, Vol. 2, Verlag von Leopold Voss, Hamburg, Germany. English translation from the German edited by J. P. C. Southall: *Helmholtz's Treatise on Physiological Optics*, Vol. 2, The Optical Society of America, 1924.

Henderson, R. L., Miller, W. J., and Grosch, C. B. 1979. "Automatic Stereo Reconstruction of Man-Made Targets," in *Proceedings of the Society of Photo-Optical Instrumentation Engineers, SPIE* Vol. 186, Huntsville, Alabama, May, pp. 240–248.

Herskovits, A., and Binford, T. O. 1970. "On Boundary Detection," MIT AI Memo 183 (July), Artificial Intelligence Laboratory, Massachusetts Institute of Technology, Cambridge, Massachusetts.

Hilbert, D., and Cohn-Vossen, S. 1952. *Geometry and the Imagination*, Chelsea Publishing Co., New York.

Hildreth, E. C. 1984. "Computations Underlying the Measurement of Visual Motion," *Artificial Intelligence*, Vol. 23, pp. 309–354.

Horaud, R., and Skordas, T. 1989. "Stereo Correspondence Through Feature Grouping and Maximal Cliques," *IEEE Transactions on Pattern Analysis and Machine Intelligence*, Vol. 11, No. 11 (November), pp. 1168–1180.

Horn, B. K. P. 1975. "Obtaining Shape from Shading Information," in *The Psychology of Computer Vision*, P. H. Winston, Ed., McGraw-Hill Book Co., New York, pp. 115–155.

Horn, B. K. P. 1977. "Understanding Image Intensities," *Artificial Intelligence*, Vol. 8, pp. 201–231.

Horn, B. K. P. 1984. "Extended Gaussian Images," *Proceedings of the IEEE*, Vol. 72, No. 12 (December), pp. 1671–1686.

Horn, B. K. P. 1986. *Robot Vision*, MIT Press, Cambridge, Massachusetts.

Horn, B. K. P. 1987. "Motion Fields Are Hardly Ever Ambiguous," *International Journal of Computer Vision*, Vol. 1, pp. 259–274.

Horn, B. K. P. 1990. "Height and Gradient from Shading," *International Journal of Computer Vision*, Vol. 5, pp. 37–75.

Horn, B. K. P., and Brooks, M. J. 1986. "The Variational Approach to Shape from Shading," *Computer Vision, Graphics, and Image Processing*, Vol. 33, pp. 174–208.

Horn, B. K. P., and Ikeuchi, K. 1984. "The Mechanical Manipulation of Randomly Oriented Parts," *Scientific American*, Vol. 251, No. 2 (August), pp. 100–111.

Horn, B. K. P., and Schunck, B. G. 1981. "Determining Optical Flow," *Artificial Intelligence*, Vol. 17, pp. 185–203.

Horn, B. K. P., and Weldon, Jr., E. J. 1988. "Direct Methods for Recovering Motion," *International Journal of Computer Vision*, Vol. 2, pp. 51–76.

Horowitz, S. L., and Pavlidis, T. 1976. "Picture Segmentation by a Tree Traversal Algorithm," *Journal of the Association for Computing Machinery*, Vol. 23, No. 2 (April), pp. 368–388.

Hubel, D. H. 1988. *Eye, Brain, and Vision*, W. H. Freeman & Co., New York.

Hueckel, M. H. 1971. "An Operator Which Locates Edges in Digitized Pictures," *Journal of the Association for Computing Machinery*, Vol. 18, No. 1 (January), pp. 113–125.

Hueckel, M. H. 1973. "A Local Visual Operator Which Recognizes Edges and Lines," *Journal of the Association for Computing Machinery*, Vol. 20, No. 4 (October), pp. 634–647.

Huffman, D. A. 1971. "Impossible Objects as Nonsense Sentences," in *Machine Intelligence 6*, B. Meltzer and D. Michie, Eds., American Elsevier Publishing Co., New York, pp. 295–323.

Huffman, D. A. 1976. "Curvature and Creases: A Primer on Paper," *IEEE Transactions on Computers*, Vol. C-25, No. 10 (October), pp. 1010–1019.

Huffman, D. A. 1977a. "A Duality Concept for the Analysis of Polyhedral Scenes," in *Machine Intelligence 8*, E. W. Elcock and D. Michie, Eds., Ellis Horwood, Chichester, U.K., pp. 475–492.

Huffman, D. A. 1977b. "Realizable Configurations of Lines in Pictures of Polyhedra," in *Machine Intelligence 8*, E. W. Elcock and D. Michie, Eds., Ellis Horwood, Chichester, U.K., pp. 493–509.

Hummel, R. A., and Zucker, S. W. 1983. "On the Foundations of Relaxation Labeling Processes," *IEEE Transactions on Pattern Analysis and Machine Intelligence*, Vol. PAMI-5, No. 3 (May), pp. 267–287.

Huttenlocher, D. P., and Ullman, S. 1990. "Recognizing Solid Objects by Alignment with an Image," *International Journal of Computer Vision*, Vol. 5, pp. 195–212.

Ikeuchi, K. 1984. "Shape from Regular Patterns," *Artificial Intelligence*, Vol. 22, pp. 49–75.

Ikeuchi, K., and Horn, B. K. P. 1981. "Numerical Shape from Shading and Occluding Boundaries," *Artificial Intelligence*, Vol. 17, pp. 141–184.

Ikeuchi, K., and Kanade, T. 1988. "Applying Sensor Models to Automatic Generation of Object Recognition Programs," in *Proceedings of the Second International Conference on Computer Vision*, Tampa, Florida, December, pp. 228–237.

Ito, M., and Ishii, A. 1986. "Three-View Stereo Analysis," *IEEE Transactions on Pattern Analysis and Machine Intelligence*, Vol. PAMI-8, No. 4 (July), pp. 524–532.

Jarvis, R. A. 1983. "A Perspective on Range Finding Techniques for Computer Vision," *IEEE Transactions on Pattern Analysis and Machine Intelligence*, Vol. PAMI-5, No. 2 (March), pp. 122–139.

Johansson, G. 1975. "Visual Motion Perception," *Scientific American*, Vol. 232, No. 6 (June), pp. 76–88.

Julesz, B. 1960. "Binocular Depth Perception of Computer-Generated Patterns," *The Bell System Technical Journal*, Vol. 39, No. 5 (September), pp. 1125–1161.

Julesz, B. 1962. "Visual Pattern Discrimination," *IRE Transactions on Information Theory*, Vol. IT-8, No. 2 (February), pp. 84–92.

Julesz, B. 1971. *Foundations of Cyclopean Perception*, University of Chicago Press, Chicago.

Julesz, B. 1975. "Experiments in the Visual Perception of Texture," *Scientific American*, Vol. 232, No. 4 (April), pp. 34–43.

Julesz, B. 1981. "Textons, the Elements of Texture Perception, and Their Interactions," *Nature*, Vol. 290, pp. 91–97.

Kailath, T. 1981. *Lectures on Wiener and Kalman Filtering*, Springer-Verlag, New York.

Kanade, T. 1980. "A Theory of Origami World," *Artificial Intelligence*, Vol. 13, pp. 279–311.

Kanade, T. 1981. "Recovery of the Three-Dimensional Shape of an Object from a Single View," *Artificial Intelligence*, Vol. 17, pp. 409–460.

Kanade, T., and Okutomi, M. 1991. "A Stereo Matching Algorithm with an Adaptive Window: Theory and Experiment," in *Proceedings of the 1991 IEEE International Conference on Robotics and Automation*, Sacramento, California, April, pp. 1088–1095.

Kanatani, K. 1984. "Detection of Surface Orientation and Motion from Texture by a Stereological Technique," *Artificial Intelligence*, Vol. 23, pp. 213–237.

Kanatani, K., and Chou, T.-C. 1989. "Shape from Texture: General Principle," *Artificial Intelligence*, Vol. 38, pp. 1–48.

Kanizsa, G. 1979. *Organization in Vision: Essays on Gestalt Perception*, Praeger Publishers, New York.

Kass, M., Witkin, A., and Terzopoulos, D. 1988. "Snakes: Active Contour Models," *International Journal of Computer Vision*, Vol. 1, pp. 321–331.

Kaufman, L. 1974. *Sight and Mind: An Introduction to Visual Perception*, Oxford University Press, New York.

Kearney, J. K., Thompson, W. B., and Boley, D. L. 1987. "Optical Flow Estimation: An Error Analysis of Gradient-Based Methods with Local Optimization," *IEEE Transactions on Pattern Analysis and Machine Intelligence*, Vol. PAMI-9, No. 2 (March), pp. 229–244.

Keating, T. J., Wolf, P. R., and Scarpace, F. L. 1975. "An Improved Method of Digital Image Correlation," *Photogrammetric Engineering and Remote Sensing*, Vol. 41, No. 8 (August), pp. 993–1002.

Keller, J. M., Chen, S., and Crownover, R. M. 1989. "Texture Description and Segmentation Through Fractal Geometry," *Computer Vision, Graphics, and Image Processing*, Vol. 45, pp. 150–166.

Kender, J. R. 1980. "Shape from Texture," Ph.D. Dissertation, Department of Computer Science, Carnegie–Mellon University, Pittsburgh, Pennsylvania.

Kender, J. R., and Kanade, T. 1980. "Mapping Image Properties into Shape Constraints: Skewed Symmetry, Affine-Transformable Patterns, and the Shape-from-Texture Paradigm," in *Proceedings of the First National Conference on Artificial Intelligence, AAAI-80*, Stanford, California, August, pp. 4–6.

Kennedy, J. M. 1974. "Icons and Information," in *Media and Symbols: The Forms of Expression, Communication, and Education*, D. R. Olson, Ed., The National Society for the Study of Education, Chicago, pp. 211–240.

Kirkpatrick, S., Gelatt, Jr., C. D., and Vecchi, M. P. 1983. "Optimization by Simulated Annealing," *Science*, Vol. 220, pp. 671–680.

Kirsch, R. A. 1971. "Computer Determination of the Constituent Structure of Biological Images," *Computers and Biomedical Research*, Vol. 4, No. 3 (June), pp. 315–328.

Kirsh, D. 1991. "Today the Earwig, Tomorrow Man?" *Artificial Intelligence*, Vol. 47, pp. 161–184.

Klinker, G. J., Shafer, S. A., and Kanade, T. 1988. "The Measurement of Highlights in Color Images," *International Journal of Computer Vision*, Vol. 2, pp. 7–32.

Koenderink, J. J. 1984a. "The Structure of Images," *Biological Cybernetics*, Vol. 50, pp. 363–370.

Koenderink, J. J. 1984b. "What Does the Occluding Contour Tell Us About Solid Shape?" *Perception*, Vol. 13, pp. 321–330.

Koenderink, J. J., and van Doorn, A. J. 1975. "Invariant Properties of the Motion Parallax Field Due to the Movement of Rigid Bodies Relative to an Observer," *Optica Acta*, Vol. 22, No. 9, pp. 773–791.

Koenderink, J. J., and van Doorn, A. J. 1976. "The Singularities of the Visual Mapping," *Biological Cybernetics*, Vol. 24, pp. 51–59.

Koenderink, J. J., and van Doorn, A. J. 1979. "The Internal Representation of Solid Shape with Respect to Vision," *Biological Cybernetics*, Vol. 32, pp. 211–216.

Koenderink, J. J., and van Doorn, A. J. 1980. "Photometric Invariants Related to Solid Shape," *Optica Acta*, Vol. 27, No. 7, pp. 981–996.

Koenderink, J. J., and van Doorn, A. J. 1982. "The Shape of Smooth Objects and the Way Contours End," *Perception*, Vol. 11, pp. 129–137.

Koenderink, J. J., and van Doorn, A. J. 1983. "Geometrical Modes as a General Method to Treat Diffuse Interreflections in Radiometry," *Journal of the Optical Society of America*, Vol. 73, No. 6 (June), pp. 843–850.

Koenderink, J. J., and van Doorn, A. J. 1986. "Dynamic Shape," *Biological Cybernetics*, Vol. 53, pp. 383–396.

Konrad, J., and Dubois, E. 1988. "Multigrid Bayesian Estimation of Image Motion Fields Using Stochastic Relaxation," in *Proceedings of the Second International Conference on Computer Vision*, Tampa, Florida, December, pp. 354–362.

Kriegman, D. J., and Ponce, J. 1990. "On Recognizing and Positioning Curved 3-D Objects from Image Contours," *IEEE Transactions on Pattern Analysis and Machine Intelligence*, Vol. 12, No. 12 (December), pp. 1127–1137.

Krotkov, E. 1987. "Focusing," *International Journal of Computer Vision*, Vol. 1, pp. 223–237.

Kuffler, S. W., Nicholls, J. G., and Martin, A. R. 1984. *From Neuron to Brain: A Cellular Approach to the Function of the Nervous System*, Second Edition, Sinauer Associates, Sunderland, Massachusetts.

Lamdan, Y., and Wolfson, H. J. 1988. "Geometric Hashing: A General and Efficient Model-Based Recognition Scheme," in *Proceedings of the Second International Conference on Computer Vision*, Tampa, Florida, December, pp. 238–249.

Laws, K. I. 1980. "Textured Image Segmentation," Ph.D. Dissertation, Department of Electrical Engineering, University of Southern California, Los Angeles.

Leclerc, Y. G. 1989. "Constructing Simple Stable Descriptions for Image Partitioning," *International Journal of Computer Vision*, Vol. 3, pp. 73–102.

Lee, D. 1988. "Some Computational Aspects of Low-Level Computer Vision," *Proceedings of the IEEE*, Vol. 76, No. 8 (August), pp. 890–898.

Lee, S. J., Haralick, R. M., and Zhang, M. C. 1985. "Understanding Objects with Curved Surfaces from a Single Perspective View of Boundaries," *Artificial Intelligence*, Vol. 26, pp. 145–169.

Lendaris, G. G., and Stanley, G. L. 1970. "Diffraction-Pattern Sampling for Automatic Pattern Recognition," *Proceedings of the IEEE*, Vol. 58, No. 2 (February), pp. 198–216.

Levine, M. D. 1985. *Vision in Man and Machine*, McGraw-Hill Book Co., New York.

Levine, M. D., O'Handley, D. A., and Yagi, G. M. 1973. "Computer Determination of Depth Maps," *Computer Graphics and Image Processing*, Vol. 2, pp. 131–150.

Levine, M. W., and Shefner, J. M. 1991. *Fundamentals of Sensation and Perception*, Second Edition, Brooks/Cole Publishing Co., Pacific Grove, California.

Lim, H. S. 1987. "Stereo Vision: Structural Correspondence and Curved Surface Reconstruction," Ph.D. Dissertation, Department of Electrical Engineering, Stanford University, Stanford, California.

Limb, J. O., and Murphy, J. A. 1975. "Estimating the Velocity of Moving Images in Television Signals," *Computer Graphics and Image Processing*, Vol. 4, pp. 311–327.

Lipschutz, M. M. 1969. *Differential Geometry*, McGraw-Hill Book Co., New York.

Longuet-Higgins, H. C. 1981. "A Computer Algorithm for Reconstructing a Scene from Two Projections," *Nature*, Vol. 293, pp. 133–135.

Longuet-Higgins, H. C. 1984a. "The Visual Ambiguity of a Moving Plane," *Proceedings of the Royal Society of London*, Series B, Vol. 223, pp. 165–175.

Longuet-Higgins, H. C. 1984b. "The Reconstruction of a Scene from Two Projections—Configurations That Defeat the 8-Point Algorithm," in *Proceedings of the First Conference on Artificial Intelligence Applications*, Denver, Colorado, December, pp. 395–397.

Longuet-Higgins, H. C. 1988. "Multiple Interpretations of a Pair of Images of a Surface," *Proceedings of the Royal Society of London*, Series A, Vol. 418, pp. 1–15.

Longuet-Higgins, H. C., and Prazdny, K. 1980. "The Interpretation of a Moving Retinal Image," *Proceedings of the Royal Society of London*, Series B, Vol. 208, pp. 385–397.

Lowe, D. G. 1987. "Three-Dimensional Object Recognition from Single Two-Dimensional Images," *Artificial Intelligence*, Vol. 31, pp. 355–395.

Lowe, D. G. 1989. "Organization of Smooth Image Curves at Multiple Scales," *International Journal of Computer Vision*, Vol. 3, pp. 119–130.

Lowe, D. G., and Binford, T. O. 1985. "The Recovery of Three-Dimensional Structure from Image Curves," *IEEE Transactions on Pattern Analysis and Machine Intelligence*, Vol. PAMI-7, No. 3 (May), pp. 320–326.

Mackworth, A. K. 1973. "Interpreting Pictures of Polyhedral Scenes," *Artificial Intelligence*, Vol. 4, pp. 121–137.

Mackworth, A. K. 1977. "How to See a Simple World: An Exegesis of Some Computer Programs for Scene Analysis," in *Machine Intelligence 8*, E. W. Elcock and D. Michie, Eds., Ellis Horwood, Chichester, U.K., pp. 510–537.

Malik, J. 1987. "Interpreting Line Drawings of Curved Objects," *International Journal of Computer Vision*, Vol. 1, pp. 73–103.

Mandelbrot, B. B. 1983. *The Fractal Geometry of Nature*, W. H. Freeman & Co., New York.

Mariotte, L'Abbe 1668. "A New Discovery Touching Vision," communicated by Monsieur Justel, *Philosophical Transactions of the Royal Society of London*, Vol. 3, pp. 668–669.

Marr, D. 1978. "Representing Visual Information—A Computational Approach," in *Computer Vision Systems*, A. R. Hanson and E. M. Riseman, Eds., Academic Press, New York, pp. 61–80.

Marr, D., and Hildreth, E. 1980. "Theory of Edge Detection," *Proceedings of the Royal Society of London*, Series B, Vol. 207, pp. 187–217.

Marr, D., and Poggio, T. 1976. "Cooperative Computation of Stereo Disparity," *Science*, Vol. 194, pp. 283–287.

Marr, D., and Poggio, T. 1979. "A Computational Theory of Human Stereo Vision," *Proceedings of the Royal Society of London*, Series B, Vol. 204, pp. 301–328.

Marroquin, J., Mitter, S., and Poggio, T. 1987. "Probabilistic Solution of Ill-Posed Problems in Computational Vision," *Journal of the American Statistical Association*, Vol. 82, No. 397 (March), pp. 76–89.

Martelli, A. 1976. "An Application of Heuristic Search Methods to Edge and Contour Detection," *Communications of the ACM*, Vol. 19, No. 2 (February), pp. 73–83.

Matthies, L., Kanade, T., and Szeliski, R. 1989. "Kalman Filter-Based Algorithms for Estimating Depth from Image Sequences," *International Journal of Computer Vision*, Vol. 3, pp. 209–238.

Matthies, L., and Shafer, S. A. 1987. "Error Modeling in Stereo Navigation," *IEEE Journal of Robotics and Automation*, Vol. RA-3, No. 3 (June), pp. 239–248.

Maybank, S. J. 1985. "The Angular Velocity Associated with the Optical Flowfield Arising from Motion Through a Rigid Environment," *Proceedings of the Royal Society of London*, Series A, Vol. 401, pp. 317–326.

Mayhew, J. E. W., and Frisby, J. P. 1981. "Psychophysical and Computational Studies Towards a Theory of Human Stereopsis," *Artificial Intelligence*, Vol. 17, pp. 349–385.

Mead, C. 1989. *Analog VLSI and Neural Systems*, Addison-Wesley Publishing Co., Reading, Massachusetts.

Medioni, G., and Nevatia, R. 1985. "Segment-Based Stereo Matching," *Computer Vision, Graphics, and Image Processing*, Vol. 31, pp. 2–18.

Metropolis, N., Rosenbluth, A. W., Rosenbluth, M. N., Teller, A. H., and Teller, E. 1953. "Equation of State Calculations by Fast Computing Machines," *The Journal of Chemical Physics*, Vol. 21, No. 6 (June), pp. 1087–1092.

Millay, E. S. V. 1923. *The Harp-Weaver and Other Poems*, Harper & Brothers, New York.

Mokhtarian, F., and Mackworth, A. 1986. "Scale-Based Description and Recognition of Planar Curves and Two-Dimensional Shapes," *IEEE Transactions on Pattern Analysis and Machine Intelligence*, Vol. PAMI-8, No. 1 (January), pp. 34–43.

Montanari, U. 1971. "On the Optimal Detection of Curves in Noisy Pictures," *Communications of the ACM*, Vol. 14, No. 5 (May), pp. 335–345.

Montanvert, A., Meer, P., and Rosenfeld, A. 1991. "Hierarchical Image Analysis Using Irregular Tessellations," *IEEE Transactions on Pattern Analysis and Machine Intelligence*, Vol. 13, No. 4 (April), pp. 307–316.

Moravec, H. P. 1977. "Towards Automatic Visual Obstacle Avoidance," in *Proceedings of the Fifth International Joint Conference on Artificial Intelligence, IJCAI-77*, Cambridge, Massachusetts, August, p. 584.

Moravec, H. P. 1979. "Visual Mapping by a Robot Rover," in *Proceedings of the Sixth International Joint Conference on Artificial Intelligence, IJCAI-79*, Tokyo, August, pp. 598–600.

Moravec, H. P. 1983. "The Stanford Cart and the CMU Rover," *Proceedings of the IEEE*, Vol. 71, No. 7 (July), pp. 872–884.

Mori, K., Kidode, M., and Asada, H. 1973. "An Iterative Prediction and Correction Method for Automatic Stereocomparison," *Computer Graphics and Image Processing*, Vol. 2, pp. 393–401.

Murray, D. W., and Buxton, B. F. 1990. *Experiments in the Machine Interpretation of Visual Motion*, MIT Press, Cambridge, Massachusetts.

Musgrave, F. K., and Mandelbrot, B. B. 1989. "Natura ex Machina," *IEEE Computer Graphics and Applications*, Vol. 9, No. 1 (January), pp. 4–7.

Nackman, L. R., and Pizer, S. M. 1985. "Three-Dimensional Shape Description Using the Symmetric Axis Transform I: Theory," *IEEE Transactions on Pattern Analysis and Machine Intelligence*, Vol. PAMI-7, No. 2 (March), pp. 187–202.

Nagel, H.-H. 1983. "Displacement Vectors Derived from Second-Order Intensity Variations in Image Sequences," *Computer Vision, Graphics, and Image Processing*, Vol. 21, pp. 85–117.

Nagel, H.-H., and Enkelmann, W. 1986. "An Investigation of Smoothness Constraints for the Estimation of Displacement Vector Fields from Image Sequences," *IEEE Transactions on Pattern Analysis and Machine Intelligence*, Vol. PAMI-8, No. 5 (September), pp. 565–593.

Nakayama, K., and Loomis, J. M. 1974. "Optical Velocity Patterns, Velocity-Sensitive Neurons, and Space Perception: A Hypothesis," *Perception*, Vol. 3, pp. 63–80.

Nalwa, V. S. 1987. "Edge-Detector Resolution Improvement by Image Interpolation," *IEEE Transactions on Pattern Analysis and Machine Intelligence*, Vol. PAMI-9, No. 3 (May), pp. 446–451.

Nalwa, V. S. 1988a. "Line-Drawing Interpretation: A Mathematical Framework," *International Journal of Computer Vision*, Vol. 2, pp. 103–124.

Nalwa, V. S. 1988b. "Line-Drawing Interpretation: Straight Lines and Conic Sections," *IEEE Transactions on Pattern Analysis and Machine Intelligence*, Vol. 10, No. 4 (July), pp. 514–529.

Nalwa, V. S. 1989a. "Line-Drawing Interpretation: Bilateral Symmetry," *IEEE Transactions on Pattern Analysis and Machine Intelligence*, Vol. 11, No. 10 (October), pp. 1117–1120.

Nalwa, V. S. 1989b. "Representing Oriented Piecewise C^2 Surfaces," *International Journal of Computer Vision*, Vol. 3, pp. 131–153.

Nalwa, V. S., and Binford, T. O. 1986. "On Detecting Edges," *IEEE Transactions on Pattern Analysis and Machine Intelligence*, Vol. PAMI-8, No. 6 (November), pp. 699–714.

Nalwa, V. S., and Pauchon, E. 1987. "Edgel Aggregation and Edge Description," *Computer Vision, Graphics, and Image Processing*, Vol. 40, pp. 79–94.

Nayar, S. K., Ikeuchi, K., and Kanade, T. 1990. "Determining Shape and Reflectance of Hybrid Surfaces by Photometric Sampling," *IEEE Transactions on Robotics and Automation*, Vol. 6, No. 4 (August), pp. 418–431.

Nayar, S. K., Ikeuchi, K., and Kanade, T. 1991a. "Surface Reflection: Physical and Geometrical Perspectives," *IEEE Transactions on Pattern Analysis and Machine Intelligence*, Vol. 13, No. 7 (July), pp. 611–634.

Nayar, S. K., Ikeuchi, K., and Kanade, T. 1991b. "Shape from Interreflections," *International Journal of Computer Vision*, Vol. 6, pp. 173–195.

Nayar, S. K., and Nakagawa, Y. 1990. "Shape from Focus: An Effective Approach for Rough Surfaces," in *Proceedings of the 1990 IEEE International Conference on Robotics and Automation*, Cincinnati, Ohio, May, pp. 218–225.

Negahdaripour, S., and Horn, B. K. P. 1987. "Direct Passive Navigation," *IEEE Transactions on Pattern Analysis and Machine Intelligence*, Vol. PAMI-9, No. 1 (January), pp. 168–176.

Nelson, R. C., and Aloimonos, J. 1988. "Finding Motion Parameters from Spherical Motion Fields," *Biological Cybernetics*, Vol. 58, pp. 261–273.

Nevatia, R. 1976. "Depth Measurement by Motion Stereo," *Computer Graphics and Image Processing*, Vol. 5, pp. 203–214.

Nevatia, R. 1982. *Machine Perception*, Prentice-Hall, Englewood Cliffs, New Jersey.

Nevatia, R., and Babu, K. R. 1980. "Linear Feature Extraction and Description," *Computer Graphics and Image Processing*, Vol. 13, pp. 257–269.

Nevatia, R., and Binford, T. O. 1977. "Description and Recognition of Curved Objects," *Artificial Intelligence*, Vol. 8, pp. 77–98.

Nilsson, N. J. 1980. *Principles of Artificial Intelligence*, Tioga Publishing Co., Palo Alto, California.

Ohlander, R., Price, K., and Reddy, D. R. 1978. "Picture Segmentation Using a Recursive Region Splitting Method," *Computer Graphics and Image Processing*, Vol. 8, pp. 313–333.

Ohta, Y., and Kanade, T. 1985. "Stereo by Intra- and Inter-Scanline Search Using Dynamic Programming," *IEEE Transactions on Pattern Analysis and Machine Intelligence*, Vol. PAMI-7, No. 2 (March), pp. 139–154.

Ohta, Y., Maenobu, K., and Sakai, T. 1981. "Obtaining Surface Orientation from Texels Under Perspective Projection," in *Proceedings of the Seventh International Joint Conference on Artificial Intelligence, IJCAI-81*, Vancouver, Canada, August, pp. 746–751.

Onn, R., and Bruckstein, A. 1990. "Integrability Disambiguates Surface Recovery in Two-Image Photometric Stereo," *International Journal of Computer Vision*, Vol. 5, pp. 105–113.

Oppenheim, A. V., and Schafer, R. W. 1975. *Digital Signal Processing*, Prentice-Hall, Englewood Cliffs, New Jersey.

Papoulis, A. 1984. *Probability, Random Variables, and Stochastic Processes*, Second Edition, McGraw-Hill Book Co., New York.

Pappas, T. N., and Jayant, N. S. 1988. "An Adaptive Clustering Algorithm for Image Segmentation," in *Proceedings of the Second International Conference on Computer Vision*, Tampa, Florida, December, pp. 310–315.

Pavlidis, T. 1972. "Segmentation of Pictures and Maps Through Functional Approximation," *Computer Graphics and Image Processing*, Vol. 1, pp. 360–372.

Pavlidis, T. 1977. *Structural Pattern Recognition*, Springer-Verlag, New York.

Pavlidis, T. 1983. "Curve Fitting with Conic Splines," *ACM Transactions on Graphics*, Vol. 2, No. 1 (January), pp. 1–31.

Penrose, R. 1989. *The Emperor's New Mind: Concerning Computers, Minds, and The Laws of Physics*, Oxford University Press, Oxford, U.K.

Penrose, L. S., and Penrose, R. 1958. "Impossible Objects: A Special Type of Visual Illusion," *The British Journal of Psychology*, Vol. 49, pp. 31–33.

Pentland, A. P. 1984. "Fractal-Based Description of Natural Scenes," *IEEE Transactions on Pattern Analysis and Machine Intelligence*, Vol. PAMI-6, No. 6 (November), pp. 661–674.

Pentland, A. P. 1986. "Perceptual Organization and the Representation of Natural Form," *Artificial Intelligence*, Vol. 28, pp. 293–331.

Perona, P., and Malik, J. 1990. "Scale-Space and Edge Detection Using Anisotropic Diffusion," *IEEE Transactions on Pattern Analysis and Machine Intelligence*, Vol. 12, No. 7 (July), pp. 629–639.

Peters, A., and Jones, E. G., Eds. 1985. *Cerebral Cortex: Volume 3, Visual Cortex*, Plenum Press, New York.

Pingle, K. K. 1969. "Visual Perception by a Computer," in *Automatic Interpretation and Classification of Images*, A. Grasselli, Ed., Academic Press, New York, pp. 277–284.

Pirenne, M. H. 1967. *Vision and the Eye*, Second Edition, Chapman and Hall, London.

Pizer, S. M., Oliver, W. R., and Bloomberg, S. H. 1987. "Hierarchical Shape Description via the Multiresolution Symmetric Axis Transform," *IEEE Transactions on Pattern Analysis and Machine Intelligence*, Vol. PAMI-9, No. 4 (July), pp. 505–511.

Poggio, T., Torre, V., and Koch, C. 1985. "Computational Vision and Regularization Theory," *Nature*, Vol. 317, pp. 314–319.

Polyak, S. 1957. *The Vertebrate Visual System*, University of Chicago Press, Chicago.

Pratt, W. K. 1991. *Digital Image Processing*, Second Edition, John Wiley & Sons, New York.

Prazdny, K. 1981. "Determining the Instantaneous Direction of Motion from Optical Flow Generated by a Curvilinearly Moving Observer," *Computer Graphics and Image Processing*, Vol. 17, pp. 238–248.

Prazdny, K. 1983. "On the Information in Optical Flows," *Computer Vision, Graphics, and Image Processing*, Vol. 22, pp. 239–259.

Preparata, F. P., and Shamos, M. I. 1985. *Computational Geometry: An Introduction*, Springer-Verlag, New York.

Prewitt, J. M. S. 1970. "Object Enhancement and Extraction," in *Picture Processing and Psychopictorics*, B. S. Lipkin and A. Rosenfeld, Eds., Academic Press, New York, pp. 75–149.

Ramachandran, V. S. 1988. "Perceiving Shape from Shading," *Scientific American*, Vol. 259, No. 2 (August), pp. 76–83.

Ramer, U. 1975. "Extraction of Line Structures from Photographs of Curved Objects," *Computer Graphics and Image Processing*, Vol. 4, pp. 81–103.

Ramón y Cajal, S. 1892–1893. "La Rétine des Vertébrés," *La Cellule*, Vol. 9, pp. 17–257. English translation from the French by D. Maguire and R. W. Rodieck: "The Vertebrate Retina," in *The Vertebrate Retina: Principles of Structure and Function*, R. W. Rodieck, W. H. Freeman & Co., San Francisco, 1973, pp. 773–904.

Regan, D., and Beverley, K. I. 1979. "Binocular and Monocular Stimuli for Motion in Depth: Changing-Disparity and Changing-Size Feed the Same Motion-in-Depth Stage," *Vision Research*, Vol. 19, pp. 1331–1342.

Requicha, A. A. G. 1980. "Representations for Rigid Solids: Theory, Methods, and Systems," *Computing Surveys*, Vol. 12, No. 4 (December), pp. 437–464.

Rieger, J. H. 1990. "The Geometry of View Space of Opaque Objects Bounded by Smooth Surfaces," *Artificial Intelligence*, Vol. 44, pp. 1–40.

Rittenhouse, D. 1786. "Explanation of an Optical Deception," *Transactions of the American Philosophical Society*, Vol. 2, pp. 37–42.

Roberts, L. G. 1965. "Machine Perception of Three-Dimensional Solids," in *Optical and Electro-Optical Information Processing*, J. T. Tippett, D. A. Berkowitz, L. C. Clapp, C. J. Koester, and A. Vanderburgh, Jr., Eds., MIT Press, Cambridge, Massachusetts, pp. 159–197.

Rodieck, R. W. 1973. *The Vertebrate Retina: Principles of Structure and Function*, W. H. Freeman & Co., San Francisco.

Rosenfeld, A., Hummel, R. A., and Zucker, S. W. 1976. "Scene Labeling by Relaxation Operations," *IEEE Transactions on Systems, Man, and Cybernetics*, Vol. SMC-6, No. 6 (June), pp. 420–433.

Rosenfeld, A., and Kak, A. C. 1982. *Digital Picture Processing*, Second Edition, Vols. 1 & 2, Academic Press, New York.

Rosenfeld, A., and Thurston, M. 1971. "Edge and Curve Detection for Visual Scene Analysis," *IEEE Transactions on Computers*, Vol. C-20, No. 5 (May), pp. 562–569.

Ross, S. M. 1983. *Stochastic Processes*, John Wiley & Sons, New York.

Roth, B. 1984. "Screws, Motors, and Wrenches That Cannot Be Bought in a Hardware Store," in *Robotics Research: The First International Symposium*, M. Brady and R. Paul, Eds., MIT Press, Cambridge, Massachusetts, pp. 679–693.

Ruechardt, E. 1958. *Light: Visible and Invisible*, University of Michigan Press, Ann Arbor, Michigan.

Sampson, P. D. 1982. "Fitting Conic Sections to 'Very Scattered' Data: An Iterative Refinement of the Bookstein Algorithm," *Computer Graphics and Image Processing*, Vol. 18, pp. 97–108.

Schachter, B. J., Davis, L. S., and Rosenfeld, A. 1979. "Some Experiments in Image Segmentation by Clustering of Local Feature Values," *Pattern Recognition*, Vol. 11, No. 1, pp. 19–28.

Shanmugam, K. S., Dickey, F. M., and Green, J. A. 1979. "An Optimal Frequency Domain Filter for Edge Detection in Digital Pictures," *IEEE Transactions on Pattern Analysis and Machine Intelligence*, Vol. PAMI-1, No. 1 (January), pp. 37–49.

Shannon, C. E. 1948. "A Mathematical Theory of Communication," *The Bell System Technical Journal*, Vol. 27, No. 3 (July), pp. 379–423, and Vol. 27, No. 4 (October), pp. 623–656.

Shapira, R., and Freeman, H. 1978. "Computer Description of Bodies Bounded by Quadric Surfaces from a Set of Imperfect Projections," *IEEE Transactions on Computers*, Vol. C-27, No. 9 (September), pp. 841–854.

Simchony, T., Chellappa, R., and Shao, M. 1990. "Direct Analytical Methods for Solving Poisson Equations in Computer Vision Problems," *IEEE Transactions on Pattern Analysis and Machine Intelligence*, Vol. 12, No. 5 (May), pp. 435–446.

Slama, C. C., Ed. 1980. *Manual of Photogrammetry*, Fourth Edition, American Society of Photogrammetry, Falls Church, Virginia.

Smith, B. G. 1967. "Lunar Surface Roughness: Shadowing and Thermal Emission," *Journal of Geophysical Research*, Vol. 72, No. 16 (August), pp. 4059–4067.

Spedding, J., Ellis, R. L., and Heath, D. D., Eds. 1875. *The Works of Francis Bacon*, Vol. 4, Longmans & Co., London.

Spivak, M. 1965. *Calculus on Manifolds: A Modern Approach to Classical Theorems of Advanced Calculus*, Benjamin/Cummings Publishing Co., Menlo Park, California.

Srinivasan, M. V., Laughlin, S. B., and Dubs, A. 1982. "Predictive Coding: A Fresh View of Inhibition in the Retina," *Proceedings of the Royal Society of London*, Series B, Vol. 216, pp. 427–459.

Stevens, K. A. 1981. "The Information Content of Texture Gradients," *Biological Cybernetics*, Vol. 42, pp. 95–105.

Stoker, J. J. 1969. *Differential Geometry*, John Wiley & Sons, New York.

Subbarao, M. 1988. "Interpretation of Image Flow: Rigid Curved Surfaces in Motion," *International Journal of Computer Vision*, Vol. 2, pp. 77–96.

Sugihara, K. 1984. "A Necessary and Sufficient Condition for a Picture to Represent a Polyhedral Scene," *IEEE Transactions on Pattern Analysis and Machine Intelligence*, Vol. PAMI-6, No. 5 (September), pp. 578–586.

Szeliski, R. 1990a. "Fast Surface Interpolation Using Hierarchical Basis Functions," *IEEE Transactions on Pattern Analysis and Machine Intelligence*, Vol. 12, No. 6 (June), pp. 513–528.

Szeliski, R. 1990b. "Bayesian Modeling of Uncertainty in Low-Level Vision," *International Journal of Computer Vision*, Vol. 5, pp. 271–301.

Tenenbaum, J. M., and Barrow, H. G. 1977. "Experiments in Interpretation-Guided Segmentation," *Artificial Intelligence*, Vol. 8, pp. 241–274.

Terzopoulos, D. 1983. "Multilevel Computational Processes for Visual Surface Reconstruction," *Computer Vision, Graphics, and Image Processing*, Vol. 24, pp. 52–96.

Terzopoulos, D. 1986. "Image Analysis Using Multigrid Relaxation Methods," *IEEE Transactions on Pattern Analysis and Machine Intelligence*, Vol. PAMI-8, No. 2 (March), pp. 129–139.

Terzopoulos, D. 1988. "The Computation of Visible-Surface Representations," *IEEE Transactions on Pattern Analysis and Machine Intelligence*, Vol. 10, No. 4 (July), pp. 417–438.

Thompson, W. B., and Barnard, S. T. 1981. "Lower-Level Estimation and Interpretation of Visual Motion," *Computer*, Vol. 14, No. 8 (August), pp. 20–28.

Thompson, W. B., and Kearney, J. K. 1986. "Inexact Vision," in *Proceedings of the Workshop on Motion: Representation and Analysis*, Charleston, South Carolina, May, pp. 15–21.

Tikhonov, A. N., and Arsenin, V. Y. 1977. *Solutions of Ill-Posed Problems*, V. H. Winston & Sons, Washington, D.C.

Tomasi, C., and Kanade, T. 1992. "Shape and Motion from Image Streams Under Orthography: A Factorization Method," *International Journal of Computer Vision*, Vol. 9, pp. 137–154.

Torrance, K. E., and Sparrow, E. M. 1967. "Theory for Off-Specular Reflection from Roughened Surfaces," *Journal of the Optical Society of America*, Vol. 57, No. 9 (September), pp. 1105–1114.

Torre, V., and Poggio, T. A. 1986. "On Edge Detection," *IEEE Transactions on Pattern Analysis and Machine Intelligence*, Vol. PAMI-8, No. 2 (March), pp. 147–163.

Tsai, R. Y. 1986. "An Efficient and Accurate Camera Calibration Technique for 3D Machine Vision," in *Proceedings of the IEEE Computer Society Conference on Computer Vision and Pattern Recognition, CVPR'86*, Miami Beach, Florida, June, pp. 364–374.

Tsai, R. Y., and Huang, T. S. 1984. "Uniqueness and Estimation of Three-Dimensional Motion Parameters of Rigid Objects with Curved Surfaces," *IEEE Transactions on Pattern Analysis and Machine Intelligence*, Vol. PAMI-6, No. 1 (January), pp. 13–27.

Tsai, R. Y., Huang, T. S., and Zhu, W.-L. 1982. "Estimating Three-Dimensional Motion Parameters of a Rigid Planar Patch, II: Singular Value Decomposition," *IEEE Transactions on Acoustics, Speech, and Signal Processing*, Vol. ASSP-30, No. 4 (August), pp. 525–534.

Turing, A. M. 1950. "Computing Machinery and Intelligence," *Mind*, Vol. 59, No. 236 (October), pp. 433–460.

Turner, K. J. 1974. "Computer Perception of Curved Objects Using a Television Camera," Ph.D. Dissertation, School of Artificial Intelligence, University of Edinburgh, Edinburgh, U.K.

Ullman, S. 1981. "Analysis of Visual Motion by Biological and Computer Systems," *Computer*, Vol. 14, No. 8 (August), pp. 57–69.

Ullman, S., and Basri, R. 1991. "Recognition by Linear Combinations of Models," *IEEE Transactions on Pattern Analysis and Machine Intelligence*, Vol. 13, No. 10 (October), pp. 992–1005.

Van Hove, P. 1987. "Silhouette-Slice Theorems," in *Proceedings of the Workshop on Computer Vision*, Miami Beach, Florida, November–December, pp. 295–297.

Verri, A., and Poggio, T. 1989. "Motion Field and Optical Flow: Qualitative Properties," *IEEE Transactions on Pattern Analysis and Machine Intelligence*, Vol. 11, No. 5 (May), pp. 490–498.

Vilnrotter, F. M., Nevatia, R., and Price, K. E. 1986. "Structural Analysis of Natural Textures," *IEEE Transactions on Pattern Analysis and Machine Intelligence*, Vol. PAMI-8, No. 1 (January), pp. 76–89.

Vistnes, R. 1989. "Texture Models and Image Measures for Texture Discrimination," *International Journal of Computer Vision*, Vol. 3, pp. 313–336.

Wallach, H. 1935. "Über Visuell Wahrgenommene Bewegungsrichtung," *Psychologische Forschung*, Vol. 20, pp. 325–380.

Wallach, H. 1976. *On Perception*, Quadrangle/The New York Times Book Co., New York.

Wallach, H., and O'Connell, D. N. 1953. "The Kinetic Depth Effect," *Journal of Experimental Psychology*, Vol. 45, No. 4 (April), pp. 205–217.

Waltz, D. 1975. "Understanding Line Drawings of Scenes with Shadows," in *The Psychology of Computer Vision*, P. H. Winston, Ed., McGraw-Hill Book Co., New York, pp. 19–91.

Waxman, A. M., and Duncan, J. H. 1986. "Binocular Image Flows: Steps Toward Stereo–Motion Fusion," *IEEE Transactions on Pattern Analysis and Machine Intelligence*, Vol. PAMI-8, No. 6 (November), pp. 715–729.

Waxman, A. M., and Ullman, S. 1985. "Surface Structure and Three-Dimensional Motion from Image Flow Kinematics," *The International Journal of Robotics Research*, Vol. 4, No. 3 (Fall), pp. 72–94.

Waxman, A. M., and Wohn, K. 1985. "Contour Evolution, Neighborhood Deformation, and Global Image Flow: Planar Surfaces in Motion," *The International Journal of Robotics Research*, Vol. 4, No. 3 (Fall), pp. 95–108.

Weng, J., Huang, T. S., and Ahuja, N. 1989. "Motion and Structure from Two Perspective Views: Algorithms, Error Analysis, and Error Estimation," *IEEE Transactions on Pattern Analysis and Machine Intelligence*, Vol. 11, No. 5 (May), pp. 451–476.

Werblin, F. S. 1973. "The Control of Sensitivity in the Retina," *Scientific American*, Vol. 228, No. 1 (January), pp. 70–79.

Weszka, J. S. 1978. "A Survey of Threshold Selection Techniques," *Computer Graphics and Image Processing*, Vol. 7, pp. 259–265.

Weszka, J. S., Dyer, C. R., and Rosenfeld, A. 1976. "A Comparative Study of Texture Measures for Terrain Classification," *IEEE Transactions on Systems, Man, and Cybernetics*, Vol. SMC-6, No. 4 (April), pp. 269–285.

Weszka, J. S., and Rosenfeld, A. 1979. "Histogram Modification for Threshold Selection," *IEEE Transactions on Systems, Man, and Cybernetics*, Vol. SMC-9, No. 1 (January), pp. 38–52.

Whitney, H. 1955. "On Singularities of Mappings of Euclidean Spaces. I. Mappings of the Plane into the Plane," *Annals of Mathematics*, Vol. 62, No. 3 (November), pp. 374–410.

Whitney, D. E. 1986. "Real Robots Don't Need Jigs," in *Proceedings of the 1986 IEEE International Conference on Robotics and Automation*, San Francisco, April, pp. 746–752.

Whittaker, E. T. 1937. *A Treatise on the Analytical Dynamics of Particles and Rigid Bodies*, Fourth Edition, Cambridge University Press, London.

Witkin, A. P. 1981. "Recovering Surface Shape and Orientation from Texture," *Artificial Intelligence*, Vol. 17, pp. 17–45.

Witkin, A. P. 1983. "Scale-Space Filtering," in *Proceedings of the Eighth International Joint Conference on Artificial Intelligence, IJCAI-83*, Karlsruhe, Germany, August, pp. 1019–1022.

Witkin, A., Terzopoulos, D., and Kass, M. 1987. "Signal Matching Through Scale Space," *International Journal of Computer Vision*, Vol. 1, pp. 133–144.

Wohlgemuth, A. 1911. *On the After-Effect of Seen Movement*, Cambridge University Press, London.

Wolberg, G. 1990. *Digital Image Warping*, IEEE Computer Society Press, Los Alamitos, California.

Wolff, L. B., and Boult, T. E. 1991. "Constraining Object Features Using a Polarization Reflectance Model," *IEEE Transactions on Pattern Analysis and Machine Intelligence*, Vol. 13, No. 7 (July), pp. 635–657.

Woodham, R. J. 1980. "Photometric Method for Determining Surface Orientation from Multiple Images," *Optical Engineering*, Vol. 19, No. 1 (January–February), pp. 139–144.

Yachida, M. 1986. "3-D Data Acquisition by Multiple Views," in *Robotics Research: The Third International Symposium*, O. D. Faugeras and G. Giralt, Eds., MIT Press, Cambridge, Massachusetts, pp. 11–18.

Yamamoto, M. 1981. "Motion Analysis by Visualized Locus Method," in Japanese, *Transactions of the Information Processing Society of Japan*, Vol. 22, No. 5 (September), pp. 442–449.

Yen, B. L., and Huang, T. S. 1983. "Determining 3-D Motion and Structure of a Rigid Body Using the Spherical Projection," *Computer Vision, Graphics, and Image Processing*, Vol. 21, pp. 21–32.

Yuille, A. L., and Grzywacz, N. M. 1989. "A Mathematical Analysis of the Motion Coherence Theory," *International Journal of Computer Vision*, Vol. 3, pp. 155–175.

Yuille, A. L., and Poggio, T. A. 1986. "Scaling Theorems for Zero Crossings," *IEEE Transactions on Pattern Analysis and Machine Intelligence*, Vol. PAMI-8, No. 1 (January), pp. 15–25.

Zhuang, X. 1989. "A Simplification to Linear Two-View Motion Algorithms," *Computer Vision, Graphics, and Image Processing*, Vol. 46, pp. 175–178.

Zucker, S. W. 1976a. "Region Growing: Childhood and Adolescence," *Computer Graphics and Image Processing*, Vol. 5, pp. 382–399.

Zucker, S. W. 1976b. "Toward a Model of Texture," *Computer Graphics and Image Processing*, Vol. 5, pp. 190–202.

Zucker, S. W., David, C., Dobbins, A., and Iverson, L. 1988. "The Organization of Curve Detection: Coarse Tangent Fields and Fine Spline Coverings," in *Proceedings of the Second International Conference on Computer Vision*, Tampa, Florida, December, pp. 568–577.

Citation Index

Page numbers in ***bold italics*** point to the figures; page numbers in *italics* point to the footnotes and the appendices; page numbers in **boldface** point to the list of references describing the cited literature.

Subject Index

Page numbers in ***bold italics*** point to the figures; page numbers in *italics* point to the footnotes and the appendices. Only the principal discussions of each topic are indexed.